PEABODY JOURNAL OF EDUCATION

James W. Pellegrino, Editor
Susan A. McDowell, Managing Editor

EDITORIAL BOARD—Peabody College of Vanderbilt University

Alfred Baumeister	Ellen Goldring
Camilla Benbow	James Guthrie
Leonard Bickman	Philip Hallinger
David Bloome	James Hogge
John Bransford	Ann Kaiser
Penelope Brooks	Mark Lipsey
Vera Chatman	Joseph Murphy
Paul Cobb	Charles Myers
David Cordray	J. R. Newbrough
Anne Corn	Daniel Reschly
Robert Crowson	Victoria Risko
Paul Dokecki	Howard Sandler
Carolyn Evertson	Sharon Shields
Douglas Fuchs	Patrick Thompson
Lynn Fuchs	Travis Thompson
Judy Garber	Tedra Walden
Susan Goldman	

SUBSCRIBER INFORMATION

Peabody Journal of Education (ISSN 0161–956X) is published quarterly by Lawrence Erlbaum Associates, Inc. (10 Industrial Avenue, Mahwah, NJ 07430–2262), and subscriptions for the 2000 volume are available on a calendar-year basis. In the United States and Canada, per-volume rates are U.S. $50 for individuals, U.S. $25 for graduate students, and U.S. $180 for institutions; in other countries, per-volume rates are U.S. $80 for individuals, U.S. $50 for graduate students, and U.S. $210 for institutions. Send subscription orders, information requests, and address changes to the Journal Subscription Department, Lawrence Erlbaum Associates, Inc., 10 Industrial Avenue, Mahwah, NJ 07430–2262. Address changes should include the mailing label or a facsimile. Claims for missing issues cannot be honored beyond 4 months after mailing date. Duplicate copies cannot be sent to replace issues not delivered due to failure to notify publisher of change of address.

Electronic: Full-price print subscribers to Volume 75, 2000 are entitled to receive the electronic version free of charge. *Electronic-only* subscriptions are available at a reduced subscription price. Please visit the LEA Web site at http://www.erlbaum.com for complete information.

Peabody Journal of Education is abstracted or indexed in: *Contents Pages in Education; Education Abstracts; Education Index; Linguistics and Language Behavior Abstracts; Sociological Abstracts.* Microform copies of this journal are available through Bell & Howell Information and Learning, P.O. Box 1346, Ann Arbor, MI 48106–1346.

Copyright © 2000, Lawrence Erlbaum Associates, Inc. No part of this publication may be reproduced, in any form or by any means, without permission of the publisher. Printed in the United States.

Send special requests for permission to the Permissions Department, Lawrence Erlbaum Associates, Inc., 10 Industrial Avenue, Mahwah, NJ 07430–2262.

Production Editor: Victoria Reed, Lawrence Erlbaum Associates, Inc.

PEABODY JOURNAL OF EDUCATION

Volume 75, Numbers 1 & 2, 2000

The Home Education Movement in Context, Practice, and Theory

    The Home Education Movement in Context,
    Practice, and Theory: Editors' Introduction   1
    Susan A. McDowell
    Brian D. Ray

    I. The Historical, Political, Legal, and International Context
            of the Home Education Movement

    Pluralism to Establishment to Dissent: The
    Religious and Educational Context of
    Home Schooling   8
    James C. Carper

    Home Schooling and the Future of
    Public Education   20
    Paul T. Hill

    From Confrontation to Accommodation: Home
    Schooling in South Carolina   32
    Zan Peters Tyler
    James C. Carper

    Home Education Regulations in Europe and Recent
    U.K. Research   49
    Lesley Ann Taylor
    Amanda J. Petrie

(Continued)

II. The Present Practice of Home Schooling: A Look at the Research

Home Schooling: The Ameliorator of Negative
Influences on Learning?   71
Brian D. Ray

Home Schooling and the Question of Socialization   107
Richard G. Medlin

Participation and Perception: Looking at Home
Schooling Through a Multicultural Lens   124
Susan A. McDowell
Annette R. Sanchez
Susan S. Jones

Defying the Stereotypes of Special Education:
Home School Students   147
Jacque Ensign

When Home Schoolers Go to School: A Partnership
Between Families and Schools   159
Patricia M. Lines

The Home Schooling Mother–Teacher: Toward a
Theory of Social Integration   187
Susan A. McDowell

III. A Dialectic Discourse: The Pros and Cons of Home Schooling

Whither the Common Good? A Critique of
Home Schooling   207
Chris Lubienski

The Future of Home Schooling   233
Michael P. Farris
Scott A. Woodruff

The Cultural Politics of Home Schooling   256
Michael W. Apple

Home Schooling for Individuals' Gain and Society's
Common Good   272
Brian D. Ray

IV. The Home Schooling Movement: An Evaluation

The Home Schooling Movement: A Few Concluding
Observations   294
Robert L. Crowson

PEABODY JOURNAL OF EDUCATION, 75(1&2), 1–7
Copyright © 2000, Lawrence Erlbaum Associates, Inc.

The Home Education Movement in Context, Practice, and Theory: Editors' Introduction

Susan A. McDowell
Brian D. Ray

As an educational movement, home schooling is growing by leaps and bounds. Currently, an estimated 1.2 million to 1.7 million children (Lines, 1998; Ray, 1999) are home schooled in the United States. Not surprisingly, the number of research studies on home schooling has grown in parallel fashion. Research on the academic achievement and social adjustment of home-schooled children abounds, as well as research presenting the beliefs, practices, socioeconomic levels, educational background, and ethnicity of home schooling parents. Although some voices have offered negative commentaries on the practice of home schooling (e.g., Franzosa, 1984; National Education Association, 1990; Peterson, 1997), research studies indicate that home-schooled students perform well in terms of both academic achievement (Ray, 1997; Wartes, 1988) and social and psychological development (Kelley, 1991; Shyers, 1992). Home education is thriving; its ranks are swelling, and its children—according to the most current research—are flourishing.

The home education movement also is experiencing a growing acceptance in the popular culture (Lines, 1996, p. 65) and finding an increas-

Requests for reprints should be sent to Susan A. McDowell, P.O. Box 148351, Nashville, TN 37214–8351. E-mail: Susan.A.McDowell@vanderbilt.edu

ingly strong and apparently expanding voice on the political front, as Belz (1997) noted,

> What special interest group in American society right now may be most effective at lobbying the U.S. Congress? If you guessed that it's a band of educators, you'd be right. But if you picked the National Educational Association—the very liberal union of public school teachers that is so active in public affairs—you might well be wrong these days. For according to Rep. William Goodling (R–PA), a 22-year veteran of Congress and Chairman now of the influential Education and Labor Committee, the homeschoolers of our country, and especially those associated with the Home School Legal Defense Association, have developed more expertise than any other group in getting the attention of our nation's lawmakers.
>
> I would suggest that Rep. Goodling's high praise of homeschoolers for their ability to win points in Congress may represent no more than the tip of an iceberg—that it's only a precursor of other ways in which homeschoolers may more and more shape society far out of proportion to their numbers and acceptability to the rest of society. (p. 5)

In sum, then, the home education movement is a growing one. Its numbers are growing, its acceptance is growing, and its power to affect the political environment is growing. With these differing elements being a matter of established fact, an issue devoted to examining the home schooling movement—both empirically and theoretically—in terms of its historical development and context, present practice, and ongoing scholarly debate as to efficacy and appropriateness would seem to be both appropriate and timely.

With this guiding purpose in mind, we have adopted and implemented a four-part organizational framework for this special issue, those four sections being "The Historical, Political, Legal, and International Context of the Home Education Movement," "The Present Practice of Home Schooling: A Look at the Research," "A Dialectic Discourse: The Pros and Cons of Home Schooling," and the concluding section, "The Home Schooling Movement: An Evaluation."

In the first section—"The Historical, Political, Legal, and International Context of the Home Education Movement"—the articles endeavor to place home education in appropriate context by addressing the movement in terms of (a) its history and development; (b) its place in the larger issue of education privatization; (c) its legal difficulties, and how these difficulties shaped current practice (a case study); and (d) its international adoption as an educational alternative.

Editors' Introduction

Specifically, in this section, James C. Carper (University of South Carolina) presents an article titled "Pluralism to Establishment to Dissent: The Religious and Educational Context of Home Schooling," in which he explores the historical background of the home schooling movement, examines the relation of home schooling to the development of institutional education, and discusses the current status of the home schooling movement. In "Home Schooling and the Future of Public Education," Paul T. Hill (University of Washington, Seattle) examines the home education movement in terms of its context within the shift toward privatization and the larger school reform movement (e.g., charter schools and the voucher system).

Also in this first section is an article by Zan Peters Tyler (Founder and President of the South Carolina Association of Independent Home Schools) and James C. Carper (University of South Carolina) titled "From Confrontation to Accommodation: Home Schooling in South Carolina." In this case study, the authors describe the historical background of home schooling in South Carolina (including examination of the original home schooling laws in that state) and discuss the development of the South Carolina Association of Independent Home Schools as a unique means of preserving parental freedom in education while satisfying the state's interest in education. Special attention is given to the shifting political climate for home schooling in South Carolina.

The first section closes with an article by Lesley Ann Taylor (Wales, United Kingdom) and Amanda J. Petrie (University of Liverpool, England) titled "Home Education Regulations in Europe and Recent U.K. Research." In this international look at the subject at hand, the authors examine and discuss the home education movement in Europe and the United Kingdom, detail the differences between the movement in the United States and in the United Kingdom and Europe, discuss national legal requirements in regard to home schooling, and look at current home schooling research in the United Kingdom.

In the second section of this issue, titled "The Present Practice of Home Schooling: A Look at the Research," the articles present research pertaining to the home schooling population and address the inherently important and integral issues of (a) academics, (b) socialization, (c) multicultural participation, (d) special needs children, (e) public school interaction with the home schooling population, and (f) the perceived impact of home schooling on the family and the mother–teacher.

Brian D. Ray (Founder and President, National Home Education Research Institute) authors the first article in this section. In "Home Schooling: The Ameliorator of Negative Influences on Learning?," Ray presents the data and findings on the 5,402 home-schooled students—and

3

S. A. McDowell and B. D. Ray

their 1,657 families—that were the subject of his latest nationwide study. This quantitative study attempted a representative national sampling of home schoolers, used descriptive statistics to describe the families and children, and employed multivariate analyses to understand which variables explain the students' high academic achievement. Ray also explores the concept that a heretofore undefined element in the home schooling process ameliorates the negative effects of background variables (e.g., low income, low parent education), and he examines the implications of these and other findings for (a) minorities in particular and families in general, (b) educational policy, and (c) the future of choice in education.

In "Home Schooling and the Question of Socialization," Richard G. Medlin (Stetson University) examines this most frequent objection to home schooling by first defining the concept of socialization, suggesting objective criteria for healthy social development and addressing the issue of what "normal" social contact should be. In the second part of his article, Medlin reviews the literature on social development in home-schooled children from three differing perspectives: Do home-schooled children participate in the daily routines of their communities? Are they acquiring the rules of behavior and systems of beliefs and attitudes they need? Can they function effectively as members of society? In conclusion, Medlin (a) suggests that home schooling seems to afford the kind of social contact that best fosters healthy social behavior, (b) examines and details the essential features of this particular kind of "contact," and (c) suggests directions for future research.

In this section, the third article—"Participation and Perception: Looking at Home Schooling Through a Multicultural Lens"—by Susan A. McDowell (Vanderbilt University) and Annette R. Sanchez and Susan S. Jones (Nashville State Tech), examines home schooling from a multicultural standpoint. McDowell, Sanchez, and Jones look at the current participation of minorities in the home schooling movement, examine the pertinent extant literature, and present the surprising results of an exploratory research study that examines the perceptions of differing ethnic groups—within the confines of the non-home schooling general population—concerning those families that choose to home school and the efficacy of the home schooling movement itself.

Jacque Ensign (Southern Connecticut State University), in her article "Defying the Stereotypes of Special Education: Home School Students," discusses cases from her 9-year longitudinal study of 100 home-schooled students. The article focuses on students who have been identified as exhibiting learning disabilities and giftedness, chronicles the academic development of several special education students, and examines their parents' educational backgrounds and pedagogical approaches.

Editors' Introduction

In "When Home Schoolers Go to School: A Partnership Between Families and Schools," Patricia M. Lines (Senior Fellow, Discovery Institute, Seattle) reports on visits with public programs in Washington State, at least 10 of which include a longitudinal look at the program over a 3- or 4-year period. According to Lines, success in launching such a program appears to require (a) superintendent support, (b) teacher support for home schooling (at least after the program is launched), (c) a flexible and responsive curriculum, and (d) the support of at least some of the home schoolers in the vicinity. The most interesting aspect of these programs is the wide variety of curricular offering and the imaginative manner in which they are presented.

In the final article of this section, Susan A. McDowell (Vanderbilt University), in her article titled "The Home Schooling Mother–Teacher: Toward a Theory of Social Integration," discusses and details the theory gleaned from her quantitative and qualitative research on the perceived effects of home schooling on the mother–teacher. In the article, McDowell argues that because social integration involves and pertains to several aspects of an individual's life—the chief of which may be termed *social capital*—and because social capital is made up, in turn, of the "norms, social networks, and the relationships between adults and children that are of value for children's growing up" (Coleman, 1987, p. 36), then the element of social integration allowed the home schooling mother–teacher is an extraordinarily empowering one. Also examined in this discussion is a surprising "feminist factor" emerging from the data.

The articles in "A Dialectic Discourse: The Pros and Cons of Home Schooling," the third part of our framework, present theoretical and/or philosophical arguments concerning the pros and cons of the home education movement. In particular, Chris Lubienski (Iowa State University), in his article "Whither the Common Good? A Critique of Home Schooling," argues that the growing movement toward home schooling does not enhance but, in fact, is likely to detract from the common good and, thus, from the democratic and moral essence and capacities of our society. To that end, he examines home schooling on two of its most cherished justifications: that the decision to focus on one's own children is in the best interest of the United States, and that, for many, such an approach is a fundamental aspect in exercising their personal religious liberty.

In the next article, Michael P. Farris (Attorney, Founder and President of the Home School Legal Defense Association) and Scott A. Woodruff (Attorney, Home School Legal Defense Association) look at "The Future of Home Schooling." These authors discuss the present state of affairs in home schooling, look at current trends, and address the future of the movement in terms of the individual and the implications for society.

S. A. McDowell and B. D. Ray

Michael W. Apple (University of Wisconsin), in "The Cultural Politics of Home Schooling," raises a number of conceptual, political, and empirical questions about (a) the home schooling movement as a whole and (b) the elements behind, and at least partly responsible for, much of the movement. In "Home Schooling for Individuals' Gain and Society's Common Good," Brian D. Ray (National Home Education Research Institute) presents his argument that "five general areas of evidence and reasoning support the claim that home schooling is a good, if not the best, form of education" for both the individual and society as a whole.

The final article of this special issue, "The Home Schooling Movement: A Few Concluding Observations," by Robert L. Crowson (Vanderbilt University), offers a highly thoughtful and analytical appraisal of the articles and arguments presented in the issue. In fact, given the very real help this article might be in placing the entire issue in appropriate context, we suggest that readers consider beginning and ending their reading of this special double issue with this piece. In sum, Crowson offers a scholarly, balanced evaluation of the movement and the issues surrounding it.

It is hoped that this issue as a whole also offers a scholarly, balanced look at the home education—also known as the home schooling—movement. It is an educational alternative that gives every indication of continuing to grow in terms of size, acceptability, and political power. It is also an educational movement that—by its very nature—often finds itself at odds not only with professional teacher organizations and public school systems, but also with state, local, and national governments. Given these various elements, differing considerations, and seemingly conflicting interests, it will be fascinating to watch the direction and development of home education as it moves into the 21st century.

References

Belz, J. (1997). Rebels of the best kind: As educational structures change, keep your eyes on the homeschoolers. *World, 12*(23), 5.

Coleman, J. S. (1987, August/September). Families and school. *Educational Researcher, 16*(6), 32–38.

Franzosa, S. D. (1984). The best and wisest parent: A critique of John Holt's philosophy of education. *Urban Education, 19*, 227–244.

Kelley, S. W. (1991). Socialization of home schooled children: A self-concept study. *Home School Researcher, 7*(4), 1–12.

Lines, P. M. (1996, October). Home schooling comes of age. *Educational Leadership, 54*(2), 63–67.

Lines, P. M. (1998). *Home schoolers: Estimating numbers and growth* (Tech. Rep). Washington, DC: U.S. Department of Education, Office of Educational Research and Improvement, National Institute on Student Achievement, Curriculum, and Assessment.

Editors' Introduction

National Education Association. (1990). *The 1990–91 resolutions of the National Education Association*. Washington, DC: Author.

Peterson, A. J. (1997, March/April). The perspective of the American Psychological Association on home schooling: Psychologists are wary of schooling children at home. *Home School Court Report, 13*(2), 3.

Ray, B. D. (1997). *Strengths of their own—home schoolers across America: Academic achievement, family characteristics, and longitudinal traits*. Salem, OR: National Home Education Research Institute.

Ray, B. D. (1999). *Home schooling on the threshold: A survey of research at the dawn of the millennium*. Salem, OR: National Home Education Research Institute.

Shyers, L. E. (1992). A comparison of social adjustment between home and traditionally schooled students. *Home School Researcher, 8*(3), 1–8.

Wartes, J. (1988). Summary of two reports from the Washington Home School Research Project, 1987. *Home School Researcher, 4*(2), 1–4.

Pluralism to Establishment to Dissent: The Religious and Educational Context of Home Schooling

James C. Carper

Although estimates of the number of children currently taught by their parents in a home setting vary considerably—from 750,000 to 1.7 million—no one doubts that their numbers have grown rapidly since the mid-1970s, when only 10,000 to 15,000 children were educated at home (Lines, 1998; Ray, 1999). Home schooling is not, however, a new approach to educating the young in this country. It was commonplace in religiously pluralistic colonial America and virtually disappeared with the establishment and expansion of common school systems in the 19th and early 20th century, but it has experienced a renaissance since the mid-1970s, particularly among evangelical Protestant "dissenters" who, ironically, once

JAMES C. CARPER *is Associate Professor of Foundations of Education, Department of Educational Psychology, University of South Carolina, Columbia.*

Portions of this article were adapted by permission of the publisher from Sears, J. T., & Carper, J. C., *Curriculum, Religion, and Public Education* (New York: Teachers College Press, © 1998 by Teachers College, Columbia University. All rights reserved), pp. 11–24.

Requests for reprints should be sent to James C. Carper, Department of Educational Psychology, Wardlaw College, University of South Carolina, Columbia, SC 29208. E-mail: jcarper@gwm.sc.edu

Religious and Educational Context

staunchly supported what historian Mead (1963) called America's "established church"—the public school.[1]

Educational Pluralism in Early America

Prior to the central, transforming event in our educational history—the advent of mandatory, state-supported and state-controlled common schooling in the middle decades of the 19th century—the rich religious diversity that characterized overwhelmingly Protestant colonial and early national America (Roman Catholics numbered only about 25,000 in 1776) was matched by an equally rich diversity of educational arrangements. With few exceptions—namely, when they were unable or unwilling to direct their children's upbringing—parents fashioned an education that was consonant with their religious beliefs (Cremin, 1970; Noll, 1992).

For the better part of the 17th and 18th centuries, the family was the primary unit of social organization and the most important educational agency. In the words of Puritan divine Mather (1699), "Families are the nurseries of all societies, and the first combinations of mankind" (pp. 3–4). Historian Mintz and anthropologist Kellogg (1988) echoed Mather's observation regarding the colonial family:

> Three centuries ago the American family was the fundamental economic, educational, political, social and religious unit of society. The family, not the isolated individual, was the unit of which church and state were made. The household was not only the locus of production, it was also the institution primarily responsible for the education of children, the transfer of craft skills, and the care of the elderly and infirm. (p. xiv)

Whether parents taught children at home primarily out of necessity or out of religious conviction is difficult to ascertain.[2]

In general, then, parents—particularly the father in the 1600s—bore the primary responsibility for teaching their children (and often those from other families who had been apprenticed or "fostered out") Christian doctrine, vocational skills, and how to read. That responsibility was not al-

---

[1] Although the resurgence of home schooling in the 1970s was in large measure led by advocates of progressive pedagogy such as John Holt, the movement rapidly became dominated by evangelical Christians. Despite the increasing diversity of the movement in the 1990s, it remains closely identified with conservative Christianity.

[2] Although contemporary home schooling has been the subject of much research, comparatively little is known about its past (Carper, 1992).

J. C. Carper

ways carried out equally or effectively. According to historian Lewis (1989), "The effectiveness of home schooling varied depending particularly upon region and gender; literacy was much higher in the North than the South, and for males than females" (p. 126). Although many 17th- and 18th-century White parents sent their children to school for short periods of time—at least in the northern colonies—much education took place in the household. Indeed, a majority of colonial children may have acquired rudimentary literacy skills at home.

In contrast to current schooling arrangements, the colonial mode of schooling was unsystematic, unregulated, and discontinuous. The initiative for school attendance resided with parents, not the state, as Reese (1983) pointed out,

> Early school laws of Massachusetts, which called for the creation of various levels of schools in response to population growth, were widely ignored and unenforceable. Whether in New England, the Middle Colonies, or the South—and regional differences would long prevail in schooling—schools were an irregular, incidental, and unsystematic part of a child's life. (p. 3)

Although schooling in colonial America was unsystematic and primarily the product of local community or church efforts and parental initiatives, it was not neglected. According to Cremin (1970), school opportunities increased more rapidly than the population during the 1700s, even though the "increase was neither linear over time nor uniform from region to region" (p. 500). By the eve of the American Revolution, most White children (more boys than girls) attended school at some point in their lives. Schooling, however, was not controversial. In great measure, this was because most schools mirrored the religious beliefs of their patrons and, like churches, were expected to assist parents in the education of the young. They were to complement rather than replace parental educational efforts in the home (Cremin, 1970; Kaestle, 1973; Vinovskis, 1987).

The diversity of educational institutions and the blurred line between "public" and "private" schools were the most salient features of colonial schooling. The colonial education landscape was dotted with an incredible variety of institutions: from the town schools, dame schools (in which women taught reading skills in their homes for a small fee), and private-venture schools of New England; to the various denominational (e.g., Lutheran, Quaker, Presbyterian, and Reformed), charity, and pay schools in the Middle Colonies; to the old-field schools and Society for the Propagation of the Gospel in Foreign Parts missionary efforts in the South; to academies that appeared throughout the provinces after 1740 (Cremin,

Religious and Educational Context

1977; Kaestle, 1983). Classifying these schools as purely public or private is problematic, as Bailyn (1960) argued: "The modern conception of public education, the very idea of a clean line of separation between 'private' and 'public,' was unknown before the end of the eighteenth century" (p. 11). To most colonials, a school was public if it served a public purpose, such as promoting civic responsibility. Public education did not require public support and control.

Toward the end of the colonial era, the family began to lose its position as American society's most important economic and social unit. The slow shift of family functions, including education, to nonfamilial institutions occurred initially in the settled areas of the eastern seaboard. According to Mintz and Kellogg (1988),

> By the middle of the eighteenth century, a variety of specialized institutions had begun to absorb traditional familial responsibility. To reduce the cost of caring for widows, orphans, the destitute, and the mentally ill, cities began to erect almshouses instead of having such cared for in their own homes or homes of others. Free schools and common pay schools educated a growing number of the sons of artisans and skilled laborers. Workshops increasingly replace individual households as centers of production. (p. 23)

Although parents increasingly looked to schools to carry out what had once been primarily a family function, the colonial approach to education continued virtually unchanged throughout the late 1700s and early 1800s. Despite proposals for more systematic, state-influenced schooling offered by luminaries such as Thomas Jefferson and Benjamin Rush, the colonial mode of schooling suited to the Protestant pluralism of the period persisted well into the 19th century. Whether or not sponsored by a church, the vast majority of schools at that time embodied some variation of Protestant Christianity, and parents decided whether children would attend them.

By the 1820s, private and quasi-public schooling (e.g., district schools) were widely available to White Americans in most settled parts of the United States, except the South. These educational opportunities were due primarily to the efforts of churches, parents, local governments, voluntary associations, entrepreneurs, and communities, not state mandates. In some areas, school attendance was nearly universal. Despite some references to common pay schools as "private" and charity schools systems as "public," these terms still lacked their modern connotations. Public funding of privately controlled institutions was still common (Gabel, 1937). With the exception of some charity schooling, most schools

11

J. C. Carper

embodied the belief system of their clientele. In sum, the structure of schooling reflected the Protestant "confessional pluralism" of the time, and public policy generally recognized and even encouraged diversity. Parents viewed schools as extensions of the household that would reinforce their educational efforts.

Establishing the Public Schools

The middle decades of the 19th century marked a period of intense educational debate and reform that led to major changes in educational beliefs and practices in the United States—namely, the genesis of the modern concept and practice of public schooling. Distressed by the social and cultural tensions wrought by mid-19th-century urbanization, industrialization, and immigration (which included a large number of Roman Catholics from Ireland) and energized by what Kaestle (1983) called the values of republicanism, Protestantism, and capitalism, educational reformers touted the messianic power of tax-supported, government-controlled compulsory schooling. Common schools, they believed, would mold a moral, disciplined, and unified population prepared to participate in American political, economic, and social life. Some reformers viewed the common school as a substitute for the family. Horace Mann, for example, often referred to the state and its schools as "parental" (Carlson, 1998). Private schools, on the other hand, often were cast as undemocratic, divisive, and inimical to the public interest (Glenn, 1988; Kaestle, 1983; Randall, 1994).

As de Tocqueville (1835/1966) recognized in the 1830s and several generations of historians have since confirmed, public schooling was nurtured by a robust evangelical Protestant culture that emerged from the Great Awakening of the 1730s and 1740s and was nourished by the Second Great Awakening—a series of religious revivals stretching from the late 1790s through the Civil War. With few exceptions, notably several Lutheran and Reformed bodies that opted for schools designed to preserve cultural and/or confessional purity, Protestants were generally supportive of common schooling. Indeed, many were in the vanguard of the reform movement. They approved of early public schooling because it reflected Protestant beliefs and was viewed as an integral part of a crusade to fashion a Christian—which, to the dismay of Roman Catholics, meant Protestant—America (Kaestle, 1983; Noll, 1992; Smith, 1967). According to church historian Handy (1971), elementary schools hardly had to be under the control of particular denominations because "their role was to prepare young Americans for participating in the broadly Christian civilization toward which all evangelicals were working" (p. 102).

Religious and Educational Context

Rather than countenance sharing public funds with Roman Catholic schools, such as requested by Bishop John Hughes in the early 1840s in the face of Protestant practices of the New York Public School Society (such as using the King James version of the Bible) or schools associated with Protestant groups, evangelicals united behind the "nonsectarian" (in reality, pan-Protestant) common school as the sole recipient of tax monies for education. Therefore, Catholic schools and those of other dissenters from the common school movement were denied not only legitimacy but tax dollars as well. Latent anti-Catholicism was rekindled by the immigration of the 1840s and 1850s; by Roman Catholic bishops' assertions of missionary intent in the United States; and by the provocative statements of Pope Pius IX (from 1846–1878), such as the Syllabus of Errors in 1864—an anthology of earlier condemnations of, among other things, liberty of religion and separation of church and state, which were looked on unfavorably in the United States. To a significant degree, then, this anti-Catholicism closed prematurely the debate on whether the education of the public could be accomplished by a variety of schools reflecting diverse moral and religious viewpoints funded by tax dollars or whether it required the creation of a government school system embodying a supposedly common belief system with a virtual monopoly on the public treasury—in other words, an educational counterpart to the traditional established church (Baer & Carper, 1998–1999; Carper & Weston, 1990; Curran, 1954; Glenn, 1988; Hicks, 1990; Hunt & Carper, 1993).

It is indeed ironic that as Protestants embarked on the "lively experiment" of religious freedom and denominationalism (Massachusetts became the last state formally to separate church and state in 1833), they, with few exceptions, abandoned an educational arrangement well suited to the Protestant pluralism of the previous 200 years, allied themselves with Unitarian reform leaders like Mann, and cast their hopes for a Protestant Kingdom of God in America with a new established church—the common school. Little did they know that in the future this pan-Protestant institution would embody a belief system at odds with their evangelical faith, which, in turn, would lead many conservative Protestants in the last decades of the 20th century to embrace educational arrangements of an earlier period (Carper, 1992).

Early Dissenters From the Public School Establishment

By 1890, about 86% of children aged 5 to 14 years were in public schools, and private schools accounted for another 11% (Wattenberg, 1976). Why did most parents turn their children over to the public schools? Why did they

J. C. Carper

give up some of their educational prerogatives to the government? (I say some because, despite the ever-increasing institutionalization of children for educational purposes, families no doubt taught and continue to teach propositions and skills as well as dispositions.) First, parents sent their children to school, usually of their own volition, because they believed that schooling offered status and opportunity for economic advancement. In other words, there was a "payoff" for relinquishing some parental authority (Kaestle, 1983). Second, with several notable exceptions (e.g., Roman Catholics), most 19th-century parents supported the public schools' goals of Christian character building and literacy training as well as the means of attaining them (Handy, 1971; Tyack & Hansot, 1981). Third, despite the oft-decried centralizing innovations (e.g., the establishment of state and county superintendencies), 19th-century public education was intensely localistic. In 1890, for example, more than 75% of American children attended school in rural areas. Even as late as 1913, around 50% of American schoolchildren were enrolled in 212,000 one-room schools (Cuban, 1984; Gulliford, 1984). Many of these schools enrolled children from only four or five families. Thus, parents looked on the school as an extension of family and community educational and religious preferences rather than an instrument of state authority. Finally, it is likely that some parents were simply pleased to have the public school relieve them of part of the responsibility of raising their children, a task made more arduous by the separation of the father and the workplace from the household.

Not all 19th-century parents shared in the often tension-filled consensus regarding common schooling. There was dissent regarding curriculum, structure, and the belief system embodied in the common school, much as there is today. Among others, Roman Catholics, Lutherans, and Reformed Protestants established alternative schools to maintain tightly knit communities in which the family, church, and school propagated the same doctrines of the faith (Carper & Hunt, 1984). For economic, religious, pedagogical, and, probably most commonly, geographical reasons, some children were schooled to a greater or lesser extent at home. Indeed, Gordon and Gordon (1990) argued that during the better part of the 19th century, literature on "domestic" or "fireside" education was widely available to those interested in the "family school" movement. We do not know how many children were schooled at home by either parents or relatives. Several, however, we know much about. In addition to the oft-cited 18th-century luminaries like Washington, Madison, and Franklin (Dobson, 1995), well-known 19th-century figures who were taught by their parents include Thomas A. Edison, who was instructed at home after school officials labeled him "addled"; Jane Addams, who received most of her precollegiate formal

Religious and Educational Context

education at home due to poor health; Andrew Taylor Still, a colleague of abolitionist John Brown and founder of osteopathic medicine, who was largely educated by his father; and Alexander Campbell, founder of the Disciplines of Christ, who received part of his education from his father (A. Johnson, 1928–1936; see also McCullough, 1987; Moore & Moore, 1984). Lesser lights, such as Daniel Dawson Carothers, Chief Engineer of the Baltimore and Ohio Railroad from 1904 to 1909, who received his primary schooling from his mother before attending an academy, eventually may be "discovered" in obituaries, memorials, diaries, and family records (Rawn et al., 1909).

20th-Century Dissenters

In addition to the well-known efforts on the part of states like Wisconsin, Illinois, and, most aggressively, Oregon to regulate or outlaw nongovernment schools, the late 1800s and early 1900s also witnessed the gradual decline of evangelical Protestantism as the dominant theme in America's public religion and the growing influence of the Enlightenment Pillar of our civic faith. Pointing out the disruptive effect on American Protestantism of, among other things, Darwinism, higher criticism of the Bible, the fundamentalist–modernist controversy, and growing cultural and religious diversity, sociologist Hunter (1983) argued, with only slight exaggeration, that in the course of roughly 35 years (1895–1930), "Protestantism had been moved from cultural domination to cognitive marginality and political impotence. The worldview of modernity [often termed secular humanism or civil humanism] had gained ascendancy in American culture" (p. 37).

Public education was affected, albeit gradually, by this shift in America's public religion. For example, prior to the U.S. Supreme Court's ruling on Bible reading in *Abington Township v. Schempp* (1963), 11 states already forbade it on the grounds that it was a "sectarian" practice. Furthermore, Bible reading in some form was practiced in fewer than half of the nation's public school districts (Dierenfeld, 1962; Stokes & Pfeffer, 1964). Christianity also became less visible in the public school curriculum after the turn of the century. For example, in his analysis of the religious content of American history textbooks, Shannon (1995) documented a gradual shift from a Christian or theistic worldview to a more secular, "democratic" orientation between 1865 and 1935.

Although the Supreme Court's decisions on prayer and Bible reading (*Abington Township v. Schempp*, 1963; *Engel v. Vitale*, 1962; *Murray v. Curlett*, 1963) merely marked the culmination of more than a half-century-long pro-

15

J. C. Carper

cess of "de-Protestantization" of public education (Nord, 1995), many conservative Protestants have interpreted the official removal of these symbols of the evangelical strain of the American civic faith as "yanking" God out of the public schools. Rather than making the schools "neutral" on matters related to religion, they have concluded that these decisions contributed to the establishment of secular humanism as the official creed of American public education. This belief, in turn, has led them to scrutinize public education to a greater extent than ever before. Once crusaders for the establishment of public education, conservative Protestants are now, ironically, among its most vociferous critics (Carper, 1984). They have awakened to the fact that public education in now officially "agnostic" vis-à-vis Christianity.

Since the mid-1960s, disgruntled conservative Protestants have responded to the "established church" and its secular "theology" in several ways. Like their Reformation ancestors of the 16th century, some have attempted to "purify" the public schools by protesting the use of curricular materials (e.g., literature series) that they believe advance "secular humanism" or by attempting to reincorporate theistic symbols (e.g., posting the Ten Commandments) and perspectives (e.g., intelligent design theories about the origin of the cosmos) in the public schools (Bates, 1993; P. E. Johnson, 1995). Others have forsaken their historic commitment to public education and founded independent Christian schools. The most radical dissenters, "educational anabaptists" if you will, have carried the reformation one step further. They have abandoned institutional education for home schooling in an attempt to restore what they believe to be education in its purest form—parents teaching their own children. As was the case with 16th-century anabaptists, these radical dissenters have been criticized and in some cases persecuted by public school establishmentarians (Mayberry, Knowles, Ray, & Marlow, 1995). Even fellow dissenters in the nongovernment sector have questioned home schooling.

Despite occasional friction between independent Christian school advocates and evangelical home schoolers, these dissenters have much in common. Both are profoundly dissatisfied with what they perceive to be the secularistic worldview embodied in the public school curriculum, unsatisfactory behavioral and academic standards, and an unsafe environment. Although the rapid growth of independent Christian schooling preceded that of home schooling by about a decade, both sectors of nonpublic education now claim more than 1 million students each (and although the home school population is certainly becoming more religiously diverse, the vast majority remains conservative Christian). Both are broadly middle-class movements comprised of persons who are deeply committed to their faith and their children. Few families with children in either are likely to return to the "established church."

16

Religious and Educational Context

Indeed, in the case of the home school sector, conservative Christians are likely to be joined by increasing numbers of dissenters whose beliefs are rooted in other faith systems, such as Islam or "romantic libertarianism." How this growing diversity will affect the home school movement and its relation to the state remains to be seen. After numerous clashes with public school officials and state authorities in the 1970s, 1980s, and early 1990s, home schoolers now are tolerated—and, in some cases, even accommodated—by the education establishment, and they enjoy legal status and considerable freedom in all 50 states. Nevertheless, parents who teach their children at home must be wary of reforms to improve education, particularly the current wave of "accountability" measures that impose uniform content and performance standards on public schools. Such measures could be extended beyond state school systems. As dissenters of the past discovered, "edicts of toleration" can be revoked in favor of "edicts of conformity."

References

Abington Township v. Schempp, 374 U.S. 203 (1963).

Baer, R. A., & Carper, J. C. (1998–1999). Spirituality and the public schools: An evangelical perspective. *Educational Leadership, 56*(4), 33–37.

Bailyn, B. (1960). *Education in the forming of American society.* New York: Norton.

Bates, S. (1993). *Battleground: One mother's crusade, the religious right, and the struggle for control of our classrooms.* New York: Poseidon.

Carlson, A. (1998, September). Will family-centered education strengthen families? *The Family in America, 12*(9), 1–7. (Available from the Howard Center for Family, Religion, and Society, 934 North Main Street, Rockford, IL 61103).

Carper, J. C. (1984). The Christian day school. In J. C. Carper & T. C. Hunt (Eds.), *Religious schooling in America* (pp. 110–129). Birmingham, AL: Religious Education Press.

Carper, J. C. (1992). Home schooling, history, and historians: The past as present. *High School Journal, 75,* 252–257.

Carper, J. C., & Hunt, T. C. (Eds.). (1984). *Religious schooling in America.* Birmingham, AL: Religious Education Press.

Carper, J. C., & Weston, W. J. (1990). Conservative Protestants in the new school wars. *History of Education Quarterly, 30,* 79–87.

Cremin, L. A. (1970). *American education: The colonial experience, 1607–1783.* New York: Harper & Row.

Cremin, L. A. (1977). *Traditions of American education.* New York: Basic Books.

Cuban, L. (1984). *How teachers taught: Constancy and change in American classrooms, 1890–1980.* New York: Longman.

Curran, F. X. (1954). *The churches and the schools: American Protestantism and popular elementary education.* Chicago: Loyola University Press.

Dierenfeld, R. B. (1962). *Religion in American public schools.* Washington, DC: Public Affairs Press.

Dobson, L. (1995). *The art of education: Reclaiming your family, community, and self.* Tonasket, WA: Home Education Press.

J. C. Carper

Engel v. Vitale, 370 U.S. 421 (1962).

Gabel, R. J. (1937). *Public funds for church and private schools.* Unpublished doctoral dissertation, Catholic University of America, Washington, DC.

Glenn, C. L. (1988). *The myth of the common school.* Amherst: University of Massachusetts Press.

Gordon, E. E., & Gordon, E. H. (1990). *Centuries of tutoring: A history of alternative education in America and Western Europe.* Lanham, MD: University Press of America.

Gulliford, A. (1984). *America's country schools.* Washington, DC: Preservation Press.

Handy, R. T. (1971). *A Christian America: Protestant hopes and historical realities.* New York: Oxford University Press.

Hicks, L. E. (1990). Republican religion and republican institutions: Alexander Campbell and the anti-Catholic movement. *Fides et Historia, 22*(3), 42–52.

Hunt, T. C., & Carper, J. C. (Eds.). (1993). *Religious schools in the United States, K–12: A source book.* New York: Garland.

Hunter, J. D. (1983). *American evangelism: Conservative religion and the quandary of modernity.* New Brunswick, NJ: Rutgers University Press.

Johnson, A. (Ed.). (1928–1936). *The dictionary of American biography* (Vols. 1–20). New York: Scribner's.

Johnson, P. E. (1995). *Reason in the balance: The case against naturalism in science, law, and education.* Downers Grove, IL: Intervarsity.

Kaestle, C. F. (1973). *The evolution of an urban school system: New York City, 1750–1850.* Cambridge, MA: Harvard University Press.

Kaestle, C. F. (1983). *Pillars of the republic: Common schools and American society, 1780–1860.* New York: Hill & Wang.

Lewis, J. (1989). Mothers as teachers: Reconceptualizing the role of the family as educator. In W. J. Weston (Ed.), *Education and the American family: A research synthesis* (pp. 122–137). New York: New York University Press.

Lines, P. M. (1998). *Homeschoolers: Estimating numbers and growth* (Tech. Rep.). Washington, DC: U.S. Department of Education, Office of Educational Research and Improvement, National Institute on Student Achievement, Curriculum, and Assessment.

Mather, C. (1699). *A family well-ordered* [Microfilm]. Boston: Green & Allen.

Mayberry, M., Knowles, J. G., Ray, B., & Marlow, S. (1995). *Home schooling: Parents as educators.* Thousand Oaks, CA: Corwin.

McCullough, D. W. (1987). *American childhoods: An anthology.* Boston: Little, Brown.

Mead, S. E. (1963). *The lively experiment.* New York: Harper & Row.

Mintz, S., & Kellogg, S. (1988). *Domestic revolutions: A social history of family life in America.* New York: Free Press.

Moore, R., & Moore, D. (1984). *Home style teaching.* Waco, TX: Word Books.

Murray v. Curlett, 374 U.S. 203 (1963).

Noll, M. A. (1992). *A history of Christianity in the United States and Canada.* Grand Rapids, MI: Eerdmans.

Nord, W. A. (1995). *Religion and American education: Rethinking a national dilemma.* Chapel Hill: University of North Carolina Press.

Randall, E. V. (1994). *Private schools and public power.* New York: Teachers College Press.

Rawn, I. G., Begien, R. N., Fritch, L. C., Grenier, J. E., Stuart, F. L., & Thompson, A. W. (1909). *Daniel Dawson Carothers: A memoir.*

Ray, B. D. (1999). Home schooling after 20 years of resurgence in America. *Private School Monitor, 20,* 1, 12.

Reese, W. J. (1983, October). *Changing conceptions of public and private in American educational history.* Paper presented at the meeting of the History of Education Society, Vancouver, BC, Canada.

Shannon, C. K. (1995). *The religious content of secondary school American history textbooks.* Unpublished doctoral dissertation, Pennsylvania State University, University Park.

Smith, T. L. (1967). Protestant schooling and American nationality, 1800–1850. *Journal of American History, 53,* 679–695.

Stokes, A. P., & Pfeffer, L. (1964). *Church and state in the United States* (3rd ed.). New York: Harper & Row.

de Tocqueville, A. (1966). *Democracy in America* (G. Lawrence, Trans.). New York: Harper & Row. (Original work published 1835)

Tyack, D., & Hansot, E. (1981). Conflict and consensus in American public education. *Daedalus, 110*(3), 1–25.

Vinovskis, M. A. (1987). Family and schooling in colonial and nineteenth century America. *Journal of Family History, 12*(1–3), 19–37.

Wattenberg, B. J. (1976). *The statistical history of the United States from colonial times to the present.* New York: Basic Books.

PEABODY JOURNAL OF EDUCATION, 75(1&2), 20–31
Copyright © 2000, Lawrence Erlbaum Associates, Inc.

Home Schooling and the Future of Public Education

Paul T. Hill

Home schooling, not a present threat to public education, is nonetheless one of the forces that will change it. If the high estimates of the number of children in home schools—1.2 million or higher—is correct, then the home schooling universe is larger than the New York City public school system and roughly the size of the Los Angeles and Chicago public school systems combined. Even if the real number of home schoolers is more like 500,000, fewer than the lowest current estimate, there are more children home schooling than in charter schools and public voucher programs combined.[1]

Home schooling is not a new phenomenon, but a very old one. In Colonial days, families, including wealthy ones, educated their children at home, combining the efforts of parents, tutors, and older children. The rural one-room schoolhouse was created by families that banded together to hire a teacher who could substitute for parents but would still use the same mixture of direct instruction, tutoring, and mentoring by older students.

PAUL T. HILL *is Research Professor in the Daniel J. Evans School of Public Affairs, University of Washington, Seattle.*

Requests for reprints should be sent to Paul T. Hill, Graduate School of Public Affairs, 327 Parrington Hall, Box 353060, University of Washington, Seattle, WA 98195. E-mail: bicycle@u.washington.edu

[1]The best estimates of the numbers of home schools are provided by Lines (1998) and Bruno and Curry (1997).

The Future of Public Education

There is nothing un-American about home schooling. Home schooling families, however, are breaking a pattern established since Colonial times of education's becoming more and more institutionalized, formal, and removed from the family. How important is the contemporary home schooling movement, and what does it portend for American public education? No one can say for sure. It is difficult even to estimate the numbers of children being schooled at home, and evidence about student learning and other outcomes is incomplete.

It is possible, however, to draw three conclusions about where home schooling is likely to go and how it will affect the broad public education enterprise—which, for the purpose of this article, includes charter schools and publicly funded voucher programs as well as conventional district-run public schools.[2]

• First, home schooling is part of a broad movement in which private groups and individuals are learning how to provide services that once were left to public bureaucracies.

• Second, as home schooling families learn to rely on one another, many are likely to create new institutions that look something like schools.

• Third, although many home schooling families are willing to accept help from public school systems, the families and the schools they create are far more likely to join the charter and voucher movements than to assimilate back into the conventional public school system.

The body of this article spells out the evidence for these conclusions, and the final section considers the implications of the home school movement for the future of public education.

Developing New Teachers

Parents who decide to school their children at home commit time and energy to an activity that once was left to specialized professionals. Even in

[2]Facts about home schooling can be hard to come by. Home schoolers do not like big organizations, often refuse government-paid assistance, and otherwise avoid doing things that make it easy for bureaucracies to count them. Many families even shun private organizations. Although home schooling associations are growing rapidly, group leaders think that the vast majority of home schoolers are not members. To date, no government or foundation has paid for a careful assessment of all home schoolers' learning or of older children's experiences in jobs and higher education. Thus, a researcher is left with interviews with home school association leaders and with school district officials who assist home schoolers and with facts that can be gleaned from the many home school Web sites. Those are the main sources of this article.

21

P. T. Hill

the states with the most permissive home schooling laws, parents must learn what is normally taught to children of a given age, find materials and projects that teach specific skills, and learn how to use their own time and that of their children productively. The vast majority of home school parents who hope their children will attend colleges and universities also must learn how to assess their children's progress against higher education admission standards.

Even a casual perusal of home schooling literature can reveal the scale and intensity of home schooling parents' search for ideas, materials, and relevant standards of performance. In only 1 month, home schooling Web sites posted new ideas and materials for teaching mathematics, history, social studies, classics, literature, art, drama, and creative and expository writing. Parents can find advice about what kind of mathematics program is likely to work for their own children and can enter chat rooms with other parents struggling with the same issues.

Without making a quality judgment about these resources, it is clear that many serious people are putting in a great deal of effort. The materials available are not amateur: They come from universities, research institutes, mutual assistance networks, school districts, and state education departments. People who contribute to home schooling Web sites and association meetings also are conducting serious research and development. Home schooling is a very large teacher training program, and many tens of thousands of people are learning how to teach, assess results, and continuously improve instruction. It also must be one of the biggest parent training programs in the country.

Home schooling is not the only area in which large numbers of people are committed to learning how to serve others effectively. Nonprofit and faith-based organizations, recently the main providers of welfare and job training services, are working hard to learn how to provide effective services, keep clients, maintain private and public funding, build stable organizations, and select and train staff. Although most such organizations are led by professional managers with experience in public administration, many organizations rely heavily on people who have never before had formal training in their jobs. Chambers of commerce and associations of retired executives are helping these organizations get their feet on the ground. A conservative Christian group, Faithworks, provides volunteer leadership and training for nonprofit groups working on poverty, education, public health, job training, prisoners' transition to freedom, and so forth.

Like charter schooling, home schooling depends on the creation of new human capital. People have to learn, in new contexts and under new rules, how to teach and motivate students, take advantage of complementary adult skills, find resources, and make effective use of scarce time and money.

The Future of Public Education

Critics charge that much of this effort is wasted and that, at best, all the new human capital developed at such cost can only duplicate what already exists in conventional public and private schools. Unlikely. Although the new people undoubtedly will reinvent some wheels, and some may go down blind alleys, these initiatives bring new blood and new ideas into human service areas that previously were dominated by civil service cartels and, thus, were rule-bound and risk-averse.

Likely to Evolve Toward Something Like Schools

Home schoolers are not all recluses living in remote log cabins. Growing numbers of home schooling families live in or near cities, are well educated, and hold down normal jobs. They are not all afraid of the modern world; many are inveterate users of the Internet, and large numbers of West Coast home school parents work in the computer and software industries.

Though large numbers of home schoolers are Christian fundamentalists and Mormons, many are members of mainstream religions. There are active home schooling organizations for Lutherans, Catholics, and Jews. In Washington, Oregon, and California, many of the new urban home schoolers are unchurched.

Home schoolers' fierce independence does not lead to isolationism. Increasingly, parents are bartering services—the mother who was a math major tutors children from several families in return for music or history lessons. Families come together to create basketball or soccer teams, hold social events, or put on plays and recitals. Growing numbers of home schoolers value the expertise of professional educators and are readily accepting help, advice, and testing assistance offered by school districts.

State home school association leaders say that some families have built their whole lives around teaching their children and are unlikely to change. But few home schooling parents want to isolate their children from other people. Many are happy to accept help, and they seize opportunities to have their children tutored by experts or tested in ways that demonstrably reflect progress toward meeting college admission standards.

In such a situation, it is highly likely that parents will come to collaborate, specialize, and exploit comparative advantages. It is too soon to say whether many such collaborations will ever become elaborate enough to include (a) cash payments for services or (b) the hiring of coordinators to schedule and integrate services and exercise quality control. However, some home schooling collaboratives already have advanced to the point that groups of parents find themselves running organizations that—to the naked eye—look like schools. In Colorado, Arizona, and Michigan, several

P. T. Hill

such groups have won charters and are operating as new public schools. Some home schooling groups also have created management firms offering to create new schools that coordinate parent efforts and incorporate many of the values and processes of home schooling.

The advantages are obvious: Parents can limit their time commitments and get for their children the benefits of others' expertise. They also can get public funds to pay for materials, facilities, management time, Internet hookups, and testing that they otherwise would have to spend their own time and money to arrange. Those who have mastered a subject or learned a great deal about instructional methods can even decide to become paid teachers.

However, home schooling parents would be skittish and demanding clients. Many have learned exactly what they want for their children and are unlikely to stick with an arrangement that does not deliver. But all the preconditions exist for the emergence of new schools based on what home schooling families have learned. Charter school heads report that former home schoolers, who know exactly how much their children can accomplish, are extremely demanding about the standards and pace of instruction.

"Reschooling" of home schoolers might have happened much more quickly if conservative Christian church leaders had been inclined to build new institutions. However, compared to "mainstream" Catholic, Lutheran, Episcopalian, and Jewish leaders, conservative Christians have devoted relatively more energy to political movements and relatively less to institution-building. Discouraged about the results of political action, many Christian leaders are now advocating intensified investment in their own communities. Coupled with major social investments led by new organizations like Social Venture Partners and Faithworks, lay and religious leaders can, and probably will, greatly accelerate the reschooling of experienced parent–teachers and their children.

Not Likely to Meld Back Into Conventional Public Education

Although growing numbers of home schoolers are receiving valuable assistance from local public school systems, mass returns to conventional public schools are unlikely. Most home schooling parents fled something they did not like about the public education system—variously perceived as lax discipline, bad manners, low standards, unsafe conditions, and hostility to religious practice. Although some also may have fled racial integration, the majority of home schoolers live in neighborhoods where virtually all public school students are White.

The Future of Public Education

In general, their Web sites make it clear that home schoolers dread bureaucracy, unions, and liberals. Parents complain about teachers who would not adjust to individual children's needs and about principals who insisted that district rules prevent using better methods, changing children's placements, accelerating instruction, or replacing bad teachers. Web sites also complain about liberal social agendas, particularly those associated with homosexuality and perceived attacks on the family. (Public schools' teaching of evolution, a persistent complaint of the religious right, gets far less attention on home school home pages than perceived advocacy of alternative life styles, as in the book *Heather Has Two Mommies* by Newman, 1989).

Although home school Web sites are full of ideas about learning projects and what conventional educators would call "authentic" performance measures, parents are openly suspicious about forms of student-directed "progressive" education used in public schools. They strongly favor reading, writing, and debating. Web sites are full of resources for teaching classic liberal arts subjects (including rhetoric) and suggestions for study of primary sources.

Complaints about state standards and performance-based education are far less prominent in home schooling materials than in religious right political agendas. Educated home schoolers are concerned about preparing their children for the real world, and they are open to state standards and testing programs that guide action and give measures of progress. Home schoolers are, however, suspicious of federally imposed rules on education of the handicapped. Their Web sites include guidance for parents who have decided to home school children with disabilities rather than keep them in public school special education programs, which they consider stigmatizing and of low quality.

These concerns, and the fact that many families began home schooling after what they perceived as "takeovers" of their local public school systems by "progressive" academics and left-of-center parents, make it unlikely that large numbers of home schooling parents can return readily to public schools. Some home schoolers will get by with the help available from public school systems, and others will seek to create charter schools. Some—the numbers depending on costs and the availability of private subsidies—also will be attracted to specially constructed private schools such as those now being created by the conservative Christian Heritage Schools.

Given American families' reliance on dual incomes, it is unlikely that home schooling will continue to grow indefinitely. But it almost certainly will continue to attract families that cannot find comfortable places in conventional public schools, and it will continue to be a channel through which parents become attached to private and charter alternatives.

25

P. T. Hill

What's the Harm?

What could be wrong with a movement that leads tens of thousands of people to spend vast amounts of time and money learning to teach, working closely with children, developing new instructional materials, and subjecting them to real-world tests? Critics charge that three things could be wrong: Home schooling could harm students academically; it could harm society by producing students who are ill-prepared to function as democratic citizens and participants in a modern economy; and it could make it more difficult for other parents to educate their children by harming public education. However, the best available evidence suggests that home schooling does not threaten children, society, or public education in any of these ways.

Student Learning

The same factors that make it hard to count home schoolers also make the phenomenon difficult to study. Home schoolers do not all show up at one place to be counted, and many see no reason to identify themselves in ways that might later lead to requests for information or demands on their time. Thus, at this point, there is no study on the experiences and outcomes for a truly representative sample of home school students.

The best available evidence, which is strongly positive about home school student learning, is based on a large sample of children whose parents use the Bob Jones University Testing Service for home schoolers. Rudner's (1999) analysis, based on test scores of more than 20,000 students, is highly positive:

> Almost 25% of home school students are enrolled one or more grades above their age-level peers in public and private schools.
>
> Home school student achievement test scores are exceptionally high. The median scores for every subtest at every grade (typically in the 70th to 80th percentile) are well above those of public and Catholic/Private school students.
>
> On average, home school students in grades 1 to 4 perform one grade level above their age-level public/private school peers on achievement tests.
>
> The achievement test score gap between home school students and public/private school students starts to widen in grade 5.
>
> Students who have been home schooled their entire academic life have higher scholastic achievement test scores than students who have also attended other educational programs.

The Future of Public Education

There are no meaningful differences in achievement by gender, whether the student is enrolled in a full-service curriculum, or whether a parent holds a state issued teaching certificate. (Rudner, 1999)[3]

However, these results are drawn from a self-selected group of home schoolers—less than 5% of the lowest estimated total—who sought a university's help in assessing student progress. Although there is no known profile of home schoolers against which to compare the sample, it is almost certainly a better-educated, higher-income, and better-supported (e.g., by church membership) group than home schoolers as a whole (see Welner & Welner, 1999). The potential importance of these differences is clear from another finding summarized in the article: "There are significant achievement differences among home school students when classified by amount of money spent on education, family income, parent education, and television viewing."

Thus, it is still impossible to say whether, on the whole and on average, home schooling students are doing much better than their public and private school counterparts than the results of the Rudner study would imply. However, it is also totally unwarranted to argue on the assumption that home schoolers are doing badly. Absent a rigorous (and given the difficulties of creating an adequate sampling frame, extremely expensive) study, the best guess must be that home schoolers are doing extremely well. The lurid image of the home school parent as a mad individualist who abuses his children by shielding them from knowledge is, in light of the best data, unwarranted.

In light of the best available facts, people who are worried about home school student learning have the burden of proof. They should be the ones urging the federal government to spend the millions it would cost to study participation and outcomes. Such a study would be based on a truly representative sample of home schoolers. It also would compare home schooling outcomes to the whole range of outcomes of public schools, asking not only whether home schoolers do as well on average but also whether extremely low performance is as prevalent among home schoolers as it is among public school students.

Preparation for Adult Life

Nobody knows whether home schooling produces any different mixture of geniuses, socially adept individuals, academic failures, or misfits than do conventional public schools. For that matter, nobody has a good

---

[3]For an excellent commentary on the Rudner article, see Welner and Welner (1999).

P. T. Hill

grasp on what the distribution of those outcomes is—or ought to be—in the population as a whole.

Some educators worry about the agendas of conservative religious leaders and parents, assuming they want children to become intolerant, insular, hypercompetitive, or convinced of religious or racial superiority. There is little basis for these fears, other than the long-standing tensions between religious groups (both conservative and mainstream) and the academic left. In the 1950s, some educators worried that Catholic schools were building an insular subpopulation tied to an authoritarian culture and intellectually unprepared for modern life. Harvard President James Conant called Catholic schools "divisive." Stories about children learning arithmetic by adding and subtracting rosary beads fed this fear. Today, however, it is hard to argue that Catholic school students, among the most socially and politically active Americans and perhaps the most economically mobile, were not being at least as well prepared for life in a modern democracy as were public school students.

Concerns about the educational motives and practices of Conservative Christians echo earlier worries about Catholic schooling. Berliner (1997), for example, worries about Christian schools' consequences for pluralism and cites examples of (presumably unacceptable) rote learning practices and underuse of modern teaching methods in Christian schools. As in the earlier case of Catholic schools, education professors' tastes in pedagogy do not necessarily predict results.

Others avoid the trap of assessing schools in terms of current pedagogical orthodoxies but worry that home schooling (along with private schooling, charters, and vouchers) pulls children away from the socially centripetal experience of the common school, in which people of all races and backgrounds are educated together to common standards. This concern, too, has little empirical basis. Home schoolers certainly do not experience "common schools," but neither, apparently, does anyone else. Whether they attend private or public schools, the vast majority of students are likely to attend classes and associate with others very like themselves. Even in public schools that serve all social classes and races, students are resegregated by race, social class, and academic performance.[4]

Moreover, contemporary public schools do not meet the aspirations of those who expect them to be incubators of young democrats. As Smith and Sikkink (1999) found, graduates of private (including conservative Chris-

---

[4]Small studies by Jay Green are about the only evidence we have on this topic, and they showed that students in private and religious schools are *more* likely to associate with children from diverse racial and income backgrounds that are children in demographically similar public schools (see, e.g., Greene & Mellow, 1998).

The Future of Public Education

tian) schools are more likely than demographically similar public school graduates to express tolerant attitudes, volunteer time and money for social causes, and participate in civic debates. My own studies of high schoolers' discourse about issues of tolerance, reciprocity, and social responsibility suggest that students in large, diverse public high schools have fewer opportunities for discussion and are kept farther away from potentially emotional topics than are students in private schools.

None of this proves that home schooling meets every aspiration Americans have for their children. But it does place the worries about home schooling in perspective, and it suggests the basis on which home schooling should be evaluated: It needs to be compared to the real performance of conventional public schools, not to some idealized aspiration.

Harm to Public Education

Home schooling limits public school enrollments and therefore reduces the amounts of money state governments provide to local school districts. It also reduces the numbers of parents who expect to enhance their own children's education by voting for taxes and bond issues. On the other hand, home schooling reduces the burdens on public school systems and, in areas with growing populations, decreases pressure for new buildings and staffs. Unlike charters and public vouchers, home schooling does not force an overt transfer of public funds from an incumbent bureaucracy to a new rival organization.

Like charters and vouchers, home schooling also is criticized for weakening the common civic enterprise represented by the public school system. To some, deliberation about education is a necessary means of making one society out of many groups. To them, public policy making through elections, legislative action, ballot initiatives, and neighborhood decision making is what makes us a society. They think that people who demand freedom from regulations, educate children themselves, or pay for private schools weaken critical public forums.

There is a contrary view, that intellectual and values diversity are so important to a democratic society that questions about education never should be settled authoritatively (see, e.g., Randall, 1994, particularly chap. 5). People who hold that view point to legislatures' susceptibility to being captured by interest groups and their inability to settle deeply controversial issues. They also question whether new mechanisms like state standards-setting processes are any less susceptible to interest group logrolling. They have reason to think that standard-setting processes have degenerated into logrolling sessions among advocates for different sub-

P. T. Hill

jects and that states have pretended false clarity about what skills young people must have in our boisterous, competitive, fast-moving, technology-driven, and unpredictable society. There are, moreover, democratic theorists who question whether a parent should defer to a majority.

Again, in a situation in which so little is understood, the potential harms of home schooling seem far smaller than the harms of trying to prevent or thwart it. Every issue raised here is amenable to evidence, but abstract arguments and fears do not stand up against home school parents' First Amendment rights and their evident willingness to back up conviction with money, time, and effort.

Conclusion

The issues raised here are far from resolved. Scholarly and political discussions about home schooling are burdened by an unrecognized ambiguity in our use of the term "public education," which in some instances refers to a commitment to use any means necessary to ensure that every child learns enough to participate fully as a citizen, earner, and parent, and in other instances refers to a specific set of political bargains, rules, programs, job rights, and bureaucratic oversight mechanisms. The difference between these two definitions of public education is evident everywhere, but most painfully in the big cities. There, aspirations for student learning, racial injustice, and introduction of disadvantaged students into the mainstream of society are high. Political and educational leaders talk endlessly about the importance of high standards. But students fall further behind the longer they are in school, and more than half of them drop out before gaining a regular high school diploma.

Our dialogue about home schooling, charters, and public vouchers is frozen by confusion of means and ends. The people who run and staff conventional public schools are convinced that the current arrangements are public education. The question, put into play by home schooling and related reforms, is, Is that definition too narrow? Should home schooling, charters, and vouchers be considered parts of a broad repertoire of methods that we as a society use to educate our children? On what grounds can those questions be resolved?

References

Berliner, D. C. (1997). Educational psychology meets the Christian right: Differing view of children, schooling, teaching, and learning. *Teachers College Record, 98,* 381–411.

The Future of Public Education

Bruno, R., & Curry, A. (1997). *Current population reports. Population characteristics: School enrollment—Social and economic characteristics of students: October 1995.* Washington, DC: U.S. Department of Commerce, Economics, and Statistics Administration.

Greene, J. P., & Mellow, N. (1998). *Integration where it counts: A study of racial integration in private school lunchrooms.* Unpublished manuscript, University of Texas at Austin, Department of Political Science.

Lines, P. M. (1998). *Home schoolers: Estimating numbers and growth.* Washington, DC: U.S. Department of Education, Office of Educational Research and Improvement, National Institute on Student Achievement, Curriculum, and Assessment.

Newman, L. (1989). *Heather has two mommies.* Boston: Alyson Wonderland.

Randall, V. (1994). *Private schools and public power: A case for pluralism.* New York: Teachers College Press.

Rudner, L. M. (1999). The scholastic achievement and demographic characteristics of home school students in 1998. *Education Policy Analysis Archives, 7*(8) [Online]. Retrieved March 2000 from the World Wide Web: http://epaa.asu.edu/epaa/v7n8/

Smith, C., & Sikkink, D. (1999, April). Is private school privatizing? *First Things, 92,* 16–20.

Welner, K. M., & Welner, K. G. (1999). Contextualizing homeschooling data: A response to Rudner. *Education Policy Analysis Archives, 7*(13) [Online]. Retrieved March 2000 from the World Wide Web: http://epaa.asu.edu/epaa/v7n13.html

From Confrontation to Accommodation: Home Schooling in South Carolina

Zan Peters Tyler
James C. Carper

Clashes between parents who wanted to teach their children at home and state school officials were commonplace throughout the United States from the 1970s through the early 1990s. State courts and legislatures struggled to balance (a) parents' assertions of free exercise of religion and parental rights to teach their children with minimal state regulations with (b) the government's claim of a compelling interest in assuring an adequate education for children. Curriculum, certification, testing, and home school "approval" were usually the focus of various "battles" between parents and government officials. By the late 1990s, however, most of these issues had been resolved to the satisfaction of most home school parents. South Carolina presents a unique model of one state's efforts to rectify the conflict between government officials and parents.

ZAN PETERS TYLER *is Founder and President of the South Carolina Association of Independent Home Schools, Irmo.*

JAMES C. CARPER *is Associate Professor of Foundations of Education, Department of Educational Psychology, University of South Carolina, Columbia.*

Requests for reprints should be sent to Zan Peters Tyler, 17 Tallawood Lane, Elgin, SC 29045. E-mail: zantyler@aol.com

Introduction

The modern history of home schooling in South Carolina can be divided into four distinct time periods: pre-1984, 1984–1988, 1988–1992, and 1992 until the present. The first three time periods were times of escalating tension and hostility between home school families and school officials, with a period of relative peace ensuing since 1992.

In the years prior to 1988, a "substantial equivalence law" governed home school programs. Section 59–65–40 (Code of Laws of South Carolina, 1976) and State Board of Education Regulation 43–246 provided the legal basis for what was then termed "instruction at a place other than school" (Carnes, 1981). Section 59–65–40 then stated,

> Instruction during the school term at a place other than school may be substituted for school attendance; provided, such instruction is approved by the State Board of Education as substantially equivalent to instruction given to children of like ages in the public or private schools where such children reside.

In 1976, the State Board of Education adopted Regulation 43–246, delegating the approval (or disapproval) of home schooling programs to the school board of the district in which the home schooling family resided. This regulation also established the State Board of Education as the first avenue of appeal in the event the local school board disapproved of a particular home instruction program.

In 1981, the South Carolina State Department of Education (SDE) adopted guidelines to aid local school boards and administrations in determining the ambiguous standard of substantial equivalence. In a letter dated June 19, 1981, Associate Superintendent Ernest B. Carnes stated that these guidelines were implemented after conducting "extensive research into the issues concerning instruction at a place other than school." The guidelines contained two separate documents: one offering suggestions to local school districts researching instruction at a place other than school, and the other providing indicators of quality of instruction at a place other than school. These indicators included the following four areas: teacher qualification, instructional program, student evaluation, and place of instruction.

Under the area of teacher qualification, the guidelines reminded local school personnel that requiring teacher certification might not be appropriate because the law allowed for substantial equivalence to be demonstrated in accord with either private or private schools. Private schools are not required by South Carolina law to employ certified teachers as are the public schools; therefore, in demonstrating substantial equivalence to a private

Z. P. Tyler and J. C. Carper

school that does not require teacher certification, a parent would not have to be a certified teacher to home school. This caveat notwithstanding, many public school districts required certification of home schooling parents.

The guidelines for instructional programs suggested requesting information as detailed as the number of minutes parents planned to devote to each subject per day, week, and year. They suggested that parents provide a daily schedule including beginning time, recess, lunch, and ending time. In a section requesting information on additional materials available at the place of instruction, even the number of books in the home was solicited. Under "Place of Instruction," the guidelines urged an "on-site evaluation of the facility ... prior to approval of the program" (Carnes, 1981).

The Years Prior to 1984

Prior to 1984, the home schooling movement in South Carolina was small, unorganized, and largely unnoticed. Although many date the beginning of the modern home schooling movement as early as 1970 (Moore, 1991), in South Carolina the development of the home schooling community lagged almost a decade behind the rest of the country—probably in part because of the state's hostile legal environment. I have been involved in home schooling since 1984 and have interacted with thousands of parents during the last 15 years (Tyler & Dorian, 1996).[1] Only one dozen to two dozen families with whom I have had contact home schooled in South Carolina prior to 1984, and, of those families, fewer than a handful home schooled prior to 1980.

Some of these families home schooled "underground"; others worked out very simple arrangements with their school districts; some were denied permission to home school by local school boards; and at least one family was taken to court. According to Phoebe Winter (1989) with the Office of Research for the South Carolina SDE,

Each local school district could establish its own criteria for determining whether a home-schooling instruction program provided "substantially equivalent" instruction. The district criteria established ranged from requiring the home instructor to hold a high school diploma to requiring the parent or guardian to be a certified teacher. At least one district disapproved all requests for home instruction. Parents wishing to teach their children at home could be eligible to do so in one district but be barred from providing home instruction in a neighboring district.

[1] In this article, *I* refers to Zan Peters Tyler.

Home Schooling in South Carolina

At least one family went to court prior to 1984. Scott and Susan Page began home schooling two children in 1982. The Calhoun County School Board initially denied their request to home school. This decision was then upheld by the State Board of Education. The matter ended in family court, when Judge Alvin Biggs rendered his decision on June 28, 1983:

I find that the Calhoun County Board's rejection of the Pages' request to teach their children in their homeschool was based upon the unfettered discretion of the Calhoun County School Board. I find the Board did not provide the Pages with any definite standards to guide them after they sent their original letter in August, 1982 requesting permission to teach at the home school, nor did they provide them with any guidelines for future compliance. I find the Calhoun County Board was guided only by their own personal ideas and concepts. ... I find the law has layed an unequal hand on anyone who wants to provide his child with a home school. ... I find that the Pages' home school qualifies under S.C. Code 59–65–10 (1976) as a "school," and that the Board's decision shall be modified accordingly.

I find that the Pages or any other person in South Carolina, if they qualify under set definite ascertainable standards, should be allowed to teach in a home school. I find this is a basic constitutional "liberty" guaranteed by the U.S. Constitution and the 14th Amendment of the U.S. Constitution. (*Calhoun County Department of Education v. Scott Page and Susan Page*, Ruling in the Family Court, June 28, 1983, pp. 177, 179, 181)

Judge Biggs's decision was the last positive ruling the home schooling community in South Carolina would see for years to come.

1984–1988

Between 1984 and 1988, the number of home schooling families in South Carolina grew dramatically. By 1987, an estimated 500 to 600 children were being home schooled ("Committee Votes," 1987), although these numbers were considerably lower than those in neighboring states. The increased interest in home education began concerning public school officials, who determined that they must do something to control the growing numbers of home schooling parents, as well as the process itself.

In the following paragraphs, I relate my experience as a home schooling mother in 1984 to demonstrate the educational establishment's absolute abhorrence of home education in the 1980s. Between 1984 and 1988, many educators in South Carolina decided, "Now is the time to tame the home-school

Z. P. Tyler and J. C. Carper

beast." When I applied to my local school board for permission to home school in June 1984, I did not know that I was inadvertently stepping into a hornet's nest and was about to become the symbolic whipping post for home schooling in South Carolina. Employees at the SDE later informed me that my case in particular, in conjunction with growing statewide interest in home schooling, prompted the SDE and local school district personnel to promulgate stringent regulations for home schooling parents.

In March 1984, I enrolled my oldest son in 5-year-old kindergarten (K–5) at our local public school. Although he would turn 6 in May, at the behest of the clinical psychologist who tested him, I decided to hold him back a year. The assistant principal who completed his enrollment assured me this was no problem; however, in May, the principal of the school informed me that due to South Carolina's Education Improvement Act of 1984, I could not hold him back a year—he would have to be put into first grade. This grade placement for my son was simply unacceptable to my husband and me, and, at that point in May, all the private kindergartens we would have considered suitable were filled for the 1984–1985 school year. I called a school district employee whom I knew very well and, after explaining our situation with my son, pleaded with him to help us secure a place for him in a K–5 class rather than a first-grade class.

When he refused, I stated, "Well, I have no choice then but to home school my son next year." It was a bluff; I was hoping to get his attention sufficiently to help us out of our predicament. I did not want to home school. Instead, he said, "Well, the school board has become lenient with that kind of thing." Later, I discovered the district had approved one family to home school, and the teaching parent was a certified teacher.

I was then baptized with fire into the home schooling movement. First of all, the school district and the State Board of Education refused to provide me with information on how to comply with the law as a home schooling parent. There was nowhere to turn for help—there were no local support groups, no Home School Legal Defense Association (HSLDA),[2] and no state organization. As a matter of fact, I did not know, nor could I find, one person in the state who was home schooling. Everything I knew about home education was contained in *Home Grown Kids* (Moore & Moore, 1981).

I had to hire an attorney simply to find out the laws governing home schooling in the state of South Carolina. In June, I delivered my lengthy application to the school district. In July, the school board denied my request to

---

[2]The HSLDA is an association led by attorneys consisting of more than 60,000 home schooling families nationwide committed to advancing and protecting the rights of parents who teach their children at home.

Home Schooling in South Carolina

home school, although I had very carefully complied with all items outlined in the "guidelines for instruction at a place other than school." Once again, I had to hire an attorney to help me navigate the appeals process. I was discovering firsthand the veracity of Judge Biggs's 1983 prophetic decision: "The law has layed an unequal hand on anyone who wants to provide his child with a home school" (*Calhoun County Department of Education v. Scott Page and Susan Page*, Ruling in the Family Court, June 28, 1983, p. 177).

During the appeals process, I paid an unannounced visit to Charlie Williams, State Superintendent of Education. He graciously agreed to see me; I had known him since my elementary school years. He had observed my mother's fourth-grade classroom for hours on end while he worked toward his doctorate. I thought surely if I explained my situation with my son rationally, he would help me. After all, I had been thrown into home schooling because of a school district error—this had not been my first choice.

Williams's response to my story shocked me. "You know, Mrs. Tyler, you can be put in jail for truancy." (Through no fault of mine, the State Board of Education decided to delay my appeal until after the commencement of school in August.) Everyone seemed to know that the State Board of Education would not reverse the local school board's denial of my home schooling program, reinforcing another portion of Judge Biggs's 1983 decision: "The State Board delegated its decision making authority to the Local Board and in effect 'rubber stamped' any decision by them" (*Calhoun County Department of Education v. Scott Page and Susan Page*, Ruling in the Family Court, June 28, 1983, p. 178).

After the State Superintendent of Education threatened me with jail, I informed my father, an attorney, of my plight. Heretofore, I had told no one (parents, friends, or neighbors) of my plans to home school. In 1984, upstanding citizens simply did not home school in South Carolina. My father immediately contacted Senator Strom Thurmond's office and explained my dire straits (I had worked for the Senator in my senior year in high school). With my hearing with the state board less than a week away, Senator Thurmond immediately flew from Washington, DC, to Columbia to meet with Superintendent Williams to advocate my position. The Senator's staff already had examined my case to make sure it met the letter of the law in every regard. After the Thurmond–Williams meeting, things changed dramatically for me, and, a week later (to no one's surprise), the State Board of Education overturned the school district's decision—authorizing me to home school for the 1984–1985 school year.

My home schooling program was approved in a relatively painless manner for the 1985–1986 school year. My plans to home school for only 1 year dissipated as I became enamored with the concept of home schooling and experienced the benefits to my family firsthand. During 1984 and

Z. P. Tyler and J. C. Carper

1985, I began collecting names of people across the state who advocated (the overwhelming majority were not actually home schooling) home schooling. My sources for these names were private education foundations and attorneys across the nation. Also, as interest in home schooling began to build somewhat, people began contacting me for information on how to get started as well as how to comply with the law. As home schooling families moved to South Carolina from out-of-state, they were given my name as a contact person. I felt compelled to help as many families as I could weather the hostility of the SDE and local school boards.

By fall 1985, I had a mailing list that consisted of approximately 400 names, although I was not at all sure what I was going to do with this list. I had learned from "sources" that public educators were not happy that my home schooling program had been approved and that they were particularly unhappy that the State Board of Education had overturned the local school board's ruling in my case. The animosity and hostility I experienced as a home schooling parent totally baffled me. One educator clarified the situation for me in remarks off the record:

> Zan, it is okay for pockets of home schoolers to exist as long as school districts feel they are still in control. Even underground home schoolers are okay—that means they're scared. But you have become a threat because they stacked the deck against you and you still won. To them you have opened Pandora's box.[3]

Almost all states experienced some type of angst in working out the intricacies of weaving home schooling families into the fabric of daily life in the community. South Carolina's sustained hostility toward home schooling was amazing to me, given the relative ease with which our neighbors in North Carolina and Georgia home schooled.

On October 22, 1985, the SDE served public notice in the State Register concerning the promulgation of home schooling regulations in South Carolina (Williams, 1985). A task force, consisting of five public school officials and three private school administrators, was appointed to draft new, stringent regulations (Quick, 1986). At least two of the five public school officials had aggressively denied parents the right to home school in their districts. None of the task force members had a working knowledge of home education, and none was a home schooling advocate, although one member was slightly sympathetic to home education.

---

[3]This article is based primarily on personal recollections, conversations, and letters. Many times, the individuals with whom I spoke or corresponded provided me with their information and insights based solely on my promise to keep their names anonymous.

Home Schooling in South Carolina

I inadvertently learned of the task force and requested a chance for home school parents to have the opportunity to testify before the committee. At the January 1986 meeting, five parents, including myself, did speak. In my testimony, I pointed out that other states in the region had made more progress in balancing parental rights and state interests and were doing so in a less adversarial manner.

After the task force endured the testimony of the participating parents, they took a short break. On reconvening, Steve Quick, Elementary Supervisor in the Accreditation Section at the SDE, handed out the predrafted regulations that the SDE would be recommending to the legislature (Quick, 1986). The task force had tolerated our testimony but had no intention of using it in any way (Tyler, 1986, pp. 1–4). The regulations apparently had been drafted before hearing our testimony. Among the most severe of the proposed regulations were these: a requirement that the teaching parent hold a college degree from an accredited, 4-year institution; a requirement that parents only be allowed to use state-approved texts in their home schooling programs; and a requirement that all home-schooled students participate in the statewide testing program.

Again, I hired an attorney to learn how to stop these regulations. He advised me that if we had 25 letters of request for a public hearing on the proposed regulations, the state agency had to grant it. This would at least postpone the regulations' submission to the Senate Education Committee and the House Education and Public Works Committee for approval from the 1986 legislative session to the 1987 session, buying us some much-needed time to organize.

For the first time, I put my mailing list to use, having no idea that there were actually 25 home schooling parents on the list and with no certainty that 25 people would respond. Within 2 weeks of that initial mailing, I received more than 100 letters requesting a public hearing in South Carolina. I hand-delivered the letters to the SDE.

In March, I was notified that the public hearing would be held on May 13, 1986. I spent 2 months working intensely with home schooling parents, attorneys, and Raymond Moore, the nationally recognized expert and author (*Home Grown Kids*, 1981; *Home-Spun Schools*, 1982; *Home Style Teaching*, 1984); we flew in for the hearing. A few weeks before the hearing, the SDE notified me that home schooling advocates would have a total of a mere 20 minutes for their comments. We had enough planned testimony to fill at least 2 hours. Once again, my father used his connections to ensure that we would have all the time we needed for testimony at the public hearing.

The day of the public hearing arrived. More than 350 parents and home schooling advocates descended on the Rutledge Building in Columbia (Tyler, 1987, pp. 1–9). Home schoolers provided almost 4 hours of well-organized

Z. P. Tyler and J. C. Carper

testimony against the regulations. Even the SDE's internal publication *Newsline* ("Parents Make Plea," 1986) reported that "a well-organized group of parents and supporters presented their cases for teaching their children at home." Nevertheless, the SDE sent the regulations to the General Assembly for approval with the objectionable portions still intact (McDonald, 1986).

The public hearing did buy home schooling proponents valuable time. During the summer, I paid a visit to my state senator, Warren K. Giese. Not only is Senator Giese a retired University of South Carolina head football coach, but he also holds an earned doctorate in education. For the first time in 2½ years, I found a public official who was genuinely outraged by the treatment that I, as well as other home schooling parents, had received. He agreed to ask the Senate Education Committee, of which he was a member, to hold a hearing on the proposed regulations during the 1987 legislative session. (The South Carolina General Assembly convenes from January through the first week in June.)

On February 4, 1987, the Senate Education Committee held a hearing on the proposed regulations and invited the House Education and Public Works Committee to attend. Almost 700 parents and home schooling advocates were in attendance. In response to the hearing and the great outcry against the regulations, both committees refused to approve the regulations.

Defeating the regulations had been both a time-consuming and expensive adventure. In my naiveté, I thought the issue was closed. The day after the hearing, a young legislator called me at home and assured me that although home schoolers had momentum on our side, we had to strike while the iron was hot. He told me, "Now is the time" to submit proactive home schooling legislation. When I hesitated, he said he had seen the legislation the SDE was planning to introduce, and he assured me that I would not like it.

A few days later, Representative David Beasley filed H. 4224 in the House, and Senator Warren Giese filed S. 457 in the Senate. Ed Garrison, Chairman of the Senate Education Committee, appointed an ad hoc committee made up of three home schooling advocates, representatives from the SDE, and senators. Our job was to draft legislation that respected both the rights of parents and the state's compelling interest in education (Tyler, 1995).

The two issues over which home schooling advocates on the committee were not prepared to compromise were the issues raised by the SDE in the defeated regulations (i.e., the minimum level of parental education for the teaching parent and the freedom of choice in textbook selection). We maintained that the minimum educational requirement for home schooling parents should be a high school diploma or a Graduate Equivalency Degree (GED) and that parents must not be limited in their choice of textbooks to only those on the state-approved list. In return, the Senate

Home Schooling in South Carolina

responded that we must be willing to document that education was occurring in the home.

The committee's deliberations resulted in compromise legislation that stipulated the following conditions for home schooling (Anderson, 1987, pp. 1–2):

1. The teaching parent must hold a high school diploma or a GED.

2. The instructional day must consist of a minimum of 4½ hours, and the instructional year must consist of a minimum of 180 days.

3. The curriculum shall include, but not be limited to, the basic instructional areas of reading, writing, mathematics, science, and social studies.

4. As evidence that a student is receiving regular instruction, the instructor shall maintain the following records: (a) a plan book, diary, or other written record indicating subjects taught and activities in which the student and instructor engage; (b) a portfolio of samples of the student's academic work; (c) a record of evaluations of the student's academic progress; and (d) a semiannual progress report including attendance records and individualized assessments of the student's academic progress in each of the basic instructional areas specified in Item 3.

5. Students must have access to library facilities.

6. Students must participate in the annual statewide testing program and the Basic Skills Assessment Program approved by the State Board of Education for their appropriate grade level.

Because the SDE and home schooling advocates had participated equally in the compromise process, I assumed that the bill would be enacted with minimal debate _(Timothy Lawrence, Richard Kaiser, Deborah Kaiser, and Maureen Deaton v. South Carolina Board of Education,_ Plaintiffs' Post Trial Memorandum by M. P. Farris, October 24, 1990). The SDE, however, immediately withdrew support of the bill. In spite of this, the bill passed the Senate Education Committee and the full Senate with few problems. The bill also was reported favorably out of the House Education and Public Works Committee for consideration by the full House. Passing the House of Representatives presented a new challenge. The bill was placed on the contested calendar and remained there as the House adjourned in June.

It was not until March of the 1988 legislative session that home schoolers,[4] after intense lobbying, finally were able to get the bill out of the

[4]In 1987 through 1988, home schoolers in South Carolina were very loosely organized through a statewide organization named the Carolina Family Schools Association (CFSA). David Waldrop, member of the ad hoc Senate committee to draft compromise home schooling legislation, served as the president. I served as the legislative liaison. In 1989, CFSA changed its name to the South Carolina Home Educators Association (SCHEA). SCHEA still functions today as a networking and information-disseminating organization for home schoolers in South Carolina.

Z. P. Tyler and J. C. Carper

Rules Committee and onto the House floor. When the bill came to a vote in late May, it was substantially amended. Although there were a few benign amendments, one so altered the substance of the bill that the home schooling community withdrew its support of the bill in the amended form. The unpalatable amendment required teaching parents without a 4-year college degree to make a passing score on the Education Entrance Examination (EEE) before they would be allowed to teach their children at home. (The EEE was developed by the state of South Carolina to screen prospective professional teachers.) The concept of "front-end credentialing" for teaching parents had been bandied about since the inception of the task force in 1985 and was vehemently opposed by the home schooling community. Nevertheless, the bill passed in its amended form.

One of the goals of passing home schooling legislation was to standardize the application process that heretofore had been left to the total discretion of local school boards. By instituting reasonable standards, home school advocates had hoped to put an end to the avalanche of home schooling litigation. Instead, the inception of the EEE ushered in a new era of litigation. At one point, HSLDA had more lawsuits filed in South Carolina than in the other 49 states combined ("Cases Filed," 1992).

Members of the home schooling community had hoped by the end of 1988 to lay to rest the hostility and legal turmoil surrounding home education in South Carolina. Instead, the problems escalated. In a letter to members in July 1988, HSLDA President Michael Farris asserted, "Home schoolers in South Carolina need to be banded together for future actions on all fronts. You are saddled with one of the most cumbersome laws in the country. Of all states, you all need to stick together" (Tyler, 1992, p. 3).

1988–1992

From July 1988 to July 1989, a deceptive calm ensued. Although the home schooling law took effect in July 1988, the EEE requirement was not imposed for another year, allowing the SDE to complete the study required by law validating the EEE for use with the home school population. Although fewer home schoolers were denied approval by their local school boards for that one year, many school districts required more information on their home school applications after the law passed than they did before. The forms became so far removed from the intent of the law that HSLDA sent a letter to South Carolina members encouraging them not to give their school districts more information than the law required.

When the EEE requirement took effect, unprecedented numbers of home schoolers were denied approval by their local school boards. Parents without college degrees who had been home schooling successfully for

Home Schooling in South Carolina

years were suddenly disqualified unless they took and passed the EEE. Some veteran home schooling families who moved to South Carolina from other states were not allowed to continue their home schooling. One of the major problems with the EEE was logistical. Although home schoolers as a group had a high pass rate for the EEE (*Timothy Lawrence, Richard Kaiser, Deborah Kaiser, and Maureen Deaton v. South Carolina Board of Education,* Opinion No. 23526 by C. J. Gregory, 1991), they experienced problems because it is only administered three times annually.

At that point, HSLDA intervened and filed a class-action suit on behalf of its 369 member families in South Carolina. The major contention of the lawsuit was that the validity study for using the EEE with the home schooling population had been done poorly and did not meet professional and governmental standards. In February 1989, HSLDA lost the lower court case in a disappointing one-sentence ruling from Judge Drew Ellis.

During 1989, SCHEA, for whom I served as the legislative liaison, developed a twofold strategy for the 1989–1990 legislative session. The first goal was to reduce the sting of the EEE by making it a requirement in the absence of a high school diploma rather than a college diploma. The second goal instituted by SCHEA involved providing for private-sector supervision of home schooling programs. I met with key legislators in both the House and the Senate before the beginning of the 1990 legislative session, and they concurred that our chances to amend the home schooling law looked fairly positive. Only a month into the session, however, the same key legislators informed me that we had no chance of making the desired strides through legislation. As one legislator told me, "You will have to find another way."

In February 1990, I began researching the legal feasibility of creating an accrediting organization for home schools in the private sector, thereby negating the need for home schooling parents to gain approval from their local school districts. On July 20, 1990, the South Carolina Association of Independent Home Schools (SCAIHS) was incorporated. SCAIHS was founded on the premise that the South Carolina compulsory attendance law provided the legal basis for its existence. According to 59–65–10 of the South Carolina Code of Laws:

> All parents or guardians shall cause their children or wards to attend regularly a public or private school or kindergarten of this State which has been approved by the State Board of Education or a member school of the South Carolina Independent Schools' Association (SCISA) or some similar organization. (p. 215)

The "some similar organization" clause served as the key element in the establishment of SCAIHS. Patterned after SCISA, SCAIHS fulfilled that

43

Z. P. Tyler and J. C. Carper

part of the compulsory attendance law allowing a private school to be a member of SCISA or some similar organization. Also key to the legal basis for SCAIHS was the establishment of member home schools as private schools. Because of our tenuous legal position, the anticipated SCAIHS membership the first year was 35 to 50 families. Within the first 2 months of existence, 120 families had joined.

SCAIHS had not been in existence for 3 months before our legal problems commenced. On October 5, 1990, 11 SCAIHS families in Lexington School District 5 were served with truancy charges. The County Solicitor agreed to delay prosecution of these families until an attorney general's opinion could be rendered on the legal status of SCAIHS and its members. Many other school districts contemplating prosecution of SCAIHS families also agreed to wait for the impending attorney general's opinion. In January 1991, the attorney general ruled that SCAIHS did not fulfill the intent of the compulsory attendance law, thus setting the stage for litigation. Early in 1991, HSLDA's Michael Farris and Dewitt Black filed a declaratory judgment suit in Lexington County on behalf of the affected SCAIHS families. This was followed by Richland County School District 1 filing a declaratory judgment to establish the school district's rights under the home schooling law. SCAIHS lost both cases and appealed both decisions to the South Carolina Supreme Court.

During fall 1991, when the future of SCAIHS looked very bleak, several events occurred that would begin to change the landscape of home schooling in South Carolina. A state attorney mentioned to me the need for new legislation to resolve the mounting legal tension surrounding SCAIHS. Newly elected State Superintendent of Education Barbara Nielsen made it clear that she did not view home schoolers as "the enemy" and was open to a legislative remedy to the "SCAIHS problem."

On December 9, 1991, the South Carolina Supreme Court rendered its ruling on the EEE Case. It reversed the lower court's decision and stated that the EEE had not been properly validated for use with home schooling parents (*Timothy Lawrence, Richard Kaiser, Deborah Kaiser, and Maureen Deaton v. South Carolina Board of Education,* Opinion No. 23526 by C. J. Gregory, 1991). This was a landmark decision for home schoolers in South Carolina, carrying with it national implications as well. In *The Home School Court Report* (Tyler, 1992), attorney Mike Farris said,

> We viewed this law with utmost seriousness as a grave danger which had the potential of spreading across the nation. Accordingly, we went after this South Carolina test with everything we had. We have learned a lot about the world of test validity. We are ready if any other state decides to try this again. ("Home Schoolers Win EEE Case," 1992, p. 4)

Home Schooling in South Carolina

The ruling had significant ramifications for SCAIHS because one of the biggest complaints leveled against the association had been its lack of minimum educational requirements for teaching parents (i.e., SCAIHS did not require a teaching parent to possess a baccalaureate degree or a passing score on the EEE). When the EEE requirement was rendered unenforceable, one of the major objections against SCAIHS was laid to rest.

In December 1991, the SCAIHS Board of Directors appointed a legislative committee, including James Carper and myself, to pursue the possibility of introducing SCAIHS legislation during the 1992 legislative session. This committee met with legislative and education officials, as well as representatives from the governor's office. By January 1992, we had members in both the House and the Senate who agreed to sponsor the following SCAIHS legislation:

In lieu of the requirements of 59–65–40 (the home-schooling law requiring school district approval), parents and guardians may teach their children at home if the instruction is conducted under the auspices of the South Carolina Association of Independent Home Schools. Bona fide membership and continuing compliance with the academic standards of SCAIHS exempts the home school from the further requirements of Section 59–65–40.

Considering the rocky road the prior home schooling legislation had encountered, the bill proceeded through the House of Representatives with relative ease and speed. This was due in large part to the expert guidance of Representative David Wright, bill sponsor and Chairman of the K–12 Subcommittee, and Representative Olin Philips, Chairman of the House Education and Public Works Committee. At the bill's final reading in the House, a threatening amendment was offered but averted, and the House unanimously approved the legislation with the following amendment: "By January thirtieth of each year the South Carolina Association of Independent Home Schools shall report the number and grade level of children home schooled through the association to the children's respective school districts."

The bill was then sent to the Senate and assigned to a subcommittee of the Senate Education Committee. On March 4, the bill was passed unanimously by the subcommittee, but we were warned that a potentially crippling amendment would be considered at the full Senate Education Committee meeting on March 18.

Following a massive phone campaign and lobbying effort initiated by SCAIHS, the Senate passed the House version of the bill, and the objectionable provisions of the threatening amendment were defeated. The Senate

Z. P. Tyler and J. C. Carper

version did contain the following amendments that were viewed as harmless, because SCAIHS already had implemented the requirements into the association's membership guidelines: A parent must hold at least a high school diploma or GED; the instructional year must be at least 180 days; and the curriculum must include, but not be limited to, the basic instructional areas of reading, writing, mathematics, science, and social studies, and, in Grades 7 through 12, composition and literature.

On March 25, the bill went to the full Senate and was unanimously approved. On March 31, the House concurred with the Senate version of the bill. On April 8, 1992, Governor Carroll A. Campbell, Jr., signed the bill, and the SCAIHS legislation became law, ending a decade of intense legal and political hostility toward home schooling parents.

Concerning the SCAIHS legislative victory, Michael P. Farris, President of HSLDA, said,

> South Carolina was the most active state in the nation in taking home schoolers to court. The South Carolina legislature responded to this bad situation by allowing responsible self-government for home schoolers. This is an advancement of an important legal principle. (Tyler, 1992, p. 3)

Confrontation had given way to accommodation.

1992 Through the Present

Since its inception in 1990, SCAIHS has grown from two employees and 120 families to 18 employees and more than 1,300 families, representing more than 2,000 children. With the cessation of political and legal problems, SCAIHS has been able to focus its energy on developing support services for home schooling families. The association has instituted the High School Program, which has grown from 5 students to 400 students. Every college and university in South Carolina accepts the SCAIHS transcript and diploma, and all of our graduates have been accepted to the college of their first choice—with many attending college on scholarships. A Special Needs Program has been implemented to provide specialized counsel to those parents of children with learning disabilities and physical handicaps. SCAIHS publishes a quarterly newsletter, provides thousands of hours of curriculum counseling, sponsors teacher-training workshops and seminars, represents the home schooling viewpoint to the community at large, and maintains an active presence in the legislature. Foundational to the association's mission to serve parents is the accountability we provide from a supportive, rather than adversarial, position.

Home Schooling in South Carolina

The SCAIHS success story has it roots in years of struggle, turmoil, and backbreaking labor. The long years of publicly hammering out the issues of parental freedom in education have born great fruit. The General Assembly, the South Carolina judicial system, state and local educators, and parents have all played important roles in forging a creative solution to the overwhelming problems that once plagued home schooling parents in South Carolina. SCAIHS is the only organization in the nation to be named specifically in state statute and vested with authority equal to that of local school boards in approving home schooling programs.[5]

SCAIHS is not a state agency, and, yet, we have been entrusted by the state with the task of responsibly governing ourselves. The arrangement is working extremely well. Our students are succeeding academically, socially, and morally. The state is benefitting from well-educated students who have cost taxpayers nothing. Families benefit from a state that has actively engaged in public debate and has reinforced its commitment to the fundamental principle that children are a sacred trust from God and "not mere creatures of the State."

References

Anderson, J. A. (1987, April 2). [Letter to ad hoc committee members providing draft of home school legislation].

Associations for Home Schools; Requirements, Volume 20, Code of Laws of South Carolina § 59–65–47 (1976).

Calhoun County Department of Education v. Scott Page and Susan Page, Ruling in the Family Court (State of South Carolina, County of Calhoun, June 28, 1983).

Carnes, E. B. (1981, June 19). *Guidelines concerning instruction at a place other than school.* Columbia: South Carolina State Department of Education.

Cases filed in South Carolina by Home School Legal Defense Association on behalf of parents challenging the validity and constitutionality of the state home school statute. (1992, January 10). Paeonian Springs, VA: Home School Legal Defense Association.

Committee votes to loosen home school regulations. (1987, February 13). *Charleston News and Courier,* 5b.

Education Improvement Act of 1984, Volume 20, Code of Laws of South Carolina (1976).

Home schoolers win EEE case. (1992, January–February). *Home School Court Report.* Paeonian Springs, VA: Home School Legal Defense Association.

Home Schooling Programs, Volume 20, Code of Laws of South Carolina § 59–65–40 (1976).

Instruction as a Place Other Than School, Regulations Volume 24, Code of Laws of South Carolina, Regulation 43–246 (1976).

McDonald, H. (1986, October 8). Motion to promulgate a regulation: R43–246.1—Home Instruction. Columbia: South Carolina State Board of Education.

---

[5]In 1996, the South Carolina General Assembly passed a third home schooling law (59–65–47), which allows for the existence of other accountability organizations in South Carolina.

Z. P. Tyler and J. C. Carper

Moore, R. S. (1991, February). *White paper—history on homeschooling*. Washougal, WA: Hewitt Research Foundation.

Moore, R. S., & Moore, D. (1981). *Home grown kids*. Washougal, WA: Hewitt Research Foundation.

Moore, R. S., & Moore, D. (1982). *Home-spun schools*. Washougal, WA: Hewitt Research Foundation.

Moore, R. S., & Moore, D. (1984). *Home style teaching*. Waco, TX: Word Books.

Parents make plea to be "home" team in education. (1986, May 16). *Newsline*.

Quick, S. (1986, January 14). *Proposed home instruction regulations for grades 1–12*. Columbia: South Carolina State Department of Education.

Responsibility of Parent or Guardian; Notification of School District Availability of Kindergarten; Transportation for Kindergarten Pupils, Volume 20, Code of Laws of South Carolina § 59–65–10 (1976 & Supp. 1999).

Timothy Lawrence, Richard Kaiser, Deborah Kaiser, and Maureen Deaton v. South Carolina State Board of Education, Opinion No. 23526 by C. J. Gregory (Supreme Court, State of South Carolina, December 9, 1991).

Timothy Lawrence, Richard Kaiser, Deborah Kaiser, and Maureen Deaton v. South Carolina Board of Education, Plaintiffs' Post Trial Memorandum by M. P. Farris (Court of Common Pleas, State of South Carolina, County of Richland, October 24, 1990).

Tyler, Z. P. (1986, January 5). [Letter to home-schooling advocates concerning home-schooling regulations and public hearing].

Tyler, Z. P. (1987, January 3). [Letter to home-schooling families and advocates concerning the Senate Education Committee's hearing on home-schooling regulations].

Tyler, Z. P. (1992, May–June). South Carolina home schoolers celebrate legislative victory. *Home School Court Report*, 3–5.

Tyler, Z. P. (1995). *Supporting home education in South Carolina. Reclaiming the legacy: A new public policy agenda for South Carolina*. Columbia: South Carolina Policy Council.

Tyler, Z. P., & Dorian, T. (1996). *Anyone can homeschool*. Lafayette, LA: Huntington House.

Williams, C. G. (1985, October 22). *South Carolina Department of Education notice of drafting period in the South Carolina State Register*. Columbia, SC: Legislative Council.

Winter, P. C. (1989, March). *Regulation of home schooling parents in South Carolina: The state's perspective*. A symposium presentation at the annual meeting of the American Educational Research Association, San Francisco.

PEABODY JOURNAL OF EDUCATION, 75(1&2), 49–70
Copyright © 2000, Lawrence Erlbaum Associates, Inc.

Home Education Regulations in Europe and Recent U.K. Research

Lesley Ann Taylor
Amanda J. Petrie

Home education is the education of children in and around the house by their parents or by those appointed by the parents. It can be seen as a temporary or permanent alternative to the education which is provided by the state or by private schooling. (Petrie, 1993, p. 139)

Home schooling has clearly caught the imagination of the American public as we approach the 21st century. Whether it is called home schooling, home education, home-based education, or home-centered learning, this age old practice has experienced a rebirth and taken hold in every state of the Union. (Ray, 1997, p. ix)

Children are born, they learn to walk, they learn to talk, they go to school. Schooling is now so ingrained in our culture we have come to believe there can be no education without it. In line with this, almost every-

LESLEY ANN TAYLOR, *who received her doctorate from Stanford University in 1993, resides in Wales, United Kingdom. E-mail: LesleyAnnTaylor@alumni.stanford.org*

AMANDA J. PETRIE *is a Research Fellow in the Department of Education at the University of Liverpool, England. www.worldzone.net/lifestyles/homeducation*

49

L. A. Taylor and A. J. Petrie

thing done to improve the quality of education through research and innovation, is based on the assumption that schooling and education are interchangeable terms. ... Yet, while good classroom practice no doubt maximizes learning within the classroom, it does not follow that there may not be other equally or more efficient ways in which children can learn. (Thomas, 1998, pp. 1, 53)

This article looks at the legal situation of home educators in the United Kingdom and other parts of Europe, outlines the law that applies to home education in the United Kingdom and France in detail, summarizes some of the more recent U.K. research, and considers ways in which recent home education research in the United Kingdom compares with that in the United States.

An Overview of the Legal Situation in Europe

Home education during the 19th and early 20th centuries was considered a natural form of education in all European countries. It is only during the 20th century that some governments have sought to limit this form of education. Sometimes the limitation has been for political reasons, as in Germany. Other governments have encouraged the child's right to education, and legislators, aware of schooling and unaware of home education, inadvertently have confused compulsory education and compulsory schooling. In Spain and France, very stringent laws were enacted because a very few children were involved in small schools of extreme religious sects, and home educators in those countries subsequently were restricted. It would seem that in those instances, information about home educators and their children and home education research results had not been studied before decisions were made by the legislators involved.

In a study of legislation concerning home education in Western European countries, Petrie (1995) found countries that

- Accommodate home educators and always have done so (Belgium, Denmark, Ireland, France, Italy, Luxembourg, Norway, Portugal, most of Switzerland, United Kingdom).
- Have not permitted home education sometime in the past, but now do so (Austria).
- Now no longer permit home education in the word of the law but would appear to permit individual instances (Spain, Greece, two Swiss cantons, the Netherlands, Germany).

Home Education Regulations

The exact numbers of home educators in each country are difficult to come by for a variety of reasons. In some countries, children who have never been to school are not required to register with the authorities. Even where it is difficult to home educate, as in Germany, children are educated at home, but the parents often do not make themselves known to others. Not all families belong to home educating support groups.

Along with differing laws throughout Europe, there are differing demands placed on home educating parents. In the United Kingdom and the Republic of Ireland, parents are responsible for providing a suitable education. In Norway, the law reads that students have the right and obligation to attend the basic school unless they are receiving a corresponding education from some other source. In Norway and also in Portugal, home-educated students must register with the local school. In Austria, the students must follow the national curriculum and are tested on it annually, and in Luxembourg, students' education must be equal with that of school. In Italy, it is traditionally the father who has a responsibility to God to see that his children are educated.

Germany is the only country where permission to home educate is extremely rare. No exceptions to the compulsory schooling laws are made for Traveler[1] children to be educated at home by their parents or via correspondence courses; these children are expected to attend boarding schools (Liegeois, 1987). In addition, home education is not permitted for river craft children. In other countries, such as the Netherlands, there is a more flexible approach that permits such families to maintain their own culture and way of life.

Some families who wished to home educate have left Germany and moved to other European countries or the United States to home educate. Petrie (1995) gave two examples. The first involved Tilmann, a child who suffered from severe school phobia. Initially, when the doctor decided Tilmann was too ill to go to school, he was taught at home by a qualified secondary school teacher. A 2-year legal process began that was "resolved" when he felt well enough to attend school. Two years later, when he was again unable to face school, his parents sent him to stay for a year with friends in the United States. When he returned, the family subsequently moved to Switzerland to live in a canton where home education is permitted. The second case involved Danny, whose mother Renata Leuffen wanted to home educate him, mainly for religious reasons. Leuffen took her case to the European court, but she did not secure the right to home educate her son in Germany. She moved to London to con-

---

[1]The term *Traveler* is used here to refer to peoples of Romany origin who move location for the major part of the year, selling handcrafted products and finding seasonal employment.

51

L. A. Taylor and A. J. Petrie

tinue home educating him; the education she provided was monitored by the Local Education Authority (LEA) and thought to be satisfactory.

An American family in Germany was prosecuted for home educating three children and fined approximately $2,300.00 (U.S.) per child; it has been reported that there are other German home educating families who also have been fined by the German government and face possible jail sentences (Grimes & Grimes, 1999).

On December 18, 1998, an Act was passed in France limiting the role of home education. Prior to this, home educators had been able to provide an education suitable to each individual child that was monitored by the regional administration when the child was 8, 10, and 12 years old. Any disputes between families and the education authorities (e.g., over the definition of *suitable education*) were decided by a visit of a representative from the Ministry of Education in Paris. The Loi No. 98–1865 now enforces compulsory registration at the local town hall and visits to the home by an employee of the Academie de l'Education and by sociologists and psychologists. If parents refuse to comply with these regulations, they can be fined 50,000 francs or have a 6-month prison sentence. The areas that the home-educated child must study are also specified:

- The French language, both written (in grammar and expression) and spoken, and a knowledge of French culture, based on literature.
- Principles of mathematics (specified in detail).
- At least one foreign language.
- The history and geography of France, Europe, and the world.
- Science and technology.
- Art and culture.
- Participation in sport.

In addition, the child must be able to

- Ask questions.
- Propose reasoned answers from observations and written evidence.
- Prove reasoning ability.
- Devise a plan of work, conduct research, and produce finished work.
- Master information technology and use it to communicate with others.
- Approach things in a mature way, using available resources and evaluating risks.

Depending on ability, the child must be at a level in all subjects similar to a child who is attending school.

Home Education Regulations

The discussion in the Assemblée Générale [Parliament] (1998–1999–45ème jour, 115ème séance du Jeudi 10 Decembre 1998) centered around a belief (expressed by M. Patrick Leroy) that at least 6,000 children between the ages of 6 and 16 did not attend school and that these children were subjected to the influence of sects and dogmatic manipulation under the auspices of original education programs. The children were at risk of being marginalized and incapable of developing an independent critical spirit:

> Il faut donc renforcer le contrôle de l'enseignement dispensé à ces enfants, pour s'assurer que les valeurs fondatrices de la République, la citoyenneté et la laïcité au premier chef, leur sont bien inculquées [It is thus necessary to be better able to verify the teaching given to these children, to be confident that the essential values of the Republic—citizenship and a high degree of secularity—are well impressed upon them.]

Mr. Leroy stated that only in schools provided by the Republic could the child learn to have an open spirit and personality and be aware of the world around him or her. He spoke against Jehovah's Witness groups in almost the same breath as the Reverend Moon, the Citadelle sect, and Krishna. At the end of his speech, he was applauded in each section of the parliament. Various other deputies spoke in a similar vein. The general discussion makes depressing reading for those knowledgeable about home education and the benefits that it can bring to individual children. There seemed to be no speaker prepared to support their needs. The broad spectrum of home educators and the great variety of education that they provide were ignored. Details of the proceedings, the Acts, and the further qualifying circular are given in Editions 5, 6 and 7 of *Grandir Sans Ecole*, the web site of *Possible* (www.multimania.com/possible), and the government web site (www.legifrance.gouv.fr/citoyen/officiels.ow/).

There is a general belief among home educators in France that when the inspector, who is used to monitoring schooling, makes a home visit, it will be possible to find fault with one aspect of all the regulations, and that many parents could unwittingly default on their responsibilities. In addition, it probably will be extremely difficult for non-French speakers to comply with the regulations. There are German, Dutch, and English families, educating children in their own language, who live for some time in France (longer than the permitted 6 months nonresidency), so that their children can "pick up" a foreign language and be aware of other ways of living. Some such home educators already have reluctantly returned to England. These and other concerns are expressed in the publications of the home educating support groups in France.

53

L. A. Taylor and A. J. Petrie

Compulsory Education in England and Wales

Education is compulsory in England and Wales for children between the ages of 5 and 16, but, although ensuring an education for every child, the law has never made schooling compulsory. The legal limitations that currently apply to home education are the 1996 Education Act, Statutory Instrument 1995 No. 2089, and clarifications that have been made in the courts and by the Ombudsman (Petrie, 1998, p. 124). The relevant section of the 1996 Education Act for home educators that currently applies is Section 7:

> The parent of every child of compulsory school age shall cause him to receive efficient full-time education suitable—
> (a) to his age, ability and aptitude, and
> (b) to any special educational needs he may have, either by regular attendance at school or otherwise.

The general definition of *education* and the definition of *efficient education* as it relates to home education were discussed in *Harrison and Harrison v. Stephenson* (1982 QB [DC] 729/81). A lower court had accepted an "autonomous method of self-directed study, recognisable as such by educationalists, and which could properly be described as systematic and which was certainly full-time." The term *efficient* was defined as achieving "that which it sets out to achieve." The court stated that "the education of these children had achieved that which [the Harrisons] had set out to achieve, with striking success."

The judge also stated that

> by any standard, education, however efficient it may be, is only suitable to the age, ability and aptitude of a child if
> (a) it is such as to prepare a child for life in a modern civilised society and
> (b) it enables a child to fulfil its best potential
> ...(iii) that the basic skills of reading, writing and arithmetic are fundamental to any education for life in the modern world as being essential for communication, research and self-education. We would not regard any system of education as suitable for any child capable of learning such skills, if that education failed to attempt to instil them (whatever the chosen method) but left it to time, chance and the inclination of the child to determine whether, if ever, the child was to attain even elementary proficiency in them.

The appeal by the Harrisons to the higher court contested that an education should be *systematic*. The appeal court judges believed that although it might not always be so, for the two Harrison children concerned, the education should be systematic because they were dyslexic. The judge stated,

> The local education authority has a duty to see that the children are properly educated. Included in that duty is something more than just seeing that the parents are doing what they like about the children. There comes a stage when, in certain circumstances, children have to be protected against the views of their parents, if those views are held with a high degree of tenacity which may ultimately be damaging to the children. ... [Children] are not possessions of their parents, and parents must realize that they are not totally in control of their children's lives ... if the children are not sent to school in accordance with a school attendance order then the only way in which parents can resist prosecution is by showing ... that the child is receiving efficient full-time education suitable to its age, ability and aptitude otherwise than at school.

Appropriately for a long-standing democracy, parents in England and Wales have a large measure of freedom to select the curriculum and pedagogy of their choice suitable for the education of their children. The 1988 Education Reform Act established a National Curriculum. This was the first time there were national guidelines on curriculum content for children of primary (5–11) and secondary (11–16) age. It does not apply to home educators. It only applies to children who are registered in maintained schools (i.e., state schools or state-supported schools). Some independent and religious schools follow the National Curriculum by choice.

Local government, in particular the LEA, is responsible for education within the area; it thus is responsible for ascertaining that home-educated children known to them are being educated:

> If it appears to a local education authority that a child of compulsory school age in their area is not receiving suitable education, either by regular attendance at school or otherwise, they shall serve a notice in writing on the parent requiring him to satisfy them within the period specified in the notice that the child is receiving such education. (Education Act, 1996, § 437[1])

It only becomes the responsibility of an LEA when it knows that a child is being home educated. A parent of a child who has never attended school is not legally bound to inform the LEA of the decision to home educate. However, if a child already is attending school, the parent who decides to home

L. A. Taylor and A. J. Petrie

educate must notify the head teacher, who in turn must remove the child's name from the attendance register and notify the LEA.

Thus, it is the responsibility of parents, the LEAs, and sometimes the courts to ensure a child is receiving a suitable education. Although some home educators enjoy a positive relationship with LEA officials, others have had negative experiences. Four areas of potential conflict were identified by Petrie (1998):

- LEA representative comparing the education provided at home with that in school. This can cause problems for parents educating in an autonomous style that is dissimilar to education in school.
- The varying definitions of words such as *full-time*, *efficient*, and *socialization*. The majority of officials are particularly concerned that home education might involve a lack of contact with others.
- LEA officials who monitor home education not always being trained in monitoring the variety of provision of education.
- Frequency of monitoring. It has not been clarified how often home educators should be monitored. A few home educating families believe that after the initial assessment to ascertain that an education is taking place there should be no further visits. In some LEAs, visits can take place 1–3 times per academic year. In one instance 10 visits per year were recorded. (Petrie, 1992)

However, the LEA has no automatic right to visit the home. The courts have clarified that evaluation of the education provided can take place in other places, agreed to in advance by both LEA officials and the parents concerned (*R v. Surrey Quarter Sessions Appeals Committee ex Parte Tweedie* [1963] 61, LGR, 464 [DC] 1208, 1209).

There currently is a reasonable balance in England and Wales between home educating parents and LEAs that benefits the home-educated children concerned. Any differences are clarified in the courts.

The Number of Home-Educated Children in England and Wales

It is difficult to establish the number of home-educated children with any accuracy. Estimates of the number of home-educated children largely have been based on those families known to LEAs, but not all home-educated children are known to them. For the period 1988 to 1992, Lowden (1994) and Petrie (1992) gave figures of approximately 4,000 recognized by LEAs. In 1995, a follow-up study by Petrie suggested that the

Home Education Regulations

number known to them had increased to 6,000. LEA officials, even those who are conscientious, rarely "discover" home educators who are not known to them. Families who are not known to them, to legally be considered as home educating, must fulfill the requirement laid down in the *Harrison* case that a child educated at home must receive "the basic skills of reading, writing and arithmetic [which] are fundamental to any education for life in the modern world as being essential for communication, research and self-education" (*Harrison and Harrison v. Stephenson* (1982 QB [DC] 729/81)). Petrie believes that with this definition, the number of home-educated children is unlikely to be more than 15,000. This figure was validated by a snap survey of individuals who have been supporting home educators for a number of years, who variously suggested between 8,000 and 15,000 home-educated children.

HERALD, a home educating support group, suggested that in Gloucestershire, the LEA only knew of 25% of the home educating population. The LEA's knowledge of home educators may depend on attitudes of the LEA staff and the frequency of previous court cases in the area. Meighan (1997) suggested that there might be as many as 50,000. Rothermel (1997c) increased this number still further, but her numbers included children whose status might not comply with definitions of education established in court cases.

National Exams and University Entrance

In England and Wales, most school children prepare for national exams (General Certificate of Education, or GCSE) at the age of 16, and some continue to take further exams (Advanced Level, or A-Level) at age 18. Home educating families resolve the acquisition of qualifications in a variety of ways. The family can decide that

- There is no great need for exams either in general or in the case of a specific child.
- The child should go to a school or a further education college (usually 16–18).
- They wish to continue home educating, study for the exams at home, and undertake the exam in a designated examination center.

Most exams now have a course work element, which can create difficulties because it must be completed and validated well ahead of the formal exam. Assuming it can be validated, an examination center also must be found in which to sit the exam. Some students must travel considerable

57

L. A. Taylor and A. J. Petrie

distances. Home-educated students must pay for the exam (and an adjudicator, in some instances) because the exams are only free to those children educated in the state system. Open learning centers and other organizations offer tuition for exams, some by correspondence course, but this also involves cost to the family.

Some home-educated children enroll in courses and sit their exams in Further Education Colleges, which offer a more flexible adult learning environment; this is part of the state provision of education and, as such, it is free. The colleges offer technical and both GCSE and A-Level courses. For A-Level, students currently study one to four subjects in depth. For entry to university, the minimum requirement is usually five GCSE passes, including two at A-Level. More A-Levels with higher grades may be required to enter the preferred university.

Home Education Support Groups in the United Kingdom and France

United Kingdom

The original support group was created more than 100 years ago by Charlotte Mason (Parents National Education Union, now Worldwide Education Service). Petrie is conducting research that shows that it was frequently used between the two world wars by people who were home educating. Many also used this correspondence course when living abroad. It gave practical suggestions of both academic and fun things to do with children.

Education Otherwise (EO). (P.O. Box 7420, London, N9 9SG). The name *education otherwise* comes from the wording of the Education Acts of 1944 and 1996 and explains the British term *otherwise education*, which sometimes is used to refer to home education.

EO is the largest of all the home education support groups in the United Kingdom. It was formed by a small group of parents in 1977. It is a self-help organization with a nationwide team of volunteers who offer their expertise to support others. It aims to help parents choose the right kind of education for their own situation and does not promote any one right way of educating all children. Members include those families who are practicing home education, those who are considering home education, and those who support the principle of home education. It benefits from local area coordinator support and can help, for example, with the

Home Education Regulations

process of deregistering a child and advice with home education for special needs children. It produces a contact list and a bimonthly newsletter, organizes local meetings and national gatherings, and provides free or reduced entry to a variety of educational sites across the country.

A further aim of EO is to raise awareness that although education is compulsory, school is not, and that families can legally choose to home educate.

Home Service. (The Hawthorns, 48 Heaton Moor Road, Heaton Moor, Stockport, SK4 4NX). Home Service is a national self-help organization providing support for Christian home educating families. It established the first national U.K. telephone service for Christian home educators. It was established in 1992 with about 20 families and now has a mailing list of 300. It has close links with the Christian Home Schools Contact List, which produces a quarterly magazine called *Home Time,* the first U.K. newsletter for Christian home educators.

Home Education Advisory Service. (P.O. Box 98, Welwyn Garden City, Hertfordshire, AL8 6AN). The Home Education Advisory Service (HEAS) also provides a national home education support network. HEAS was established as a national charity in 1995 to provide reliable support and consistent information to home educators across England. It offers quarterly bulletins and a registration card for free and reduced-rate access to places of interest. It also runs a central daily telephone hotline for information about home education. It has chosen not to operate with voluntary local coordinators, but prefers a centrally run organization to provide a more consistent interface with home educators, LEAs, and the media.

Home Education Resource and Learning Development (HERALD).
(Kelda Cottage, Lydbrook, Gloucestershire, GL17 9SX). HERALD was established in 1997 and claims to offer " ... a stepping stone between the rigors of schooling and the autonomous approach which many home-based educators strive to achieve by suggesting a structured yet flexible framework as a basis for study." Student work schemes are part of the membership package. The founders of the organization realized that some people, especially those who have just removed a child from school, were not sure how to approach the task of home education; although not advocating a very structured school day, some rhythm or pattern to the home educator's day could be beneficial for both parents and children. HERALD organizes very specific but flexible practical

L. A. Taylor and A. J. Petrie

support for home educators. A 5-day work plan for each week is produced that encourages parents to give five tasks a day to children. The work plan covers all aspects of the curriculum that would be found in schools. Topic-based schemes are sent out three times a year with comprehensive notes suggesting ways to organize the child's education. Parents are encouraged to produce a daily journal both for themselves and for LEA inspectors who might show an interest.

Northstar UK. (www.northstar-academy.org/UK/). Northstar UK is a community of 11- to 16-year-old learners. Christian teachers aim to provide a flexible online learning environment emulating traditional school interactions with lectures, discussions, social chatter, peer learning, group work, and student presentations. Northstar UK is not an online school; rather, it aspires to create a new institutional context within which learning can take place. Using conferencing software called *FirstClass*, tutors provide tutorial support, facilitate group discussion, and mark assignments. Northstar UK offers a U.K.-produced curriculum leading to GCSE. Not only can students study when they want to, but they can study as much or as little of Northstar UK curriculum that suits them. Northstar UK is available for home educating families, missionary families, and small Christian schools at home and abroad. However, students must find their own examination centers and make their own arrangements to sit the exams. There are some links with Northstar in the United States.

There are other specialist group networks for home educators, of which we provide some examples.

Schoolhouse (Scotland). (311 Perth Road, Dundee, DD2 1LG; Tel: 01382 646964; E-mail: jafkd@lineone.net; http://www.welcome.to/schoolhouse). Schoolhouse is a national Scottish charity, providing information and support about home education in Scotland.

Catholic Home-schooling Network. (P.O. Box 52, Skegness, PO25 1UE). This is an informal network for Catholic families who are educating children at home. There is a newsletter and a resources list.

France

It has been estimated by Sophie Haesen, editor of the newsletter *Grandir Sans Ecole,* that there are about 2,200 children who are home educated in France and about 12,000 children who are taught with the state correspondence course, both within France and abroad.

Home Education Regulations

Grandir Sans Ecole. (B P 5, 68480 Ferrette). This publication is produced quarterly to inform home educators about legal developments and the possibilities of home educating using different educational philosophies. It also includes articles written by home educators from a variety of countries. Books are reviewed, and home educators can make contact with others.

Les Enfants d'Abord. (Elyane Delmares, La Croix Saint Fiacre, 03110 Vendat). This is a home educating support group with four newsletters annually. They are edited by a member family and contain accounts of home education by the members. There is a membership list for those members who are home educating. Regional groups organize meetings to support home educators and discuss current issues. The annual national meeting is held in a different location each year involving as many of the members as possible.

Possible. This organization is concerned with the dissemination of information about all forms of alternative education, including home education. In the newsletters and the web page there are articles about the law, differing philosophies of education, and extracts from other journals of interest to members. Information is available from www.multimania.com/possible.

Recent Home Education Research in the United Kingdom
Compared With the U.S. Research

The Context of Four U.K. Studies

Home education research in the United Kingdom is rarely funded and is therefore not as extensive as that conducted in the United States, where it sometimes is funded by the government (e.g., Lines, 1991), by the National Home Education Research Institute (e.g., Ray, 1997), or by the Home School Legal Defense Association (e.g., Rudner, 1999). However, details of four studies undertaken in the U.K. setting by Goymer, Page, Rothermel, and Thomas are given here.

Stephen Goymer (in press), who is head of special needs in a large comprehensive school (2,000 pupils) in Norwich, studied seven families in Norfolk, England. The families came from contacts with students in his school, with friends and family acquaintances, and with EO. The families all practiced home education on a nonreligious basis, although they may have belonged to a religious group or have had their own religious philosophy. The research is ongoing, but in an initial analysis, some findings resonated with those of three Christian home educating families in the United States studied by L. A. Taylor (1993). Taylor studied these families in depth, and they are listed subsequently and compared with Goymer's research.

61

L. A. Taylor and A. J. Petrie

In L. A. Taylor's Home School 1, mother Joan talked about keeping many of the worldly distractions at bay and expressed concerns about peer pressure; Goymer found this concern raised in his study especially among the families with daughters. Joan also expressed a fear of her children being distracted in school and wasting time as she had done; Goymer found that two families expressed a concern that the children would have the same problems in school as the mother had exhibited. Finally, one of Goymer's families, like Joan, taught the children as she had been taught, perhaps without realizing that the school model is only one of many possible ways to educate.

In L. A. Taylor's Home School 2, mother Susan designated an area of the house as a schoolroom area; Goymer found two of his families did this. Also, Goymer's families shared Susan's experience of not liking what she observed at the local school. Susan's opinion, which was shared by people in four of Goymer's families, was that schools do not work children hard enough and do not stretch them. Susan's husband Robert stated that it is possible to affect the children's character, manner, and thinking more easily at home, and this was a sentiment shared by three of Goymer's families. All of Goymer's families shared Susan's belief that closer relationships between parents and children were established by parents living out their lives in front of the children, thus permitting children to see parents as they really are. Other examples of areas of similarity were theme days with other home educators, lots of read-aloud time, networking projects with other groups so parents or older children take some teaching responsibility, and families learning new skills together (e.g., bicycle maintenance). A concern to make the child feel important was expressed by Susan and shared by all the families in Goymer's sample. Some off-the-shelf curriculum was used by Susan, and Robert did a little of the teaching. In Goymer's group, similarly, some off-the-shelf curriculum was used, and some of the fathers became involved in teaching. Just as Susan stressed the role of teacher as guide, so did all of Goymer's families.

In L. A. Taylor's Home School 3, the mother Martha mentioned that when her oldest daughter returned to school for fifth grade, she found a lot of time wasted—a focus on irrelevant issues (such as how to shape the letter "A"), competition, and grade chasing. In Goymer's group, three of the four families who returned children to some aspect of mainstream schooling reflected these concerns. Martha stressed that learning should be seen as part of life; home and school learning activities should not be separated. All of Goymer's families held this philosophy. Martha's family had made good progress when compared to schooled peers on test scores. All but one of Goymer's families found the same result.

However, although the previous comparison indicated that there were some similarities between the three Christian home educating families

62

Home Education Regulations

that L. A. Taylor studied in the Stanford, California, area and the seven families Goymer studied in Norfolk, England, Taylor believed there may be fundamental differences between the Christian home educators in both places. John Hay (whose work in Christian education addresses some of the inadequacies of the Christian schools movement; see, e.g., Hay, 1998) stated that

> These schools often looked to the programs and "successes" of the public schools as their model. Instead of developing unique and alternative (Biblical) approaches to education, they just followed, instead of led. Because of this, many have compromised Biblical standards and become not unlike their secular counterparts. The pressure to conform to government accreditation standards, etc. has also influenced this conformity. (John Hay, personal communication, May 31, 1999)

L. A. Taylor's (1993, 1997) research indicated that Christian home educators in the United States largely modeled home education on Christian schools; they accepted the traditional school paradigm and made wide use of curriculum originally marketed for private Christian schools. In contrast, in the United Kingdom, there has never been a large Christian schools movement; U.K. Christian home educators seem to choose a wider variety of paths and seem more ready to define models of education for themselves (L. A. Taylor, in press). As further evidence of this tendency, at a Christian home education conference at Cliff House in 1996, the keynote speaker ended with these words: "Now we have taken our children out of school, we need to decide what to do with them." There was no assumption that the traditional school paradigm should be modeled in any way.

Page (1997) studied 20 home schooling families living within a 100-mile radius of his home in East Anglia, England. He described his sample as White, mostly Christian, and mainly well educated and noted that although the results were based on a limited and perhaps unrepresentative sample, the consistency of the results is very persuasive. In his sample, a traditional view of the family was held by all participants—that of the father, mother, and their children living together as one unit. He conducted his research by interview, in the form of a general discussion. He interviewed all 20 mothers and 11 of the fathers.

Page (1997) found that the parents all wanted to give their children a general education that included the formation of a well-rounded individual as well as good academic standards. The parents valued two things in particular: the one-to-one contact with their children that home education afforded and the freedom from such things as school hours and peer pressure. In addition, they enjoyed more family time, and, in some instances,

63

L. A. Taylor and A. J. Petrie

friendships within the family grew. They all tended to support other home educating families.

Parents were happy to confess to their children that they did not know something, and the child's education became an adventure for all the family. As Page (1997) noted, "One thing all the parents, who were deeply involved in the home schooling, had discovered was a new joy in learning; this was matched by their own children's joy in discovery" (p. 48). The mothers found deep meaning and contentment in their roles both as mothers and home educators; most of the fathers interviewed were much more involved in the life of the family as a consequence. Page concluded,

> I began with the theological idea that we are not merely affected by our own actions, but actually formed by those actions. In this study of home schooling I have found that the parents are not merely forming their children but they are themselves being both formed and educated in the process. (p. 49)

Although some research has been done in the United States on how home educating parents perceive their home education (e.g., Knowles, 1988; McDowell, 1998; Medlin, 1994), Page's work seems to be unique in its focus on how mothers in particular have grown because of their home educating experience.

Paula Rothermel is in the last phase of a 4-year study exploring the aims and practices of home educators in the United Kingdom. Her study involved use of questionnaire data from 1,000 families and educational and psychological data for children of various age groups (including administration of Performance Indicators in Primary Schools, or PIPS; use of the Children's Assertiveness Behavior Scale, the Rutter Scale, and the Goodman Strengths and Difficulties Scale) and interview data with 100 families.

Although the study has not yet been published, Rothermel (1999a) reported the results from a pilot analysis of 50 completed questionnaires. This sample involved 123 children—16 with special needs—and 88 parents. She found 23% of the parents were trained schoolteachers, and, although there was no consensus on whether teacher training had helped or hindered them in their home education, there was a consensus that it had helped parents to communicate better with LEA staff. The national curriculum was followed by only 14% of the families, 28% referred to it occasionally, and 58% stated that they did not use it. Some kind of learning routine was followed by 74% of the families.

Reading skills were more spread than the normal distribution for children in schools, with more home-educated children reading either very early or very late. She noted that children with religious backgrounds read the earliest. More recently, Rothermel (personal communication, June 26, 1999) found, when analyzing the National Literacy Project assessment results, that the percentage of U.K. home-educated "late readers" in her sample exactly replicated that of the national figure, as provided by the Department for Education and Employment (England and Wales).

Rothermel (1999b) provided results from the PIPS study of 36 four-year-olds. The sample was taken from the first 312 questionnaire returns. The initial sample were all found via an appeal in the EO newsletter, although not all respondents were EO members. Using a PIPS indicator, children aged 4 years were assessed at the beginning and end of a 9-month period. She tested children at the beginning and end of what would be their reception year in school. For the beginning of the year, the results were as follows: Her analysis of the PIPS baseline data indicated that 64% (23 children) scored over 75%; nationally, the figure for children scoring over 75% was 5.1%. The average score for the sample was 81%, whereas the national score was only 45%. In other words, the home-educated children were well ahead. However, when they were assessed 9 months later, the home-educated children had made less progress in terms of the PIPS measure than had their school-based counterparts, although being so far ahead in the beginning meant that many were still ahead of the schooled children. The national average score for mathematics was found to be 51.5%, and the average for the home-educated sample was 68.7%; the national average for reading was 44.9%, and the average for the sample was 59.3%. However, Rothermel (personal communication, June 23, 1999) believed that the difference could be accounted for by the fact that the tests—although apparently having universal appeal—are biased toward children in school, using data collection criteria adapted to a reception class environment.

Rothermel summarized the early indications of her study in four main findings:

1. The home educators came from mixed socioeconomic classes.

2. The educational methods adopted by the families varied. Parents adapted to individual children's needs, where appropriate employing different approaches at varying stages of the child's development.

3. In general, the children were competent social beings with the ability to interact with others, adults and peers alike, as equals. The children were generally confident and independent.

4. When subjected to a program of assessment measures attached to this research, the home-educated children (aged 4–11 years) were generally progressing more positively in developmental and academic terms than were their school counterparts.

L. A. Taylor and A. J. Petrie

Rothermel was keen to point out that these findings relate to the sample as a group and that there were exceptions at both extremes.

A nationwide study in the United States conducted by Ray (1997) collected data on 1,657 families and their 5,402 children. In that study, the students—like Rothermel's students—scored at above-average percentiles:

Total reading 87th percentile
Total language 80th
Total math 82nd
Total listening 85th
Science 84th
Social studies 85th
Study skills 81st
Basic battery (reading language and math) 85th
Complete battery 87th
The national average is the 50th percentile.

However, Ray's sample of parents had a higher than average educational attainment—46% of the fathers and 42% of the mothers had a bachelor's degree. Some might argue that this correlated with the high educational achievement of their youngsters. However, Havens (1991), Rakestraw (1988), and Ray (1992), who all studied the correlation between academic achievement and other variables, found no relation between the academic achievement of home-educated children and the educational attainment of their parents.

Rothermel's positive results for children's social development also confirm similar findings in the United States. J. W. Taylor (1986) studied self-concept among 224 home educators in Grades 4 through 12. He administered the Piers–Harris Self Concept Scale and found the home-schooled children scored significantly higher that did the public norm group on the global scale and on all six subscales. He concluded, "Insofar as self-concept is a reflector of socialization ... the findings of this study would suggest that few home-schooling children are socially deprived" (pp. 160–161).

Shyers (1992) studied 140 children, 70 of whom were traditionally schooled and 70 who were home educated. Using the Piers–Harris Self Concept Scale, he found that both groups of children had higher-than-average measured self-concept. However, using a technique in which children's behaviors are recorded by trained observers, the home-educated students received significantly lower problem behavior scores than did their traditionally schooled counterparts. He found that al-

Home Education Regulations

though schooled children may not be socially well-adjusted, home-schooled children are socially well-adjusted.

Smedley (1992), in a study of 20 home-educated children and 17 traditionally educated students, used the Vineland Adaptive Behavior Scale to investigate the socialization issue from a communication perspective. Like Shyers, Smedley concluded, "The findings of this study indicate that children kept at home are more mature and better socialized than those who are sent to school" (p. 12). Rothermel's findings have supported those of both Shyers (1992) and Smedley (1992).

Thomas (1998) studied 50 home educating families in England and 50 in Australia to investigate how parents went about the day-to-day task of educating their children. From his findings, Thomas divided his families into three types: more formal learning, less formal learning, and informal learning. The tendency was for parents to become less formal as they proceeded. He made no claims for any one best method, but he stated that different methods worked well for different families at different times.

1. Formal Learning. This was the type most similar to a school situation, but there were several differences. Learning at home is more intensive, giving children more free time. It is flexible, so topics can be selected and pursued at length or dropped, and learning becomes more of a process than a series of tasks, so a parent becomes more of a guide than a teacher. When challenges arise, there is an attitude of "Let's sort it out" rather than a sense of failure on the part of the child or loss of self-worth. Children learn that an important part of learning is knowing how to find out.

2. Less Formal Learning. A second group operates less formally. These are parents who believe that children can learn a great deal without being deliberately taught.

3. Informal Learning. Others continue simply to "apprentice their children to the culture" as they did when the children were preschool age. Thomas concluded,

> There can be few professional educators, or anyone else for that matter, who would expect much learning could accrue from simply living at home. There is no doubt, however, that school-age children who learn informally really do learn, which is intriguing at the very least. It challenges nearly every assumption about how children of school age should learn. (p. 67)

Thomas also noted that children learned to read anywhere between the ages of 2 and 12, and that this had no effect on their ultimate enjoyment of reading.

67

L. A. Taylor and A. J. Petrie

Conclusion

As policies in education are in a constant state of flux and change, home education, conducted for centuries according to the perceived needs of the child, is perhaps the only education by which the effectiveness of schooling can be measured; it therefore should only be regulated by governments in a limited way to protect the child from harm. Holt (1983) stated,

> [Home education] is—in effect, though certainly not by design—a laboratory for the intensive and long range study of children's learning and of the ways in which friendly and concerned adults can help them learn. It is a research project, done at no cost, of a kind for which neither the public schools nor the government could afford to pay. (p. 393)

During the last 20 years, a large body of research has been conducted into home education in the United States. Initially in the United Kingdom, as in the United States, studies reflected an inadequate knowledge of the law and the need to clarify the legal boundaries. Gradually, a large body of research findings has emerged, documenting the successes of home schooling both academically and socially (Meighan, 1997; Ray, 1997). Some interesting studies on home educating families have been undertaken in the United Kingdom that reflect a research interest in both the families involved and the methods of teaching and learning employed. Some of the findings, such as those of Rothermel, were similar to those in the United States. Others, such as those of L. A. Taylor (in press), begin to pinpoint possible differences regarding the approach of Christian home educators. Much research remains to be done.

More important even than new research undertakings, however, is how (a) these research findings might be disseminated to legislators and those working in educational administration, (b) research into home education can be seen to be relevant to children in school and their parents, and (c) research into home education that has been undertaken in one country can be seen to be applicable to home educators in other countries.

It was quite apparent, for example, that the legislators in France either did not know or did not want to know the findings of international research from studies into home educating families or did not think they were relevant to education in France. In the United Kingdom, those working in education also can be unaware of home education research. Bentley (1998), who works for Demos (the independent think tank and research institute based in London) and who is an advisor to David Blunkett, a Member of Parliament and Secretary of State for Education and Employment, is one example. His book, hailed as one of the key education manuals of the decade (*Times Educational Supple-*

ment, October 23, 1998), made no reference to home education or to any of the major research findings of families' experiences of home education. In his last chapter, titled "New Landscape of Learning," he suggested that

From the age of 14, compulsory schooling might come to an end, to be followed by a number of different community-based learning packages which continued for five years or more. ... Young people would have the power to choose what they did, but this choice would be guided by a rich network of resources, guidance and support contexts for learning. The student's education would step outside the classroom, integrating diverse perspectives and experiences into a rounded, disciplined, individual view of the world. (p. 185)

Much of what Bentley suggested is already under way in many guises among home-educated children. They already can experience this "rounded, disciplined, and individual view of the world," supplemented by learning environments such as Northstar UK, if required. In addition, Bentley, in his concern to focus on social problems and how to resolve them through education, missed the fact that among home educators, many of these problems are resolving themselves. Home-educated children in general enjoy strong family ties and a healthy academic and social development.

References

Bentley, T. (1998). *Learning beyond the classroom: Education for a changing world*. London: Routledge & Kegan Paul.

Goymer, S. (in press). Getting inside families: Exploring a case study research issue in home schooling. *Home School Researcher*.

Grimes, D., & Grimes, S. (1999, May/June). Supporting home schoolers in foreign countries. *The Teaching Home*, 17(3), 61.

Havens, J. E. (1991). *A study of parent education levels as they relate to academic achievement among home schooled children*. Unpublished doctoral dissertation, Southwestern Baptist Theological Seminary, Fort Worth, TX.

Hay, J. (1998, January). *Raising up the foundations: A curriculum project for developing a Biblical Christian worldview and an integrated perspective of school subjects in students ages 6–12*. Paper presented at the Stapleford Centre Conference, Nottingham, England.

Holt, J. C. (1983, February). School and home schooling: A fruitful partnership. *Phi Delta Kappan*, 391–394.

Knowles, J. G. (1988). Parents' rationales and teaching methods for home schooling: The role of biography. *Education and Urban Society*, 21(1), 64–84.

Liegeois, J. (1987). *School provision for gypsy and traveller children: A synthesis report*. Luxembourg: Commission of the European Communities.

Lines, P. M. (1991, October). *Estimating the home schooled population* (Working Paper No. OR 91–537). Washington, DC: U.S. Department of Education, Office of Education Research and Improvement.

Lowden, S. (1994). *The scope and implications of home based education.* Unpublished doctoral dissertation, University of Nottingham, Nottingham, England.

McDowell, S. A. (1998). *Home sweet school: The perceived impact of home schooling on the family in general and the mother–teacher in particular.* Unpublished doctoral dissertation, Peabody College of Vanderbilt University, Nashville, TN.

Medlin, R. G. (1994). Homeschooling: What's hard? What helps? *Home School Researcher, 11*(4), 1–6.

Meighan, R. (1997). *The next learning system: And why home-schoolers are trailblazers.* Nottinghamshire, England: Educational Heretics Press.

Page, R. E. (1997). *Families growing together: A study of the effects of home schooling on the development of the family.* Unpublished master's thesis, Maryvale Institute, Birmingham, England.

Petrie, A. J. (1992). *Home education and the Local Education Authority: From conflict to cooperation.* Unpublished doctoral dissertation, Liverpool University, Liverpool, England.

Petrie, A. J. (1993). Education at home and the law. *Education and the Law, 5*(3), 139–144.

Petrie, A. J. (1995). Home educators and the law within Europe. *International Review of Education, 41*(3–4), 285–296.

Petrie, A. J. (1998). Home education and the law. *Education and the Law, 10*(2–3), 123–134.

Rakestraw, J. F. (1988). Home schooling in Alabama. *Home School Researcher, 4*(4), 1–6.

Ray, B. D. (1992). *Home education in Oklahoma: Family characteristics, student achievement, and policy matters.* (Available from the National Home Education Research Institute, P.O. Box 13939, Salem, OR 97309)

Ray, B. (1997). *Strengths of their own—Home-schoolers across America.* Salem, OR: National Home Education Research Institute. (Available from the National Home Education Research Institute, P.O. Box 13939, Salem, OR 97309)

Rothermel, P. (1999a, April). *Home-education: A critical evaluation.* Paper presented at the British Psychological Society annual conference, Belfast, Northern Ireland.

Rothermel, P. (1999b, March). *Home-education: A critical evaluation involving 36 families with at least one child aged 4 years.* Conference paper presented at the New Directions for Primary Education conference, Association for the Study of Primary Education, Ambleside, England.

Rothermel, P. (1999c, Summer). A study of home-education: Early indications and wider implications. *Education Now News and Review,* (24), 5.

Rudner, L. M. (1999). The scholastic achievement and demographic characteristics of home school students in 1998. *Education Policy Analysis Archives* [Online], *7*(8). Retrieved October 24, 1999 from the World Wide Web: http://epaa.asu.edu/epaa/v7n8/

Shyers, L. E. (1992). A comparison of social adjustment between home and traditionally schooled students. *Home School Researcher, 8*(3), 1–8.

Smedley, T. C. (1992). Socialization of home school children. *Home School Researcher, 8*(3), 9–16.

Taylor, J. W. (1986). Self concept in home schooling children. *Home School Researcher, 2*(2), 1–3.

Taylor, L. A. (1993). *At home in school: A qualitative inquiry into three Christian home schools.* Unpublished doctoral dissertation, Stanford University, Stanford, CA.

Taylor, L. A. (1997). Home in school: Insights on education through the lens of home schoolers. *Theory Into Practice, 36*(2), 110–116.

Taylor, L. A. (in press). Portraits of Christian home education in the UK. *Home School Researcher.*

Thomas, A. (1998). *Educating children at home.* London: Cassell.

Home Schooling: The Ameliorator of Negative Influences on Learning?

Brian D. Ray

The modern home school movement appears to be making a noticeable mark on society in general and on education in particular (Clark, 1994; Kantrowitz & Wingert, 1998; Lines, 1994; Toch, 1991a). *Home schooling* is the practice in which the education of children is clearly parent-controlled or parent-directed (and sometimes student-directed) during the conventional-school hours during the conventional-school days of the week. Although it did not begin a resurgence in the United States until the 1970s, parent-led and home- and family-based education have been practiced by many cultures throughout history, and it never disappeared in some of them. Gordon and Gordon (1990) made it clear that education centered in and around the home and family has played a key role throughout the history of Western civilization. An examination of education in America indicates that home education, in one form or another, was prevalent until the late 19th century. "In general, then, seventeenth and eighteenth century parents—particularly the father—bore the primary responsibility for teaching their children. ... Christian doctrine, vocational skills, and how to read and, to a lesser extent, write and figure" (Carper, 1992, p. 254). During the 19th century, "the school was a voluntary and incidental institution: attendance varied enormously from day to day and season to season" (Tyack, 1974, p.

BRIAN D. RAY *is Founder and President of the National Home Education Research Institute.*

Requests for reprints should be sent to Brian D. Ray, National Home Education Research Institute, Box 13939, Salem, OR 97309. E-mail: bray@nheri.org

B. D. Ray

16). Furthermore, the parents and community controlled the school during that period of history. Schooling or book learning was only a small and often incidental part of the total education of a child because he "acquired his values and skills from his family and from neighbors of all ages and conditions" (Tyack, 1974, pp. 14–15). The growth in popularity of compulsory school attendance at the end of the 19th and the early 20th centuries, along with the idea that trained professionals could best teach children, decidedly moved the education of children into the hands of school personnel as the 20th century began. The Gordons' brief couple of pages dedicated to home schooling at the end of the 20th century puts into perspective that today's home education has a rich heritage and is one more significant expression of the importance of the historical concept and practice of home- and family-based learning. A fast-growing number of parents in the United States and in other countries (Farris, 1998; Klicka, 1997; Meighan, 1984, 1997; Ray, 1994; D. S. Smith, 1993) are renewing this practice, and their activities are attracting researchers of various interests.

Kirschner (1991) surveyed the shifting roles of family and school as educator to make sense of the surge in home education:

> We find many Americans turning to "family values" and scriptural religion in a search for stability and something to believe in. ... In the home-school movement one finds a hint of optimism in this age of cynicism not seen in quite a while. (p. 156)

Even the secular media by the mid-1990s was addressing the breakdown of the traditional nuclear family that had occurred during the preceding 3 decades (Leo, 1992, p. 24).

Mayberry (1988, pp. 12, 13), a sociologist, also perceived home education as a way for parents to regain control of their children's and their own lives, a way to make the impact they want on the next generation (see also Caldwell, 1999). This choice is being made by a wide variety of people. For example, despite the unfounded claim of some critics (e.g., a representative of the National Education Association) that many parents choose home schooling due to their racism (Caldwell, 1999), it appears that an increasing proportion of African Americans, Hispanics, and other minorities are choosing home education (Home School Legal Defense Association [HSLDA], 1996; Romm, 1993). Romm, for example, found that a variety of families in Atlanta, Georgia, including African American Muslims, African American Christians, American Indian Christians, European American secular humanists, European American Christians, and others were practicing home education to transmit particular cultural and ethnic values to their offspring. Research suggests that currently more than 90% of

Home Schooling: The Ameliorator?

home schoolers are non-Hispanic White in terms of racial or ethnic background (Ray, 1990b, 1997b), but it appears that a rapidly increasing number of minorities are engaging in home-based education (HSLDA, 1996; Romm, 1993; Safley, 1998).

This educational life that closely integrates parents and children, however, is contrary to the modern trend toward the institutionalization and professionalization of education. In 1980, close to 100% of children and youth aged 6 to 18 were in institutional schools; about 88% of those were in state-operated (public) schools (U.S. Department of Education [USDE], 1998b). Over the course of just 2 decades, the United States has changed to the point where 1.3 million to 1.7 million school-aged children and youth are home schooled (Lines, 1998; Ray, 1998b, 1999). In the fall of 1996, it was estimated that there were more home school students than public school students in nine states combined (Ray, 1999; USDE, 1998a). If these estimates are correct, the home school population is now about 24% of the size of the private school student population (USDE, 1998b). This represents a very notable change in the educational choices of parents and students. If this trend were to continue at a modest 7% annual growth rate (Lines, 1998; Ray, 1998b), about 3 million students would be home educated during the fall of 2010. It now appears that what some observers thought would be a passing fad—home schooling—has become a visible movement animated by a robust mix of parents and children and capable local and national leaders (Caldwell, 1999; Clark, 1994; Hadeed, 1991; Kantrowitz & Wingert, 1998; Lines, 1994; Toch, 1991a).

Purpose of the Study

Twenty years ago, the public and researchers began asking many questions about home schooling related to topics such as the social and psychological development of the home educated, whether home school families are sufficiently participating in important social and political aspects of American life, the proper role of the government and law in the education of children, and the history of parent-directed and family-based education. The public and researchers also asked, Does it work? Is it possible for parents, who are not professionally trained teachers, to teach and guide their children's education successfully? More specifically, how will these students perform in terms of academic achievement?

The purpose of this study was twofold and could be addressed by the following questions:

1. How were the home educated, across the nation, performing in terms of academic achievement in the mid-1990s compared to their performance nationwide and in state-specific studies in the past?

B. D. Ray

2. Perhaps more important, are selected background variables more or less helpful with respect to explaining the academic achievement of the home educated compared to that of the conventionally schooled?

Review of Related Literature

Dozens of studies have been completed regarding the academic achievement of home-educated students. In general, children who are taught by their parents score above national averages on standardized achievement tests. Following are summaries of several characteristic studies.

Wartes (1987, 1988, 1989, 1990b, 1991), a public high school counselor, studied the Stanford Achievement Test scores of thousands of home-educated students, from kindergarten to Grade 12, in Washington State for several years. He found that these students consistently scored above the national average in all academic areas, with the median score at about the 67th percentile on national norms.

Students in Alaska's Centralized Correspondence Study, a state-managed form of home education, consistently have scored higher than conventional school students nationwide on the California Achievement Test in math, reading, language, and science (Alaska Department of Education, 1984, 1985, 1986; Falle, 1986). These students also scored higher on achievement tests than did their conventional school Alaskan peers (Alaska Department of Education, 1985, 1986; Falle, 1986).

State departments of education often report that the home-educated students (for whom they have scores) in their states are scoring well above average on standardized achievement tests. The Oregon Department of Education (1990, 1998) found their median percentile range to be the 71st to 80th, and the Tennessee Department of Education (1988) reported they were generally in the 70th to 80th percentile range.

Ray's (1990b) nationwide study, the largest of its kind at that time, involved approximately 1,500 families and 4,600 children in them. The home-educated students averaged at or above the 80th percentile on standardized achievement tests in all subject areas.

The HSLDA (1994–1995) provided a summary of the Iowa Test of Basic Skills (ITBS) scores (in several subject areas) of 16,311 home-educated students in kindergarten through Grade 12; the scores were obtained from a national testing service. The basic battery scores, by grade level, ranged from a low of the 62nd percentile to a high of the 87th percentile, with a majority of the percentile scores in the 70s.

A number of other studies have resulted in similar findings: Home-educated students in Canada averaged at the 79th percentile on the

Home Schooling: The Ameliorator?

basic battery (Ray, 1994); Indiana students averaged at the 86th percentile on the basic battery (Ray, 1997a); Massachusetts students were at the 85th percentile on the basic battery (Ray, 1998a); Montana students were at the 72nd and 70th percentile on the basic battery in two separate studies (Ray, 1990a, 1995); North Dakota students taught at home had averages at about the 85th percentile (Ray, 1991); those taught by their parents in Oklahoma scored, on average, at the 88th percentile in the combination of their reading, language, and mathematics performance (Ray, 1992); the home educated in Pennsylvania scored from the 60th to 74th percentiles (Richman, Girten, & Snyder, 1990; see also Butler, 1994; Frost, 1987; Havens, 1991).

Not all studies, however, show home-educated students scoring above average. A study in California by Delahooke (1986) compared the intelligence and academic achievement of home school and private school 9-year-olds. She found no significant differences between the two groups in terms of intelligence and achievement test scores, and both were average on national norms. Rakestraw (1987, 1988) found first- and fourth-grade home education students to be scoring below the national average in mathematics, and the home educated in Grades 2, 3, 5, and 6 were above average; average reading scores for the first- through sixth-grade students were at the 54th through 97th percentile. The Washington State Superintendent of Public Instruction (1985) also found scores that were not particularly high, with the home educated scoring at the 62nd percentile in reading, 53rd percentile in mathematics, and the 56th percentile in language. The New Mexico State Department of Education once reported that their records showed that the academic achievement of the home educated was generally above average, but not as high as reported in most research studies (Pat Rael, personal communication, February 17, 1998).

Overall, the research base to date (see also Ray, 1988, 1993, 1999) indicates that home school students perform at least as well as public school students in the subject areas considered to be the "basics" of American education.

Relations Between Academic Achievement and
Other Variables

Several researchers have explored whether the academic achievement of the home educated is related to selected variables that might be of particular interest to policymakers, educators, and others. One of these factors is whether the home school parents are government-certified teachers. Studies in Alabama, Oklahoma, Pennsylvania, Texas, nationwide in the United States, and nationwide in Canada all revealed that there was no significant relation between student achievement and the teacher certification

75

status of their parents (Havens, 1991; Rakestraw, 1988; Ray, 1990b, 1992, 1994). Duvall, Ward, Delquadri, and Greenwood (1997) and Duvall (Steven F. Duvall, personal communication, January 23, 1999) found that special-needs children were successfully home educated by parents who were not certified teachers. One study in Montana found that whether the father was a certified teacher was not significant, whereas the mother's certification status was significant (Ray, 1995). Medlin (1994), on the other hand, found a weak relation between achievement and whether the mother was a certified teacher.

The formal educational attainment of parents and its relation to student achievement is another factor that is of interest to policymakers and some researchers. In three studies, Havens (1991), Rakestraw (1988), and Ray (1992) found no relation between parents' educational attainment and the academic achievement scores of their home-educated children in Texas, Alabama, and Oklahoma, respectively. On the other hand, Ray (1990b, 1991) found statistically significant relations, which were relatively weak in practical terms, between parents' educational attainment and their children's achievement scores in his earlier nationwide and North Dakota studies. Likewise, Wartes (1990a) found weak to moderate relations in his Washington research. Even with these correlations, the home educated of lower education level parents still tended to score above average on achievement tests.

The relation between family income and student achievement has been of interest to policymakers and researchers. As Wartes (1990a) wrote, "Within the general school population ... the children of parents who earn more money tend to do better than those where the parents earn less" (p. 50; see also Coleman et al., 1966; Coleman & Hoffer, 1987, chap. 5; "Outstanding High Schools," 1999; Snow, Barnes, Chandler, Goodman, & Hemphill, 1991; Toch, 1991b). There was no significant relation between family income and student achievement in home school studies done in North Dakota (Ray, 1991), in most comparisons in an Oklahoma study (Ray, 1992), and in Washington (Russell, 1994). On the other hand, Wartes (1990a) and Ray (1990b) found mixed results with some weak relations between income and test scores in Washington and in a nationwide study. Even with these correlations, the home educated of lower income families scored above average.

Many policymakers are interested in whether home schoolers should be regulated more heavily by the state. Research to date has shown little to no relation between the degree of regulation by the state and the students' academic achievement (Ray, 1990b).

Economists, sociologists, and policymakers also wonder whether the money spent on home education is related to student achievement. Research findings have suggested there is no relation (Ray, 1990b, 1998a).

76

Home Schooling: The Ameliorator?

Various researchers have studied many factors and their relation to the academic achievement of the home educated. Table 1 provides a summary of these relations before this study was conducted.

Based on some generally recognized correlates of academic achievement performance in conventional schools, past research on home education, and the goals of this exploratory study, several independent variables were selected for analysis and are listed subsequently in the methodology section.

Methodology

The larger study (Ray, 1997b) on which this study was based included cross-sectional descriptive, multivariate, and longitudinal design elements; detailed methodology was provided by Ray.

The Instrument

The data collection instrument used in this study was based on the surveys used by Ray (1990b, 1994). It also contained selected items from the

Table 1
Relation Between Various Independent Variables and Academic Achievement Test Scores of Home School Students

Variable of Interest	*Relation to Academic Achievement in Home Schooling*
Money spent on education	No relation
Family income	No relation most studies; a few studies found weak positive
Degree of state regulation	No relation
Legal status of family	Typically no relation; one study found underground performed better
Father's formal education level	Mixed results
Mother's formal education level	Mixed results
Father been certified teacher	Typically no relation; few studies found weak positive
Mother been certified teacher	Typically no relation; few studies found weak positive
Gender of student	No relation
Years student home educated	Typically no relation; few studies slight positive
Time spent in formal instruction	No relation
Age began formal instruction	No relation
Use of libraries	Typically no relation; occasional slight positive
Use of computer	Typically no relation; occasional slight positive
Who administered test to student	Typically no relation; occasional slight

Note. This is a summary of the findings of many studies preceding the study reported here.

B. D. Ray

National Assessment of Educational Progress (USDE, 1992) and the National Education Longitudinal Survey (USDE, 1996). Guidelines for survey research delineated by Borg and Gall (1989) were followed; the instrument was reviewed and revised by experts on home education (e.g., home school leaders and researchers), and consensus was reached on the validity of the items and their wording. The instrument addressed variables regarding descriptive information about parents and family, the home education legal status of the family, information on the students (e.g., demographics, achievement scores), and volunteering to participate in a longitudinal study. The instrument resulted in 190 variables being available for analysis, 99 per family and 91 per child. The entire instrument is reproduced in Ray's (1997b) book.

Definitions

For this study, *academic achievement* was defined as the demonstration of learning (including knowledge, understanding, and thinking skills) attained by a student as measured by standardized academic achievement tests. *Degree of structure* in the practice of home education varies greatly; it ranges from a very unstructured (e.g., unschooling) learning approach, centered on the child's interests, to the use of a planned, structured, and highly prescribed curriculum. Given the preceding explanation, parents rated their own practice on a 7-point scale, ranging from 1 (*very unstructured*) to 7 (*very structured*). *Formal instruction* was defined as planned or intentional instruction in areas such as reading, writing, spelling, or arithmetic; it is done to meet a learning objective. *Structured learning* was defined as time during which the child is engaged in learning activities planned by the parent; it is a time during which the child is not free to do whatever he or she chooses.

Population and Sample

The target population was all families in the United States who were educating their school-age children at home. Linear systematic sampling was used to select families from the lists of various national and statewide organizations. Home education support organizations—and contacts via word-of-mouth and personal networks—assisted in contacting home education families throughout the country. This combination of using support organizations, publications, and word-of-mouth was the best way to contact the widest variety of home educators in a practical and efficient man-

Home Schooling: The Ameliorator?

ner. This method of using support organizations for making contact with a variety of home education families has been used successfully in prior research (e.g., Knowles, Mayberry, & Ray, 1991; Ray, 1990b, 1991, 1992, 1994; Richman et al., 1990). Neither this method, nor any other reasonable method, would either (a) necessarily result in a representative sample of home education families or (b) necessarily introduce sampling bias.

Distribution and Collection of the Instrument, and Response Rate

First-class mail was used to distribute a total of 5,995 copies of the instrument to individual home education families and home education support groups in all states from late January to late February 1996. All usable instruments returned were included in this study. The total number of completed and usable instruments included in the study was 1,657 (i.e., 1,657 families, including information on 5,200 children), which is equivalent to a response rate of 28.8% or more. The minimum response rate of 28.8% compares favorably with that of 24.7% reported by Knowles et al. (1991), who dealt with a wide variety of home education organizations and a variety of means of obtaining names and addresses of home educators, and with the 31.3% response rate reported by Ray (1994). The response rate for this study is typical of what can be expected in this type of social science research (Fowler, 1988).

Data Analysis and Statistical Hypotheses

Students' test score percentiles were converted to z scores (Hopkins, Glass, & Hopkins, 1987, Appendix Table A) for statistical analyses. Z scores were used because they provided the most reasonable way to aggregate scores from many students using a variety of tests and to analyze how those scores compared to standardized test norms and to each other. It was not assumed in this study that scores on different tests meant, necessarily, the same thing about the students who took them (Gronlund & Linn, 1990), nor was it assumed that students in this study were perfectly analogous to those students represented by norms for the standardized tests that these students took. It was assumed, however, that the use of aggregated scores from a variety of standardized achievement tests is an acceptable practice, provides valuable information (Frisbie, 1992; Hunter & Schmidt, 1990, pp. 516–518), and would provide the best data for this study.

Multiple regression analysis (stepwise) was used to determine whether any of several independent variables explained significant amounts of variance in students' total reading, total language, total mathematics, and complete battery on standardized achievement tests. The researcher decided that only these four dependent variables would be used, for two reasons. First, past research that has explored many independent variables and test scores has shown that few independent variables explain statistically significant and practically significant amounts of variance in home-educated students' test scores (Rakestraw, 1988; Ray, 1990b, 1992, 1994; Russell, 1994; Wartes, 1990a). Second, reducing the number of dependent variables reduces the number of statistical tests to be performed, which, in turn, reduces multiple error rate (R. Good, 1984).

Furthermore, the researcher originally planned to include the student's age and the degree of structure in the home education environment as independent variables. Analyses of collinearity between independent variables, however, gave evidence that these two variables should be excluded from analyses to increase the likelihood of valid and meaningful multiple regression results.

The statistical hypothesis tested in all cases was the null hypothesis. Alpha was set at 0.01 for statistical tests in this study for several reasons. First, this level of alpha (rather than a larger one) helps to take into account multiple error rate (R. Good, 1984). Second, this approach was consistent with prior research (Ray, 1990b, 1994). Finally, this level of alpha helps reduce the probability of Type I error in this situation in which the rejection of a true null hypothesis might involve potential harm to people like those involved in the study (Shavelson, 1988, p. 286)—for example, suggesting government policy that could jeopardize family integrity and children's learning. The study was designed to provide basic descriptive statistics and to test the following hypothesis: There is no significant relation between the dependent variable of student academic achievement and the following independent variables: (a) highest formal education level attained by the father, (b) highest formal education level attained by the mother, (c) teacher certification status of the father (i.e., whether the father had ever been a certified teacher), (d) teacher certification status of the mother (i.e., whether the mother had ever been a certified teacher), (e) family income, (f) amount of money spent on the home education of the student, (g) legal status of the family (i.e., underground, notified district but not attempting to fully comply with statute, satisfied statutory requirements, in a current legal dispute, and other), (h) gender of the student, (i) the number of years the student was home educated, (j) the extent to which the family visits public libraries, (k) the time spent in formal educational activities, (l) the age at which formal education of the student commenced,

Home Schooling: The Ameliorator?

(m) the degree of regulation of home education by the state (i.e., low, moderate, and high, which are defined in the Findings section), (n) who administered the achievement test (which is explained in the Findings section), and (o) the use of a computer in the education of the student. Independent variables (a) through (l) were addressed using multiple regression; (m) through (o) were addressed via tests of comparison.

Assumptions

The researcher assumed that parents and their children (their students) were honest and accurate in completing the surveys. It was assumed that parents and their students were the ones who would have the most accurate information, for the purposes of this study, about the functioning of home education for their family. The researcher also assumed that only one survey per family was completed. Finally, it was assumed that the standardized academic achievement tests, from which scores were reported in this study, were reasonably reliable and valid (e.g., Borg & Gall, 1989; Hopkins, Stanley, & Hopkins, 1990; Mitchell, 1983, 1985) and that they were properly administered and scored.

Delimitations and Limitations

The first delimitation is that this study does not examine the extent to which several objectives of home education parents (e.g., productive adulthood, adherence to a particular belief and value system) are met (Cizek, 1991, 1993; Ray, 1988). Second, this is not a causal-comparative study (Borg & Gall, 1989); background variables in this ex post facto study are not controlled in such a way as to make possible conclusions about the causes of academic achievement test scores being higher or lower than those of students in conventional schools. The first limitation is that the sample in this study is composed of volunteers, and, therefore, characteristics of volunteers must be considered when interpreting the findings (Borg & Gall, 1989, p. 228). Second, it is practically impossible to include a random sample of all home education families in the United States, and, therefore, one should keep in mind the limitations of representativeness and generalizability. Third, this study is descriptive and exploratory in nature. It is one of the relatively few nationwide studies that have been completed on home education.

Findings

For 1,952 students in this study, the most frequently used (by 37.3%) academic achievement test was the ITBS; 29.8% took the Stanford Achieve-

B. D. Ray

ment Test; 15.6% used the California Achievement Test; 6.7% used the Comprehensive Test of Basic Skills; 2.7% used the Metropolitan Achievement Test; 0.2% used the Tests of Achievement and Proficiency; 7.9% used one of a variety of other tests (and the total exceeds 100% due to rounding error). The average age of students taking achievement tests was 11.00 (*SD* = 2.89, *n* = 1,864), and the average grade level of the tests was 5.43 (*SD* = 2.89, *n* = 1,824). The person who administered the test was a public school teacher in 10.3% of the cases, a private school teacher in 12.3% of the cases, the parent in 43.9% of the cases, and some other administrator (such as a home education support group member or a qualified test administrator) in 33.5% of the cases. Copies of test results from the test publisher or test administrator were submitted for 77% of the students.

The students scored, on the average, at the following percentiles on standardized achievement tests: (a) total reading, 87th; (b) total language, 80th; (c) total math, 82nd; (d) total listening, 85th; (e) science, 84th; (f) social studies, 85th; (g) study skills, 81st; (h) basic battery (typically reading, language, and mathematics), 85th; and (i) complete battery (all subject areas in which student was tested), 87th. Table 2 presents summary statistics on academic achievement. Not all students were tested in all subject areas; therefore, sample sizes varied.

The reading, language, and math test score data were examined to determine whether low scores were ever reported by the parents. In reading, scores at or below the 16th percentile (−1.0 SD) were reported for 26 students. In language, scores at or below the 16th percentile were reported for 39 students. In math, scores at or below the 16th percentile were reported

Table 2
Summary of Home Educated Students' Standardized Achievement Test Scores

Variable	National Percentile[a]	M z	SD z	N
Reading, total	87	1.15	.84	1,594
Listening, total	85	1.05	.85	580
Language, total	80	.85	.90	1,486
Math, total	82	.90	.87	1,613
Science	84	1.00	.82	1,133
Social studies	85	1.03	.82	1,099
Study skills	81	.87	.81	916
Basic battery	85	1.05	.81	1,338
Complete battery	87	1.11	.80	1,092

Note. A given percentile may have slightly different z scores associated with it due to lack of precision in conversion.

[a]All means for the home educated were significantly higher (*p* < .001) than the 50th percentile national average (Ray, 1997b).

Home Schooling: The Ameliorator?

for 35 students. The lowest score possible on achievement tests was reported for both language and math.

Variables that explain achievement scores—multivariate analyses. Seven of the 12 independent variables did not explain statistically significant amounts of variance in students' test scores. These 7 were (a) father's certification status, (b) mother's certification status, (c) family income, (d) money spent on home education, (e) legal status of family, (f) time spent in formal educational activities, and (g) age at which formal education began.

Five of the 12 independent variables explained statistically significant amounts of variance in students' test scores for any of the subject areas explored. The 5 significant variables were (a) father's education level, (b) mother's education level, (c) years taught at home, (d) gender of the student, and (e) number of visits to the public library. The maximum amount of variance in the test scores that any one of these independent variables explained was 5.0% (and this was by father's education level for the complete battery scores).

Father's education level, years the student was taught at home, and number of visits to the public library explained statistically significant amounts of variance in total reading scores (see Table 3). The strongest predictor of the reading score was the father's education level. The reading z score would be .048 higher per additional year of the father's formal education. This would be .02 to 1.9 percentiles of reading score per year of father's education (in this study). Father's educational level explained 2.5% of the variance in reading scores. The number of years home educated and number of visits to the public library per month were positively related to reading scores.

Father's education level, gender of the student, mother's education level, and number of years home educated explained statistically significant amounts of variance in the total language scores (see Table 4). Father's education was the strongest predictor. The student's language z score would be .054 (or .01–2.2 percentiles) higher per additional year of father's formal education. The number of years home educated and mother's education level were positively related to language scores. Girls scored somewhat higher in language than did boys.

Mother's education level, father's education level, and gender of student explained statistically significant amounts of variance in the total math scores (see Table 5). Mother's education was the strongest predictor. The student's language z score would be .056 (or .02–2.2 percentiles) higher per additional year of mother's formal education. The father's education level was positively related to math scores. In addition, boys scored somewhat higher in math than did girls.

83

B. D. Ray

Table 3

Coefficients of Determination, Analysis of Variance, and Other Statistics Regarding the Multiple Regression for Total Reading Test Scores With Three Significant Independent Variables

Independent Variable	R^2 Adjusted	R^2 Change
FATHED	.02472	
HOMEYRS	.03385	.009
LIBRPUB	.03825	.004

Analysis of Variance			
	df	SS	MS
Regression	3	38.01040	12.67013
Residual	1,331	902.59261	.67813

Variables in the Equation					
Variable	B	SE B	β	T	Significant T
FATHED	.047810	.007834	.163971	6.103	.0000
HOMEYRS	.033061	.008748	.101579	3.779	.0002
LIBRPUB	.026689	.010019	.071580	2.664	.0078
Constant	.140582	.138328		1.016	.3097

Note. FATHED = father's education level; HOMEYRS = years home educated; LIBRPUB = visits to public library. $F(3, 1331) = 18.68390$, $p < .01$.

Father's education level and mother's education level explained statistically significant amounts of variance in the complete battery scores (see Table 6). Father's education was the strongest predictor. The student's language z score would be .050 (or .01–2.0 percentiles) higher per additional year of father's formal education. The mother's education level was positively related to complete battery scores.

Correlation coefficients between the test scores and the interval-data independent variables mentioned in the preceding section on multiple regression are relatively small in magnitude. Ray (1997b, p. 123) provided these correlations and accompanying statistics in detail.

Degree of regulation of home education in the state and test scores. An analysis of variance was conducted to test whether the degree of regulation of home education by a state has an effect on students' basic battery test scores. States were categorized as having either low regulation, moderate regulation, or high regulation (see Table 7). *Low regulation* was defined as

Home Schooling: The Ameliorator?

no state requirement on the part of the home school parents to initiate any contact with the state. *Moderate regulation* was defined as the state requiring home school parents to send to the state notification or achievement test scores and/or evaluation of the student's learning by a professional. *High regulation* was defined as the state requiring home school parents to send to the state notification or achievement test scores and/or evaluation by a professional and, in addition, having other requirements (e.g., curriculum approval by the state, teacher qualifications of parents, or home visits by state officials). There was no significant difference between students' scores in the three groups.

Test administrator and test scores. There was a significant difference between basic battery scores of students based on who administered the test (i.e., public school teacher, private school teacher, parent, and other), $F(3,$

Table 4
Coefficients of Determination, Analysis of Variance, and Other Statistics Regarding the Multiple Regression for Total Language Test Scores With Four Significant Independent Variables

Independent Variable	R^2 Adjusted	R^2 Change
FATHED	.04149	
SEX	.06103	.020
MOTHED	.06568	.005
HOMEYRS	.07014	.004

Analysis of Variance			
	df	SS	MS
Regression	4	72.55888	18.13972
Residual	1,234	919.40706	.74506

Variables in the Equation					
Variable	B	SE B	β	T	Significant T
FATHED	.054312	.009601	.174736	5.657	.0000
MOTHED	.036936	.013567	.084083	2.722	.0066
SEX	−.253990	.049130	−.141909	−5.170	.0000
HOMEYRS	.025061	.009519	.072232	2.633	.0086
Constant	−.547542	.196476		−2.787	.0054

Note. FATHED = father's education level; SEX = sex of student; MOTHED = mother's education level; HOMEYRS = years home educated. $F(4, 1234) = 24.34658$, $p < .01$.

Table 5

Coefficients of Determination, Analysis of Variance, and Other Statistics Regarding the Multiple
Regression for Total Math Test Scores With Three Significant Independent Variables

Independent Variable	R^2 Adjusted	R^2 Change
MOTHED	.03577	
FATHED	.04749	.012
SEX	.05487	.007

Analysis of Variance			
	df	SS	MS
Regression	3	58.81049	19.60350
Residual	1,347	973.51453	.72273

Variables in the Equation					
Variable	B	SE B	β	T	Significant T
FATHED	.037344	.009053	.122984	4.125	.0000
MOTHED	.056156	.012794	.130859	4.389	.0000
SEX	.157257	.046314	.089939	3.395	.0007
Constant	−.585768	.177116		−3.307	.0010

Note. MOTHED = mother's education level; FATHED = father's education level; SEX = sex of student. $F(3, 1347) = 27.12431$, $p < .01$.

Table 6

Coefficients of Determination, Analysis of Variance, and Other Statistics Regarding the Multiple
Regression for Complete Battery Test Scores With Two Significant Independent Variables

Independent Variable	R^2 Adjusted	R^2 Change
FATHED	.04997	
MOTHED	.05621	.006

Analysis of Variance			
	df	SS	MS
Regression	2	33.70664	16.85332
Residual	908	544.61842	.59980

Variables in the Equation					
Variable	B	SE B	β	T	Significant T
FATHED	.050286	.010042	.181658	5.007	.0000
MOTHED	.037568	.014193	.096028	2.647	.0083
Constant	−.232221	.195413		−1.188	.2350

Note. FATHED = father's education level; MOTHED = mother's education level. $F(2, 908) = 28.09823$, $p < .01$.

Home Schooling: The Ameliorator?

Table 7
Basic Battery Test Scores Compared According to Degree of Regulation of Home Education by the State

			Analysis of Variance		
Source	df	Sum of Squares	M Squares	F Ratio	F Probability
Between groups	2	.1179	.0589	.0898	.9141
Within groups	1,236	811.3733	.6565		
Total	1,238	811.4911			

Group	Count	M	SD	SE	95% Confidence Interval
1	187	1.0721	.8437	.0617	.9504 to 1.1938
2	758	1.0515	.7921	.0288	.9950 to 1.1079
3	294	1.0711	.8343	.0487	.9753 to 1.1668
Total	1,239	1.0592	.8096	.0230	1.0141 to 1.1043

Note. Group 1 (low regulation) = states of ID, IL, IN, MI, MO, NJ, OK, and TX. Group 2 (moderate regulation) = states of AK, AL, AZ, CA, CO, CT, DC, DE, FL, GA, HI, IA, KS, KY, LA, MD, MS, MT, NC, NE, NH, NM, OH, OR, SC, SD, TN, VA, WI, and WY. Group 3 (high regulation) = states of AR, MA, ME, MN, ND, NV, NY, PA, RI, UT, VT, WA, and WV.

1258) = 7.9542, p = .000. All four groups had scores that were above average. The least significant difference multiple range test (with a set at .05) revealed that there was no significant difference in basic battery scores when students were tested by public school teachers (M = 85th percentile) compared to when they were administered tests by their parents (M = 88th percentile); scores of students who were tested by their parents, however, were significantly higher than scores of those tested by private school teachers (M = 81st percentile) and by others (M = 84th percentile).

Use of computer for education of the child and test scores. A comparison was made between achievement scores of children who used a computer for their education and those who did not. The t tests revealed no significant differences in language, $t(1448)$ = 2.27, p = .02; math, $t(1571)$ = 1.32, p = .19; science, $t(1112)$ = .06, p = .95; and social studies, $t(1079)$ = .19, p = .85. There was a significant difference in reading, $t(1554)$ = 2.59, p = .01; those using computers for their education scored higher (M = 88 percentile) than did those not using computers (M = 85 percentile).

B. D. Ray

Conclusions and Discussion

The home-educated students in this study fared well on standardized academic achievement tests. The average age of students taking achievement tests was 11, and the average grade level of the tests was fifth. The students scored, on the average, at or above the 80th percentile in all areas tested. These scores were consistent with those average scores, typically in the 65th to 85th percentile range, found by most researchers who have studied the home schooled in state-specific studies and nationwide in the United States and in Canada. In addition, very few demographic or learning environment factors were significantly related to their achievement.

Variables That Explain Academic Achievement Scores

Several analyses were conducted to determine which independent variables were significantly related to academic achievement. Five of the 12 independent variables used in multiple regression explained statistically significant amounts of variance in students' test scores for any of the subject areas explored. Only 1 of these significant variables (i.e., father's education level) was significant in all regressions performed. The 5 significant variables were father's education level, mother's education level, years taught at home, gender of the student, and frequency of visits to the public library. The maximum amount of variance in the test scores that any 1 of these independent variables explained was 5.0% (and this was by father's education level for the complete battery scores).

Father's education level, years the student was taught at home, and number of visits to the public library were all positively related to and together explained 3.8% of the variance in total reading scores. This explanatory power is, practically speaking, unremarkable. Father's education level (i.e., a positive relation), gender of the student (i.e., girls outperformed boys), mother's education level (i.e., a positive relation), and number of years home educated (i.e., a positive relation) together explained 7.0% of the variance in total language scores. This explanatory power is, practically speaking, not very remarkable. Mother's education level (i.e., a positive relation), father's education level (i.e., a positive relation), and gender of student (i.e., boys outperformed girls) explained 5.5% of the variance in total math scores. Again, this explanatory power is, practically speaking, rather unremarkable. Father's education level and mother's education level were positively related to and explained 5.6% of the variance in complete battery scores (which are partially based on reading, language, and math scores).

Home Schooling: The Ameliorator?

The effect of three other variables on achievement was considered using tests of comparison. The degree of regulation of home education by the state, who administered the tests to students, and the use of computers for the education of the student all had little to no effect on academic achievement.

Table 8 provides a summary of all the statistical analyses that explored the relation between the several independent variables and various achievement test scores in this study.

The father's education level was the only variable that consistently (i.e., four of four analyses) explained significant amounts of variance in achievement. The education level of the mother (who does most of the formal teaching of the students) was significant in three of four analyses and was a weaker predictor than was the father's education level. In sum, relatively little variance in achievement was explained by the variables examined in this study. Variables such as parent education level and family income may be better predictors of achievement in public schools (Coleman & Hoffer, 1987; Coleman, Hoffer, & Kilgore, 1982; Snow et al., 1991) than they are in home schooling.

One explanation for why little variance in academic achievement was explained by the independent variables in this study is range restriction. It is difficult to know for certain to what extent range restriction, in this study, affected the regression coefficients (Cohen & Cohen, 1983, p. 71). Furthermore, if range restriction does exist, it would be very difficult (if at all possible) to estimate the true correlations adjusted for range restriction. Future research that includes more home school students with more varied backgrounds and characteristics and research that entails a careful causal-comparative design will reveal more about the effects of home schooling on academic achievement and whether selected background variables have positive or negative effects within the practice of home schooling and compared to the effects within conventional schooling. Based on the findings at hand and those from other research, however, some implications can be suggested.

While this report was being written, Rudner (1999) published some findings that add to those of this study and others. He examined the ITBS and Tests of Achievement and Proficiency scores of 20,760 home school students from 11,930 families across the United States:

> The median scores for home school students are well above their public/private school counterparts in every subject and in every grade. The corresponding percentiles range from the 62nd to the 91st percentile; most percentiles are between the 75th and 85th percentile. (Rudner, 1999, p. 15)

Table 8

Summary of Statistical Analyses Showing Which of the Selected Independent Variables Were Statistically Significantly Related to Achievement Test Scores in This Study

Independent Variable	Reading	Language	Math	Science	Social Studies	Basic Battery	Complete Battery
Father's education	Yes, positive	Yes, positive	Yes	n/a	n/a	n/a	Yes, positive
Mother's education	No	Yes, positive	Yes, positive	n/a	n/a	n/a	Yes, positive
Father is certified teacher	No	No	No	n/a	n/a	n/a	No
Mother is certified teacher	No	No	No	n/a	n/a	n/a	No
Family income	No	No	No	n/a	n/a	n/a	No
Money spent on education	No	No	No	n/a	n/a	n/a	No
Legal status	No	No	No	n/a	n/a	n/a	No
Sex	No	Yes, girls higher	Yes, boys higher	n/a	n/a	n/a	No
Years home educated	Yes, positive	Yes, positive	No	n/a	n/a	n/a	No
Use of libraries	Yes, positive	No	No	n/a	n/a	n/a	No
Time in formal instruction	No	No	No	n/a	n/a	n/a	No
Age began formal instruction	No	No	No	n/a	n/a	n/a	No
Degree of state regulation	n/a	n/a	n/a	n/a	n/a	No	n/a
Test administrator	n/a	n/a	n/a	n/a	n/a	Yes, mixed results	n/a
Use of computer	Yes, positive	No	No	No	No	n/a	n/a

Note. n/a = not applicable—no statistical test was done.

Home Schooling: The Ameliorator?

As in some of the previous studies that examined the three independent variables of number of years the student was home educated, family income, and parent's formal education level, Rudner (1999) found significant positive relations between these and achievement. Contrary to previous research, Rudner found a significant relation between amount of money spent on home education and achievement. Consistent with most previous research, he found no relation between achievement and whether at least one of the parents was a certified teacher. Consistent with critiques of the methodology involved in many studies on home schooling, Welner and Welner (1999) argued that Rudner should have more clearly described the possible bias in his sample.

The Home Schooling "Treatment" and its Possible
Ameliorative Effects

Decades of research on what causes or is associated with improved learning (i.e., academic achievement) in conventional classroom schools have provided wide-ranging findings and conclusions. The factors that are associated with increased achievement, at the macrolevel, include (but are not limited to) the following (which are listed in no particular order):

1. Clear and articulated objectives for schools and teachers—for example, learning and achievement are of the highest priority (Brophy & Good, 1986; Oswald, 1995; USDE, 1986).
2. Rewarding teachers, administrators, and students for high achievement (Oswald, 1995).
3. Holding high and reasonable expectations of students (Brophy & Good, 1986; Lumsden, 1997; USDE, 1986).
4. Individualization of curriculum for each student (Brophy & Good, 1986; T. L. Good & Brophy, 1987).
5. Increased feedback to the student (Brophy & Good, 1986; Educational Resources Information Center/Languages and Linguistics [ERIC/LL], 1997).
6. Emphasis on direct instruction by a teacher (Brophy & Good, 1986; USDE, 1986).
7. Increased academic learning time (and/or academic engaged time [AET]; Brophy & Good, 1986; Medley, 1982; USDE, 1986).
8. Greater amounts of social capital (Coleman & Hoffer, 1987; Stockard & Mayberry, 1992).
9. Greater amounts of human capital.
10. Smaller class size (Colorado Department of Education, 1996; Finn, 1998; Glass & Smith, 1979).

B. D. Ray

11. Tutoring versus group instruction, especially in certain situations—for example, beginning reading instruction (Brophy & Good, 1986; T. L. Good & Brophy, 1987; USDE, 1986).

12. Mastery learning (Brophy & Good, 1986; T. L. Good & Brophy, 1987).

13. Cooperative learning (Stahl, 1994).

14. Increased contextualization (or helping students link new concepts and information to the already familiar) of teaching and curriculum in experiences and skills of home and community (Brophy & Good, 1986; ERIC/LL, 1997).

15. Increased parent involvement (Baker & Soden, 1998; Chavkin, 1993; Giles, 1998; Henderson, 1987; Henderson & Berla, 1994; USDE, 1986, 1991, 1994).

16. Certain teacher traits—for example, knowledgeable, able to structure information for students, able to present with clarity, enthusiastic, caring, able to explain concepts, and capable in managing a classroom (Brophy & Good, 1986; Medley, 1982).

Assuming, for the sake of discussion and based on a multitude of studies, that home schooling is associated with high academic achievement (and possibly causes it), one could ask whether there is any link between the preceding list of positive factors and the nature of the educational "treatment" known as home schooling.

Before proceeding, several comments are in order. First, it should be recognized that research on what makes for effective teaching and learning in schools may be neither conceptually nor theoretically applicable to what makes for effective teaching and learning in the home-based environment (see, e.g., Sheffer, 1995, pp. 22, 23). Enough is known, however, about home schooling and its practices (e.g., Bliss, 1989; Breshears, 1996; Colfax & Colfax, 1988; Gustavsen, 1980; Guterson, 1992; Howshall, 1998; Johnson, 1991; Knowles, 1987; Macdonald & Marchant, 1992; Mayberry, 1988; Mayberry, Knowles, Ray, & Marlow, 1995; Medlin, 1994, 1996; Ray, 1990b, 1997b; Sheffer, 1995; Taylor, 1992, 1993; Van Galen, 1988) that it is possible to address whether it is likely that the features of effective schools that might reasonably apply to home schooling are generally, in fact, a part of home schooling. If they are a part of home schooling, then it may be likely they would work to the academic advantage of home school students. Second, proposing ideas about home schooling that appear to ascribe only "positive" attributes to home schooling may make a scholar vulnerable to charges of partiality. It may be that until more scholars whose focus has always been state-run education and whose preferences have clearly lain with the modern common school study home schooling and discuss its potential benefits and positive traits that the topic of parent-directed and

Home Schooling: The Ameliorator?

family-based education will be held in abeyance within academe (on the topic of scholars avoiding the topic of white racism, cf. Scheurich & Young, 1998, p. 28).

The following, therefore, is a brief consideration of certain features of effective schools that might be features of typical home school situations and may contribute to the apparent high academic achievement of the home educated. This is not to suggest that research findings clearly substantiate that all of these positive traits exist in all (or even most) home school families. The following comments are offered to encourage researchers to make sure that these considerations are made in future research on home schooling.

Value consistency, value communities, and social capital. Social capital "exists in the relations between persons" (Coleman & Hoffer, 1987, p. 221). Coleman and Hoffer presented trust as a form of social capital. "A group within which there is extensive trustworthiness and extensive trust is able to accomplish much more than a comparable group without that trustworthiness and trust" (Coleman & Hoffer, 1987, p. 221). They gave evidence that even if families possess high levels of human capital (i.e., skills and capacities in people as may be acquired in schools), the children may be at an academic disadvantage if there is little social capital in the family. This low level of social capital might be caused by the physical absence of family members (i.e., a "structural deficiency") or the absence of strong relationships between children and parents (i.e., a "functional deficiency"). Coleman and Hoffer used the construct of social capital to explain why private school students outperform public school students in terms of academic achievement. Based on research regarding the characteristics and practices of home school families (cited previously), it appears that home school families likely possess a large measure of social capital (Ray, 1989, 1990c).

As a part of their overall analysis that hinges on social capital, Coleman and Hoffer (1987) discussed the importance of value consistency and value communities—that is, the sharing of values between school personnel, parents, and students leads to efficient social function and schools in which students learn effectively. It may be that the home education environment and home education communities provide a high level of value consistency and a shared-value community in which children may learn successfully. Children who engage in home-based education are presented by their parents, friends, home education communities, and religious groups with a relatively coherent worldview—rather than the menagerie of competing value systems that often is encountered in state schools (Glanzer, 1998; Nord, 1995; Vitz, 1985).

B. D. Ray

Class size and tutoring.   Although there have been mixed results, the weight of evidence on class size shows that smaller classes generally are associated with higher achievement (Colorado Department of Education, 1996; Finn, 1998; Glass & Smith, 1979). Most home school students find themselves in a group of two to four children or youth for the majority of the time they spend on their more-structured studies and learning. Many home-educated children are, therefore, essentially tutored—that is, they have private instructors, their parents and others, in a one-to-one or small-group instructional setting. The average home school family has about three children; one of these is preschool age, and two are in the conventional kindergarten to Grade 12 range. Thus, there is one adult teaching only two school-age children most of the day. When the other parent is not at work, there are potentially two adults to teach two children. Even when the family is larger—for example, with six children—the parent who conducts most of the formal instruction is still only teaching five children. In these larger families, furthermore, it is often the case that the older children help teach the younger ones. Again, then, this approaches a one-to-one tutoring situation for most of the children most of the time.

Literature on tutoring defines it and explains its advantages, as seen in Bloom (1984):

> Students learn the subject matter with a good tutor for each student, or for two or three students simultaneously. This tutoring instruction is followed periodically by formative tests, feedback-corrective procedures, and parallel formative tests as in the mastery learning classes. The need for corrective work under tutoring is very small. (p. 4)

Bloom (1984) and his associates tried to find teaching-learning methods that were as effective as tutoring. Bloom wrote on some controlled research settings:

> The most striking of the findings is that under the best learning conditions we can devise—(tutoring)—the average student is 2 sigmas [2 standard deviations of the control group] above the average control student taught under conventional group methods of instruction. (p. 6)

In the home education setting, qualitative researchers have witnessed ongoing feedback, formative evaluation, intimate interaction during academic learning, and efforts by parents to holistically affect every area of their children's lives (e.g., Taylor, 1993, pp. 85, 133; Treat, 1990, pp. vii, 120–136).

Home Schooling: The Ameliorator?

From a more historical perspective, Gordon and Gordon (1990) said, "Tutoring, as we will use it, encompasses the academic, moral and philosophical growth of the individual child. Tutors identified themselves closely with their pupils" (p. 6). Tutors often became quasi-family members, and tutoring made education a family affair:

> It often involved the parents with the tutor in combining education and the family as a unified life-long experience. This is what distinguished a "tutor" from a "classroom teacher." The tutor's highly individualistic approach transcended education's academic lessons. At its best tutoring attempted to reach out and touch a child's intellectual, moral and spiritual fiber in a dynamic personal process. The tutor remained a counselor into adulthood, long after the lessons had ceased. These concepts were found originally in the "tutorial ideal" of the ancient world. (Gordon & Gordon, 1990, p. 6)

Individualization and flexibility. About 70% of home educators say that they design the curriculum for their children (Ray, 1990b, 1997b)—that is, they hand-pick the materials that they think are best fit to the individual student. This may be an indication that they are individualizing the curriculum for their students, which may cause high achievement (T. L. Good & Brophy, 1987).

Academic learning time and academic engaged time. Academic learning time (ALT) is "the amount of time a student spends performing relevant academic tasks with a high level of success" (T. L. Good & Brophy, 1987, p. 35). High ALT generally is associated with high academic achievement. Students at home may experience more ALT and AET than do students in conventional schools. Data show that home-educated students spend only 3 to 4 hr per day in planned structured learning, compared to the 6 or more hr per day in school plus homework that conventional school students experience. The relatively small amount of time that the home educated spend in academics may be, in fact, largely ALT. Duvall et al. (1997) found that special-needs students who were home educated were involved in AET 59.0% of the time versus 22.5% of the time for special-needs students in public schools. A new study corroborates this finding (Steven F. Duvall, personal communication, January 23, 1999).

Positive social interactions, cooperative learning, and age integration. Educators have struggled perennially to ensure that same-age peer-group so-

B. D. Ray

cial interactions are positive and conducive to learning (academic achievement). The reality in the classroom is that the social interactions are not always of this nature. One line of research and practice that appears to have met reasonable success in this area is cooperative learning. Stahl (1994) delineated the essential elements of successful cooperative learning. Although it would be inappropriate to casually claim that the technical aspects of conventional school cooperative learning apply to the typical home school setting, some of the essential elements of cooperative learning may be inherent to home schooling. These might be positive social interaction behaviors and attitudes, heterogeneous groups (both within the family and outside the family at events and classes organized for home schoolers), individual accountability, and sufficient time being spent on learning (Stahl, 1994).

Although the integration of variously aged students in a learning environment has a long history (e.g., one-room schoolhouses, dame schools, agrarian societies), it has been largely uncharacteristic of American schools for many decades. Recent research, however, suggests that age mixing among children and adolescents may have educational and other benefits (Feldman & Gray, 1999). These researchers concluded, regarding age mixing, that (a) younger children actively use older children to learn and acquire skills and take responsibility for their own learning, (b) "age-mixed play offers unique opportunities for creativity and the practice of skills" (Feldman & Gray, 1999, pp. 509–510), (c) it is sometimes a means of matching abilities, and (d) "Older children feel a sense of responsibility for younger children and develop an increasingly sophisticated understanding of that responsibility" (Feldman & Gray, 1999, p. 511). It should be noted that age mixing is the everyday and yearly experience of the majority of home school students. They are born into a family and regularly interact with their parents and other adults, their siblings, other home school students, neighborhood peers, and children and youth at community activities such as scouts, 4-H, group sports, Sunday school, and dance classes. Their world, including the conventional school "school hours," is an age-integrated world. It may be that the typical individual home schooler is not aware that he or she "should" think of himself or herself as part of a peer group or "a tribe apart," as Hersch described adolescents in schools who feel isolated from the grown-up world and alienated from parents (as cited in Mattox, 1999; cf. Delahooke, 1986; Sheffer, 1995; Shyers, 1992).

Although peer pressure can be positive and motivate students to higher achievement and better behavior, in many instances peer pressure distracts students from academic pursuits, reduces their efficient use of time, and draws students into behaviors that are neither beneficial nor virtuous (Coleman, 1961, as cited in T. E. Smith, 1992; Larson, 1983, as cited in T. E.

Home Schooling: The Ameliorator?

Smith, 1992; T. E. Smith, 1992). Many parents recognize this social problem that accompanies conventional schools.

Although much of the verbal and nonverbal behavior that permeates a conventional school is that which many adults consider normal and relatively harmless, the physical violence in schools is a more extreme but obvious example of what few consider to be harmless (USDE, 1994, p. 15). Toch (1991a) reported that the exodus from public schools was largely fueled by the fact that "many parents view the public schools as ineffective and dangerous, and are exploring other options before it's too late" (p. 66). Home school parents cite safety as one of their reasons for home schooling their children (Mayberry et al., 1995; Ray, 1997a; Sheffer, 1995). Students whose learning is based in the home may be experiencing a safe and relatively orderly daily environment—one that often may not exist in public schools (USDE, 1994).

Expectations of students.　　One of the main reasons why parents choose home education is success in academics. With this in mind and the probability that these parents want their children to do well and live up to their intellectual potential, it is plausible that they generally hold high expectations of them. Research findings have suggested repeatedly that high expectations lead to children doing well. Perhaps this cycle is typically at work within home school families.

Human capital.　　A large body of evidence positively links the formal education level of parents to the achievement of their children in public schools. Generally speaking, the education level of home educators is somewhat above the national average, and this appears to explain, in some vague way, some of their children's high academic achievement (Ray, 1990b, 1997b; Rudner, 1999; Russell, 1994).

Parent involvement.　　Within the milieu of conventional public and private schools, the overwhelming opinion of practitioners and research evidence indicate that parent involvement is an important key, if not the primary key, to students' academic success. It may not be obvious to everyone, but most people with whom I have had extended conversations about home schooling—both detractors from and advocates of home schooling—have opined that home educators are the paragon of parent involvement. To be sure, there are likely exceptions to this stereotype among the 700,000 or so home school families in the United States; generally, however,

97

these parents direct, engage in, monitor, and enjoy their children's educational lives. In fact, many of them do not even think of their children's educational lives as constructs distinctly separate from their own lives in general—that is, the parents' involvement in the children's lives, and vice versa, is one rather continuous, roughly seamless intertwining of the learning, applying, and practicing of values, knowledge, and culture and familial, social, religious, and political activities as the children move from the womb to adulthood and the parents move from being parental novitiates to veterans to grandparents. Home schooling, generally speaking, is, de facto parent involvement and family-within-community life.

I have heard many negative critics of home schooling—and others who are simply trying to explain the positive success of the home educated—suggest that any child who has parents as involved in his or her education as are the parents of the home-educated child would probably do just as well in conventional public schools as in home schooling. This hypothesis has a ring of truth to it. This suggestion ignores, however, at least two important points. First, parents who send their children away from themselves and their home for 6 to 9 hr per day do not have the available time to be as involved with their children as do home school parents. Second, conventional schools, systemically speaking, are in many ways impervious to efforts by parents to be wholly involved in their children's educational lives (see, e.g., Epstein, as cited in Baker & Soden, 1998; USDE, 1994). It is possible, then, that the suggestion that if only public school parents would be as involved in the lives of their children as are home school parents then the public school children would have just as high achievement as the home educated is an example of the logical fallacy of a hypothesis contrary to fact; perhaps this level of parent involvement simply cannot exist when a child is enrolled in a conventional classroom school.

Despite the fact that various professional educators (e.g., National Association of Elementary School Principals, 1989–1990, 1993; National Association of State Boards of Education, 1996; National Education Association, 1990, 1999) claim that home education is not good for students, research evidence continues to mount that home education benefits children and youth. The conjectural advantages of state-run, conventional schools are things such as professionally trained and state-certified teachers; experiencing a wide variety of cultures and worldviews; academic and extracurricular activities that are not available to the home educated; a quality and quantity of laboratory and technical equipment that exceeds what most families possess; school personnel who are receptive to and tolerant of a variety of philosophical and religious beliefs and the expression thereof; 6 to 9 hr of daily social interaction with a large number of same-age peers; and 6 to 9 hr per day with a variety of adults outside the family who are,

Home Schooling: The Ameliorator?

generally, neither psychologically nor emotionally close to the child. The weight of research evidence, however, suggests that the lack of these things, which allegedly benefit students in conventional schools, are not harming the home educated.

In summary, the various studies related to the learning and thinking skills of home-educated students, almost without exception, lead to the conclusion that a variety of families who represent varied philosophical and religious worldviews, socioeconomic statuses, and races and ethnicities are clearly successful at teaching their children via home education. Regarding the cause of these children's high academic achievement, however, there is little consensus, and the problem has not been thoroughly investigated.

An observer might be tempted to suggest that the significance of this study and others on academic achievement is that home schooling is generally associated with or causes higher achievement than does public schooling. It has been pointed out, however, that this topic was only one part of this study and this article, and that very limited research of a causal-comparative design has been done. This work, rather, in addition to other studies, might suggest that there is something inherent to the modern practice of home education that could (or does) ameliorate the effect of background factors that are associated with lower academic achievement when students are placed in conventional public schools. One might submit, therefore, that the "treatment" that is currently called home schooling is simply a combination, or at least is potentially a combination, of many factors that make for effective schooling and learning in conventional classroom schools. Furthermore, it should be noted that home schooling may be not only comprised of these factors, but may include some that have neither been identified nor about which anyone has thought and presented to the world of scholarship.

Perhaps most home school parents and students naturally—that is, without formal training—practice many of the things that researchers have found to be effective for teaching and learning. In the estimation of T. L. Good and Brophy (1987), private individualized tutoring "is the method of choice for most educational purposes, because both curriculum (what is taught) and instruction (how it is taught) can be individualized and because the teacher can provide the student with sustained personalized attention" (p. 352). Perhaps it should not surprise anyone—state- or private-school teacher, educational policymaker, teacher union leader, or parent—that the home educated do well in terms of learning. T. L. Good and Brophy went on to say, "Unfortunately, private tutoring is too expensive for most families to afford" (p. 352). Perhaps they were not aware, while writing their book, of the then-burgeoning home education movement. It now appears that both low- and high-income families, and both

99

B. D. Ray

families that professional educators and policymakers would consider low- and at-risk, have been finding a way to make a form of tutoring affordable and effective through the practice of home schooling.

References

Alaska Department of Education. (1984). *Summary of SRA testing for Centralized Correspondence Study April/May 1984.* Juneau, AK: Author.

Alaska Department of Education. (1985). *SRA survey of basic skills and Alaska Statewide Assessment, Spring of 1985* [for Centralized Correspondence Study Students]. Juneau, AK: Author.

Alaska Department of Education. (1986). *Results from 1981 CAT* [for CCS]. Juneau, AK: Author.

Baker, A. J. L., & Soden, L. M. (1998). The challenges of parent involvement research. *ERIC/CUE Digest, 134.* Retrieved April 13, 2000 from the World Wide Web: http://www.ed.gov/databases/ERIC_Digests/ed419030.html (ERIC Document Reproduction Service No. 419 030 98)

Bliss, B. A. (1989, February 20). *Home education: A look at current practices.* A research project. East Lansing: Michigan State University. (ERIC Document Reproduction Service No. ED 304 233)

Bloom, B. S. (1984, May). The search for methods of group instruction as effective as one-to-one tutoring. *Educational Leadership, 41*(8), 4–17.

Borg, W. R., & Gall, M. D. (1989). *Educational research: An introduction* (5th ed.). New York: Longman.

Breshears, S. M. (1996). *Characteristics of home schools and home school families in Idaho.* Unpublished doctoral dissertation, University of Idaho, Moscow.

Brophy, J., & Good, T. L. (1986). Teacher behavior and student achievement. In M. C. Wittrock (Ed.), *Handbook of research on teaching* (3rd ed., pp. 328–371). New York: Macmillan.

Butler, R. W. (1994). *Home schooling: An effective setting for programmed learning.* Unpublished doctoral dissertation, California Coast University, Santa Ana.

Caldwell, D. K. (1999, January 30). Death to the schools: Leaders of religious right calling for a Christian exodus out of public education. *Dallas Morning News,* 1G.

Carper, J. C. (1992, April/May). Home schooling, history, and historians: The past as present. *High School Journal, 75,* 252–257.

Chavkin, N. F. (Ed.). (1993). *Families and schools in a pluralistic society.* Albany: State University of New York Press.

Cizek, G. J. (1991). Alternative assessments: Promises and problems for home-based education policy. *Home School Researcher, 7*(4), 13–21.

Cizek, G. J. (1993). The mismeasure of home schooling effectiveness: A commentary. *Home School Researcher, 9*(3), 1–4.

Clark, C. S. (1994). Home schooling: Is it a healthy alternative to public education? *Congressional Quarterly Researcher, 4,* 769–792.

Cohen, J., & Cohen, P. (1983). *Applied multiple regression/correlation analysis for the behavioral sciences* (2nd ed.). Hillsdale, NJ: Lawrence Erlbaum Associates, Inc.

Coleman, J. S., Campbell, E., Hobson, C., McPartland, J., Mood, A., Weinfeld, F., & York, R. (1966). *Equality of educational opportunity.* Washington, DC: U.S. Office of Education, National Center for Educational Statistics.

Coleman, J. S., & Hoffer, T. (1987). *Public and private high schools: The impact of communities.* New York: Basic Books.

Coleman, J. S., Hoffer, T., & Kilgore, S. (1982). *High school achievement: Public, Catholic, and private schools compared.* New York: Basic Books.

Home Schooling: The Ameliorator?

Colfax, D., & Colfax, M. (1988). *Homeschooling for excellence.* New York: Warner Books.

Colorado Department of Education. (1996). Class-size effects in the primary grades: Research in Tennessee. *Of Primary Interest, 3*(3).

Delahooke, M. M. (1986). *Home educated children's social/emotional adjustment and academic achievement: A comparative study.* Unpublished doctoral dissertation, California School of Professional Psychology, Los Angeles.

Duvall, S. F., Ward, D. L., Delquadri, J. C., & Greenwood, C. R. (1997). An exploratory study of home school instructional environments and their effects on the basic skills of students with learning disabilities. *Education and Treatment of Children, 20,* 150–172.

ERIC [Educational Resources Information Center]/LL [Languages and Linguistics]. (1997). *From at-risk to excellence: Principles for practice.* Washington, DC: Author. (ERIC Document Reproduction Service No. 413 765)

Falle, B. (1986). Standardized tests for home study students: Administration and results. *Method: Alaskan Perspectives, 7*(1), 22–24.

Farris, M. P. (1998). Vida nueva—New life in Mexico. *Home School Court Report, 14*(6), 37, 40.

Feldman, J., & Gray, P. (1999, March). Some educational benefits of freely chosen age mixing among children and adolescents. *Phi Delta Kappan, 80,* 507–512.

Finn, J. D. (1998). *Class size and students at risk: What is known? What is next? A commissioned paper.* Washington, DC: National Institute on the Education of At-Risk Students. (ERIC Document Reproduction Service No. 418 208)

Fowler, F. J., Jr. (1988). *Survey research methods (revised edition).* Newbury Park, CA: Sage.

Frisbie, D. A. (1992). Book review: Understanding achievement tests: A guide for school administrators. *Journal of Educational Measurement, 29*(3), 273–278.

Frost, E. A. (1987). A descriptive study of the academic achievement of selected elementary school-aged children educated at home in five Illinois counties. *Dissertation Abstracts International, 48,* 1589A.

Giles, H. C. (1998). Parent engagement as a school reform strategy. *ERIC/CUE Digest, 135.* New York: Author. Retrieved from the World Wide Web: http://www.ed.gov/databases/ERIC_Digests/ed419031.html (ERIC Document Reproduction Service No. ED 419 031)

Glanzer, P. (1998). Religion in public schools: In search of fairness. *Phi Delta Kappan, 80,* 219–222.

Glass, G., & Smith, M. L. (1979). Meta-analysis of research on class size and achievement. *Educational Evaluation and Policy Analysis, 1*(1), 2–16.

Good, R. (1984). A problem of multiple significance tests. *Journal of Research in Science Teaching, 21*(1), 105–106.

Good, T. L., & Brophy, J. E. (1987). *Looking in classrooms* (4th ed.). New York: Harper & Row.

Gordon, E. E., & Gordon, E. H. (1990). *Centuries of tutoring: A history of alternative education in America and Western Europe.* Lanham, MD: University Press of America.

Gronlund, N. E., & Linn, R. L. (1990). *Measurement and evaluation in teaching* (6th ed.). New York: Macmillan.

Gustavsen, G. A. (1980). *Selected characteristics of home schools and parents who operate them.* Unpublished doctoral dissertation, Andrews University, Berrien Springs, MI.

Guterson, D. (1992). *Family matters: Why homeschooling makes sense.* New York: Harcourt Brace.

Hadeed, H. V. (1991). Home schooling movement participation: A theoretical framework. *Home School Researcher, 7*(2), 1–9.

Havens, J. E. (1991). *A study of parent education levels as they relate to academic achievement among home schooled children.* Unpublished doctoral dissertation, Southwestern Baptist Theological Seminary, Fort Worth, TX.

Henderson, A. (1987). *The evidence continues to grow: Parent involvement improves student achievement.* Columbia, MD: National Committee for Citizens in Education.

B. D. Ray

Henderson, A. T., & Berla, N. (Eds.). (1994). *A new generation of evidence: The family is critical to student achievement.* Washington, DC: National Committee for Citizens in Education. (ERIC Document Reproduction Service No. ED 375 968)

Home School Legal Defense Association. (1994–1995). Home schoolers score significantly above national average. *Home School Court Report, 10*(6), 3.

Home School Legal Defense Association. (1996, September/October). District of Columbia. *Home School Court Report, 12*(5), 9.

Hopkins, K. D., Glass, G. V., & Hopkins, B. R. (1987). *Basic statistics for the behavioral sciences* (2nd ed.). Englewood Cliffs, NJ: Prentice Hall.

Hopkins, K. D., Stanley, J. C., & Hopkins, B. R. (1990). *Educational and psychological measurement and evaluation* (7th ed.). Englewood Cliffs, NJ: Prentice Hall.

Howshall, M. (1998). *The lifestyle of learning approach.* Eatonville, WA: Howshall Home Publications.

Hunter, J. E., & Schmidt, F. L. (1990). *Methods of meta-analysis: Correcting error and bias in research findings.* Newbury Park, CA: Sage.

Johnson, K. C. (1991). Socialization practices of Christian home school educators in the state of Virginia. *Home School Researcher, 7*(1), 9–16.

Kantrowitz, B., & Wingert, P. (1998, October 5). Learning at home: Does it pass the test? *Newsweek, 132*, 64–70.

Kirschner, J. (1991). The shifting roles of family and school as educator: A historical perspective. In J. A. Van Galen & M. A. Pitman (Eds.), *Home schooling: Political, historical, and pedagogical perspectives* (pp. 137–158). Norwood, NJ: Ablex.

Klicka, C. J. (1997). Home schooling is alive and well in South Africa. *Home School Court Report, 13*(5), 6–7.

Knowles, J. G. (1987, December 3–6). *Understanding parents who teach their children at home: The value of a life history approach.* Paper presented at the First Joint Conference of the Australian and New Zealand Associations for Research in Education, University of Canterbury, Christchurch, New Zealand.

Knowles, J. G., Mayberry, M., & Ray, B. D. (1991, December 24). *An assessment of home schools in Nevada, Oregon, Utah, and Washington: Implications for public education and a vehicle for informed policy decision, summary report* (Field Initiated Research Project Grant No. R117E90220). Washington, DC: U.S. Department of Education.

Leo, J. (1992, September 14). Sneer not at "Ozzie and Harriet." *U.S. News & World Report, 113*(10), 24.

Lines, P. M. (1994). Homeschooling: Private choices and public obligations. *Home School Researcher, 10*(3), 9–26.

Lines, P. M. (1998). *Homeschoolers: Estimating numbers and growth.* Washington, DC: U.S. Department of Education, Office of Educational Research and Improvement, National Institute on Student Achievement, Curriculum, and Assessment.

Lumsden, L. (1997, July). Expectations for students. *ERIC Digest, 116.* Retrieved April 13, 2000 from the World Wide Web: http://eric.uoregon.edu/publications/digests/digest116.html

MacDonald, S., & Marchant, G. (1992, April). *How home schoolers school: A study of home schooling parents' teaching practices.* Paper presented at the annual meeting of the American Educational Research Association, San Francisco.

Mattox, W. R., Jr. (1999, March 19). Homeschooling benefits: Children less preoccupied with peer acceptance. *San Francisco Chronicle,* A23.

Mayberry, M. (1988). Why home schooling? A profile of four categories of home schoolers. *Home School Researcher, 4*(3), 7–14.

Home Schooling: The Ameliorator?

Mayberry, M., Knowles, J. G., Ray, B. D., & Marlow, S. (1995). *Home schooling: Parents as educators*. Newbury Park, CA: Corwin.

Medley, D. M. (1982). Teacher effectiveness. In H. E. Mitzel (Ed.), *Encyclopedia of educational research* (pp. 1894–1904). New York: Free Press.

Medlin, R. G. (1994). Predictors of academic achievement in home educated children: Aptitude, self-concept, and pedagogical practices. *Home School Researcher, 10*(3), 1–7.

Medlin, R. G. (1996). Creativity in home schooled children. *Home School Researcher, 12*(1), 7–13.

Meighan, R. (1984). Home-based educators and education authorities: The attempt to maintain a mythology. *Educational Studies, 10*(3), 273–286.

Meighan, R. (1997). *The next learning system: And why home-schoolers are trailblazers.* Nottingham, England: Educational Heretics Press.

Mitchell, J. V., Jr. (1983). *Tests in print III.* Lincoln: University of Nebraska Press.

Mitchell, J. V., Jr. (1985). *The ninth mental measurements yearbook.* Lincoln, NE: Buros Institute of Mental Measurements.

National Association of Elementary School Principals. (1989–1990). *Platform 1989–1990.* Alexandria, VA: Author.

National Association of Elementary School Principals. (1993). *Position statement on home schooling.* Alexandria, VA: Author.

National Association of State Boards of Education. (1996, January). Home schooling. *Policy Update, 4*(1), 1–2.

National Education Association. (1990). *The 1990–91 resolutions of the National Education Association.* Washington, DC: Author.

National Education Association. (1999). *NEA 1999–2000 resolutions, B–67, home schooling.* Retrieved April 13, 2000 from the World Wide Web: http://www.nea.org/resolutions/99/99b-67.html

Nord, W. A. (1995). *Religion and American education: Rethinking a national dilemma.* Chapel Hill: University of North Carolina Press.

Oregon Department of Education. (1990). *Summary of home schooling data, 1986–1990.* Salem, OR: Author.

Oregon Department of Education, Office of Student Services. (1998). *Home school statistics, 1997–98.* Salem, OR: Author.

Oswald, L. J. (1995, August). Priority on learning: Efficient use of resources. *ERIC Digest, 100.* Eugene, OR: ERIC Clearinghouse on Educational Management. (ERIC Document Reproduction Service No. ED 384 951)

Outstanding high schools. (1999, January 18). *U.S. News & World Report, 126*(2), 46–87.

Rakestraw, J. F. (1987). *An analysis of home schooling for elementary school-age children in Alabama.* Unpublished doctoral dissertation, University of Alabama, Tuscaloosa.

Rakestraw, J. F. (1988). Home schooling in Alabama. *Home School Researcher, 4*(4), 1–6.

Ray, B. D. (1988). Home schools: A synthesis of research on characteristics and learner outcomes. *Education and Urban Society, 21*(1), 16–31.

Ray, B. D. (1989). Understanding public, private, and home school students' beliefs, attitudes, and intentions related to science learning. *Home School Researcher, 5*(3), 1–11.

Ray, B. D. (1990a). *Home education in Montana: Family characteristics and student achievement.* Salem, OR: National Home Education Research Institute. (Available from the National Home Education Research Institute, P.O. Box 13939, Salem, OR 97309)

Ray, B. D. (1990b). *A nationwide study of home education: Family characteristics, legal matters, and student achievement.* Salem, OR: National Home Education Research Institute. (Available from the National Home Education Research Institute, P.O. Box 13939, Salem, OR 97309)

B. D. Ray

Ray, B. D. (1990c, April). *Social capital, value consistency, and the achievement outcomes of home education.* Paper presented at the annual meeting of the American Educational Research Association, Boston.

Ray, B. D. (1991). *Home education in North Dakota: Family characteristics and student achievement.* Salem, OR: National Home Education Research Institute. (Available from the National Home Education Research Institute, P.O. Box 13939, Salem, OR 97309)

Ray, B. D. (1992). *Home education in Oklahoma: Family characteristics, student achievement, and policy matters.* Salem, OR: National Home Education Research Institute. (Available from the National Home Education Research Institute, P.O. Box 13939, Salem, OR 97309)

Ray, B. D. (1993). Practices and effects of home education in the United States of America: A synthesis of recent research. *Journal of Research on Christian Education, 2*(1), 135–154.

Ray, B. D. (1994). *A nationwide study of home education in Canada: Family characteristics, student achievement, and other topics.* Salem, OR: National Home Education Research Institute.

Ray, B. D. (1995). *Learning at home in Montana: Student achievement and family characteristics.* Salem, OR: National Home Education Research Institute. (Available from the National Home Education Research Institute, P.O. Box 13939, Salem, OR 97309)

Ray, B. D. (1997a). *Home education in Indiana: Family characteristics, reasons for home schooling, and academic achievement.* Salem, OR: National Home Education Research Institute. (Available from the National Home Education Research Institute, P.O. Box 13939, Salem, OR 97309)

Ray, B. D. (1997b). *Strengths of their own—Home schoolers across America: Academic achievement, family characteristics, and longitudinal traits.* Salem, OR: National Home Education Research Institute. (Available from the National Home Education Research Institute, P.O. Box 13939, Salem, OR 97309)

Ray, B. D. (1998a). *Home education in Massachusetts: Family characteristics, academic achievement, and social activities.* Salem, OR: National Home Education Research Institute. (Available from the National Home Education Research Institute, P.O. Box 13939, Salem, OR 97309)

Ray, B. D. (1998b). *Home education research fact sheet (IIc).* Salem, OR: National Home Education Research Institute.

Ray, B. D. (1999). *Home schooling on the threshold: A survey of research at the dawn of the new millennium.* Salem, OR: National Home Education Research Institute.

Richman, H. B., Girten, W., & Snyder, J. (1990). Academic achievement and its relationship to selected variables among Pennsylvania homeschoolers. *Home School Researcher, 6*(4), 9–16.

Romm, T. (1993). *Home schooling and the transmission of civic culture.* Unpublished doctoral dissertation, Clark Atlanta University, Atlanta, GA.

Rudner, L. M. (1999). The scholastic achievement and demographic characteristics of home school students in 1998. *Education Policy Analysis Archives, 7*(8) [Online]. Retrieved April 13, 2000 from the World Wide Web: http://epaa.asu.edu/epaa/v7n8/

Russell, T. (1994). Cross-validation of a multivariate path analysis of predictors of home school student academic achievement. *Home School Researcher, 10*(1), 1–13.

Safley, L. (1998, September 11). Minorities out to consider home-schooling. *The State* [Online]. Retrieved September 11, 1998 from the World Wide Web: http://www.thestate.com/opinion/opcolumn/safley.htm

Scheurich, J. J., & Young, M. D. (1998). Rejoinder: In the United States of America, in both our souls and our sciences, we are avoiding white racism. *Educational Researcher, 27*(9), 27–32.

Shavelson, R. J. (1988). *Statistical reasoning for the behavioral sciences* (2nd ed.). Boston: Allyn & Bacon.

Sheffer, S. (1995). *A sense of self: Listening to homeschooled adolescent girls.* Portsmouth, NH: Boynton/Cook.

Shyers, L. E. (1992). A comparison of social adjustment between home and traditionally schooled students. *Home School Researcher, 8*(3), 1–8.

Home Schooling: The Ameliorator?

Smith, D. S. (1993, September 30). *Parent-generated home study in Canada.* Westfield, NB: Francombe Place/Research Associates. (Available from The Francombe Place/Research Associates, Box 2000, Westfield R. R. 1, New Brunswick, E0G 3J0, Canada)

Smith, T. E. (1992). Time use and change in academic achievement: A longitudinal follow-up. *Journal of Youth and Adolescence, 21*(6), 725–747.

Snow, C. E., Barnes, W. S., Chandler, J., Goodman, I. F., & Hemphill, L. (1991). *Unfulfilled expectations: Home and school influences on literacy.* Cambridge, MA: Harvard University Press.

Stahl, R. J. (1994, March). The essential elements of cooperative learning in the classroom. *ERIC Digest.* Bloomington, IN: ERIC Clearinghouse for Social Studies/Social Science Education. (ERIC Document Reproduction Service No. 370 881)

Stockard, J., & Mayberry, M. (1992). *Effective educational environments.* Newbury Park, CA: Corwin.

Taylor, L. A. (1992, April). *At home in school: An empirical, observational, and interpretative study of home education.* Paper presented at the annual meeting of the American Educational Research Association, San Francisco.

Taylor, L. A. (1993). *At home in school: A qualitative inquiry into three Christian home schools.* Unpublished doctoral dissertation, Stanford University, Stanford, CA.

Tennessee Department of Education. (1988). *Tennessee statewide averages, home school student test results, Stanford Achievement Test, grades 2, 5, 7 and 9.* Nashville, TN: Author.

Toch, T. (1991a, December 9). The exodus [from public schools]. *U.S. News & World Report, 111*(24), 66–68, 71–74, 76, 77.

Toch, T. (1991b). *In the name of excellence: The struggle to reform the nation's schools, why it's failing, and what should be done.* New York: Oxford University Press.

Treat, E. B. (1990). Parents teaching reading and writing at home: An ethnographic study. *Home School Researcher, 6*(2), 9–19.

Tyack, D. B. (1974). *The one best system: A history of American urban education.* Cambridge, MA: Harvard University Press.

U.S. Department of Education. (1986). *What works: Research about teaching and learning.* Washington, DC: U.S. Government Printing Office.

U.S. Department of Education. (1994). *Strong families, strong schools: Building community partnerships for learning.* Washington, DC: Author.

U.S. Department of Education, National Center for Education Statistics. (1998a). *Common core of data, state nonfiscal survey. Public school student, staff and graduate counts by state, school year 1996–97/Table 1—Public school membership, by grade and state: Fall 1996* [Online]. Retrieved April 13, 2000 from the World Wide Web: http://nces.ed.gov/pubs98/98219t01.html

U.S. Department of Education, National Center for Education Statistics. (1998b, February). *Mini-digest of education statistics, 1997.* Washington, DC: Author.

U.S. Department of Education, Office of Educational Research and Improvement. (1991, September). *Schools have key role to play in nurturing parent involvement* (executive summary). Washington, DC: Author.

U.S. Department of Education, Office of Educational Research and Improvement. (1992). *NAEP [National Assessment of Educational Progress] data on disk: 1992 almanac viewer.* Washington, DC: Author.

U.S. Department of Education, Office of Educational Research and Improvement. (1996). *National Education Longitudinal Study [NELS 88]: 1988–94; data files and electronic codebook system* (CD-ROM). Washington, DC: Author.

Van Galen, J. A. (1988). Ideology, curriculum, and pedagogy in home education. *Education and Urban Society, 21*(1), 52–68.

Vitz, P. C. (1985). *Religion and traditional values in public school textbooks: An empirical study.* Washington, DC: National Institute of Education.

B. D. Ray

Wartes, J. (1987, March). Report from the 1986 home school testing and other descriptive information about Washington's home schoolers: A summary. *Home School Researcher, 3*(1), 1–4.

Wartes, J. (1988). Summary of two reports from the Washington Home School Research Project, 1987. *Home School Researcher, 4*(2), 1–4.

Wartes, J. (1989). *Report from the 1988 Washington homeschool testing.* Woodinville, WA: Washington Homeschool Research Project. (Available from the Washington Homeschool Research Project, 16109 N.E. 169 Pl., Woodinville, WA 98072)

Wartes, J. (1990a, September). *The relationship of selected input variables to academic achievement among Washington's homeschoolers.* Woodinville, WA: Washington Homeschool Research Project. (Available from the Washington Homeschool Research Project, 16109 N.E. 169 Pl., Woodinville, WA 98072)

Wartes, J. (1990b, September). *Report from the 1986 through 1989 Washington homeschool testing.* Woodinville, WA: Washington Homeschool Research Project. (Available from the Washington Homeschool Research Project, 16109 N.E. 169 Pl., Woodinville, WA 98072)

Wartes, J. (1991, December). *Five years of homeschool testing within Washington State.* Woodinville, WA: Washington Homeschool Research Project. (Available from the Washington Homeschool Research Project, 16109 N.E. 169 Pl., Woodinville, WA 98072)

Washington State Superintendent of Public Instruction. (1985). *Washington State's experimental programs using the parent as tutor under the supervision of a Washington State certificated teacher 1984–1985.* Olympia, WA: Author.

Welner, K. M., & Welner, K. G. (1999). Contextualizing homeschooling data: A response to Rudner. *Education Policy Analysis Archives, 7*(13) [Online]. Retrieved April 13, 2000 from the World Wide Web: http://epaa.asu.edu/epaa/v7n13.html

Home Schooling and the Question of Socialization

Richard G. Medlin

"Why aren't your kids in school? Do you have experience as a teacher? How do you know if you're teaching the right things? Aren't you worried that your kids won't be able to get into college? Whatever made you decide to keep your children at home?"

Home schooling parents, if they have been at it very long at all, have been asked these questions countless times by the curious and the disapproving. But of the customary questions home schoolers face, "What about socialization?" is perhaps the most familiar and the most puzzling.

What makes this question so puzzling is that different people mean different things by the word *socialization*. Some people mean social activity: giving children the chance to play with friends and participate in traditional extracurricular activities like sports, school plays, and the senior prom. Others mean social influence: teaching children to conform to majority norms. And some mean social exposure: introducing children to the culture and values of different groups of people. All these things may be a part of socialization, but socialization can be more accurately defined as "the process whereby people acquire the rules of behavior and systems of

RICHARD G. MEDLIN *is Professor of Psychology and Chair of the Department of Psychology, Stetson University, DeLand, Florida.*

Requests for reprints should be sent to Richard G. Medlin, Department of Psychology, College of Arts and Sciences, Stetson University, Campus Box 8321, DeLand, FL 32720-3756. E-mail: rmedlin@stetson.edu

R. G. Medlin

beliefs and attitudes that equip a person to function effectively as a member of a particular society" (Durkin, 1995b, p. 614).

Ordinarily, this process occurs naturally as children take part in "daily routines which immerse them directly in the values of their community" (Durkin, 1995b, p. 618). For example, as parents hurry children along to avoid being late, organize children's activities around specific hours like "bedtime" or "dinnertime," and consult their watches and say "I don't have time" when children want them to play, they are teaching children to think in terms of minutes and hours and schedules and deadlines (Durkin, 1995b; Goodnow, 1990; Pitman & Smith, 1991). This kind of thinking, of course, helps people function more successfully in a culture like ours.

Naturally, these daily routines often involve parents. They also encompass other family members, peers, neighbors, friends of the family, books, television, movies, coaches, music teachers, camp counselors, religious leaders—in fact, any point of contact between children and other members of their community, whether direct or indirect (Bronfenbrenner, 1989; Durkin, 1995b; Gecas, 1992; Harris, 1995). Furthermore, children themselves actively participate in the process as they interact with others in a reciprocal way and as they form their own unique understandings of the social world around them (Bandura, 1986; Durkin, 1995a, 1995b; Goodnow, 1990; Ruble, 1987). How important, then, is school as one agent of socialization among many?

The goals of American education always have been mixed (Shaffer, 1988), but, in the last 50 years or so, "school has been made responsible for an expanding range of socializing activities that previously were considered the proper roles of other social institutions, such as the family"(Nyberg & Egan, 1981, p. 3) and are not necessarily related to academics. Perhaps because of this, education and socialization have become closely linked in our cultural consciousness (Nyberg & Egan, 1981). Many people now assume that traditional schooling offers essential socialization experiences that home schooling cannot (Harris, 1995; Mayberry, Knowles, Ray, & Marlow, 1995). For example, the American Psychological Association, in an effort to bring professional psychology to bear on current issues, presented the opinions of educational psychologists about home schooling in the *APA Monitor* (Murray, 1996). These psychologists warned that home-schooled children may be unable to get along with others and may experience difficulty entering "mainstream life." Home-schooled children, they said, "only hear their parents' philosophies and have little chance to form their own views," whereas conventional schools teach "what society as a whole values." Home schooling shelters children from society, they suggested, but traditional schools ensure that children will grow up to be "complete people" by teaching key social skills such as cooperation, respect for others, and self-control.

The Question of Socialization

The harshest critics charge that isolating children from larger society and inhibiting their social development are the principal goals home schooling parents have in mind. A survey of public school superintendents found that 92% believed home-schooled children do not receive adequate socialization experiences (Mayberry et al., 1995). When asked to explain their views, some of these superintendents commented that home schoolers "don't want any influence other than parents" in their children's lives, believe "communities at large are evil," and "want to ensure their children's ignorance" (pp. 92, 94). The parents "have real emotional problems themselves," one superintendent asserted, and do not realize "the serious harm they are doing to their children in the long run, educationally and socially" (p. 94).

Home schooling parents, not surprisingly, disagree on every point. They describe conventional schools as rigid and authoritarian institutions where passive conformity is rewarded, where peer interactions are too often hostile or derisive or manipulative, and where children must contend with a dispiriting ideological and moral climate. Home schooling parents argue that this kind of environment can stifle children's individuality and harm their self-esteem. They say it can make children dependent, insecure, or even antisocial. They believe it can undermine their efforts to teach their children positive values and appropriate behavior. Finally, they insist that it is unlikely to cultivate the kind of rewarding and supportive relationships that foster healthy personal and moral development (Allie-Carson, 1990; Gatto, 1992; Holt, 1981; Linden, 1983; Martin, 1997; Mayberry et al., 1995; Medlin, 1993b; Shirkey, 1987; Williams, Arnoldsen, & Reynolds, 1984). From this perspective, the "social environment of formal schools is actually a compelling argument for operating a home school" (Mayberry et al., 1995, p. 3).

Nevertheless, when parents decide to home school, they are thinking more of the advantages of home schooling than the disadvantages of conventional schooling (Parker, 1992). Home schooling parents are strongly committed to providing positive socialization experiences for their children (Johnson, 1991; Mayberry et al., 1995; Montgomery, 1989), but they "believe that socialization is best achieved in an age-integrated setting under the auspices of the family" (Tillman, 1995, p. 5) rather than in an institution. They "seek to provide safe, secure, positive environments for their children to grow and learn" (Tillman, 1995, p. 5). Then, they say, "skills learned at home are put into practice in the greater world, ... the success which follows builds self-esteem and prepares the child for adulthood" (Tillman, 1995, p. 5). Parents choose to home school for many reasons, but often it is because they believe that home schooling is most likely to offer the kind of socialization experiences they want for their children (Gray, 1993; Gustafson, 1988;

109

R. G. Medlin

Howell, 1989; Martin, 1997; Mayberry, 1989; Mayberry et al., 1995; Tillman, 1995; Van Galen, 1987; Van Galen & Pitman, 1991).

Of course, home schooling parents realize that extra effort may be required to give their children certain kinds of social experiences (Gustafson, 1988). For example, they report that home schooling can make it harder to find playmates for their children who share their children's interests, and that activities such as drama and band are less accessible (Gustafson, 1988; Montgomery, 1989). Nevertheless, they are not particularly worried about socialization and do not consider that extra effort stressful (Breshears, 1996; Martin, 1997; Medlin, 1995; Selke, 1996). They believe that their children are receiving positive socialization experiences through their relationships both inside and outside the family and that their children's social development is coming along quite nicely (Pitman & Smith, 1991; Reynolds, 1985; Tillman, 1995; Wartes, 1987).

Such a difference of opinion between professional educators and home schooling parents highlights the importance of research on the question of socialization. Could home-schooled children be growing up without the kind of social experiences that will prepare them to live capably in society? Or could home schooling allow children to have much better socialization experiences than those most children receive? Either way, "What about socialization?" is a critical question. But for this question to be answered properly, it must be recast into three more specific questions that are consistent with an accurate definition of socialization: Do home-schooled children participate in the daily routines of their communities? Are they acquiring the rules of behavior and systems of beliefs and attitudes they need? Can they function effectively as members of society?

Do Home-Schooled Children Participate in the Daily Routines of Their Communities?

Review of the Research

Research on home schooling appeared in the mid-1980s, and an early case study first hinted that home-schooled children were perhaps not so isolated as most people seemed to think. Schemmer (1985) observed four home schooling families and noted (with a trace of surprise?) that the children participated in activities outside the home and were "able to communicate with the researcher" (Ray & Wartes, 1991, p. 56). Since then, several surveys—some of them quite large—asked home schooling parents to report their children's activities. These surveys showed that almost all home-schooled children regularly took part in extracurricular activities

The Question of Socialization

(Delahooke, 1986; Gustafson, 1988; Montgomery, 1989; Rakestraw, 1988; Ray, 1990, 1997; Rudner, 1999; Tillman, 1995; Wartes, 1988, 1990). In fact, Delahooke found that home-schooled children actually participated in more activities than did children attending a conventional school.

The activities parents reported in these surveys covered a wide range: organized sports, scouts and 4-H clubs, paid jobs, volunteer work, church activities, music and dance lessons, hobby groups, playing with friends, and more. Perhaps one of the reasons home-schooled children take part in so many different extracurricular activities is that they spend little time watching television. Rudner (1999), in a huge survey of home schooling families, found that fewer than 3% of home-schooled fourth graders watch more than 3 hr of television a day. The comparable figure for fourth graders nationwide is 38%.

After examining the nature of home-schooled children's activities, Montgomery (1989) concluded that home schooling parents were purposefully giving their children opportunities to develop leadership abilities. And Johnson (1991) found that home schooling parents were actively fostering their children's development in seven key areas: personal identity, morality, career goals, independence, social relationships, social skills, and sexuality. The strategies these parents used went beyond arranging for children to take part in extracurricular activities to include such things as giving children regular responsibilities around the house, letting children direct their own studies, and holding high expectations for children's behavior (Groover & Endsley, 1988).

In a closer look at social contacts, Chatham-Carpenter (1994) asked home-schooled children and children attending public schools to keep a record of all their interactions with others for 1 month. The children, aged 12 to 18, wrote down to whom they talked and what they talked about for every interaction lasting more than 2 min. They also rated how accepting and understanding each person on their list was and how close their relationship with each person was.

Chatham-Carpenter (1994) found that home schoolers had contact with 49 different people in a month's time, and public school students met with 56 individuals—a difference that was not statistically significant. Although most of the people on the public school children's lists were peers, home-schooled children often met with younger children and adults as well as peers. Nevertheless, home-schooled children rated the people on their lists as just as accepting and understanding as the public school children did. Public school students, however, had more frequent contact with others and rated their relationships with others as closer—that is, public school students were more willing overall to share their inner feelings with their contacts and to go to them for advice.

R. G. Medlin

In a similar study, Medlin (1998) asked home schooling parents to report how often their children associated with specific groups of people during a typical month and to describe how close their children's relationships were to individuals from each group. The point of this study was to measure how diverse home-schooled children's social contacts were. The results showed that home-schooled children regularly associated with adults outside their own family; the elderly; people from a different socio-economic, religious, or ethnic background than their own; and children attending conventional schools. Parents reported that their children had close relationships with adults outside the family, the elderly, and children attending conventional schools. Children's relationships with people from different socioeconomic, religious, or ethnic backgrounds were described as moderately close.

Whether home-schooled children are unhappy with the frequency and intimacy of their social contacts is unclear. Shirkey (1987) asked home-schooled children (who, apparently, previously had attended traditional schools) aged 6 to 13 to list the advantages and disadvantages of the two types of schools. As disadvantages of home schooling, the older children said they missed their friends who were still attending conventional schools, felt left out of school dances and parties, and were not sure they knew "what's in style" anymore. Shirkey concluded that home-schooled children "feel they have few friends and are socially isolated" (p. 120).

In contrast, Mullins (1992), who interviewed home-schooled children of middle-school age, reported that "the majority of the students viewed socialization in the home school in a positive manner" (p. 1), especially if they were involved in the family's decision to home school. Home-schooled teenagers in a study by Montgomery (1989) overwhelmingly preferred to be home schooled rather than to attend a conventional school, and only 2 of 87 mentioned "having few friends" as a disadvantage of home schooling. (Some, by the way, said not worrying about what's in style was one of the reasons they liked home schooling so well.) And Natale (1995) found that even while at home, many home-schooled children kept in touch with their friends via E-mail.

Commentary

Despite the widespread belief that home schooling is socially isolating (Gray, 1993), the research documents quite clearly that home-schooled children are very much engaged in the social routines of their communities. They are involved in many different kinds of activities with many different kinds of people. In fact, the flexible schedule and more efficient use of time home schooling affords may allow home-schooled children to participate in

The Question of Socialization

more extracurricular activities than children attending conventional schools (Delahooke, 1986; Montgomery, 1989). As Montgomery concluded, "The perception of homeschooled students as being isolated, uninvolved, and protected from peer contact is simply not supported by the data" (p. 9).

Nevertheless, home-schooled children's social contacts may be somewhat different than those of children attending traditional schools. Shirkey's (1987) study probably said more about children's adjustment as they make the transition from conventional schooling to home schooling than anything else. And Chatham-Carpenter's (1994) finding that home-schooled children's relationships were not as close as those of public school students was most likely an artifact of the difference in the makeup of their social networks. Who, after all, goes to younger children for advice, or to share their inner feelings? Her research does suggest, however, that home-schooled children have less frequent contact with peers.

Friends are important to children. When asked which of seven things they liked best about school, students attending conventional high schools ranked friends first (Benham, Giesen, & Oates, 1980). Friends "foster self-esteem and a sense of well-being ... and support one another in coping with developmental transitions and life stress" (Hartup & Stevens, 1999, p. 76). But all peers, of course, are not friends. Chatham-Carpenter's (1994) public school students had more contact with peers than did home-schooled children, but children that age typically have only three to five close friends (Hartup & Stevens, 1999). Therefore, Chatham-Carpenter's (1994) results should not be taken to mean that home-schooled children have few friends or do not spend enough time with them. Shirkey's (1987) study aside, home-schooled children do not seem to feel socially deprived.

The real issue raised by Chatham-Carpenter's (1994) research is whether the kind of social network that children attending conventional schools have, which consists mostly of peers, provides more effective socialization experiences than the kind of social network that home-schooled children have, which consists of people of all ages. The next question addresses this issue by focusing more directly on the process of socialization.

Are Home-Schooled Children Acquiring the Rules of Behavior and Systems of Beliefs and Attitudes They Need?

Review of the Research

The earliest studies of home-schooled children's social behavior used somewhat dubious measures, but they invariably suggested that nothing was seriously amiss. Reynolds (1985) rated a small number of home-schooled chil-

R. G. Medlin

dren on eight positive traits such as "friendly," "helpful," and "trustworthy" and gave the children above-average scores. In a large survey, Wartes (1987) asked home schooling parents to rate their children's sense of responsibility, ability to interact constructively with others, and leadership skills. Only 6% rated their children below average. Delahooke (1986) compared home-schooled children to children attending a private conventional school using the Roberts Apperception Test for Children (McArthur & Roberts, 1982). Both groups scored in the "well-adjusted" range overall. The only differences between the groups were that the private school group was "more influenced by or concerned with peers" (p. 85) and perhaps better at resolving conflicts with peers.

Stough (1992) and Smedley (1992) both tested home-schooled children and children attending traditional schools with a more widely used measure of social development, the Vineland Adaptive Behavior Scales (Sparrow, Balla, & Cicchetti, 1984). Whereas Stough found no significant differences between the groups, Smedley reported that home-schooled children scored higher on the communication, daily living skills, socialization, and social maturity subscales of the test. The mean score overall for the home school group fell at the 84th percentile and for the conventional school group at the 23rd percentile. Smedley concluded that "children kept home are more mature and better socialized than those who are sent to school" (p. 12).

In a similar study, Lee (1994) found that home-schooled children scored higher than traditionally schooled children on the family and community subscales of the Adaptive Behavior Inventory for Children (Mercer & Lewis, 1977) and had higher total scores as well. Lee wrote that the "socialization of children in home schools is effective without exposure to large groups of children. … Home school parents are imparting positive family socialization, which is not inferior to the public school culture" (p. 1).

Shyers (1992a, 1992b), in the most thorough study of home-schooled children's social behavior to date, tested 70 children who had been entirely home-schooled and 70 children who had always attended traditional schools. The two groups were matched in age (all were 8–10 years old), race, gender, family size, socioeconomic status, and number and frequency of extracurricular activities. Shyers measured self-concept and assertiveness and found no significant differences between the two groups. The most intriguing part of the study, however, involved observing the children as they played and worked together. Small groups of children who all had the same school background were videotaped while playing in a large room equipped with toys such as puzzles, puppets, and dolls. The children were then videotaped again in a structured activity: working in teams putting puzzles together for prizes.

The Question of Socialization

Each child's behavior was rated by two observers who did not know whether the children they were rating were home-schooled or traditionally schooled. The observers used the Direct Observation Form of the Child Behavior Checklist (Achenbach & Edelbrock, 1983), a checklist of 97 problem behaviors such as argues, brags or boasts, doesn't pay attention long, cries, disturbs other children, isolates self from others, shy or timid, and shows off. The results were striking—the mean problem behavior score for children attending conventional schools was more than eight times higher than that of the home-schooled group. Shyers (1992a) described the traditionally schooled children as "aggressive, loud, and competitive" (p. 6). In contrast, the home-schooled children acted in friendly, positive ways:

> During the brief period allowed for children to become acquainted, home school children introduced themselves and sought common interests for conversation. ... Home schooled children from each age group tended to play well together, cooperated in the group interaction activity, and were quiet. In several settings, children would invite others within their group to join them in group play. During games they cooperated by taking turns. When they "lost" in the games they would often smile or otherwise indicate that it was "okay" and continue to play. ... As the activities ended, several of the home schooled children exchanged addresses or telephone numbers for future contact. (Shyers, 1992b, p. 194)

Shyers (1992a) concluded, "The results of this study, therefore, draw into question the conclusions made by many educators and courts that traditionally educated children are more socially well-adjusted than are those who are home schooled" (p. 6). In fact, Shyers proposed, the study suggests that just the opposite may be true.

Research on home-schooled children's systems of beliefs and attitudes has so far focused on self-concept. Studies directly comparing home-schooled children to children attending conventional schools have found either no difference between the two (Hedin, 1991; Lee, 1994; Shyers, 1992a, 1992b; Stough, 1992) or a slight difference favoring home-schooled children (Kitchen, 1991). For example, Kitchen reported that although home-schooled children scored higher than traditionally schooled children on the personal security, academic competence, and family acceptance subscales of the Self-Esteem Index (Pro-Ed, 1991), the difference was statistically significant only for the academic competence subscale.

In several studies, only home-schooled children were tested, and their scores were compared to published norms based on public-school sam-

R. G. Medlin

ples. These studies consistently have found that home-schooled children score better than average (Kelley, 1991; Medlin, 1993a, 1994; Taylor, 1986; Tillman, 1995). In the largest of these (Taylor, 1986), more than 220 home-schooled children completed the Piers–Harris Children's Self-Concept Scale (Piers & Harris, 1969). Their mean scores were significantly higher than test norms for the physical appearance and attributes, anxiety (which is reverse-scored), intellectual and school status, behavior, happiness, and satisfaction subscales of the test.

Commentary

The research confirms that home-schooled children are learning rules for appropriate social behavior and forming healthy attitudes toward themselves. Their social behavior and self-esteem are certainly no worse than those of children attending conventional schools and are probably better (Meighan, 1995; Ray & Wartes, 1991). In fact, their social behavior may be much better if Shyers's (1992a, 1992b) results prove to be typical. Social behavior is, however, very complex, and these few studies have too little to tell. Although it would appear that home-schooled children's socialization experiences are more effective than those of traditionally schooled children, the next question, which focuses on the end result of socialization, must be considered also.

Can Home-Schooled Children Function Effectively as Members of Society?

Review of the Research

There is little research on the long-term consequences of home schooling. The modern home schooling movement is, after all, very young, and research on home schooling is younger still. However, a few studies have analyzed the college and workplace experiences of students who have "graduated" from home school.

Ray (1997) surveyed more than 230 graduates of home education and found that 69% had gone on to some kind of postsecondary education, and 31% had become employed. These figures, he reported, were almost identical to those of high school graduates in general. Webb (1990) interviewed adults in England who had been home schooled as children and found that they were successful in obtaining both higher education and employment and were perhaps "much better prepared socially than some of their

The Question of Socialization

schooled peers" (p. 121). In a similar study in the United States, Knowles and Muchmore (1995) reported that adults who had been home schooled as children were satisfied with both their education and their employment.

Galloway (Galloway, 1998; Galloway & Sutton, 1997) identified 60 students at a small private college who had been exclusively home schooled throughout high school. She then composed two matched comparison groups from the other students at the college: one of students who had attended private high schools and another of students who had attended public high schools. Galloway evaluated the three groups on 63 indicators of college performance, grouped into five categories: academic, cognitive, social, spiritual, and psychomotor. Academic indicators included standard measures such as grade point average and class rank. The cognitive category involved more subtle indicators of academic success, such as the difficulty of the student's major and membership in honorary organizations. Extracurricular activities such as dance, music, and drama made up the social category, and spiritual indicators included such things as records of personal conduct and religious activities. Finally, psychomotor indicators involved activities like sports and cheerleading.

For each of these 63 indicators, Galloway (1998) computed averages for the three groups of students and compared the averages to see which group had the highest score. For 42 of the 63 measures, home-schooled students came in first. In fact, they led by a large margin in every category except psychomotor skills. Because many indicators for which home-schooled students took first place involved positions of leadership, Galloway concluded that home-schooled students were readily recognized for their leadership abilities. She stated flatly, "They are the leaders on campus."

Commentary

Because it is so meager, little can be concluded from this research except, as Knowles and Muchmore (1995) reported, "grown-up homeschooled kids" are apparently "doing just fine" (p. 35). There is a suggestion from Galloway's (Galloway, 1998; Galloway & Sutton, 1997) study that adults who were home schooled as children may have exceptional social and leadership skills. But Galloway's results, as impressive as they are, should not be generalized too freely. The particular college environment she studied was probably especially suited to home-schooled students, given that so many chose to enroll there. That does not mean, however, that her results are irrelevant. They show quite clearly that the home-schooled college students she observed were functioning effectively in "a particular society" (Durkin, 1995b, p. 614).

R. G. Medlin

Conclusions

Studies of home schooling and socialization have the customary faults of research in a very young field: no guiding theory, inadequate experimental design, poorly defined research questions, untried and weak measures, unorthodox treatment and presentation of data, and conclusions based on subjective judgments. Even a cursory look at the research reveals that many studies are qualitative descriptions of so few participants that the results cannot be generalized. Many are surveys that rely exclusively on parental reports but offer no idea of how reliable those reports may be. Many test only home-schooled children without comparing them to children attending conventional schools, making it very difficult to know what the results might mean. Furthermore, as Ray and Wartes (1991) pointed out, all home school research is correlational (because researchers have no way to control the type of schooling children experience), samples are usually self-selected (because researchers cannot require home schooling families to participate), and, however carefully researchers try to match their home-schooled and traditionally schooled groups, there are probably still important differences between the two.

Fortunately, against a background of questionable research, a few solid studies stand out—Rudner's (1999) survey of more than 20,000 home-schooled children and their families, Chatham-Carpenter's (1994) analysis of home-schooled children's social networks, and Shyers's (1992a, 1992b) research on social behavior. Shyers's study, especially, offers features worth emulating. He composed his two groups of children who had always been either home schooled or traditionally schooled. He matched the participants in each group on several relevant variables. He used widely known and reliable tests. He tested for both positive and negative social behaviors. Information was collected from both the children themselves and impartial observers. The behavioral observation took place in two different situations and was videotaped for later analysis. Every child's behavior was rated by two independent observers. Observers were trained carefully and were unaware of children's group status. Statistical procedures were orthodox and appropriate. Conclusions were objective, not subjective.

But these few examples are clearly not enough. More than anything else, they simply underscore that more—and better—research is needed (Aiex, 1994). And the questions addressed by that research need to cut a little deeper. What does socialization within the home schooling family look like? Are parents meeting their own goals for their children's social development (Ray & Wartes, 1991)? What are home-schooled children's closest friendships like? Are home-schooled children more independent,

The Question of Socialization

open-minded, or self-controlled than other children? Are they better able to get along with people of all ages? Is their moral development more advanced? How does their home schooling experience affect the kind of adult lives they lead?

Although there are still far too many unanswered questions about home schooling and socialization, some preliminary conclusions can be stated. Home-schooled children are taking part in the daily routines of their communities. They are certainly not isolated; in fact, they associate with—and feel close to—all sorts of people. Home schooling parents can take much of the credit for this. For, with their children's long-term social development in mind, they actively encourage their children to take advantage of social opportunities outside the family. Home-schooled children are acquiring the rules of behavior and systems of beliefs and attitudes they need. They have good self-esteem and are likely to display fewer behavior problems than do other children. They may be more socially mature and have better leadership skills than other children as well. And they appear to be functioning effectively as members of adult society.

Perhaps the most intriguing unanswered question is, "Why?" Why should home-schooled children seem, in the words of Smedley (1992), to be "better socialized" (p. 12) than children attending conventional schools? Smedley speculated that the family "more accurately mirrors the outside society" (p. 13) than does the traditional school environment, with its "unnatural" age segregation. Galloway (Galloway, 1998; Galloway & Sutton, 1997) agreed, stating that because they are not peer-grouped in school, home-schooled children learn to get along with a variety of people, making them socially mature and able to adjust to new and challenging situations. She added two further explanations: She argued that the highly individualized academic program afforded by home schooling creates an ideal learning environment, giving children an excellent chance to do well both in college and in a career. She also said that because home-schooled children learn and grow in the nurturing environment of secure family relationships, they develop a confidence and resiliency that helps them to succeed as adults.

If Galloway proves to be right about the importance of family relationships, then much of the answer to the question "Why?" may have been found. Many parents choose to home school not for academic reasons at all but to surround their children with the kind of nurturing atmosphere that will support their development as individuals (Gustafson, 1988; Howell, 1989; Mayberry & Knowles, 1989; Van Galen, 1987). They believe this can be accomplished far better by situating their children's education within the family rather than within an impersonal institution. As one home schooling mother said about her children, "It is my responsibility to see

119

R. G. Medlin

that they grow up to be conscientious, responsible and intelligent people. This is too important a job to be given to someone I don't even know" (Mayberry et al., 1995, p. 39). Research on the question of socialization suggests that children are thriving in the home school environment and that much can be learned from looking more closely at what home schooling families are doing.

References

Achenbach, T. M., & Edelbrock, C. S. (1983). *Manual for the Child Behavior Checklist and Revised Child Behavior Profile*. Burlington: University of Vermont, Department of Psychiatry.

Aiex, N. K. (1994). *Home schooling and socialization of children* (Report No. EDO–CS–94–07). Bloomington, IN: ERIC Clearinghouse on Reading, English and Communication. (ERIC Document Reproduction Service No. ED 372 460)

Allie-Carson, J. (1990). Structure and interaction patterns of home school families. *Home School Researcher, 6*(3), 11–18.

Bandura, A. (1986). *Social foundations of thought and action*. Englewood Cliffs, NJ: Prentice Hall.

Benham, B., Giesen, P., & Oates, J. (1980). A study of schooling: Students' experiences in schools. *Phi Delta Kappan, 61*, 337–340.

Breshears, S. M. (1996). *Characteristics of home schools and home school families in Idaho*. Unpublished doctoral dissertation, University of Idaho, Moscow.

Bronfenbrenner, U. (1989). Ecological systems theory. *Annals of Child Development, 6*, 187–249.

Chatham-Carpenter, A. (1994). Home versus public schoolers: Differing social opportunities. *Home School Researcher, 10*(1), 15–24.

Delahooke, M. M. (1986). *Home educated children's social/emotional adjustment and academic achievement: A comparative study*. Unpublished doctoral dissertation, California School of Professional Psychology, Los Angeles.

Durkin, K. (1995a). *Developmental social psychology: From infancy to old age*. Cambridge, MA: Basil Blackwell.

Durkin, K. (1995b). Socialization. In A. S. R. Manstead & M. Hewstone (Eds.), *The Blackwell encyclopedia of social psychology* (pp. 614–618). Cambridge, MA: Basil Blackwell.

Galloway, R. S. (1998, June). *The home schooled students' potential for success in college*. Speech presented at the Florida Homeschool Convention, Orlando, FL.

Galloway, R. S., & Sutton, J. P. (1997, October). *College success of students from three high school settings: Christian school, home school, and public school*. Paper presented at the National Christian Home Educators Leadership Conference, Boston.

Gatto, J. T. (1992). *Dumbing us down*. Philadelphia: New Society.

Gecas, V. (1992). Socialization. In E. F. Borgatta & M. L. Borgatta (Eds.), *Encyclopedia of sociology* (Vol. 4, pp. 1863–1872). New York: Macmillan.

Goodnow, J. J. (1990). The socialization of cognition: What's involved? In J. W. Stigler, R. A. Shweder, & G. Herdt (Eds.), *Cultural psychology: Essays on comparative human development* (pp. 259–286). Cambridge, England: Cambridge University Press.

Gray, S. (1993). Why some parents choose to home school. *Home School Researcher, 9*(4), 1–12.

Groover, S. V., & Endsley, R. C. (1988). *Family environment and attitudes of homeschoolers and non-homeschoolers*. Champaign, IL: ERIC Clearinghouse on Elementary and Early Childhood Education. (ERIC Document Reproduction Service No. ED 323 027)

The Question of Socialization

Gustafson, S. K. (1988). A study of home schooling: Parental motivation and goals. *Home School Researcher, 4*(2), 4–12.

Harris, J. R. (1995). Where is the child's environment? A group socialization theory of development. *Psychological Review, 102,* 458–489.

Hartup, W. W., & Stevens, N. (1999). Friendships and adaptation across the life span. *Current Directions in Psychological Science, 8,* 76–79.

Hedin, N. S. (1991). Self-concept of Baptist children in three educational settings. *Home School Researcher, 7*(3), 1–5.

Holt, J. (1981). *Teach your own.* New York: Delacorte.

Howell, J. R. (1989). Reasons for selecting home schooling in the Chattanooga, Tennessee vicinity. *Home School Researcher, 5*(2), 11–14.

Johnson, K. C. (1991). Socialization practices of Christian home school educators in the state of Virginia. *Home School Researcher, 7*(1), 9–16.

Kelley, S. W. (1991). Socialization of home schooled children: A self-concept study. *Home School Researcher, 7*(4), 1–12.

Kitchen, P. (1991). Socialization of home school children versus conventional school children. *Home School Researcher, 7*(3), 7–13.

Knowles, G. J., & Muchmore, J. A. (1995). Yep! We're grown-up home-schooled kids and we're doing just fine, thank you! *Journal of Research on Christian Education, 4*(1), 35–56.

Lee, W. J. (1994). *The socialization of home-schooled and public-schooled children.* Unpublished doctoral dissertation, University of La Verne, La Verne, CA.

Linden, N. J. F. (1983). An investigation of alternative education: Home schooling. *Dissertation Abstracts International, 44,* 3547A. (University Microfilms No. 84–03319, 94)

Martin, M. (1997). *Homeschooling: Parents' reactions.* Unpublished manuscript. (ERIC Document Reproduction Service No. ED 415 984)

Mayberry, M. (1989). Home-based education in the United States: Demographics, motivations and educational implications. *Educational Review, 41,* 171–180.

Mayberry, M., & Knowles, J. G. (1989). Family unit objectives of parents who teach their children: Ideological and pedagogical orientations to home schooling. *Urban Review, 21,* 209–225.

Mayberry, M., Knowles, J. G., Ray, B., & Marlow, S. (1995). *Home schooling: Parents as educators.* Thousand Oaks, CA: Corwin.

McArthur, D. S., & Roberts, G. E. (1982). *Roberts Apperception Test for Children: A manual.* Los Angeles: Western Psychological Services.

Medlin, R. G. (1993a). [Home educated children's scores on the Piers–Harris Children's Self-Concept Scale]. Unpublished raw data.

Medlin, R. G. (1993b). [Reasons parents give for teaching their children at home]. Unpublished raw data.

Medlin, R. G. (1994). Predictors of academic achievement in home educated children: Aptitude, self-concept, and pedagogical practices. *Home School Researcher, 10*(3), 1–7.

Medlin, R. G. (1995). Homeschooling: What's hard? What helps? *Home School Researcher, 11*(4), 1–6.

Medlin, R. G. (1998, September/October). For homeschooled children, the social contacts are diverse. *Homeschooling Today, 7*(5), 51–52.

Meighan, R. (1995). Home-based education effectiveness research and some of its implications. *Educational Review, 47,* 275–287.

Mercer, J. R., & Lewis, J. F. (1977). *System of multicultural pluralistic assessment: Parent interview manual.* New York: Psychological Corporation.

Montgomery, L. (1989). The effect of home schooling on the leadership skills of home schooled students. *Home School Researcher, 5*(1), 1–10.

R. G. Medlin

Mullins, B. A. B. (1992). *Christian home-school students' perception of their socialization.* Unpublished doctoral dissertation, University of Virginia, Charlottesville.

Murray, B. (1996, December). Home schools: How do they affect children? *APA Monitor, 7* [Online]. Retrieved January 28, 1997 from the World Wide Web: www.apa.org/monitor /dec96/home.html

Natale, J. A. (1995). Home, but not alone. *American School Board Journal, 182*(7), 34–36.

Nyberg, D., & Egan, K. (1981). *Socialization and the schools.* New York: Teachers College Press.

Parker, R. D. (1992). *Inside home schools: A portrait of eighty-four Texas families and the schools in their homes.* Unpublished doctoral dissertation, Texas Tech University, Lubbock.

Piers, E. V., & Harris, D. B. (1969). *Piers–Harris Children's Self-Concept Scale.* Los Angeles: Western Psychological Services.

Pitman, M. A., & Smith, M. L. (1991). Culture acquisition in an intentional American community: A single case. In J. Van Galen & M. A. Pitman (Eds.), *Home schooling: Political, historical, and pedagogical perspectives* (pp. 77–97). Norwood, NJ: Ablex.

PRO-ED, Inc. (1991). *Self Esteem Index: Examiner's manual.* Austin, TX: Author.

Rakestraw, J. F. (1988). Home schooling in Alabama. *Home School Researcher, 4*(4), 1–6.

Ray, B. D. (1990). *A nationwide study of home education: Family characteristics, legal matters, and student achievement.* Salem, OR: National Home Education Research Institute.

Ray, B. D. (1997). *Strengths of their own—Home schoolers across America: Academic achievement, family characteristics, and longitudinal traits.* Salem, OR: National Home Education Research Institute.

Ray, B. D., & Wartes, J. (1991). The academic achievement and affective development of home-schooled children. In J. Van Galen & M. A. Pitman (Eds.), *Home schooling: Political, historical, and pedagogical perspectives* (pp. 43–62). Norwood, NJ: Ablex.

Reynolds, P. L. (1985). *How home school families operate on a day-to-day basis: Three case studies.* Unpublished doctoral dissertation, Brigham Young University, Provo, UT.

Ruble, D. N. (1987). The acquisition of self-knowledge: A self-socialization perspective. In N. Eisenberg (Ed.), *Contemporary topics in developmental psychology* (pp. 281–312). New York: Wiley.

Rudner, L. M. (1999). Scholastic achievement and demographic characteristics of home school students in 1998. *Education Policy Analysis Archives, 7*(8) [Online]. Retrieved April 18, 1999 from the World Wide Web: http://epaa.asu.edu/epaa/v7n8/

Schemmer, B. A. S. (1985). *Case studies of four families engaged in home education.* Unpublished doctoral dissertation, Brigham Young University, Provo, UT.

Selke, J. H. (1996). *Homeschooling Parental Stress and Social Support Scale: Initial psychometric evidence.* Unpublished manuscript, University of California at Berkeley.

Shaffer, D. R. (1988). *Social and personality development* (2nd ed.). Pacific Grove, CA: Brooks/Cole.

Shirkey, B. T. (1987). *Students' perspectives of home schools: A descriptive study.* Unpublished doctoral dissertation, University of Florida, Gainesville.

Shyers, L. E. (1992a). A comparison of social adjustment between home and traditionally schooled students. *Home School Researcher, 8*(3), 1–8.

Shyers, L. E. (1992b). *A comparison of social adjustment between home and traditionally schooled students.* Unpublished doctoral dissertation, University of Florida, Gainesville.

Smedley, T. C. (1992). Socialization of home school children. *Home School Researcher, 8*(3), 9–16.

Sparrow, S. S., Balla, D. A., & Cicchetti, D. V. (1984). *Vineland Adaptive Behavior Scales: Survey form manual, interview edition.* Circle Pines, MN: American Guidance Service.

Stough, L. (1992). *Social and emotional status of home schooled children and conventionally schooled children in West Virginia.* Unpublished master's thesis, University of West Virginia, Morgantown.

The Question of Socialization

Taylor, J. W. V. (1986). Self-concept in home-schooling children. *Home School Researcher, 2*(2), 1–3.

Tillman, V. D. (1995). Home schoolers, self-esteem, and socialization. *Home School Researcher, 11*(3), 1–6.

Van Galen, J. A. (1987). Explaining home education: Parents' accounts of their decisions to teach their own children. *Urban Review, 19,* 161–177.

Van Galen, J., & Pitman, M. A. (1991). *Home schooling: Political, historical, and pedagogical perspectives.* Norwood, NJ: Ablex.

Wartes, J. (1987). Report from the 1986 home school testing and descriptive information about Washington's home schoolers: A summary. *Home School Researcher, 3*(1), 1–4.

Wartes, J. (1988). Summary of two reports from the Washington Homeschool Research Project, 1987. *Home School Researcher, 4*(2), 1–4.

Wartes, J. (1990). Recent results from the Washington Homeschool Research Project. *Home School Researcher, 6*(4), 1–7.

Webb, J. (1990). *Children learning at home.* New York: Falmer.

Williams, D. D., Arnoldsen, L. M., & Reynolds, P. (1984, April). *Understanding home education: Case studies of home schools.* Paper presented at the annual meeting of the American Educational Research Association, New Orleans, LA.

PEABODY JOURNAL OF EDUCATION, 75(1&2), 124–146
Copyright © 2000, Lawrence Erlbaum Associates, Inc.

Participation and Perception: Looking at Home Schooling Through a Multicultural Lens

Susan A. McDowell
Annette R. Sanchez and Susan S. Jones

Home education as a movement is not only growing and expanding in terms of the number of participants involved, but it also is increasing in

---

SUSAN A. MCDOWELL *is an educational researcher and writer and is Managing Editor of the* Peabody Journal of Education, *Peabody College of Vanderbilt University, Nashville, Tennessee.*

ANNETTE R. SANCHEZ *is Associate Professor in the Department of Academic Skills, Nashville State Tech, Tennessee.*

SUSAN S. JONES *is Professor in the Department of Mathematics, Nashville State Tech, Tennessee.*

Portions of this article are from *Freedom Challenge: African American Homeschoolers,* edited by G. Llewellyn, 1996, Eugene, OR: Lowry House. Copyright 1996 by Lowry House. Reprinted with permission.

An earlier version of this article was presented at the 1999 annual meeting of the American Educational Research Association, Montreal, Canada.

We thank Patricia M. Lines (who was at the time a Senior Research Analyst, Office of Educational Research and Improvement, U.S. Department of Education) for her comments on an earlier draft of this article.

Requests for reprints should be sent to Susan A. McDowell, P.O. Box 148351, Nashville, TN 37214–8351. E-mail: Susan.A.McDowell@vanderbilt.edu

124

A Multicultural Lens

terms of its credibility as a viable educational alternative, as the very existence of this special issue of the *Peabody Journal of Education* would seem to attest. When considering this burgeoning home schooling population, a simple question arises: What is the participation of differing ethnic groups within this particular educational movement? The answer is a surprising one, especially when considered in light of national demographics.

According to President Bill Clinton (1997) in his *One America: The President's Initiative on Race,* the "face of America is 72.7% White, 11% Hispanic, 12.1% Black, 3.6% Asian/Pacific Islander, and 0.7% American Indian." As the home education community is currently approximately 96% White, 1.5% Hispanic, 1% Asian/Pacific Islander, 0.5% American Indian, and only 0.5% Black (Ray, 1997, p. 41),[1] it is evident that the participation of ethnic groups within the home schooling community is highly disproportionate to the larger society (see Figure 1). Why? What are the perceptions of these differing ethnic groups as to the efficacy of home schooling? Is there a difference in perceptions of ethnic groups within the confines of the general, non-home schooling population as to the efficacy of home schooling? What do they believe about those families who choose to home school and

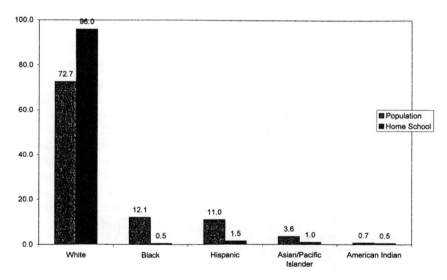

Figure 1. 1997 U.S. ethnic populations and home schooling population.

[1]Given the difficulties inherent in researching the home school population (see, e.g., Mayberry, Knowles, Ray, & Marlow, 1995; McDowell, 1998; Page, 1996; Ray, 1997; Schnaiberg, 1996), no statistical data exist at this point that claims to be 100% accurate and/or representative of the entire home schooling population.

125

S. A. McDowell, A. R. Sanchez, S. S. Jones

the reasons for their choice? If significant differences in perception between and among ethnic groups do exist, could these differences explain the disparity in participation?

This article attempts to address many of these questions by (a) presenting the current statistical level of participation of differing ethnic groups in home schooling (see Ray, 1997); (b) exploring the perceptions of these groups through an examination of the extant literature; and (c) presenting the surprising results of an exploratory research study that examines the perceptions of differing ethnic groups—within the non-home schooling general population—concerning those families that choose to home school, and the efficacy of the home schooling movement itself. In the course of examining this research study, we, of course, (a) discuss the methodology used in the study of perceptions of ethnic groups within the general population, (b) present findings, (c) discuss said findings, and (d) offer appropriate conclusions.

Having detailed the current participation of differing ethnic groups in the home schooling movement, we continue with a look at the extant research on multicultural home schooling, as well as other pertinent literature.

A Look at the Literature

Given the size of the population involved, it should not be at all surprising, perhaps, that very little research or literature dealing with home schooling's multicultural participants exists. One such study, which provides important information as to the participation of ethnic groups, already has been detailed (Ray, 1997). It also should be noted that although multicultural home schooling web sites (e.g., Jewish Home Educators Network, http://snj.com/jnen; Muslim Home Education, http://home.ici.net/customers/taadah/foyer.html) may be found on the Internet and are certainly of interest, they provide very little in the way of answers to the questions driving this study. Fortunately, however, two important sources of information do exist—a dissertation research study (Romm, 1993) and a book on African American home schoolers (Llewellyn, 1996)—both of which provide a fascinating and often disturbing glimpse of home schooling as seen through a multicultural lens.

The Dissertation Research Study and Freedom Challenge

One of the most interesting aspects of these two sources is their striking similarity. Both sources—when exploring ethnic minorities in home schooling—deal almost exclusively with the African American population, and both detail (a) the differences between African American home schoolers and the larger home schooling population, (b) the existence of racial tension within the home schooling community, and (c) the unhappy paradoxes that explain both the probable reason why many African Americans consider home schooling to be an unacceptable educational alternative and why the majority of African American home schoolers feel the need to follow a highly structured and traditional curriculum.

The differences. For his 1993 research study, *Home Schooling and the Transmission of Civic Culture,* Romm interviewed eight home schooling families in the Atlanta, Georgia, area. Four of the families interviewed were White, and four were African American. According to Romm (1993), one of the most significant findings of his study was the discovery

> that there appears to be a set of concerns which are held in common by African-American home schoolers and which distinguish them from European-American home schoolers. ... Despite their strong religious backgrounds, these parents were more likely to describe their decision to home school as motivated by political beliefs than were European-Americans. These beliefs have their root in parents' perceptions of the negative status of African-Americans in the society and of the contribution of schools to perpetuating it. Thus their goals emphasize the necessity of developing a secure cultural identity, the skills of critical analysis and communication to counter stereotypes of African-Americans, and the ability to cope effectively with experiences of racial discrimination. (pp. 359–360)

In *Freedom Challenge: African American Homeschoolers,* Llewellyn (1996) acted as editor for a collection of 15 essays written by African American home schooling parents and their children. In her introduction, Llewellyn also detailed some of the differing reasons why African Americans decide on home schooling as an educational alternative:

> As the writers in the book show, African Americans homeschool for all these [standard] reasons and then some. Some homeschool because they see that racial integration in the schools has not always worked for their benefit. (Among other things, they feel that it has disrupted community life and thrust children into hate-filled classrooms where few people encourage or hope for their success.) Some homeschool because they see that schools perpetuate institutionalized racism. Some homeschool be-

S. A. McDowell, A. R. Sanchez, S. S. Jones

cause they are tired of curriculums emphasizing Europe and excluding Africa. Some homeschool because their children are overwhelmingly treated as problems, and quickly labeled Attention Deficit Disordered or Learning Disabled. Some homeschool because they want to continue the Civil Rights struggle for equal educational rights, and they feel that they can best do so by reclaiming their right to help their own children develop fully—rather than by working to get them equal access to conventional schooling. (p. 15)

What other elements are different for the African American home schooling parent? According to both Romm and Llewellyn, problems often arise within the home schooling community itself, as is evidenced in the following section.

Racism within the home schooling community. Apparently, some African American home schoolers find that elements of racism

extend to interactions with others within the home schooling movement as well. The problem described was not so much one of outright racism, but of a more subtle variety. On the one hand, this takes the form of an assumption that all home schoolers are white, middle class, and Christian. This comes across when books at home schooling conferences or the texts used by curriculum publishers focus on Western European literature and history to the exclusion of other cultures and perspectives. It also comes across when the African-American home schoolers in attendance overhear remarks made by other parents that strike them as racially-biased or when they feel excluded socially at these events. (Romm, 1993, pp. 345–346)

Detra Rose Hood, one of the contributors to Llewellyn's (1996) collection, also felt uncomfortable with the available curriculum, especially when she

picked up the A Beka [a widely used home schooling curriculum] math book … and began to go through it carefully. I had noticed that many private schools used A Beka books, but I felt, at the time, that by using a Christian curriculum that I would be pushing religion, and I didn't want to do that. At first glance the math book seemed interesting, though, so I continued to look. It was presented in a colorful fashion, but the majority of the images of people were white; the few people of color were illustrated in a caricature kind of way. (p. 213)

A Multicultural Lens

Feeling "unsatisfied" with the home schooling networks available to them, as they were often "the only Black people" (Llewellyn, 1996, p. 223) present, many African American home schoolers began their own home schooling groups, as Donna Nichols-White—who began such a group, as well as a multicultural newsletter— explained,

> In the homeschooling world, I have noticed that white families have supports that are non-existent for Black families. Our history, needs, and desires are different. No matter how much equality society thinks we enjoy, we are still far from equal in opportunity. In order to improve our lives as homeschoolers, we must again pave our own path. (Llewellyn, 1996, p. 72)

Two unhappy paradoxes. One of the most enlightening findings arising from this brief look into the existing literature was the discovery of what may be termed "unhappy paradoxes." The first paradox may be explained as follows: Although African Americans believe that the current public school system is failing their children in record numbers—and current statistics certainly support this belief (see, e.g., Bankston & Caldas, 1997; "Event, Status, and Cohort Dropout Rates," 1998; Hu, 1997; Lewis, 1992; Nadler, 1998)—it is this very system that "has historically been associated with the ideology of upward mobility for cultural minorities in America" (Romm, 1993, p. 341). "Education has historically provided a central means of access to personal and social advancement for the African American community" (p. 315), Romm continued, and many parents believe that "their children cannot afford the 'luxury' of a totally experimental pedagogy" (p. 315). In essence, then, despite the fact that the very system they have trusted to pull them up the socioeconomic "ladder" is the same system that has failed them extraordinarily badly, many African Americans choose not to pursue home education as an educational alternative because of fear of lack of acceptance.

Perhaps this particular belief can be summed up most effectively by "Michael," a young African American student who had just heard Grace Llewellyn give a talk detailing the virtues of home schooling. Llewellyn (1996) related the encounter after her speech:

> The final bell rang, and most of the students hoisted their textbook-filled backpacks and went home. But several stayed and clustered around me, their eyes intense. Among them stood a young man whose voice wavered between resignation and longing. He told me his name was Michael. "I totally see what you're saying about school, how it's a waste of

129

S. A. McDowell, A. R. Sanchez, S. S. Jones

time," he said, "and I know there's a lot more I could learn and do on my own. But I can't do it, because I'm black. I walk into some business to get a job, they want to see my diploma, I tell them I educated myself according to my own interests, and it's over. They say, 'Right. Another dropped out nigger.'" (p. 12)

Interestingly, elsewhere in Llewellyn's book, a young home-schooled African American woman's experience seems at once to both confirm and repudiate Michael's perception:

I have actually been turned down for some jobs because they don't understand the concept of being unschooled. And even when I do get a job, they sit there and they just constantly ask questions. It winds up not being an interview about me, but about my schooling. That prejudice is not a problem because I can overcome those hurdles. (p. 54)

Clearly, the decision to home school for African American parents contains a great many critical and diverse elements that are simply not a factor for Euro-Americans.

Sadly, those African Americans who do choose to home school often find themselves the victim of a second unhappy paradox, specifically: Although home schooling by its very nature offers participants a great deal of freedom both in implementation and curriculum, the majority of African American home schoolers believe that they must adhere to a more standard, "tight" curriculum so that their efforts—and their children—will be accepted by society in general. In essence, then, even though the experience of home schooling is a freeing one in theory, in actuality it still can retain elements of "bondage" for those African Americans participating in it.

As Romm (1993) explained, African Americans as a group "are inclined toward a more rigorous curriculum than an 'unschooling' family would be" (p. 315):

[They] are considerably more structured in their home schooling than the European-American Pedagogues. They are not "unschoolers," even though they may incorporate similar methods into their programs such as self-directed and experiential learning. They are far more likely to look to educational authorities for their guides, however, and to establish a regimen which must be adhered to by their children–students. Such firmness is portrayed as a "necessity" in working with African-American children in general, the sense of which may be heightened among African-Americans pursuing an educational alternative such as home schooling. (p. 344)

A Multicultural Lens

Llewellyn's (1996) experience would seem, again, to echo that of Tracy Romm, as she relates in her introduction:

> Several African American homeschoolers have told me that black people are much more likely than whites to emphasize academics and a structured curriculum. And their observations were indeed borne out by my contact with some of the essayists and potential essayists for this book. ... If more black homeschoolers (than white) follow a structured curriculum, it's *not* necessarily because they value conformity or because they don't trust their children to acquire the skills they need to become happy, well-educated adults. Rather, for obvious reasons, they don't trust *society* to recognize their kids' intelligence without benefit of, at least, a list of textbooks completed or classes taken through an academic summer program. (Llewellyn, 1996, pp. 15–16)

Despite the seemingly overwhelming trend toward highly structured home schooling, at least one African American home schooling parent has adopted a different approach:

> Over the years I have discovered that [conventional schooling] is how children are *taught*—not necessarily how they *learn*. I have concluded that it's schooling, rather than "learning disabilities," that impinges on a child's learning. I have also decided I will not waste precious time competing with the schools. Schooling damages Black students the most; no other group of students fail in school at the rate they do. Why copy failure? (Llewellyn, 1996, p. 62)

Why, indeed? We must echo Llewellyn's (1996) hope

> that this somewhat school-like approach to education [as currently adopted by the majority of African American home schoolers] is a temporary trend among black homeschoolers. Where a strong emphasis on conventional academics is based on fear, I hope that this fear will give way to the joyous confidence that many white unschoolers enjoy. (Largely, but not completely, what this boils down to is that I fervently hope *society* will get a lot saner and make it easier for black homeschoolers to feel that it's safe for them to give their kids more freedom.) (p. 16)

Summary

This brief look at the scant available literature on multicultural home schooling informs us of the following: (a) powerful differences exist be-

S. A. McDowell, A. R. Sanchez, S. S. Jones

tween African American home schooling families and the larger home schooling population, (b) these differences extend—sometimes uncomfortably—into the home schooling community itself, and (c) the existing relationship between African Americans and institutionalized learning often seems to paralyze their choices in the education realm—including both the decision to home school itself and the decision as to how to home school.

There is a difference, then, among some ethnic groups within the home schooling population. What about ethnic groups within the general population? Do they, too, perceive the home schooling movement in significantly different ways? Does this perception, in turn, affect their willingness to consider home schooling as a viable educational alternative? In the following sections, the details of an exploratory study whose purpose it was to investigate these and other questions are presented, beginning with the methodology used.

Methodology

Sample

The rationale. The units of analysis for this research study were college students. The reasons for this particular choice were twofold. First, access to a broad spectrum of different ethnic groups within the general population was critical to the study's success, and the chosen population—college students attending either Vanderbilt University or Nashville State Tech—provided the necessary ethnic diversity. Clearly, it is not possible to discover why different ethnic groups choose to stay away from or participate in home schooling—according to current participation levels—without surveying members of these ethnic groups. The young adults that make up the college student sample population are authentic members of their respective ethnic groups and, as such, comprise a valid population for research.

Second, and most important, college students (especially undergraduates) may be seen to constitute a group that—if they have not done so already—will in the near future most probably get married, start families, and make important educational decisions for their children. They form a pool of possible future home schooling parents, and, as a result, the perceptions of this particular population in regard to the efficacy of the home education movement are of particular interest.

Using a sample population comprised of students enrolled at Vanderbilt University or Nashville State Tech ensured appropriate diversity. These institutions have widely divergent goals and serve distinctly different student populations, as the following details reveal.

A Multicultural Lens

The institutions: Vanderbilt University and Nashville State Tech. The histories, missions, costs, and entrance requirements are but a few of the areas in which these two institutions differ. One of the areas in which they diverge most sharply is in the ethnic diversity of their student bodies, as the information provided in Table 1 clearly demonstrates.

A commuter college, Nashville State Tech is a public 2-year college established in 1970, serving a geographic area comprised primarily of metropolitan Davidson County and surrounding counties. However, many foreign countries are represented as well. The institution offers associate's degrees and certificate programs in addition to courses that target business and industry. Nashville State Tech serves a student body that is diverse in age, race, and educational goals by attempting to provide high-quality education that is, at the same time, low in cost (Nashville State Tech Web Site, http://www.nsti.tec.tn.us/oir/ethnicorg.htm).

As the Vanderbilt University Web Site (http://excite.collegeedge.com/details/col..._1260.asp#UndergraduateStudentBodyProfile) reveals, Vanderbilt University is a selective private university, founded in 1873, which serves as a teaching and research university. The university is comprised of 10 schools and offers undergraduate programs as well as a wide range of graduate and professional programs. Students from all 50 states and more than 90 foreign countries attend Vanderbilt.

The average cost of tuition for the 1998–1999 academic year for a full-time undergraduate student attending Vanderbilt is $21,930 (*Vanderbilt University Undergraduate Catalog,* 1998–1999), and the average student at Nashville State Tech can expect to spend $1,086 for tuition (*Nashville State Tech Catalog,* 1998–1999) for the same course load during the same time period.

Table 1
Racial and Ethnic Representation in the Student Body: Fall 1998

Ethnic Group	Nashville State Tech	Vanderbilt Undergraduate
Native American or Alaskan native	29	12
African American	1,494	239
White	5,227	4,462
Hispanic	113	169
Asian or Pacific Islander	318	319
Other unclassified	90	651
Total	7,271	5,852

Note. From Ruben Mercado, Jr., Director of Institutional Research, Nashville State Tech, personal communication, February 1999; Vanderbilt University Web Site (http://excite.collegeedge.com/details/col..._1260.asp#UndergraduateStudentBodyProfile).

S. A. McDowell, A. R. Sanchez, S. S. Jones

Academic entrance requirements differ greatly between the two schools as well. To be admitted into Vanderbilt University, an undergraduate's high school record must contain at least 15 academic units of college preparatory work (a unit being a year of study in one subject). In addition, the student must possess "grades indicating intellectual ability and promise. The pattern of courses should show purpose and continuity and furnish a background for the freshman curriculum offered at Vanderbilt" (*Vanderbilt University Undergraduate Catalog,* 1998–1999, p. 45). Applicants who may be lacking in some of these requirements can request special consideration if they are "applicants of ability and achievement" (p. 45). As is stated in the catalog,

> Admission as a freshman represents a selection based on the personal and academic records of applicants. All available information is considered, including school record, evidence of academic maturity and independence, extracurricular activities, contributions to the school and community, and scores on standardized tests. (*Vanderbilt University Undergraduate Catalog,* 1998–1999, p. 45)

In sharp contrast, Nashville State Tech is an open-door institution into which any student with a high school degree or its equivalent (Graduate Equivalency Diploma) may enter. Entering students 21 years of age or older or those with low ACT scores may be required to take one or more tests to assess academic levels. Students with academic deficiencies based on these assessments are required to complete remedial courses successfully, courses that do not carry college credit, before their college-level study may begin. Unlike Vanderbilt, Nashville State Tech merely recommends that high school students who plan to enter college prepare themselves for these college-level courses by completing two units of algebra, one unit of geometry, and four units of English (*Nashville State Tech Catalog,* 1998–1999, pp. 12–13).

Having examined our sample base in detail at this point, an explanation of the methodological approach used to tap into this sample base is in order and is detailed in the following section.

Methodological Details of the Research Study

This research study used a nonprobability sample of the convenience variety, with researchers giving 100 surveys to students enrolled at Vanderbilt and 160 to students enrolled at Nashville State Tech. Of those surveys, 5 from Nashville State Tech and 1 from Vanderbilt University were discarded as unusable (lacking responses to 10 or more questions), resulting in a final

A Multicultural Lens

sample size of 254 ($N = 254$). The different ethnic groups sampled were White ($n = 128$), African American ($n = 53$), Asian ($n = 29$), Hispanic ($n = 5$), Native American ($n = 3$), and other ($n = 36$). Due to the low level of representation in some ethnic groups—and to run the appropriate and necessary statistical analyses—the Asian, Hispanic, Native American, and other ethnic respondents were collapsed into one category, termed "Other." As a result, three primary ethnic groups are dealt with in the data analysis: White ($n = 128$), African American ($n = 53$), and Other ($n = 73$).

The survey itself was composed of three sections: (a) the first section—using close-ended questions—included inquiries designed to gather critical information about the respondent (i.e., gender, educational level, age, income, ethnicity, whether the respondent had ever been home schooled, and respondent belief as to the probability of home schooling his or her own children at some point in the future); (b) the second section—using close-ended questions—asked respondents questions pertaining to their perception of those families who choose to home school their children (i.e., reasons for home schooling, educational level of parents, income, etc.); and (c) the final section—which used a Likert-type format—asked participants to respond to statements concerning home schooled children in both the academic and the social realm.

Method of Data Analysis

Chi-square tests of independence were used to explore the relations between the ethnic groups and their responses in Section II of the survey. This particular set of questions focused on participant perception of the home schooling family's (a) reason for home schooling, (b) annual income, (c) educational level, (d) primary home schooling instructor (i.e., mother, father, or both equally), (e) father's occupation, and (f) mother's occupation. To increase the power of the responses, some response categories within the questions were combined.

A chi-square test of independence also was used to determine the relation between the participants' ethnic group and the response given when asked about the likelihood of their home schooling their own children in the future. This particular question was found in Section I of the survey.

One-way analyses of variance (ANOVA) tests were chosen to examine the questions in Section III of the survey. The questions in that section dealt with the participant's perception of how the home-schooled child fares both academically and socially. The odd questions were combined to compare the mean responses per ethnic group on the perceived academic performance of home-schooled children, and the even questions

135

S. A. McDowell, A. R. Sanchez, S. S. Jones

were combined to compare the mean responses per ethnic group on the perceived socialization of home-schooled children.

Findings

The relation between the ethnic group of the respondents and their perceptions of the primary reason families choose to home school was investigated with a chi-square test of independence (see Table 2). This relation was not statistically significant, $\chi^2(2, N = 253) = 1.052, p = .591$. However, each ethnic group appeared to believe that most home schooling families choose to home school their children for pedagogical reasons.

Another chi-square test of independence was used to examine the relation between the ethnic group of the respondents and their perceptions of the income of the families participating in home schooling (see Table 3). This relation was highly statistically significant, $\chi^2(4, N = 252) = 30.453, p < .0005$. The largest percentage of perceived income being in the lowest category (less than $29,999) was reported by the Other ethnic group. About the same percentage (just less than 50%) of each ethnic group thought that the incomes of home schooling families would be at the middle income level. The highest percentage of the perceived income being high was reported by the White group.

A third chi-square test of independence evaluated the relation between the ethnic group of the respondents and their perceptions of the educational level of home schooling parents (see Table 4). This relation was statistically significant, $\chi^2(4, N = 253) = 9.498, p = .050$. The majority in each ethnic group believed that the home schooling parents had some college or a bachelor's degree; this category was selected by the largest percentage of the Whites.

The inferential statistical analysis of the relation between the ethnic group of the respondents and their perceptions of the primary home schooling parent was unreliable (see Table 5). However, the numbers were negligible for those who reported thinking that the father alone was the home schooling parent. Both the African Americans and the Whites perceived the mother to be the primary parent involved in the home schooling process. The ethnic group termed *Other* believed that the mother and father shared the responsibilities equally.

The perceived occupation of the father in the home schooling family was reported by the respondents (see Table 6). Using the chi-square test of independence, no statistical significance was found for the relation between the ethnic group of the respondents and their perceptions of the occupations of the father, $\chi^2(4, N = 248) = 7.245, p = .123$.

The perceived occupation of the mother in the home schooling family also was reported by the respondents (see Table 7). Using the chi-square

Table 2

Participants' Perceptions of the Reason Why Families Choose to Home School Their Children

| | Ethnic Group | | | | | |
| | White | | African American | | Other[a] | |
Reasons	Count	%	Count	%	Count	%
Ideological	33	26.0	10	18.9	18	24.7
Pedagogical	94	74.0	43	81.1	55	75.3

Note. $\chi^2(2, N = 253) = 1.052, p = .591.$
[a]Includes Asian, Hispanic, Native American, and Other.

Table 3

Participants' Perceptions of the Annual Gross Income of Home Schooling Families

| | Ethnic Group | | | | | |
| | White | | African American | | Other[a] | |
Income	Count	%	Count	%	Count	%
Less than $29,999	10	7.9	13	24.5	25	34.7
$30,000 to $49,999	60	47.2	26	49.1	35	48.6
$50,000 and above	57	44.9	14	26.4	12	16.7

Note. $\chi^2(4, N = 252) = 30.453, p < .0005.$
[a]Includes Asian, Hispanic, Native American, and Other.

Table 4

Participant's Perceptions of the Average Educational Level of Home School Parents

| | Ethnic Group | | | | | |
| | White | | African American | | Other[a] | |
Educational Level	Count	%	Count	%	Count	%
High school	19	14.8	13	24.5	19	26.4
Some college/Bachelor's Degree	97	75.8	31	58.5	41	56.9
Advanced degree	12	9.4	9	17.0	12	16.7

Note. $\chi^2(4, N = 253) = 9.498, p = .050.$
[a]Includes Asian, Hispanic, Native American, and Other.

Table 5

Participants' Perception Concerning the Primary Home Schooling Parent

| | Ethnic Group | | | | | |
| | White | | African American | | Other[a] | |
Parent	Count	%	Count	%	Count	%
Mother	121	94.5	42	80.8	29	40.3
Father	0	0.0	0	0.0	4	5.6
Mother and father share equally	7	5.5	10	19.2	39	54.2

[a]Includes Asian, Hispanic, Native American, and Other.

Table 6

Participants' Perceptions of the Occupation of the Father in Home Schooling Families

| | Ethnic Group | | | | | |
| | White | | African American | | Other[a] | |
Occupation of Father	Count	%	Count	%	Count	%
Accountant, engineer, doctor	46	37.1	19	36.5	35	48.6
Small business owner, manager	53	42.7	16	30.8	25	34.7
Technical field, tradesman	25	20.2	17	32.7	12	16.7

Note. $\chi^2(4, N = 248) = 7.245, p = .123$.
[a]Includes Asian, Hispanic, Native American, and Other.

Table 7

Participants' Perceptions of the Occupation of the Mother in Home Schooling Families

| | Ethnic Group | | | | | |
| | White | | African American | | Other[a] | |
Occupation of Mother	Count	%	Count	%	Count	%
Homemaker	110	87.3	30	58.8	36	49.3
Nurse, small business owner, doctor, teacher, office worker	16	12.7	21	41.2	37	50.7

Note. $\chi^2(2, N = 250) = 36.127, p < .0005$.
[a]Includes Asian, Hispanic, Native American, and Other.

A Multicultural Lens

test of independence, high statistical significance was found for the relation between the ethnic group of the respondents and their perceptions of the occupations for the mother, $\chi^2(2, N = 250) = 36.127, p < .0005$. Whites overwhelmingly believed that the mother was a homemaker, and more than 50% of the African Americans agreed. About equal percentages of the Other ethnic group perceived the home schooling mother as a homemaker or as having a career.

A one-way ANOVA was run to compare the perceptions held by the ethnic group of the respondents toward the academic performance of home-schooled children (see Table 8). No statistically significant difference in perception was found among the ethnic groups, $F(2, N = 248) = 0.517, p = .597$.

Another one-way ANOVA was used to compare the perceptions held by the ethnic group of the respondents toward the socialization of home-schooled children (see Table 9). There was a highly statistically significant difference in perception among the ethnic groups, $F(2, N = 248) = 8.077, p < .0005$. The Other group perceived the home-schooled children as

Table 8
Participants' Perception of Academic Performance of Home-Schooled Children

Ethnic Group	n	Mean Response[a]
White	124	16.9919
African American	52	17.2115
Other[b]	72	16.5417

Note. $F(2, N = 248) = 0.517, p = .597$.
[a]For the mean response, a range of 7.00 to 28.00 is in effect (midrange = 17.5), with the lower numbers indicating a favorable response to the academic element of home schooling and the higher numbers indicating a negative response. [b]Includes Asian, Hispanic, Native American, and Other.

Table 9
Participants' Perception of Socialization of Home-Schooled Children

Ethnic Group	n	Mean Response[a]
White	127	19.1339
African American	51	18.7451
Other[b]	70	16.7714

Note. $F(2, N = 248) = 8.077, p < .0005$.
[a]For the mean response, a range of 7.00 to 28.00 is in effect (midrange = 17.5), with the lower numbers indicating a favorable response to the academic element of home schooling and the higher numbers indicating a negative response. [b]Includes Asian, Hispanic, Native American, and Other.

S. A. McDowell, A. R. Sanchez, S. S. Jones

Table 10

Participants' Response When Asked if They Would Home School Their Own Children in the Future

| | Ethnic Group | | | | | |
| | White | | African American | | Other[a] | |
Response	Count	%	Count	%	Count	%
Yes	6	4.7	7	13.2	14	19.4
Maybe	22	17.2	17	32.1	34	47.2
No	100	78.1	29	54.7	24	33.3

Note. $\chi^2(4, N = 253) = 40.109, p < .0005$.

[a]Includes Asian, Hispanic, Native American, and Other.

adequately socialized, followed by the African Americans. The Whites were less inclined to believe that the home schooling environment provided adequate socialization.

An additional chi-square test of independence was used to determine the relation between the ethnic group of the participants and their response when asked whether they would choose to home school their own children in the future (see Table 10). This relation was highly statistically significant, $\chi^2(4, N = 253) = 40.109, p < .0005$. The largest percentage (78.1%) of the Whites did not appear to plan to home school their children. A little more than half (54.7%) of the African Americans did not seem to be interested in home schooling either. A little less than half (47.2%) of the Other group reported that they might consider home schooling their children in the future.

The findings presented in this section are not only of interest, but they were also altogether unexpected. How do respondents' perceptions about home schooling families and the effectiveness of the home schooling process compare with what is known about these differing elements? Are their perceptions accurate, and does their ethnicity seem to affect their response in important ways? What conclusions, if any, may be appropriately gleaned from this research? In the following section, these and other components of the findings are explored in detail.

Discussion

Respondent Perceptions Versus the Research

One of the more surprising aspects of the data analysis was the fact that often respondents' beliefs about certain aspects of home schooling families

A Multicultural Lens

and the home schooling process aligned exactly with what is known about the population, and at other times their perceptions were completely "off base," so to speak. For instance, when asked about the annual gross income of home schooling families, the majority of respondents judged correctly when they chose the $30,000 to $49,999 range (see Table 3); current research indicates that the median income is $43,000 (Ray, 1997, p. 30). Respondents were also correct when ascertaining the average educational level of home schooling parents as being "Some college/Bachelor's Degree" (see Table 4; see also Ray, 1997, pp. 28–30). Respondents discerned correctly once again when most of them perceived the mother to be the primary instructor (see Table 5; see also Ray, 1997, p. 28). Perhaps not surprisingly, the bulk of respondents were also correct in their perception of the primary occupation of home schooling mothers as being "Homemaker" (see Table 7). Indeed, the research indicates that approximately 88% of home schooling mothers fall into this category (Ray, 1997, p. 39).

Respondents' perceptions did not always line up so precisely with the facts, however. For instance, when asked why they believed families chose to home school their children (see Table 2), the vast majority of each ethnic grouping (Whites, 74.0%, African Americans, 81.1%, and Other, 75.3%) chose the "Pedagogical" response. This is in sharp contrast to what is known about the population, as the research data indicate that ideological concerns, rather than pedagogical ones, are the primary reason parents choose to home school their children (see, e.g., Mayberry, 1988; Mayberry et al., 1995; McDowell, 1998; Wartes, 1987, 1988a).

Another instance in which respondent response differed somewhat from the known data occurred when participants indicated their beliefs about the occupation of the father in home schooling families (see Table 6). The current research indicates that the highest percentage of home schooling fathers (34%) pursue a career or occupation that falls into the "professional" category (i.e., accountant, engineer, banker, doctor, lawyer, professor, etc.; see Ray, 1997, p. 28). Interestingly enough, although no statistical significance exists between the ethnicity of respondents and their choice, the majority of African Americans (36.5%) and Other (48.6%) judged correctly that home schooling fathers' occupations fell in the realm of the "professional" category, whereas the majority of Whites (42.7%) believed the correct response to be "Small business owner, manager."

Perhaps the most telling misperceptions of the participants had to do with their response to statements dealing with the academic and social aspects of the home schooling process (see Tables 8 and 9). Research abounds that details the fact that in academic matters, home-schooled children perform at least as well as, and usually better than, their public school counterparts (see, e.g., Medlin, 1994; Ray, 1990, 1997; Ray & Wartes, 1991;

S. A. McDowell, A. R. Sanchez, S. S. Jones

Richman, 1988; Wartes, 1988b, 1990). However, the mean response of all ethnic groups to questions concerning the academic performance of home-schooled children was basically "lukewarm," in that their perceptions were neither strongly positive nor strongly negative (see Table 8). Participant response to questions concerning the socialization of home-schooled children tended to be slightly more negative, but not strongly so (see Table 9), despite the fact that current research informs us that such children are socialized at least as well as, if not better than, their public/private schooled counterparts (see, e.g., Delahooke, 1986; Kelley, 1991; Montgomery, 1989; Shyers, 1992; Smedley, 1992; Taylor, 1986).

From this detailed examination and comparison of respondent perceptions and the known data about the population, the following conclusion may be safely drawn: The respondents taking part in this study seemed to be rarely well informed, often misinformed, and totally uninformed about many aspects of the home schooling community and, most important, the efficacy of the home schooling process itself. This finding is particularly important in light of participant response when asked if they would choose to home school their own children in the future. If, as a group, they had been better informed about the home schooling movement and its participants, would that have altered their response to this particular question? More important—especially when considering the questions driving this study—did the respondents' ethnicity have any bearing on their response to this and other questions? As we see in the following section, data analyses revealed that ethnicity had a significant bearing on participant response in five areas of inquiry and no bearing at all in the four remaining areas.

Participant Response and Ethnicity

When analyzing participant response, it was most interesting to note that ethnicity had no impact on perceptions of (a) why families choose to home school their children, (b) the primary home schooling parent, (c) the occupation of the father in home schooling families, and (d) the academic performance of home-schooled children. More interesting still is the fact that ethnicity did have a very real impact on perceptions of (a) the annual gross income of home schooling families, (b) the average educational level of home school parents, (c) the occupation of the mother in home schooling families, (d) the socialization of home-schooled children, and (e) whether respondents would choose to home school their own children in the future.

What, precisely, does this mean? It means that our African American and Other respondents—despite the fact that the majority of both chose the "$30,000 to $49,999" category—were more likely than Whites to believe that the annual gross income of home school parents was "Less than

142

A Multicultural Lens

$29,999"; Whites, as it turns out, were also more likely than the other ethnic groups to choose the "$50,000 or above" category (see Table 3). It also means that our African American and Other respondents—despite the fact that the majority of both chose the "Some college/Bachelor's Degree" category—were more likely than Caucasians to believe that the average educational level of home school parents was "High school" or "Advanced degree" (see Table 4).

Whites and African Americans were much more likely than the Other category to believe that the occupation of the home schooling mother was "Homemaker"; indeed, the respondents in the Other ethnic grouping were almost evenly divided in their beliefs as to whether the mother was a homemaker or employed outside the home (see Table 7). The socialization of home-schooled children was another area of inquiry in which the ethnicity of the respondent was statistically significant. The Other ethnic group seemed to perceive home-schooled children as being adequately socialized, whereas African Americans were more negative in their perceptions. More negative still, however, were the Whites, who gave the highest (and therefore, the most negative) response (see Table 9).

The final area in which ethnicity made a statistically significant difference in response was the question concerning whether respondents would choose to home school their own children in the future (see Table 10). The Other ethnic group had the highest percentage of any ethnicity answering in the affirmative to this question (19.4%); they also had the highest percentage answering in the "Maybe" category (47.2%), and the lowest percentage giving a negative response (33.3%). Interestingly enough, African Americans (13.2%) were more than twice as likely as Whites (4.7%) to indicate that they would home school their children in the future and also almost twice as likely (African Americans, 32.1%; Whites, 17.2%) to indicate that they might home school in the future. Perhaps the most interesting finding of all is that the vast majority of Whites (78.1%) seemed to be quite firm in their belief that they would not choose to home school their children in the future.

Summary

What conclusions can be appropriately drawn at this point? It should be noted again that—given the exploratory nature of this research study, as well as the nonprobability, convenience-type sampling used—the generalizability of the findings is limited in the extreme. That having been said, however, it is certainly appropriate to draw conclusions about our particular sample and their responses.

143

S. A. McDowell, A. R. Sanchez, S. S. Jones

Given the "hit-or-miss" aspect of the correctness of their responses—as compared to what is known about the population—it is clear that our sample population was both misinformed and uninformed about several different aspects of the home schooling movement. It is also clear that in (a) the area of socialization of home-schooled children and (b) the choice as to whether to home school in the future, Whites were much more strongly inclined to be negative than were their African American and Other counterparts. Why?

Given the current participation of Whites in the home education movement—especially as compared to other ethnic groups (see Figure 1)—this finding was completely unexpected. Not only were Whites not the most positive in their responses, but they were more negative than any other ethnic group. Given the "unhappy paradox" of African Americans and the educational system cited in the literature review, one naturally would have expected African Americans to be the most ardently opposed to certain aspects of home schooling. Why, then, would it seem to be Whites who are more negative in their perceptions? Why are the African American and Other groups more positive?

We can, of course, only make suppositions at this point. Perhaps those participants with the more negative response simply presuppose that their children will learn best and be happiest in a public/private school environment. Or, perhaps—as this sample population was made up of college students—current and/or future career plans seem more real right now than do children and family issues. The possibility also exists that these findings represent the beginnings of a subtle, positive shift among African American and Other populations in favor of home schooling. Finally, and most simply, perhaps if the sample as a whole had been better educated about the home schooling movement and its effectiveness, the responses would have been more positive.

Some Concluding Thoughts

As might be expected with an exploratory study, it seems we are left with more questions than answers. Why did the White group respond so negatively to some questions, and, by the same token, why did the African American and Other ethnic groups respond so positively? Are age, educational level, and/or economic level significant factors in participant response? As a very high percentage of the home schooling population is Christian in their religious affiliation (see, e.g., Mayberry et al., 1995; Ray, 1997), is it possible that the religious affinity—or lack thereof—of the participants played a significant role in their response? Do the often surprising results of this re-

A Multicultural Lens

search study indicate a subtle turning within certain ethnic groups toward home schooling? So much more needs to be known, and more research—with a bigger and more diverse sample population, including larger numbers of differing ethnic groups—needs to be conducted.

Again, why is the ethnic breakdown of the home schooling community so highly disproportionate to the larger society? This is an important question, and it is one that this research study has taken a first step toward answering. It will be fascinating to see what future research uncovers and discovers about differing ethnic groups and their perception of—and participation in—the educational alternative known as home schooling.

References

Bankston, C. L., & Caldas, S. J. (1997, Summer). The American school dilemma: Race and scholastic performance. *Sociological Quarterly, 38,* 423–429.

Clinton, W. J. (1997). *One America: The president's initiative on race.* Retrieved January 15, 1999 from the World Wide Web: http://www.whitehouse.gov/ Initiatives/OneAmerica/events.html#oaotm

Delahooke, M. M. (1986). *Home educated children's social/emotional adjustment and academic achievement: A comparative study.* Unpublished doctoral dissertation, California School of Professional Psychology, Los Angeles.

Event, status, and cohort dropout rates. (1998). Retrieved November 18, 1998 from the World Wide Web: http://nces.ed.gov/pubs/dp95/97473-2.html

Hu, A. (1997, September). Education and race. *National Review, 49*(17), 52–54.

Kelley, S. W. (1991). Socialization of home schooled children: A self-concept study. *Home School Researcher, 7*(4), 1–12.

Lewis, A. C. (1992, January). Dropout figures. *Education Digest, 57*(5), 56.

Llewellyn, G. (Ed.). (1996). *Freedom challenge: African American homeschoolers.* Eugene, OR: Lowry House.

Mayberry, M. (1988). The 1987–88 Oregon home school survey: An overview of the findings. *Home School Researcher, 4*(1), 1–9.

Mayberry, M., Knowles, J. G., Ray, B. D., & Marlow, S. (1995). *Home schooling: Parents as educators.* Thousand Oaks, CA: Corwin.

McDowell, S. A. (1998). *Home sweet school: The perceived impact of home schooling on the family in general and the mother–teacher in general.* Unpublished doctoral dissertation, Peabody College of Vanderbilt University, Nashville, TN.

Medlin, R. (1994). *Predictors of academic achievement in home educated children: Aptitude, self-concept, and pedagogical practices.* Unpublished doctoral dissertation, University of Florida, Miami.

Montgomery, L. (1989). The effect of home schooling on the leadership skills of home schooled students. *Home School Researcher, 5*(1), 1–10.

Nadler, R. (1998, December 21). Low class: How progressive education hurts the poor and minorities. *National Review,* 31–32.

Nashville State Tech Catalog. (1998–1999). 26, 12–13.

Page, L. A. (1996). *Beliefs and practices of home schoolers about responsibility in a democracy.* Unpublished doctoral dissertation, Peabody College of Vanderbilt University, Nashville, TN.

145

S. A. McDowell, A. R. Sanchez, S. S. Jones

Ray, B. D. (1990). *A nationwide study of home education: Family characteristics, legal matters, and student achievement.* Salem, OR: National Home Education Research Institute.

Ray, B. D. (1997). *Strengths of their own—Home schoolers across America: Academic achievement, family characteristics, and longitudinal traits.* Salem, OR: National Home Education Research Institute.

Ray, B. D., & Wartes, J. (1991). The academic achievement and affective development of home-schooled children. In J. Van Galen & M. A. Pitman (Eds.), *Home schooling: Political, historical, and pedagogical perspectives* (pp. 43–62). Norwood, NJ: Ablex.

Richman, H. (1988). *Homeschoolers score higher: A replicable result.* Kittanning, PA: Pennsylvania Homeschoolers Association. (Available from Pennsylvania Homeschoolers, RD2, Box 117, Kittanning, PA 16201)

Romm, T. (1993). *Home schooling and the transmission of civic culture.* Unpublished doctoral dissertation, Clark Atlanta University, Atlanta, GA.

Schnaiberg, L. (1996, June 12). Staying home from school. *Education Week, 15.* Retrieved October 1, 1998 from the World Wide Web: http://www.edweek.org/ew/vol-15/38home.h15

Shyers, L. E. (1992). A comparison of social adjustment between home and traditionally schooled students. *Home School Researcher, 8*(3), 1–8.

Smedley, T. C. (1992). *Socialization of home schooled children: A communication approach.* Unpublished master's thesis, Radford University, Radford, VA.

Taylor, J. W. (1986). *Self-concept in home schooling children.* Unpublished doctoral dissertation, Andrews University, Berrien Springs, MI.

Vanderbilt University undergraduate catalog. (1998–1999). *98*(3), 45.

Wartes, J. (1987). *Washington Homeschool Research Project report from the 1986 homeschool testing and other descriptive information about Washington's homeschoolers.* Woodinville, WA: Washington Homeschool Research Project. (Available from Washington Homeschool Research Project, 16109 N.E. 169 Pl., Woodinville, WA 98072)

Wartes, J. (1988a). *Washington Homeschool Research Project report from the 1987 Washington homeschool testing.* Woodinville, WA: Washington Homeschool Research Project. (Available from Washington Homeschool Research Project, 16109 N.E. 169 Pl., Woodinville, WA 98072)

Wartes, J. (1988b, June). Summary of two reports from the Washington Home School Research Project, 1987. *Home School Researcher, 4*(2), 1–4.

Wartes, J. (1990). *The relationship of selected input variables to academic achievement among Washington's homeschoolers.* Woodinville, WA: Washington Homeschool Research Project. (Available from Washington Homeschool Research Project, 16109 N.E. 169 Pl., Woodinville, WA 98072)

PEABODY JOURNAL OF EDUCATION, 75(1&2), 147–158
Copyright © 2000, Lawrence Erlbaum Associates, Inc.

Defying the Stereotypes of Special Education: Home School[1] Students

Jacque Ensign

This article discusses cases from my 9-year longitudinal study of 100 home school students. The article focuses on students who have been identified as exhibiting learning disabilities and giftedness. There has been widespread concern that parents who are not trained in special education cannot adequately teach children with special needs. This article chronicles the academic development of 6 special education students and examines their parents' educational backgrounds and pedagogical approaches. I conclude that these students have not followed the expected patterns for students with their classifications and they have not been taught with the same assumptions and techniques used by special educators. These cases raise serious questions about the stereotypes that influence current practices in special education.

Historically, expectations for student performance and school outcomes in special education have been based on research in which all the participants attended some version of what Tyack (1974) called the "one best sys-

---

JACQUE ENSIGN *is Associate Professor at Southern Connecticut State University, New Haven, where she teaches special education and foundations of education.*

Requests for reprints should be sent to Jacque Ensign, Davis Hall, Southern Connecticut State University, 501 Crescent Street, New Haven, CT 06515. E-mail: ensign@southernct.edu

[1]Jacque Ensign prefers to use the one-word spelling, "homeschool," for philosophical reasons to denote a way of learning rather than school at home. However, for uniformity in this issue of the *Peabody Journal of Education,* the editors have chosen to use the two-word spelling, "home school," in the text of this article.

147

J. Ensign

tem." As we begin to recognize more plurality in both private and public education, researchers can no longer assume that students are taught the same way. Researchers need to look closely at student outcomes in nontraditional settings to expand understandings of academic and social skills development. By teaching outside the norms of teacher preparation and pedagogy, home schoolers are offering researchers many opportunities to observe this educational alternative's effects on students (Holt, 1983).

Research in the 1970s and 1980s frequently focused on whether home-schooled children who were taught by parents who were untrained as teachers could do as well academically as public school students. Now, special education students are increasingly joining the ranks of those who are home schooled, and the initial question is being raised again, this time about teaching special education students at home. There has been widespread concern that parents who are not trained in special education cannot adequately teach children with special needs.

This article, in an effort to contribute to the research community's critique of educational outcomes, represents a contextualized outcome approach to research by a researcher who has extensive experience in both traditional and home school teaching. Researchers who have personal experience teaching in both home school and traditional school settings have what Donmeyer (1997) characterized as different life experiences from those researchers who know only mainstream school settings. Also, an ongoing debate in the American Educational Research Association has focused on whether research must be based on standardized or contextualized outcome measures. Although the most cited research on home education has been based on standardized measures, other research has been based on contextualized measures, such as that advocated for whole language research by Edelsky (1990).

After teaching in traditional schools for 10 years, I home schooled my three children for 11 years. Since 1990, I have evaluated the academic progress of more than 100 home-schooled students annually. Because many of these students have continued to home school, I have amassed a wealth of longitudinal data on these students. Now that I am teaching in a teacher education program to prepare teachers for inclusive classrooms, I find that the textbook descriptions of educating special education students are often at odds with what I have observed in many home school settings.

This article questions accepted expectations for special education students that are found in current introductory textbooks for teacher education. By looking outside traditional systems, this researcher has found exceptions to many of the textbook patterns for academic and social development. My work with special education home-schooled students has included students who are in most of the categories that special education programs serve. Although I have worked with home-schooled students with autism, commu-

Defying the Stereotypes

nication disorders, mental retardation, emotional and behavioral disorders, attention deficit hyperactivity disorder, and physical disabilities, only the categories of learning disabilities (LD) and giftedness have had enough students in them for a number of years for me to feel confident that I am seeing some general trends. Therefore, in this article, I focus only on the categories of LD and giftedness. This article (a) highlights cases from a 9-year longitudinal study of 100 home-schooled students who represent regular and special education categories; (b) chronicles the academic and social development of 6 special education students who have been identified as exhibiting LD, giftedness, or both; and (c) examines their parents' educational backgrounds and pedagogical approaches.

Related Literature

One educational anthropologist who has documented how schools construct disabilities is Ray McDermott. In a recent book with Hervé Varenne, the school experiences of an elementary school boy who was labeled as learning disabled are chronicled:

> Learning Disability moments were built for all to notice Adam as a problem and thus give Adam a problem he experienced keenly, as we also did. We might just as well say that *these are the moments when Learning Disability acquired Adam*. (Varenne & McDermott, 1999, p. 33)

Again and again, McDermott and Varenne documented how the culture of school orchestrated labeling and disabling Adam to confirm his differentness from his classmates.

> The problems many people have in the American school system stem only incidentally from what they can or cannot do and much more radically from the way they are treated by others in relation to the designation, assignment, and distribution of more or less temporary or partial difficulties interpreted as success or failure and responded to in the terms of the Testing world. (p. 135)

They noted that in the United States, LD is considered to be a category that refers to something inherently in the child, and they contend that the culture of the United States demands that schools mark students' differences and educate them differently, thereby creating categories of disabilities and abilities that "acquire" students.

In "An Exploratory Study of Home School Instructional Environments and Their Effects on the Basic Skills of Students With Learning Disabilities,"

149

J. Ensign

Duvall, Ward, Delquadri, and Greenwood (1997) documented that home-schooled students with LD were engaged in academic learning two and a half times as often as their counterparts in public schools. In addition to being more academically engaged, the home-schooled students made "relatively large gains in reading and written language while the public school students experienced losses in reading and only small gains in written language. In math, the home school and public school groups made equivalent gains" (Duvall et al., 1997, p. 167). They contended that being more academically engaged may contribute to home schoolers' higher academic achievement, despite differences in teacher training and methodology.

Kate Donegan is Director of Services for the Matrix Research Institute in Philadelphia, where she directs a large federally funded transition program for young people who have been labeled as special education students. Donegan commented while in an online discussion of the cultural effects of special education:

> The biggest challenge my staff face is building even an ounce of self-esteem in these kids—who have been through the special education/labeling ringer—once they can do that, the change, almost like blossoming, is unbelievable. ... They have scores of problems and issues to cope with; it would be nice if their "educational experience" was not one of the things we had to overcome!! (Donegan, 1998)

Donegan sounded a warning to schools as to the side-effects of special education policies.

The researchers cited previously suggest that schools may be responsible for some of the negative educational outcomes of students with LD. The following are details on a 9-year longitudinal study of 6 home-schooled gifted and/or students with LD to determine whether they are experiencing different educational experiences and outcomes than are their counterparts in schools. Although 6 students are featured in this research, they were chosen as representative of more than 50 gifted students or students with LD whom I have evaluated over the past 9 years.

LD

From a textbook on special education, the following is a typical excerpt describing studies of outcomes of students with LD:

> Educational experiences are frustrating for youth who have learning disabilities. Their drop-out rate is high (38 percent versus 25 percent for

Defying the Stereotypes

nondisabled youth). Only 28 percent attempt postsecondary education (versus 56 percent for nondisabled youth), and most do not have the study skills, reading and math skills, or academic coping skills to successfully persevere through a 4-year college career. (Peraino, 1992, as cited in Turnbull, Turnbull, Shank, & Leal, 1995, p. 22)

Only one of the four home-schooled students with LD described in this study is old enough to have graduated from high school. Projecting from the data so far on their study skills, reading and math skills, and academic coping skills, I expect all of these students to graduate and many to continue with postsecondary education. Why is there such a stark difference in expected outcomes for traditionally schooled versus these home-schooled students with LD? A look at the home schoolers' pedagogy and underlying assumptions about these special education students suggests some possible reasons.

The educational background of the parents home schooling these students ranges from 2 years of community college to a master's degree. Most do not have degrees in teaching, and none has had courses in special education. When asked how these parents learn how to teach these students, most replied that they use a combination of books, home school magazines, talking with other home schoolers, and watching their own child with LD to see what works and what does not. One parent also uses online bulletin boards. None uses traditional forms of inservice training, workshops, or courses.

When asked what specialized attention the student with LD gets from the primary home school teacher, all responded first by describing one-on-one teaching with much encouragement and love. All have read extensively to the child, even after the child mastered reading. Many of the students were taught phonics, but most never mastered phonics, being more global readers instead. Most have tried many approaches to spelling, with minimal success. All parents interviewed continually work on organizational skills with the child.

When asked what specialized attention the students with LD get from specialists, all use an educational consultant for helping plan and annually monitor the academic progress of the student. Many have used specialists for testing for LD and reading. One student is getting specialized LD tutoring twice a week, year-round. All the others get no specialized help from specialists on a regular basis throughout the academic year.

Because many schools rely on classmates and peers to provide some of the academic assistance to mainstreamed students with LD, I asked these parents what specialized attention the students get from classmates and peers. In home schools, generally the classmates are siblings who are not peers. Parents noted that siblings who are quicker in academics sometimes

151

J. Ensign

assist the students with LD. They noted that siblings sometimes provide motivation, although the ease with which the siblings do academics is occasionally discouraging for the students with LD who struggle with academics. All noted that they give careful counseling to the siblings to not make fun of the child with LD and that generally this is successful. A few of the students were in traditional classrooms prior to being home schooled, and parents noted that the LD students had more behavior and motivation problems in the traditional than in the home school situations. With peers, home schoolers appear to face similar problems to those faced by traditionally schooled students. They learn ways to hide their disability in scouts, in clubs, and with friends. Often, their fear of being noticed drives them to practice at home such skills as reading prescribed texts or signing their names in cursive so that they can do these when they are with their peers.

When asked about their philosophy toward the LD of their student, parents responded noticeably differently than I have heard from teachers in traditional schools. I asked whether they considered the LD to be an excuse, an inconvenience, a bother, part of the package, a challenge, or "what." Several responded by noting that the LD is a big challenge, but that it is also a part of the strengths of the child, such as being very creative or having the ability to see through chaos. For instance, a child who is intuitively (rather than methodically) able to see through chaos in a cluttered room will approach reading in the same intuitive way. Another parent said, "It was just a timing issue. I knew he'd eventually read—and he did at age 14." This parent reflected the attitude of many of these parents that children with LD follow a different timetable in academic development but that they would develop if they were given time and support. (Note how similar this is to the stance that Louise Spear-Swerling and Robert Sternberg have taken in their 1996 book *Off Track*.) Behind these strongly held philosophies, all admitted to underlying concerns that these children might not succeed, because they knew many cases of traditionally schooled students who do not succeed. Overall, parents saw the child as normal rather than abnormal.

When asked about their pedagogical approaches for these students with LD, parents noted that they went at the speed of the child, expecting the child to blossom when ready. All noted that they were constantly having to find ways to help the child accommodate to the LD. They worked on problem areas, but also encouraged acceleration in areas of strengths, be it flying private airplanes, doing electronics, or puppetry. Parents hoped that when the child moved on to other schooling, the colleges or schools also would see beyond the LD and allow the student to shine in the areas of abilities. One parent of a gifted student with LD expected overall excellence while realizing that some accommodations had to be made for the

Defying the Stereotypes

LD. The general approach of these parents was to work around the LD while expecting overall learning to progress continually.

Briefly, here is a synopsis of four cases of students with LD in this study.

I have followed Eileen since she was in first grade. She is now a 10th grader. For the first 6 years, she struggled to read and to do any academics. Having finally mastered reading and basic academic skills, she is now taking high school correspondence courses. Her mother said recently,

> You can tell when they are ready for a change. She's finally able to blossom and the motivation is there. So much of her energy has been on learning. After so long a wait, we'll take it at her speed.

They are guardedly optimistic that she will continue her education at a technical or community college after she finishes high school.

I have followed Jamie for the last 7 years. At 13, he is still struggling to read. For the last year and a half, he has been in individual LD therapy twice a week for an hour and a half each time. Recently, noting that reading is still not progressing very easily, his family has begun to focus on how his LD is part of his personality, in that he learns by doing, not by symbols or being told. They have decided to capitalize on his interests in flying and are now allowing him to be in the cockpit with his father in their private plane, making frequent flights to other states for his father's work. Realizing how touch is involved in his learning, they have included touch in reading, with his mother giving him neck massages while he reads. They are amazed how much better he reads during these massages. Because he loves animals and tends to be reticent in social situations, he is now training a dog so that he can take it into retirement homes for "touch therapy" for the seniors and to help him develop more social skills.

I have followed Daniel since third grade. He is now in 10th grade. He was labeled LD at age 9 while in school. The family tried specialized help for LD when he was in public school, but noted that his self-confidence was rapidly eroding and behavior problems were growing. In home schooling, they tried a number of approaches to reading—including Orton-Gilligan and several phonics programs—but none worked. Because he was classified as LD, he was able to get books on audiotapes through the Library of Congress program for the blind. During the years that he devoured books on tapes, his family called him a "tape-worm." He did not read until he was 14, when he finally began reading Frog and Toad books. Three months later, he was reading Hardy Boys books and in 2 more months he was reading adult books. One year later, he read faster than his sister, who had been avidly reading chapter books for 7 years. He is presently immersed in reading J. R. R. Tolkien's books, and his family lovingly

J. Ensign

refers to him as a "bookworm." Because he still finds math and writing difficult, his family is focusing on those skills and trusting that, in time, they will develop, just as the reading finally did.

Tristan is the oldest of the students with LD whom I have followed. I worked with him during his 11 years of home school and have continued to follow his progress in the 6 years after home school. At age 6, he was tested for LD, and at 8 he was tested for reading because he was still not reading beyond a preprimer level. He began reading independently at 9½, and by 11 he was reading college texts, though he still could not read isolated words. Also, being gifted, he wrote reams on the computer, where he could use a spell checker to make his writing understood. He did advanced course work throughout most of his schooling, but struggled with foreign language, spelling, and memorizing math facts. At 14, he became proficient in electronics, and, several years later, did computer repair to earn money. At 16, he went to an elite high school where they noticed his LD but also noticed that somehow he read and comprehended more books than any other student in his class. After high school, he spent half a year in Ecuador learning Spanish and the culture there by immersion, rather than in a school. A year later, while a freshman in college, he conducted a month-long anthropology research project in the back country of the Dominican Republic. He did all the research, in books and in interviews, in Spanish. He was a teaching assistant for an introductory anthropology class during his sophomore year. In his junior year, he conducted 7 months of independent anthropological research in Bolivia—again, all in Spanish. He has been on the dean's list at a tier-one liberal arts college throughout his college years, and he is graduating this year with honors. He is known for his independence, his ability to ferret out information in unusual places, and his horrible spelling. All of his anthropological research has been planned and executed by him, including securing grants, writing, and presenting final reports.

Overall, these home-schooled students with LD are expected to be and are treated as normal. They are often not as aware of their disabilities as are traditionally schooled students because they are not labeled as disabled by their families. Even those who read very late catch up quickly, and some become excellent readers. All love literature. Usually, these students have good self-esteem because they have areas of expertise and are respected for what they do, rather than known for what they do not do well.

Gifted

Increasingly, in today's schools with tightening budgets, gifted students are not receiving the specialized education that is recommended by

Defying the Stereotypes

authorities in gifted education. Many gifted students find themselves relegated to easy, repetitive academics in mainstreamed classes. As Hallahan and Kauffman (1997) noted, underachievement for gifted students is frequently caused by

> inappropriate school programs—schoolwork that is unchallenging and boring because gifted students have already mastered most of the material or because teachers have low expectations or mark students down for their misbehavior (Kolb & Jussim, 1994). A related problem is that gifted underachievers often develop negative self-images and negative attitudes toward school (Delisle, 1982; Gallagher & Gallagher, 1994). (Hallahan & Kauffman, 1997, p. 472)

In the cases of home-schooled gifted students, parents are consciously trying to stimulate and encourage their gifted students to prevent boredom and underachievement. What is notable is the way in which they are teaching these gifted students; the students themselves are not aware that they are any more exceptional than other students because all the students are treated as unique. Their high level of achievement and self-confidence is evident, as is the length to which these parents go to expand these students' horizons.

The educational backgrounds of the parents home schooling the gifted students in the cases in this article range from a high school education to a master's degree. Of those who have degrees in teaching, one has a degree in teaching mentally retarded elementary school students, and one has an early childhood degree. Like the parents of students with LD, these parents use a combination of observing the child and consulting relevant literature and/or people to learn how to teach these gifted students.

When asked what specialized attention the gifted student gets from the primary home school teacher, all responded first by describing a lot of independent time for the student. Time actually spent with the teacher is mostly in long discussions with the student, with the rest of the time going to overseeing school assignments.

When asked what specialized attention the gifted student gets from specialists, all use a combination of mentors and special-interest classes or activities such as Space Camp, art classes, science museum classes, and summer programs for the gifted. Adults who share common interests with the student are often key mentors for these students. This is usually on an informal basis, with the student having long conversations with a neighbor or family friend who is knowledgeable and willing to talk or work with the student. Informality seems to be a critical aspect of these relationships, as the students do not want to be "taught" so much as to be treated as coexplorers.

J. Ensign

Interestingly, contrary to the stereotypical concern that gifted students may have difficulty with peers, these gifted students are very social, with a wide variety of peers and classmates. Neighbors, classmates in special courses, and siblings are all part of their lives (Ensign, 1997). Typically, the gifted students are in a leadership role when they are with their peers and classmates.

When asked about their philosophy toward the giftedness of their students, parents responded by saying the giftedness is a challenge, a precious gift, a joy, and a responsibility. When asked about their pedagogical approaches for these gifted students, parents noted that they basically follow the students' interests, supplementing and expanding their horizons as much as possible. They try to provide a stimulating environment in which the student can pursue interests and find new interests. They feel that attention to academic and social skills that the student needs to develop is important in providing a well-rounded education for these students.

Following are the synopses of three cases of home-schooled gifted students in this study. Tristan's summary was the last one in the section on LD.

Philip is now 13 years old. I have followed him since he was 5. As a kindergartner, he was an avid inventor, more interested in the theory and process of his inventions than in their ultimate success. Reading has always been a love of Philip's. He rapidly learned to read in kindergarten, and, since then, has always read quantities of high-quality books each year. A natural leader, he was organizing group displays of collections in first grade and by seventh grade was foreman for a $1,000 mapping and inventory project of a junkyard to help it comply with Environmental Protection Agency standards. Although his mother is the daily teacher, his father is instrumental in making sure that his children have as broad an experience with the world as they can get. His father is constantly finding new experiences for Philip, such as a recent course in Hypertext Markup Language (HTML) programming and an online writing class.

Audin is a 10-year-old whom I have followed since he was in kindergarten. His mother, his primary home school teacher, has a high school education. His grandparents were initially very concerned that this gifted child of Color was being cheated to be taught at home. Now that Audin is 10, they are no longer concerned as they see how much he is learning at home. When he was in kindergarten, he had his own gem jewelry business and amazed customers at craft fairs when he mentally totaled sales and gave accurate change for transactions. At 9, he read Stephen Hawking's books on theoretical physics and spent a lot of time discussing those concepts with a neighbor who is an engineer. Neighborhood peers come over to his house after they get home from school so that they can play chess, math games, and talk about science. He is a child who absorbs information and who finds formal

Defying the Stereotypes

classes frustrating. His parents are eager explorers of new territory with him and continually find new people, books, and experiences for him.

Summary

In conclusion, these students with LD and giftedness have not been taught with the same assumptions and techniques used by special educators. The hallmarks of the educational philosophies and pedagogies of the home schoolers in this study are (a) focus on the whole child rather than primarily on the child's disability or extreme ability; (b) individualized attention; and (c) care, patience, and respect for the child to lead the teacher in both the timing and the content of what the child is ready to be taught. These students with LD and giftedness have not followed the expected patterns for students with their classifications. The educational outcomes for these home-schooled special education students may be summed up as follows: They are self-confident students who have developed academic skills at very uneven rates, but who usually have achieved academic proficiency by high school.

Renzulli (1998), director of the National Research Center on the Gifted and Talented, argued for talent development programs for all children rather than just for gifted children. He stressed the importance of allowing students to pursue their interests and talents, no matter what their academic or supposed ability level. By allowing students to forge into new territory, they develop higher self-esteem and become more excited and engaged in educational pursuits. It appears that his approach is similar to the approaches parents in this study successfully adopted in teaching their special education students, regardless of the students' ascribed abilities or disabilities.

Although some attention is being given to race as being socially constructed, little attention has been given to how special education may be socially constructed. Perhaps the reticence to question the social construction of special education has its roots in the same psychology that has kept the concept of IQ as being biologically intact and innate rather than being significantly socially constructed. In considerations of IQ, nature has been emphasized, with only a cursory nod to nurture. Both special education categories and IQ have not been seen as being very permeable. Both have been seen as being descriptions of what is in the child rather than being descriptions of the culture interacting with the child. By stepping outside the box of traditional schools as the context for educating special education students, this article has examined the role that nurture may play in special education students. This study suggests that the academic development of those special education students whose nurture occurs in home schools differs markedly from that of special education students whose nurture occurs in traditional schools.

157

J. Ensign

Meier, in a recent article, emphasized why "oddball" schools that are successful should be noticed:

> Rather than ignore such schools because their solutions lie in unreplicable individuals or circumstances, it's precisely such unreplicability that should be celebrated. Maybe what these "special" schools demonstrate is that every school must have the power and the responsibility to select and design its own particulars and thus to surround all young people with powerful adults who are in a position to act on their behalf in open and publicly responsible ways. (Meier, 1998, p. 359)

The home schooling of the special education students in this study can be viewed as an "oddball" schooling that works because of caring, powerful adults and children who have not lost faith in quality education and achievement. These home school cases raise serious questions about the stereotypes that influence current practices in special education.

References

Delisle, J. (1982). The gifted underachiever: Learning to underachieve. *Roeper Review, 4*, 16–18.

Donegan, K. (1998, July 23). Self-esteem. *AERA–G Division G: Social Context of Education* [Online]. Available via E-mail at AERA-G@ASUVM.INRE.ASU.EDU

Donmeyer, R. (1997). Editorial: Research as advocacy and storytelling. *Educational Researcher, 26*(5), 2.

Duvall, S. F., Ward, D. L., Delquadri, J. C., & Greenwood, C. R. (1997). An exploratory study of home school instructional environments and their effects on the basic skills of students with learning disabilities. *Education and Treatment of Children, 20*(2), 150–172.

Edelsky, C. (1990). Whose agenda is this anyway? A response to McKenna, Robinson, and Miller. *Educational Researcher, 19*(8), 7–10.

Ensign, J. (1997). Homeschooling gifted students: An introductory guide for parents. *ERIC Digest, E543.*

Gallagher, J. J., & Gallagher, S. A. (1994). *Teaching the gifted child* (4th ed.). Boston: Allyn and Bacon.

Hallahan, D., & Kauffman, J. (1997). *Exceptional learners: Introduction to special education.* Boston: Allyn & Bacon.

Holt, J. C. (1983). Schools and home schoolers: A fruitful partnership. *Phi Delta Kappan, 64*, 391–394.

Kolb, K. J., & Jussim, L. (1994). Teacher expectations and underachieving gifted children. *Roeper Review, 17*, 26–30.

Meier, D. (1998). Can the odds be changed? *Phi Delta Kappan, 79*, 358.

Renzulli, J. S. (1998, October). A rising tide lifts all ships: Developing the gifts and talents of all students. *Phi Delta Kappan, 79*, 105–111.

Spear-Swerling, L., & Sternberg, R. (1996). *Off track: When poor readers become "learning disabled."* Boulder, CO: Westview.

Turnbull, A., Turnbull, R., III, Shank, R. M., & Leal, D. (1995). *Exceptional lives: Special education in today's schools.* Englewood Cliffs, NJ: Prentice Hall.

Tyack, D. (1974). *The one best system.* Cambridge, MA: Harvard University Press.

Varenne, H., & McDermott, R. (1999). *Successful failure: The school America builds.* Boulder, CO: Westview.

PEABODY JOURNAL OF EDUCATION, 75(1&2), 159–186
Copyright © 2000, Lawrence Erlbaum Associates, Inc.

When Home Schoolers Go to School: A Partnership Between Families and Schools

Patricia M. Lines

Several years ago, as I was approaching the Maywood Center, a public school facility operated by the Highline Public School District in Seatac, Washington, an odd and contradictory sign pointed the way. It announced, "Homeschooling Program, North Entrance." The sign was a symbol of new partnerships between public school professionals and home schooling parents. This article offers a preliminary examination of public programs like this one. These are programs that accept parents as the child's primary teacher.

There are a number of such programs throughout the country now. California may have the largest number. There, the state's charter school law has encouraged their development. About 10% of California's more than 100 charter schools cater to students who do most of their learning off-campus. To be sure, such programs existed before California adopted charter school legislation. California's compulsory education law recognizes enrollment in a public school's independent study program as a way

---

PATRICIA M. LINES *is a senior fellow at the Discovery Institute in Seattle, Washington. She is a former associate at the National Institute on Student Achievement, Curriculum and Assessment, a part of the U.S. Department of Education, where she managed research on issues relating to charter schools and related policy issues.*

Requests for reprints should be sent to Patricia M. Lines, Discovery Institute, 1402 Third Avenue, Suite 400, Seattle, WA 98101.

159

P. M. Lines

to educate a child at home. As a result, a number of districts—the largest being San Diego—started actively recruiting home schooling children, enticing them with free curricular supplies and services from the district and, in some cases, a voucher for additional materials. These districts then include the children enrolled when calculating state per pupil assistance.

Public educators also have jumped into these unchartered waters (no pun intended) in other states. A program in Des Moines, Iowa, has been operating successfully for many years (Dahm, 1996). Alaska founded the grandfather of public programs for home schoolers with its correspondence school—now known as its distance learning school—in Juneau. The Alaska program started decades ago to serve children in isolated areas, but today well more than half its enrollment live in the Anchorage area. Recent surveys in Texas (Yeager, 1999) and Minnesota (Ricke, 1999) indicate that some public schools in those states are also offering at least limited support to home schoolers.

This article describes two different types of programs in eastern Washington state. In one, parents are independently home schooling, taking responsibility for curriculum and evaluation of student progress. They may enroll the child part-time in specific activities or classes, and they may consult with school faculty, borrow district texts and materials, and obtain testing services from the local public school system. However, they retain control, and the district may count only a part of the child's time. These parents file a declaration of intent to home school.

The other program is a home schooling "look alike." It is called public school "independent study" in California, and there the state department of education carefully distinguishes it from home schooling. In Washington state, the usage increasingly favors "parent-partnered" public education for this option. In both California's independent study and Washington's parent-partnered option, the public school sets the curriculum, at least theoretically. The school decides when and how to evaluate the child's progress and what tests to use. Most of the work takes place under a parent's supervision, but overall direction is with the school. In Washington state, there is a minimum amount of time required on campus for younger children. In Washington state, parents must revoke their declaration of intent to home school. There is nonetheless some confusion between home schooling and the independent study and parent-partnered programs. Those who enroll in these full-time programs often consider themselves home schoolers, and the faculty working with them often call them home schoolers. California charter schools, for example, sometimes announce a program of home schooling when they intend to follow the state law for independent study (and they intend to claim 100% Full Time Equivalent, or FTE, in state support for each child). If the public school fac-

A Partnership Between Families and Schools

ulty are sensitive to the parents' desires, there may be little difference between an independent study or part-time program for home schoolers.

These programs, whether home schooling or independent study, are, in the jargon of public school reform efforts, site-based managed programs, schools of choice, schools within schools, and schools that make parental involvement a key component. In both types of programs, much of the work takes place off-campus under the general supervision of a parent.

Until recently, there has been virtually nothing in the popular or the scholarly literature on such programs. There seems to be very little awareness, outside their immediate spheres, that they exist. The home schooling community is aware of them, of course. Indeed, many home schoolers greet these public efforts with extreme suspicion: At one center I found a pamphlet by an organization called the Inland Empire Home School Center, which advocated home schooling and argued that public school centers for home schoolers are a "Trojan Horse," through which public educators gain control over the child's education. Loss of a religious orientation in the program is also a serious issue to many home schoolers (Home School Legal Defense Association, 1998).

The most intensive survey of home schoolers' attitudes toward these public programs, based on a sample of home schooling families affiliated with the Texas Home School Coalition, a Christian organization, revealed some interest in using relatively neutral public school resources. The most attractive offering would be an opportunity to participate in group activity such as band or choir, with 49% of respondents saying they agreed[1] that they needed or would like to have access to such a resource. Respondents also were interested in part-time enrollment in courses (41%) and use of a public school library (36%). Except for use of the library, there was a greater preference for using these same resources at a private school. For every resource, there were more respondents who indicated antipathy to using these public school resources (indicating they disagreed that they needed such a resource). Most of the distributions were bimodal; the middle category of "undecided" usually claimed the smallest proportion of respondents (Yeager, 1999, Tables 39, 68, 69).

In Yeager's (1999) survey, home schoolers rejected the use of public school teachers for counseling on effective teaching (87% indicating that they disagreed with the statement that they needed or would like to use such service), use of public school counselors (85% disinclined), health screening (79% disinclined), and psychological services (92% disinclined). In contrast, there was greater interest in using such services at private

---

[1]The term *agree* or *disagree* includes those who said "strongly agree" or "strongly disagree" on the survey.

161

P. M. Lines

schools, although even there a majority of parents were disinclined to use the services (Yeager, 1999).

The use of a computer lab was not specifically covered in the Yeager survey, but it is popular among public school programs in Washington state. On a survey, this probably would rank in popularity at least with part-time enrollment in public school courses, and because of the family control over choice among many software offerings, it could be more popular.

As noted, many home schoolers are suspicious of such programs. Many public educators and the families who send their children full-time to public schools also often look askance at these programs. "It's not fair," complained one public school parent, "for them to want the best of what the public school has to offer without paying the dues" (Hawkins, 1996). In Yeager's survey, a majority of Texas public school superintendents indicated indifference to home schooling. Even so, most had a fair picture of home schooling: A large majority (65%) thought lack of religious integration was a large motivating factor, and a majority also named "curriculum incompatible with beliefs," "negative peer socialization" and "safety decline" (Yeager, 1999, p. 94) as reasons for home schooling. These superintendents were correctly reflecting home schoolers' frequently cited reasons for their decision. Yeager also uncovered hostile unstructured responses from a tiny minority of responding superintendents who claimed that home schoolers were "idiots," "dropouts," "unable to cope" with public school, or "exploiting" their children for free farm labor. For most superintendents, the issue is probably simply a fiscal one. The Minnesota survey revealed that about 70% of superintendents were ready to consider changes in the state funding formula to allow home school involvement in the public program (Ricke, 1999, p. 40). Where state seat-time requirements are lax, it is even possible for a home schooling program to turn into a "cash cow" (as one administrator put it) for the district. A superintendent (from another state) once told me that he built a new school building for his very low-income predominantly minority students with "profits" reaped from a distance learning program the district offered to home schoolers throughout his state.

Even if a majority of home schoolers stay away, these school–parent partnerships can be made viable. The school must have an attractive program and be sensitive to the parents' hopes and wishes for their child. There must be a large enough home schooling population that the school can afford to make at least one teacher available to the program. Put the two together, and interesting educational experiments emerge.

This article provides a descriptive analysis of 11 public school districts offering programs for parent-partnered (or independent public school study) and part-time programs for home schoolers and examines how they

A Partnership Between Families and Schools

changed over 4 years. These were the universe of such programs operating by the school year 1994–1995 in eastern Washington state. Observations are based on one or more site visits in either spring 1994 or 1995 and a follow-up telephone interview in spring or fall 1999. The analysis discusses features common to programs that remained stable over time and how families interact with other families in their host school, where there is one.

Before these programs emerged, eastern Washington state had a relatively large and active home schooling population. There, one can find families in their third generation of home schooling. On the other hand, in the 1980s the state seemed a poor candidate for the flowering of a partnership between public schools and home schoolers. Home schooling at that time violated the state's compulsory education law. However, the state also had a strong tradition of local control, and, in the more neighborly communities of the state, home schooling had won acceptance even though the law disallowed it. During that early era, for example, a group of local prosecutors in a joint press conference announced that they would not prosecute home schooling parents, as they had their hands full with real criminals. Likewise, a number of public school superintendents offered enrollment to local home schoolers, allowing children to enroll in independent study and sheltering their parents from prosecution.

Finally, the Washington legislature revised its laws to allow home schooling. The legislature also required local districts to admit home schoolers to courses on a part-time basis. The legal environment went immediately from difficult to one of the most friendly environments for home schoolers. In addition, Washington state law allowed interdistrict transfers, with state funds following the pupil. State per-pupil support is relatively generous (Gold, Smith, Lawton, & Hyary, 1992). In addition, the new law provided $300 per pupil for ancillary services such as testing. (State law requires that home schooling students undergo periodic testing, although results are not sent to the state education agency.) This and the state support for part-time enrolled students was a small incentive to offer programs to attract otherwise unenrolled students within and outside the district. In 1994–1995, the state changed its alternative education law to allow students to be full-time enrolled while remaining off-campus much of the time. This provided an even bigger incentive to districts to enroll home-based students full-time to earn 100% FTE for each.

It was just as the law was changing that I visited the 11 programs for the first time. Each was unique. Fully half the programs had a primary or exclusive focus on computer-assisted instruction in a computer lab, usually with some computer courses and with support services from a professional. However, most of these also offered field trips and some additional instruction, and those that did not were moving toward greater diversifi-

163

P. M. Lines

cation. Most of the programs were started by enthusiastic teachers working with a handful of home schooling leaders. In the smaller number of cases, although computer-assisted instruction or parent training was available, the programs focused more on subject-area offerings.

I observed the actual teaching in most of the centers that offered courses. All were good, and all enjoyed attentive pupils. Some were outstanding. One outstanding example, which was short-lived, pivoted around a charismatic teacher who had originated the program. The other, in another district, depended on an equally talented teacher who applied when the district decided to have a program and advertised for a candidate.

The Seventh Planet

In the first case, Forest Adams had once been the principal of an alternative school in the eastern United States, chosen, as he claims, not because of his education credentials, but because the district saw him, an educated African American man, as a role model for the children at the school. When the building burned and the district determined not to replace it, Adams migrated West. There, he earned a living as a management consultant, settling into a picturesque middle-class, mostly White suburban area nestled in the foothills of the Snoqualmie Mountains. Observing a substantial home schooling population, Adams decided to combine his interest in education and consulting. He developed and offered a unique program of science instruction to home schooling children. He called it the Seventh Planet, and he challenged elementary-age children to determine how to populate a seventh planet. He required each student to devise experiments to acquire knowledge on how to move a colony through space and establish it in a hostile terrain. This private operation, located in a storefront, charged $100 per child per month.

Adams's private program went public in 1993 when the assistant superintendent of the Lake Washington School District noticed a gaggle of school-age children entering a nearby storefront during school hours. Curious and concerned, he followed them and so discovered the Seventh Planet. This was a tense moment. Chances are often high that local public school officials might be hostile and try to close down such a program. But this official was not hostile. To the contrary, he was impressed. He asked if he could return with the district's elementary school principals. The full retinue of principals who visited were likewise impressed. Thom Dramer, the principal of Samantha Smith Elementary School, had brought along a sixth-grade teacher whose judgment he valued. Both liked what they saw. Before they left, they learned that Adams's lease was running out, and they offered to Adams a temporary classroom—and a deal. The school would

A Partnership Between Families and Schools

pay Adams the state FTE less 5% for administrative costs. Adams also charged the family a lab fee of $24 per month.

As a public program, the Seventh Planet enrolled three groups of children, each group meeting once per week for 5 hours. In addition to group projects, each child worked on an experiment that would further the knowledge that could allow colonizing a distant planet. Each child was to identify his or her own project. The rules were: First, the child, not the teacher, must choose the project; second, the child must finish the project; third, the project must work; and fourth, the student must present findings to a jury of peers who would grade it for clarity. The grading criteria required an explanation of the steps involved in reaching the goal, explanation of concepts, making eye contact, and use of clear graphics and other presentation aids. The student who did not receive better than a 3 on a scale of 1 to 5 had to revise and present the project again.

During the site visit in spring 1994, I met a young girl, age 9, who had designed an experiment to determine the effect of temperature on hatching chicks to understand the extent to which the space ship and the new colony would require temperature control for chickens to be transplanted. She had identified a list of control variables, including genetic selection (the eggs were to come from the same batch of hens and be randomly assigned to a control and an experimental group), hen's feed and water, and chick's feed and water. The temperature would vary for the experimental group, and she would record the hatching dates, weight, and other development of the chicks. This was only the second time I had met a child this young who understood what a control variable was. (The first time also involved an out-of-school experience in an after-school activity.) A young boy, about the same age, was building and shooting rockets into the air and taking temperature readings under varied conditions. Although enthusiastic and successful at rocket-building and launching, he was not able to indicate quite what he expected to discover.

The Samantha Smith School was considering ways it could expand the program for its full-time children in the regular classroom setting. But for personal reasons, Adams left the program. The district had no way to replicate his unique approach and this unique arrangement. It was clearly personality driven. The program had offered a valuable part-time experience for home schoolers while it was in operation.

South Whidbey School District

South Whidbey Island is about 1½ hours from Seattle by car and ferry. The largest town is Langley, home to perhaps 800 people, with summer

P. M. Lines

tourists doubling the population. Elizabeth Itaya runs the Wellington Day School, a preschool and child care establishment. As a member of the district's Strategic Planning Board, a part of a statewide restructuring effort, she proposed that the district provide services to home schooling families. Itaya hoped only for vision and hearing screening. In December 1992, the school board approved Policy No. 2115, recognizing home schooling "as a valid instructional option for children" and encouraging home schoolers to enroll in academic, cocurricular, and extracurricular activities in the district on a part-time basis and to take advantage of district testing and other services. In July 1993, the district posted a notice of vacancy for a new position—the "off campus/home school extension program coordinator." Nancy Thompson was the successful candidate in a field of 25 applicants. She had the required state certificate for teaching K through Grade 12, the desired flexibility, and a willingness to collaborate with students and parents from a wide variety of backgrounds.

In spring 1994, I observed Thompson deliver a class on health. The Wellington Day School donated the classroom space. Some of the children who had just attended a computer lab at a nearby public school rode to the site with Thompson. More children arrived with their mothers, some of whom left and some of whom stayed. All told, there were 15 children and a toddler, the younger sibling of a participating child. The mother amused the toddler with toys in one corner while four other mothers participated in the class session.

Thompson had a challenge: The age range of the children in the room, excluding the toddler, was from 6 to 16. She began with questions about parts of the body. The brightest answers came from a precocious younger girl. Thompson asked what the body needed to be healthy. Older children mentioned food, water, and shelter. The younger girl added exercise and sleep. Thompson asked what kinds of foods are good for the body. A discussion of minerals, vitamins, and food allergies followed. Then Thompson asked the children, "What's inside your body?" Several organs were named, and Thompson was ready to focus on the heart. She passed around a bottle containing a pig's heart in formaldehyde, with a word of caution and a comment about the carcinogenic effects of formaldehyde. All the children, regardless of age, were interested in the pig's heart ("cool!").

Thompson talked about the heart, how it beats and rests between beats, and then asked all the children to trace the outline of their body on a large sheet of paper, mothers and older children helping younger children where needed. She instructed the children to color and cut out the heart, and paste it in the right location on the outline of his or her body. After the session Thompson distributed kits with pictures of human organs, along with text about each organ's function. The children went home with the

A Partnership Between Families and Schools

kits and with directions to complete all the organs. Older children received additional and more advanced material. Thompson lamented later that she should have thought to require parental attendance at this particular class, as the mothers who did attend would be better equipped to help the child complete the course. She did not seem to realize what a magnificent job she had done in captivating a room of children of all ages.

In addition to developing and delivering a fine one-room schoolhouse learning experience, Thompson provided, and still provides, assistance to parents in finding curricular materials and designing their home program. She spends 1 to 2 hours with each, advising them on materials, going through catalogs, discussing how the older child can get high school credit, and so forth. She often can provide free materials—samples from publishers sent to the district. In addition, the district offers up to $100 in materials to the family. Some children dropped out of the program when their families acquired computers. Observing that some of her families are low-income and cannot afford computers, Thompson remarked, "I feel more than I ever have in my teaching that I am helping people."

Partnership in Education (II)

When I called the Partnership in Education (II; or PI) program in Chimacum, Washington, explaining that I was visiting public school programs for home schoolers, Kit Pennell admonished, "We have nothing to do with home schooling. We're public! Public! Public!" One of the teachers, Marci VanCleve, started a predecessor program, the Chimacum Studies Program, for home schoolers, in the school year 1984–1985. Originally, the Office of the Superintendent of Public Instruction (the OSPI) had funded the off-campus program easily. However, in 1992–1993, the OSPI became more rigorous about demanding seat time as a condition to receiving state foundation aid. Since then, Chimacum has considered its program a full-time alternative program, with a strong parent component. VanCleve calls it a "33–33–33 student–parent–teacher partnership." Under the classification used in this article, it is a public school independent study program.

As a public school teacher, VanCleve had become concerned that seat time seemed ineffective, at least for some students. She felt many students needed more individualized attention. She recognized that "a kid can sit at home at a computer and have the world at his or her fingertips." However, she quickly added that this was now an off-campus program. "We are not home-based. Students use the Chimacum curriculum, materials, and so forth." This is, then, exclusively an independent study program, although

167

P. M. Lines

the teachers are so sensitive to the individual wishes of families that there will appear to be little difference between this and part-time home schooling, from the family point of view. The district tends to treat the program as an intervention rather than an option for families, although the families often tend to see it in another light.

The program kicks off each year with a potluck. Throughout the year, there are parent conferences of ½ to 1 hour each week for each child. A parent who feels that this is unnecessary may reduce that time and use a report form on the child's program. The program offers 4-hour classes aimed at various cultural learning, including research on the art, foods, and games of different cultures. Some of the formal classes are offered every other year. In 1997–1998, there was some thought about abandoning the individual services to families, but about 100 families indicated that they wished to keep them.

At the time of the site visit (spring 1995), there were four teachers, mostly part time, at 2.6 FTEs. The program shared an administrator busy with other programs, leaving the teachers to do almost all the planning, developing, scheduling, evaluating, and training. The program enrolled 67 K–12 students (full-time). In addition, the program served one English-as-a-second-language student (who was Russian) and four special education students attending the adjacent elementary school, and one part-time and one home-schooled student. The last two received no conference time or record keeping. They could attend as long as there was room in a class. The teachers also tutored a number of at-risk children who were regularly enrolled.

The program for the day of the site visit involved training parents for their role in the education of kindergartners and first graders. Four mothers and five small children arrived about 9:00 a.m. One mother had questions before they started about placement at a private school. One of the teachers advised her to be cautious. "You can get lost over there ... all ages ... big kids ... It's a little scary." She advised the parent to write down what she wanted for her child, and to remember that certain approaches work best in classrooms with children of varied abilities and school officials usually want to maintain that balance.

The parent training sprang from one of the teacher's weekend training sessions and focused on child-led education. Topics ranged from the attention span of a small child for structured learning (not more than 1 hr) to letter formation and writing. The children nearby worked with computers or made play-dough sculptures. One small girl left her activity to sit on her mother's lap and diverted her mother's attention. Although the teacher tried to persuade her to return to the activity, the child remained. Another girl also appeared, but she made no effort to distract her mother.

Students tend to stay in the program for about 2 years. Some students go back to the campus school; some go to home schooling. They believe that

A Partnership Between Families and Schools

part-time school and part-time in the PI Program does not work well for elementary school students because of "conflict with the classroom teacher." Evidence of success is anecdotal. The teachers believe that the program serves children who do not fit into a regular classroom on campus, including those operating at very low and very high achievement levels. It's an "eccentric population" of "those that can't settle into a campus." VanCleve remarked, "Joey Johnson [not his real name] would fail in five minutes on campus." Wester added that "60 to 90% of our children won't respond to the methods you are supposed to use on campus."

The teachers talked about their experience in positive terms. Nita Wester remarked, "I can't go back to a regular classroom. I would be too worried about being ineffective." She subscribes to Gardner's theory of multiple intelligences and talks about how the program allows development for different children. VanCleve added, "You have to be dedicated to it. It's a unique philosophy." She talked about the ideas of W. Edward Deming and William Glasser's transference of these ideas to schools. "Boss management doesn't work." Schools must be responsive to customers; individualized program leads to success, not efficiency. Wester, who has a contract for 80% of her time, believes she is working about 60 hours a week:

We're doing this because we are all committed educators. I'm striving to change the education structure. The faster we have some options and a practical working model, the better it is. Money is a big program. We don't value kids in our society.

VanCleve also noted that in regular classes, "teachers become defensive; they cling to old ways; they are afraid of change; they have low self-esteem." Finally, to the extent that the program attracts hard-to-teach children, it can ease the task of the regular classroom teacher.

The program had not changed much by 1998–1999. There were five part-time teachers, for 2.8 FTE on the faculty, and 63 students in Grades 1 to 12. VanCleve and Wester are still there. The emphasis has remained family-centered, with a conscious effort to provide child-directed education, following the ideas of John Holt, an early writer and advocate of home schooling. VanCleve is now also interested in the ideas of Stephen Covey and considering how they might be applied to the program.

Bainbridge Island School District Options Program

In 1992, David Guterson, the novelist, was an English teacher at the Bainbridge Island High School, an author of a popular book on home

P. M. Lines

schooling, and a home schooling parent. He joined forces with an assistant superintendent, and together they planned a program in summer 1992. By fall, the district created its new Options Program, providing only an empty room and a newly hired coordinator, Marilyn Place, who had a K–8 certificate. Place worked on a flexible, part-time basis; students enrolled part-time and participated for an agreed-on number of hours per week, on a flexible schedule. By spring 1995, 38 children were enrolled, ages 6 to 13, in Grades 1 to 8. This represented more than a third of the 107 home-schooled children registered in the district at the time. Place believed compliance with the filing law was good and that she did in fact serve about one third of the district's home schoolers.

There is one program for the K–3 contingent and another for the older group. There are courses in writing and art, and a book and drama club. The center offers a room with materials where parents may work with their own children. The center plans field trips twice a month to such places as a children's museum, art museums, and so forth. A number of families who have not enrolled their children come in for ancillary services, including consulting, use of facilities, and assessment. A parent steering committee, originally meeting monthly, meets three times a year. Parents also volunteer to help with the program.

On the day of the site visit in spring 1995, the older group was meeting to learn about stream quality and was starting a project to help the county measure quality in its streams. In attendance were two fathers, seven mothers, an interested property owner, 15 children in the 7- to 9-year age range, one child age 12, and one child age 6. The session began with more or less conventional classroom instruction. A county ecologist specializing in community education passed around preserved stream insects, explaining their life cycle and habitat. With another teacher, she told two children's stories, which incidentally related to the lesson involving the condition of streams and wetlands. One was the story of a crayfish, who strayed too far from the water and whose eyes dried out. Blind, the crayfish found his way back by identifying the trees he bumped into: When he found an alder he knew he was near water, and when he found a willow he knew he was on the water's edge. The ecology expert also showed a short video on insects in streams, discussing signs of a healthy stream, what to look for, and how to do a water survey.

The group then left in private vehicles for a stream nearby, where they took two samples, following instructions. Some of the boys tended to stray, chasing each other around the field. All of the children, including the boys, gathered around when the ecology expert summarized the findings from the first stream sample. Most of the children were attentive to the procedures and helped out. The work consisted of dredging the bottom

170

A Partnership Between Families and Schools

and sifting through the mud on screens for insects, placing the insects in containers, and classifying and counting them. The first stream sample was accomplished with much adult work. The second was almost exclusively managed by the children. Students and parents planned to continue gathering samples for a year, at different sites, conveying results via modem to a city computer that would track stream quality for the island.

By 1998–1999, the number of children participating in the Options program had grown from about 40 to about 80, about half of whom were receiving only ancillary services such as testing. The other half accounted for five FTEs, with each child spending only about 2 to 4 hours on site. After some talk of expansion, most of the participants urged the district to keep it small. This means that there would be, at the most, two FTE teaching faculty, including Place and two other part-time faculty, and a secretary. Plans are to offer more multiage classroom opportunities and to mandate parental involvement. The program allows high school students to obtain a degree from the Bainbridge Island High School. The center plans to move to a new location, as the district's building program makes space available. The decision to keep the program small means that there is usually a waiting list.

Parent Assisted Learning Services

The Tacoma School District, third largest in the state, at the outset of the study offered a program, Parent Assisted Learning Services (PALS), for children in Grades 1 to 8. PALS had focused on counseling parents and considered the children to be full-time enrolled. Ninety percent of the students in the program previously had attended a regular public school setting and had been floundering. School counselors steered these children into the program because of their specific needs. Since its inception in January 1990 until the time of the visit in spring 1994, the program had enrolled approximately 40 students, of which about 20 were currently active, from among more than 300 home schoolers registered with the school district aged 8 and older. The Instructional Resource Lab is open from 2:00 to 4:30 p.m. Monday through Friday. The program also offered testing for children in Grades 4, 8, 9, 10, and 11 (the testing sequence for public school students). The teacher provided parents with a copy of the learning objectives for Grades 1 to 8 as well as the tests reflecting these objectives. The lab had eight computer stations in a large and pleasant room, conference tables, and a few books.

Parents would begin with a conference with the PALS teacher and continue to meet weekly between 9:30 a.m. and 5:00 p.m., Monday through

P. M. Lines

Friday, with the teacher to plan instruction. The parents also could borrow textbooks and workbooks (regularly adopted materials for Tacoma School District). The teacher maintained a portfolio for each child. The teacher, who was in her first year and was African American, talked about the African American home schooling parents. They recently developed their own support group, having found that the nearby White groups were heavily involved either in a religious or philosophical orientation that did not appeal to them. This teacher's supervisor, in contrast, expressed some disapproval of home schooling. "It is an intellectual isolationism. One of the reasons the parents take their kids out of school is because they don't want them exposed to their peer groups or their teacher." The program was offering the kinds of services that Yeager's study suggests interest home schoolers the least (Yeager, 1999). Over time, the program transformed completely, moved to another facility, changed its name to the Alternative Learning Center, and became available for high school students only. This new program enrolled only full-time students in school-supervised independent study, with 170 enrollees as of fall 1999.

The Maywood Center and Successors

The remainder of the programs visited initially pivoted around a computer lab, often with field trips and other classes added on the side. The largest of these at the time of the site visits was the Maywood Center. It began in 1987 as a technology center offering computer-aided instruction and services to students at risk of dropping out. The Center began as a project of the Highline Foundation, a local nonprofit organization formed to support the public schools, with grants from the Control Data Corporation and the Boeing Company. At the prompting of the district superintendent, in January 1991 the Maywood Center opened its doors to home schoolers, accepting a handful of home schooling children on a pilot basis. Despite the lack of publicity, applications came flooding in, prompting the center to close its doors to new enrollees temporarily. With 200 applicants on a waiting list, the district had to rewire the center, which had insufficient power to support the computer network housed there.

By the 1993–1994 school year, the Maywood Center was serving more than 500 students. Approximately 300 were part-time home schoolers; another 100 students had dropped out of high school and were preparing for the General Educational Development (GED) test; about 110 students had transferred recently into the district and needed an interim program because their new classroom has progressed too far into the semester. Finally, about 40 high school seniors, a few credits shy of that needed for

A Partnership Between Families and Schools

graduation, were taking up to 1.5 credits after school hours to fill the gap. Maywood required all seniors to enroll at a public high school.

In addition to access to computer hardware and software, the Center offered early childhood programs and assistance to secondary students in making the transition from school to career training, work, or college. It provided advice and information on scholarships for these students. The center was a registered site for GED testing, which took place at least monthly. It had a state-of-the-art computer lab, with two large interconnected file servers, each capable of handing five CD-ROMs. One server managed the PLATO 2000 Integrated Learning System, a sequenced Grade 3 to 12 instructional program in mathematics, language arts, social studies, science, computer technology, and career information. The other managed computer stations available for use of other computer instruction programs for K through Grade 12. There was a library of more than 200 commercial programs, which was growing, and 9,000 titles in the public domain. The center tested Microsoft educational programs before their release to the general public and so obtained some software free of charge. There were 60 workstations, and 50 used computers purchased from a Boeing surplus sale waiting to be upgraded. The center had a full-time teacher, certified for K through Grade 12, and a computer specialist. The computer specialist was then the official manager of the homeschool program, as well as the person who would install the new chips in the 50 second-hand Boeing computers and assist students at their stations. The center offered workshops on such things as the use of Microsoft Windows, Write, Terminal, Notebook, Works, Word, Publish, and other programs; search tools; and how to use the National Science Foundation's Internet electronic resources. Like several other of the programs described, the Maywood Center required parents to remain with their children while at the center. By the winter of 1992–1993, the center remained open 8 hours daily, including Saturday and Tuesday evening. Home schoolers were requesting more evening hours.

In summer 1997, the Maywood Center closed. The Highline Foundation changed its name to the Foundation for Education Choice and determined to leave Highline and start a new center in nearby Kent. The plan became one of starting such a center every year in a different location and leaving the old center to be operated by the district where it was located. The first full-time teacher at the old center, Marcus Watkins, took over the new center, which was renamed the Manhattan Homeschool Center and relocated to the Manhattan School. (The original building was found unsafe for children.) The new building offered more spacious rooms. Watkins, reporting to a busy principal in another building, found that he had virtual direction of the program. Although the number of home schoolers dropped (a large

173

P. M. Lines

number migrated to the new Kent Learning Center), he established a similar program in the new building. It has a preschool corner for younger siblings, about 20 computer stations, and two pleasant and spacious classrooms. The Manhattan School continued the home schooling component but not the other components of the old Maywood Center. It also added a small on-site school for children who were enrolled full-time. The two classrooms house these children, many of whom have siblings in home schooling in the computer lab next door. The classrooms are mixed-age, with one devoted to math and science and the other to language arts, history, and related topics. The home schooling children sometimes participate in the class offerings.

Watkins stresses that his center still actively encourages the part-time home schooling student to use the facilities and does not try to steer them into the full-time option. In the home school section, other classes are offered. Watkins, who is, among other things, a history teacher, is planning a home schooling class on naval warfare and was readying tiny replicas of ships for a reenactment of the Battle of Trafalgar. He also would like to teach Russian and German, but he finds the children interested mainly in learning Spanish. There are about 100 home schooling children at the Manhattan Center, in addition to the children enrolled full-time in the school.

The Kent Choice Learning Center opened in fall 1997 with about 200 full-time students; they are on campus full-time. It started with Grades 3 to 12 and now serves Grade 2 as well. Unlike the Maywood Center, it emphasizes the campus school and has only a handful of part-time home schooling students. It also serves about 50 older students who are at risk of dropping out and some high school students needing special courses. It offers multiage and multigrade classrooms, with a strong parental participation component. Parents are required to volunteer at least 10 hr per month in the classroom. Approximately 70% of the students were home schooled prior to enrolling. Part-time students who are registered with the center may use the computer lab and take workshops on an occasional class. This may be the first public school established almost entirely by former home schoolers.

HomeLink Technology Center

Larry Pierson and Gary Albers are teachers with the Battle Ground School District, who have, despite their youthful appearances, almost 50 years of combined teaching experience. They have team taught for almost as many years, and together they planned the HomeLink Technology Center. The long years as a team shows in the way they hand their presentation back and forth. After Albers observed, "You can't do this from the top

A Partnership Between Families and Schools

down," Pierson added, "Parents can be the best teachers." Then Albers gave the example. One of their families determined the number of speed bumps per foot based on the hum of the tires. The matter came up spontaneously, and the father adjusted the speed of the car to match "C" on a son's trombone. Knowing the frequency of "C" and the speed of the car, the boys calculated the bumps per foot. The family then stopped to measure the distance and confirm the calculation. Albers concluded, "Home schooling parents are serious about education."

Starting in about 1992, and for nearly 3 years, Albers and Pierson researched the state law and talked to people about the idea of a home schooling program in their district. The superintendent supported them from the start. When HomeLink Center opened in the 1992–1993 school year, about 3% of the school-age children in Battle Ground were home schooling—284 out of 8,500 total students. As there was little space, the center rented a storefront in a business mall. By spring 1994, the center boasted 30 Macintosh computers and 170 computer programs. It offered instruction for K through Grade 12 in technology, field trips, and a contract-based high school program leading to a diploma. Parents were required to attend with their child. The program established a parent advisory team to help with the overall direction of the school. Parents served (and still serve) rotating 2-year terms. The program relied mainly on the computer lab. However, in addition to Albers and Pierson, in 1994 the center hired a half-time teacher to consult with parents and students; she also began planning about 50 field trips per year. The hours of operation are school hours and one evening per week. From the start, parents were requesting expanded classes.

By the close of the 1998–1999 school year, the center had grown to become the largest of all the programs visited. It was serving 1,120 active students from Battle Ground and other nearby districts. It continued to offer part-time enrollment to home schooling students. Such students could take up to 9 hr of elective classes per week on-site for K through Grade 3, or 12 hr for Grades 4 through 8. HomeLink also had developed a variety of full-time enrollment options with required on-campus attendance for part of each week. One such option is a full-time program for Grades 7 through 12 leading to a diploma (with further options within the plan involving full-time on-campus attendance for 4-day classes) or public school independent study supported by consulting. Another is a "ParentPartnered" program for K through Grade 8, involving some required on-campus time, regular consultations with parents, and testing. There is an option for children who have experienced academic difficulty in a traditional classroom setting.

HomeLink also added a campus in nearby Camas, Washington. In response to parent demand, the most dramatic expansion came in classroom

175

P. M. Lines

offerings—more than 100 classes, many using a wide range of teachers under contract with the Battle Ground School District. From a modest storefront, it has moved into facilities that include 37 classrooms and offices. The parental participation requirement now varies according to the option chosen. For example, parents of children in Grades 5 to 8 promise to assist in the classroom for a half a day each month. Other parents promise to attend conferences and participate in other ways. Its lively World Wide Web page is http://www.parentpartners.net.

Extended Learning Family

For more than 25 years, the Bethel Public Schools has operated the Extended Learning Family, a complex of three schools and a day care center: Challenger High, Voyager Junior High, Explorer Elementary, and Discovery Day Care. The complex serves a student body 20% to 25% of which are racial minorities, including African American, Korean (military families), Guamanian, and Samoan. This is a larger proportion than is found in the district as a whole.

The complex is largely teacher-founded and teacher-led. A teacher had initiated the program and became its first director. Pat Dempsey, the head teacher in the Challenger High School program, was teacher of the year statewide in 1991–1992. In the early 1990s, several home-schooled students enrolled in Dempsey's high school program. Dempsey believes they did so because they liked the teaching and learning style offered in the program. By spring 1995, the center was promoting its program for home schoolers and had 27 home schooling students, all of high school age, for an equivalent of 21 FTEs. A number were on campus full-time, mostly seniors who were satisfying a local school board requirement for full-time on-campus attendance in the senior year to receive a high school degree. Those on campus full-time still considered themselves "home schoolers." As Dempsey put it, it's "an attitude, a commitment that the parents make, a desire for shared responsibility in the child's schooling." The bulk of the home schooling students came in part-time and chiefly used the PLATO software available in the computer lab. Two had signed up for a full-time contract with a teacher, just as would the students at risk of dropping out. Dempsey has found PLATO excellent for use with high-risk students and was pleased to find it useful to home schoolers as well. Some of the home schooling group also have attended classes at the high school. In addition, the center provided ancillary services to 48 students. The computer lab was open and staffed 10 to 12 hours a day, including most evenings of the week. Some students came in during the day, but the early evening was most popular.

176

A Partnership Between Families and Schools

In the 1994–1995 school year, Dempsey had 292 contacts with 171 different families. This was at a time when the district could account for 306 home schooling students meeting filing requirements. Dempsey, who keeps a log of these contacts, believed that of those she talked to, 33.8% of the contacts indicated academic reasons for home schooling, 17.9% indicated personal safety reasons, 12.3% indicated values (including philosophical and religious), 12.3% indicated special education, and 5.6% indicated health. Twenty percent indicated other reasons. The concern for personal safety may be a reflection of this district. In the 1985–1986 school year, three students were killed on the grounds of the Spanaway Junior High School. By the 1998–1999 school year, the number of total registered home schoolers in Bethel was 525. The home schooling program has continued much as it had at its founding, with 20 FTEs using the program and with early evening lab hours three nights a week and parent participation. Dempsey is still heading the project, and she has begun to think about ways in which the program might evolve.

Central Kitsap Off-Campus Program

The Central Kitsap School District encompasses Silverdale and Bremerton, home to a large naval facility. In 1990, home schoolers asked the superintendent to create a program for them. Many families already had enrolled their children part-time in classes in the district, but they thought a center could offer expanded services. Some hoped this would help their older child secure a high school diploma. The program began with a budget of $20,000 for materials, housing in a portable behind the administration building, and Bill Dunn as a teacher. The district routinely transferred a second teacher, who lasted 5 days. After a more careful search and more detailed explanation of the program to the prospective candidate, it picked Al Parker, a junior high school teacher of 22 years. Parker took to the new challenge like a duck to water. He allowed that he missed his seventh graders, but quickly added, "I like doing this. I can't tell you how much I like this. ... Someone is always saying thanks."

About 35 children started using the program, and within a year it had grown to serve 100. During the first year, Dunn and Parker started developing curricula. They then relied heavily on education contracts entered between teacher, parent, and child, but they now use regular curricular materials. The center required students to have at least 6 hours of instructional contact a month, excluding field trips. Parents had to meet with an off-campus instructor once a quarter to discuss design of educational programs and the student's progress. The program also administered tests of

P. M. Lines

reading and mathematics, on request. By the 1994–1995 school year, there were 260 children (110 FTEs), about 65 of whom were of high school age, and a waiting list of 100. The children were a diverse group, including national merit scholars, pregnant girls, and young mothers, with their parent or grandparent providing the home supervision. In that year, the center added a director, a teaching/consulting staff of five, and a special education instructor. On Fridays, 60 or 70 of the students went bowling.

Parker described the program as "a classic help system for homeschoolers" and for a handful of students whom no one else has been able to help. A typical schedule would involve enrichment classes on Wednesday, tutoring on Tuesday, testing on Mondays, and four to five field trips in a month. One involved a 3-day camping trip to Blake Island, home of the Tillicum Indians. In addition to planned instruction in geology, astronomy, marine sciences, boat safety, and wilderness first aid, students watched the Tillicum Dancers and participated in a beach cleanup along with state parks personnel and the Tillicum Tribe.

I joined a field trip planned around Kitsap Peninsula Day. The teachers and about 30 children of all ages and approximately 20 mothers and fathers took a bus to Olympia to tour the state capitol. I later sat in on a parent advisory committee in spring 1995. Parents were contemplating a junior/senior high school social activity for the approximately 80 children in that grade range. Some argued for a social event, others for participation in community work for credit. The committee consulted a parent questionnaire. Some parents wanted to end the requirement that a parent attend with the child, some wanted to see more team projects, and others wanted more science and arts instruction. Many wanted academic credit for field trips. There was a complaint that the enrichment classes were overcrowded. Much more was discussed. Parents were ready to pay extra for a specialist to lead classes and help those using the school science lab in the late afternoon.

By the 1998–1999 school year, the program had undergone major changes. It was emphasizing on-campus and independent study, and it had 275 children enrolled full-time. Many were in classes taking university-track courses. A tutor was helping children with college mathematics preparation. A parent who had enrolled a child until she was transferred to Virginia by the Navy continued to participate and offered an on-line advanced mathematics class. The computer lab was operating on extended time. Transfer students were using the program to help catch up on selected subjects that they had missed in their prior schools. There were seven full-time faculty members, three secretaries, a librarian, and two assistant teachers in the enrichment programs. The teachers, who were part-time, offered such rare courses as astronomy and deaf-language

A Partnership Between Families and Schools

courses. Four children were graduating. Enrolled students were taking up to three classes at a time, with the remainder of their studies continued under parent supervision off-campus. Students included a large segment of those requiring special education; another large segment included military families with a parent stationed at a nearby naval base. There was a waiting list of 100, with room for only about 35 new students each year. The district now limits enrollment to children from the district.

Pathways Storefront School

In spring 1994, two friendly adversaries—Bill Hainer, a retired leader of the Washington Education Association (an affiliate of the National Educational Association) and Ben Edland, a former school superintendent—got together with Marion Cupp, director of special education, and planned a computer-managed learning program for Grades 7 through 12. They sold the Franklin Pierce School District on the idea and, by fall, they had a storefront location, with easy parking and bus service. Among the goals of the program was "Recognition of parents as primary teachers for their students." This was to be an alternative education program that allowed students to meet graduation requirements. It would provide diagnostic assistance to help design an individual learning plan for each student and involve self-paced and self-directed study. Plans were to give a large role to learning software, videotapes, and similar resource material, although during the site visit, text books were in greater use than the computers. Sports participation would be made available at the student's "home school" (the school that the student would attend if in attendance). The program allowed students to attend part-time at the Storefront School and part-time "somewhere else the rest of the time." Early in the program, as the state rules on state foundation support became more stringent on seat time for younger students, the program scaled back to Grades 9 through 12. Many students are now enrolled full-time, although some are part-time and retain their home schooling status. In addition, a few students are enrolled at other schools and attended selected classes. Once enrolled, the full-time students may complete their work in local libraries, their home, or other locations within the district and still take advantage of the Storefront services.

The day of the visit, many high school-age students were using the computers or obtaining tutoring. Those present included a handful of pregnant girls and other students considered at risk of dropping out. As the program matured, it continued to attract at-risk students, but the growth was among students who were doing well in high school but who were not happy there.

179

P. M. Lines

According to Al Prentice, the new head teacher, the majority are "intro-verted" girls, often in honors courses and above grade level. In the 1998–1999 school year, the program attracted about 125 FTEs, or about 150 students. It had added grade levels and was serving Grades 6 to 12. There were 4.9 FTE faculty, with plans to add another next year, for 5.4 FTE faculty.

Home/School Academic Learning Lab

Tom Snyder, a graphics designer, had worked with the Gig Harbor School District for 2 months tutoring students needing extra help to remain in a regular classroom or needing independent study for a special reason, as in the case, for example, of a student ready for fifth-grade reading and first-grade math. Snyder, who knew a number of home schooling parents, thought the tutoring program might appeal to them. Together, they presented the idea of a home schooling learning center to the district. The board was receptive, and space was made available at the Henderson Alternative School, a district school then in operation for more than 20 years, serving mostly teenagers in need of special counseling and guidance.

Home/School Academic Learning Lab (HALL) began by offering individualized curriculum aimed at the K to Grade 8 range. The program combined parental involvement, technology, and a few extra opportunities. For example, the home schoolers had access to the gymnasium for 2 to 3 hours per day, swimming lessons at a local high school, and a period for free swimming there. District textbooks were also available. HALL remained mostly self-contained, although the principal of Henderson approved purchases. In the 1993–1994 school year, HALL began using the Henderson school for high school credits, an attraction to older home schoolers who wanted a graded transcript and a diploma. The two programs also shared a teacher. For the most part, however, the home schoolers did not interact with the alternative school students, because, as the principal explained, the age differences did not lend itself to the practice. By spring 1994, there was a faculty of 2.5 FTEs and 160 children (about 50 FTEs). The following year, after some disagreement over program direction, Snyder had left and a new teacher had taken his place. The number of enrolled students fell somewhat, to 135 (41 FTE) children in K–8 range. Parents provide classroom instruction 2 days a week. In the 1994–1995 year, 185 home schooling students requested and received testing. Gig Harbor offers home schoolers the California Achievement Test and provides results to parents only.

By spring 1995, the program was experimenting with some integration with the alternative school. It offered a combined Washington state history class and combined student assemblies. Vision testing was open to all. The

A Partnership Between Families and Schools

students at Henderson Bay use the HALL computer lab. The Hall students sometimes use the Henderson program, including use of contract learning. The teacher–consultant for K–8 students, Lynn Whitener, remarked, "Getting away from the traditional school day has allowed creative programming."

By the 1998–1999 school year, the basic facilities were much the same, with a principal and two teachers, a computer lab specialist, and an office assistant. A small lending library was added. However, the program rules were emphasizing the parent-partnered or independent study option, with its full-time enrollment requirements. Contract learning was used extensively in K through Grade 12. As required by state law, a minimum of 5 hours on site was required for all. A meeting with a teacher consultant was required every 45 days to review the plan and evaluate the student's portfolio. On-site class offerings range from art; an integrated science, math, and art curriculum; some music and dramatic classes; and computer classes. Four times each year, students display their work at a curriculum fair.

Part-time contracted learning is also available, but only for students who are part-time enrolled in another district school. There are a limited number of true home schooling students—that is, those whose parents have filed and not surrendered their state-required declaration of intent to provide home schooling. HALL enrolls 15 home schoolers on a space-available basis; they must live in the district. These students use the computer lab, enroll in classes, use textbooks, and receive testing and consulting services. The district obtains state per-pupil support only for the proportion of actual seat time to full-time for these students. These students account for only five FTEs at the most in a year. There is a waiting list.

A Composite of Computer Lab Experiences

To give the flavor of the programs with computer labs, I describe a composite of the programs. One is likely to find a handful of children, often with a parent. For example, at one center, one finds two boys playing computer games while their mother reads by herself. In a separate room, a group of families are learning Japanese with videotapes. All the members of each family are participating. They are planning a trip to Japan together. In the outer area, programs are on display, including music, material on the French impressionists, a visit to Sesame Street (Letters!), and a story machine. There are brochures for various other learning experiences, including one from a nearby parks department.

On the next day, five younger home schoolers and five of junior or senior high school age are very busy. The older children are using word processors. Two are siblings, with their mother. The mother remains most of

181

P. M. Lines

the time with the daughter, who is writing a poem and using a graphics program to produce a greeting card. At points during this session, the girl enlists help from both her mother and from the district's home schooling teacher. The two women turn to the program manual and finally ask the computer teacher for help. When the card is done, she and her daughter play a game based on geometrical concepts. She moves over to her son's station briefly, after he has indicated that he has a problem. Her son begins writing a story, but after about half an hour begins playing the same computer game with the other boy. They spend some of the time just talking. The teacher moves around and offers help where it is needed. She spends extra time with one girl. The two boys work almost without adult assistance the entire session, although a computer hardware problem provoked a flurry of attention until it was resolved. A second girl works alone. She asks for and receives no attention from the teachers. She stops working for about 15 min and watches the others. Then she turns to a typing tutor.

A third girl is working on a geometric drawing program (LOGO). She has a problem. Several times, the computer teacher from the next classroom offers help, as does the teacher and the mother of another home schooler. The girl remains frustrated. She needs the formula for the hypotenuse of a right triangle. Finally, I abandon my role as observer and provide it (and receive the girl's instant gratitude). Although three certified teachers were available, none seemed to recognize the problem she was facing. This slip was not a weakness of home schooling but of schools. Only 60% of 17-year-olds can compute with decimals, simple fractions, and percents; recognize geometric figures; solve simple equations; or use moderately complex mathematical reasoning (Campbell, Voelkl, & Donahue, 1997).

The third day, one finds a father with his two daughters, six mothers with eight children among them. The older children are working on a newsletter. Some of the mothers are using the photocopier, browsing materials, and talking to staff and each other about a project they have undertaken, while their children work at the computers alone. Late in the afternoon, a large number of parents file in for a parents' governing meeting. There is talk about the strain on the facility. "Let's not publicize it too much. It's getting harder to get in." Some of the parents wonder about the children in the same building who are in alternative schooling. One parent asks if weapons in the building might be a problem. Another asks about the number of pregnant girls. A teacher mentions that the alternative school has a 12-year-old girl expecting her second child. One mother is shocked. "My God, our life revolves around our little family!" There is some talk of how to serve the children from the alternative school. More than one parent group was considering a social event involving all the chil-

A Partnership Between Families and Schools

dren in the building, those in an alternative school and in the home schooling program.

Conclusions: Common Features, Trends, Sensitive Issues, and the Future

This intensive study of a small number of programs provides an initial
understanding of these programs, but it does not permit generalization to
similar programs in other policy environments. The study may suggest
hypotheses to be tested over time against observations of a larger number
of such programs. In that spirit, I offer a number of observations about the
common features in the programs, trends, and sensitive issues relating to
race, social status, control of education, and the future of such programs.

The state's interdistrict transfer law and substantial state funding per
child provide some incentive to offer these programs. The financial picture
is interesting, with most of the teachers running the programs feeling that
they were underfunded. Some careful study seems warranted to determine what the appropriate level of support would be for a program in
which parents participate so heavily. Although teacher time with students
may be reduced, time with parents increases.

These programs require interested home schooling families, of course.
Even if a majority of home schooling families would prefer not to use public school resources (Yeager, 1999), it appears that most districts will find
sufficient interest to support a program. In fact, there are now approximately twice as many such programs in eastern Washington. Second, interested public school teachers are critical to the success of the program. In
more than half of the programs examined, a teacher had started or helped
start the program. In the case of the Seventh Planet, this included the public school adoption of a previously private program, at the initiative of a
school principal acting in consultation with one of his teachers. In about a
third of the programs, the initiative was shared in a very quiet way: Home
schoolers simply began taking advantage of a program offered to at-risk
students. A responsive faculty then began tailoring the program to the
new constituency. School board support is essential, of course, as such programs almost always require budgetary and other authorizations at that
level. Finally, a key element appears to be the support of the superintendent. In every case, the superintendent actively supported the program, although in one case he did not promote it publicly.

The teachers who are drawn to these programs often prefer to work
part-time. In almost all the programs, there were several part-time teachers. Many of these had young children and were interested in home

183

P. M. Lines

schooling at a personal level. In addition, the teachers in all the programs were excited by the possibilities before them. All genuinely supported the home schooling option, even as they began to encourage home schoolers to enroll full-time in the program. In some cases, the teachers offer charismatic leadership, but most of the time the teachers were simply good, solid teachers who were selected by their district.

The most noticeable change over time was the growing tendency to encourage full-time enrollment. This was not, in my opinion, a case of a public school Trojan horse, as it has been called by one home schooling advocate. The motive seemed not to gain control of the curriculum, but to maximize the fiscal intake based on student count. State law allows almost $5,000 per student for full-time enrollment, compared to $300 per student for ancillary services and only a pro rata share of state assistance only for the time a student spends in direct contact with a teacher. Administrative costs mount as a center attempts to serve 80 children who constitute only 20 FTEs. Just keeping track of the seat time of a part-time child can generate considerable paperwork. (The most workable solution seems to be a low-tech sign-up sheet at the door.) Because of more lenient on-site requirements for older children, a handful of centers decided to offer programs to older children only. In any case, fiscal considerations have induced most of the centers to encourage parents to surrender their home schooling declaration of intent and to enroll their child full-time. The full-time enrollment option seems acceptable to most parents who probably learned to trust the teachers and others during the part-time enrollment period. Moreover, at this point, most of the parents in the full-time programs have had experience with home schooling, and most seem prepared to withdraw if they thought the curriculum or instructional practices were taking a wrong turn.

A second change over time was the tendency for those programs relying on computer labs as their focus to develop formal class offerings. The shift may be partially related to the drive to enroll children full-time, but there is ample evidence that parents were asking for these class offerings. Examination of programs in other policy environments would help sort out the causal factors behind this trend.

Race did not seem to be an issue, despite a belief among some professional educators that home schoolers are seeking to escape the public school melting pot. Most of the centers were located in predominantly White areas. Like home schoolers nationwide, those using these programs were predominantly White, but there were some persons of Color present in all the larger programs and some of the smaller programs. The somewhat greater proportion of minority-race children in alternative schools did not deter those home schoolers who initiated a program by first enroll-

184

A Partnership Between Families and Schools

ing their children part-time in such a school. The different ethnicity of the teacher was clearly irrelevant to the families choosing the Seventh Planet. One of the teachers in one of the centers thought there might be some home schoolers who were trying to avoid people with different cultural values and indicated that avoidance of minority-race persons did not seem to be the issue. Some home schoolers have expressed discomfort at sharing facilities with former dropouts. One teacher thought that this could be race-based but noted that the focus was on a boy who had witnessed a violent crime and a concern that one's child could be caught in the crossfire of a revenge shooting. In a few cases, home schooling families sharing facilities with an alternative school have considered joint social activities, but none of these vague plans have yet crystallized.

Another major issue, although one that was surmounted by almost all the public school teachers and administrators working in these programs, is philosophical. When public schools open their doors to home schooling families, they must operate in a very different way. Indeed, it looks as if the Trojan horse, if there is one, is sneaking into public school turf rather than into the home schooling enclave—that is, rather than losing control over home schooling, it seems more likely that home schoolers' ideas will influence public practices and curriculum. This new frontier for state and local education agencies represents a radically new service orientation toward families. Because home schooling parents are unlikely to send their children to a conventional school, public educators will attract home schoolers only if they are sensitive to their needs, preferences, and goals.

Certain fundamental features of these programs could become the model for tomorrow's education. The present paradigm calls for scheduling of groups of 30 same-age children for 5 to 6 hours a day for 180 days a year. It is possible that home schooling will produce a shift in the basic paradigm for education of children. In the new paradigm, children can learn alone or in groups from 2 to 30; they can be of widely different ages. Schools, teachers, and other professionals would provide the services; families would make the choices. Schools can advise them; offer curricular support; offer classes—on and off campus—and provide testing, transportation, and other auxiliary services. Parents and children can determine the mix each individual child will have of on- and off-campus classes, of independent study and guided study, of computer-assisted instruction, and of personal attention from a teacher.

If school districts are to attract home schoolers into a school, as these Washington districts are doing, they must be more flexible than school districts have been since parents gathered together to construct the one-room country schoolhouse. They must be ready to view each child as an individual, with an individual program. They must be ready to relinquish consid-

185

P. M. Lines

erable decision making to parents. They must heed advice from persons such as Jane Roland Martin, who urged professional educators to share their responsibilities with parents and community. She urged schools to see themselves, as they once did, as just one part of "the whole range of cultural custodians" (Martin, 1996). Professionals must stop treating their other partners like "humble assistants" or "dangerous rivals" (p. 10):

If we can envision an array of institutions, all of which share the tasks of preserving our vast cultural assets, see themselves and are seen by others as legitimate educational agents, and work together to transmit the [cultural] wealth, we will at least have a better idea of what to strive for.

References

Campbell, J. R., Voelkl, K. E., & Donahue, P. L. (1997). *NAEP 1996 trends in academic progress.* Washington, DC: National Center for Educational Statistics.

Dahm, L. (1996, October). Education at home, with help from school. *Education Leadership, 54*(2), 68–71.

Gold, S. D., Smith, D. M., Lawton, S. B., & Hyary, A. C. (Eds.). (1992). *Public school finance programs of the United States and Canada* (2 vols.). New York: American Education Finance Association.

Hawkins, D. (1996, February 12). Culture and ideas: Homeschool battles. *U.S. News & World Report* [Online]. Retrieved April 2, 1999 from the World Wide Web: http://www.usnews.com/usnews/issue/school.htm

Home School Legal Defense Association. (1998). *Analysis of the Edmonds school district "cyberschool" program.* Purcellville, VA: Author.

Martin, J. R. (1996). There's too much to teach: Cultural wealth in an age of scarcity. *Education Researcher, 25*(2), 4–10.

Ricke, K. M. (1999). *Public school superintendents' perceptions of cooperative sponsorships with home schools for extracurricular activities in Minnesota.* Unpublished master's thesis, St. Cloud State University, St. Cloud, MN.

Yeager, E. T. (1999). *A study of cooperation between home schools and public and private schools, K–12.* Unpublished doctoral dissertation, Texas A&M University, Commerce.

The Home Schooling Mother–Teacher: Toward a Theory of Social Integration

Susan A. McDowell

As a result of the findings emerging from a two-part research study, I have come to a very surprising and altogether unexpected conclusion concerning the majority of home schooling mother–teachers. They are closet feminists. Not feminists in the classic National-Organization-of-Women sense, mind you, but feminists nonetheless. Whereas the standard dictionary definition of *feminism* is "the doctrine advocating the same social, political, and economic rights for women as for men" (*Wordsmyth English Dictionary*, 1999), I believe that an appropriate definition of feminism—as operative for the home schooling mother—would read "the doctrine advocating the same social, political, and economic rights for home schooling mother–teachers as for the public and/or private educational system." As a group, home schooling mother–teachers are passionate about the education of their children,

SUSAN A. McDOWELL *is an educational researcher and writer and is Managing Editor of the* Peabody Journal of Education, *Peabody College of Vanderbilt University, Nashville, Tennessee.*

I thank Robert Crowson, David Bloome, and John Braxton (all of Peabody College of Vanderbilt University) for their comments on an earlier version of this article.

Requests for reprints should be sent to Susan A. McDowell, P.O. Box 148351, Nashville, TN 37214–8351. E-mail: Susan.A.McDowell@vanderbilt.edu

S. A. McDowell

highly informed concerning their legal rights and obligations, unhesitat-
ingly vocal in their opposition to any perceived infringement on or lessening of these rights, and generally suspicious and untrusting of
established institutions (Mayberry, Knowles, Ray, & Marlow, 1995).

One would scarcely allow that such "radical" feminist-seeming attitudes might spring from a group known to be primarily conservative
(77%), Republican (76%), and Christian (approximately 80%; Mayberry et
al., 1995, pp. 38–39). Nevertheless, the results of a quantitative and qualitative research study on the perceived impact of home schooling on the family in general and mother–teacher in particular led to this conclusion. The
results led in particular to the formation of a theory of social integration, of
which the previously cited "feminist factor" is an integral part.

It is the purpose of the article to present—as briefly and concisely as possible—the details of the qualitative portion of this research study in terms of
its (a) methodology; (b) research questions; (c) participant and site selection;
and (d) analysis and interpretation of interview, observational, and document data. The final section includes appropriate conclusions and details
the extrapolation of these conclusions into a theory of social integration.

Although the findings of the quantitative study are mentioned in the concluding section of this article, that particular portion of the research is not
detailed here for the simple reason that its findings—although supportive of
the qualitative study's findings—did not lead directly to the theory of social
integration that is the subject of this article. In brief, the quantitative study
indicated that the home schooling mother–teachers surveyed believed that
the process of home schooling had a positive impact on both their families
and themselves. Given its nature, however, the quantitative[1] study could
only tell us *how* home schooling mother–teachers felt, not *why* they felt the
way they did. It was the qualitative study, detailed in the following sections,
that provided some fascinating answers to that question.

Methodology

Selection of Research Design

Qualitative research presents the ideal framework with which to investigate the perceptions of the mother–teacher regarding home schooling
and its impact on both the family and herself, as one of the tenets of its research is the importance of letting the participants speak, and hearing the

[1]For a detailed look at the quantitative portion of this research study, please see
McDowell (1998).

The Home Schooling Mother–Teacher

participants speak, in their own voices. As LeCompte and Preissle (1993) pointed out, ethnographers "who describe cultural and behavioral patterns as they are viewed by the group under investigation reconstruct the categories that participants use to conceptualize their own experiences and world view" (p. 45). As home schoolers are the ones dealing with and living with—in every sense of the word—the home schooling process, they were logically the ones to inform the researcher about its perceived impact on family structure, roles, responsibilities, and so forth.

Qualitative methodology is particularly conducive to this variety of research; the only question remaining is what specific type of qualitative methodology to employ. According to Miles and Huberman (1994), "Qualitative research may be conducted in dozens of ways" (p. 5). For purposes of this research study, a grounded theory qualitative methodology was used; this methodology employs a social anthropological approach to data analysis:

[It] stays close to the naturalist profile ... extended contact with a given community, concern for mundane, day-to-day events, as well as for unusual ones, direct or indirect participation in local activities, with particular care given to the description of local particularities. (p. 8)

Grounded theory—in direct contrast to the quantitative portion of this study—is inductive in approach, as LeCompte and Preissle (1993) explained:

In a sense, deductive researchers hope to find data to match a theory; inductive researchers hope to find a theory that explains their data. ... That is, inductive research starts with examination of a phenomenon and then, from successive examinations of similar and dissimilar phenomena, develops a theory to explain what was studied. (p. 42)

Barney G. Glaser and Anselm L. Strauss are, as Lincoln and Guba (1985) noted, "generally credited with having coined the term" (p. 205) *grounded theory*. It is "theory that follows from data rather than preceding them" (Lincoln & Guba, 1985, p. 204). Glaser and Strauss (1967), in *The Discovery of Grounded Theory*, explained that "the basic theme in our book is the discovery of theory from data systematically obtained from social research" (p. 2). They elaborated on this concept further by explaining that

[Theory] must fit the situation being researched, and work when put into use. By "fit" we mean that the categories must be readily (not forcibly) applicable to and indicated by the data under study; by "work" we mean that they must be meaningfully relevant to and be able to explain the behavior under study. (Glaser & Strauss, 1967, p. 3)

189

S. A. McDowell

Over the last several years, Glaser and Strauss evidently have become sharply divided in their individual beliefs concerning the true definition of grounded theory, especially as concerns the "readily (not forcibly)" element described previously. According to Miles and Huberman (1994), Glaser continues to clarify "his own strongly inductive, emergent approach as the true version of grounded theory development, and suggests that Strauss's later work should be called 'full conceptual description'" (p. 238).

Because this research study used a guiding research question, Glaser most likely would consider that a true and pure version of grounded theory was not employed. However, as Miles and Huberman (1994) so logically pointed out,

> Highly inductive, loosely designed studies make good sense when experienced researchers have plenty of time and are exploring exotic cultures, understudied phenomena, or very complex social phenomena. But if you're new to qualitative studies, and are looking at a better understood phenomenon within a familiar culture or subculture, a loose, inductive design may be a waste of time. ... As Wolcott (1982) puts it, there is merit in openmindedness and willingness to enter a research setting looking for questions as well as answers, but it is "impossible to embark upon research without some idea of what one is looking for and foolish not to make that quest explicit" (p. 157). (p. 17)

As I was researching within the framework of a very familiar culture, a somewhat "tighter" (as in using a guiding research question) as opposed to a "looser" grounded theory approach was called for and implemented.

Research Methods

To provide effective triangulation, the research methods chosen for this study included (a) interviews, (b) observations, and (c) document analysis (home schooling magazines, newsletters, and Internet web sites). Each of these elements is detailed in the following sections.

Interviews.   The researcher interviewed a total of nine home schooling mothers, with the interviews taking place in a variety of locations, including the home schoolers' homes ($n = 5$), a large library at a church where two home schooling mothers worked part-time ($n = 2$), a conference room ($n = 1$), and a restaurant ($n = 1$). With the participant's permission, each interview was audiotaped, with the researcher privately dictating notes about

The Home Schooling Mother–Teacher

details of the interview (setting, impressions, etc.) into a cassette recorder immediately after each interview took place. To establish validity, transcripts of interviews were returned to participants for their approval.[2]

Observations. To conduct observations—the second element of the qualitative triangulated approach—in the most effective manner possible, a Checklist of Observational Elements was adapted from Merriam's (1988) *Case Study Research in Education: A Qualitative Approach.* This checklist was not physically carried to either interviews or observations, but I did endeavor to maintain an awareness of its elements throughout the observation process. I also took to heart other recommendations offered by Merriam (1988):

- Observers should be relatively passive and unobtrusive, put people at ease, learn how to act and dress in the setting.
- Collecting data is secondary to becoming familiar with the setting.
- Keep the first observations fairly short to avoid becoming overwhelmed with the novelty of the situation.
- Be honest but not overly technical or detailed in explaining what you are doing. (p. 91)

The actual observations of home schooling families took place (a) during the interview process itself, (b) at the 11th Annual Family Resource Fair sponsored by the Smoky Mountain Chapter of the Tennessee Home Education Association, (c) during a visit to a church attended primarily by home schoolers (The Church with the Home Schooling Heart), (d) while attending two distinct "learning" seminars presented by another local church and aimed specifically at home schooling parents and children, (e) during the 13th Annual Middle Tennessee Home Educators Association (MTHEA) conference held at another local church, and (f) while participating in a home schooling group's skating party. Photographs were taken at the curriculum fair (the 11th Annual Family Resource Fair), the conference of the MTHEA, and the skating party. Out of respect for the participants—and the inappropriateness of photography in the midst of these events—no photographs were taken during observations that were reli-

---

[2] Each participant was assigned a code name/number containing essential description information about the interviewee. For example, the participant who was coded "P3-I&P-Info1" was the third participant to be interviewed ("P3"), gave both ideological and pedagogical reasons as being equally important in the decision to home school ("I&P"), and was the first informant giving names of other potential study participants ("Info1"). For ease of discussion, participants also were assigned appropriate pseudonyms.

S. A. McDowell

gious in nature (i.e., attendance at a service of The Church with the Home Schooling Heart and the two "Learning How to Learn" seminars, which were offered as a part of a regular Wednesday night church service).

Analysis of documents.   The analysis of documents included examination of newsletters distributed by three home schooling organizations ("Smoke Signals," from the Smoky Mountain Chapter of the Tennessee Home Education Association; "Heart"—an acronym for "Home Educators Are Rutherford's Treasures"—from a home schooling group in Rutherford County, Tennessee; and "Family Christian Academy Newsletter: Dedicated to Helping Home Educators," published by the academy of the same name in a middle Tennessee county). Also examined were several home schooling magazines, and 61 home schooling sites on the Internet (for the full text of the literature review, as well as a listing of the home schooling Internet sites visited, see McDowell, 1998).

Research Questions

The Guiding Research Question

The guiding research question for the qualitative portion of this research project was, as was noted earlier, What effect does home schooling, as perceived by the mothers–teachers engaged in it, have on the family in general and the home schooling mother in particular?

Research Probes

Selected study participants (i.e., the mother–teacher in the home schooling family) were asked some very general questions—of a variety appropriate for a grounded theory approach—intended to simply "get the participant talking" about home schooling. Following is a list of the primary questions asked each participant, although, to preserve the conversational "feel" of an interview, they were not necessarily asked in the order presented:

1. How many children do you have? How many do you home school?
2. How long have you home schooled?
3. Why did you decide to home school?
4. Please describe a typical home schooling day.
5. What do you like best about home schooling?

The Home Schooling Mother–Teacher

6. What do you like least about home schooling?
7. Is there anything else you'd like to say about home schooling?

Selection and Recruitment of Participants

Selection and Sampling

Although some research into home schooling finds that only "89% of parent/tutors are female" (Lines, 1991, p. 17), other data conclude that "mothers were virtually always the primary teacher" (p. 17). Mayberry et al. (1995) reported that

> the results of previous studies demonstrated that the tasks associated with running home-based education programs were almost always carried out by mothers not employed in the paid labor force (Gladin, 1987; Mayberry, 1988; Wartes, 1988). Our study supports that finding: 63% of the mothers that we surveyed are responsible for 90% or more of the day-to-day operation of the home school. (p. 32)

Clearly, the major figure in home schooling—other than the children, of course—is the mother. As a result, this study interviewed and observed home schooling families wherein the mother was the primary instructor.

From this group of home schooling families, three smaller subsets were selected.[3] Miles and Huberman (1994) termed this sampling strategy "stratified purposeful," in that it "illustrates subgroups" and "facilitates comparisons" (p. 28). The first subset, made up of three families, consisted of those whose primary reason for home schooling was given as ideological (religious/philosophical). The second subset, composed of four families, consisted of those who cited pedagogical (academic/curriculum) concerns as their primary reason for choosing to home school. The final subset, made up of two families, consisted of those who cited ideological and pedagogical reasons as being equally important and as bearing equal weight in their decision to home school. The first two subsets were based on data that indicated that all the reasons given by families for home schooling could be condensed into two basic categories—the ideological and the pedagogical (Kutter, 1987; Van Galen, 1986). The third subset was added as a result of actual home schooling mother interview experiences.

Another sampling strategy was implemented, in conjunction with the stratified purposeful strategy cited previously, that strategy being the

---

[3]It should be noted that all mother–teachers interviewed were White.

S. A. McDowell

"snowball" or "chain" strategy. This sampling approach "identifies cases of interest from people who know people who know what cases are information-rich" (Miles & Huberman, 1994, p. 28). Because it was my intent to sample as wide and as diverse a population as possible, I used the services of more than one informant and, as a result, had several small "snowballs" rather than one large one.

Recruitment

Despite admonitions similar to the ones other researchers have experienced—"drop the home schoolers because they are way too secretive and will never let you in" (Page, 1996, p. 107)—I felt confident of easy admission and acceptance into home schoolers' homes, organizations, and functions. The reasons for this confidence were based primarily on a close relationship with my sister, who has home schooled her son for the past 8 years. In the role of sister, friend, and aunt, I have on occasion accompanied my home schooling sister to home schooling curriculum fairs, meetings, and group field trips. I believe that the reason I was not perceived as an outsider with possible negative intent, but was accepted and trusted by study participants, was due to this relationship.

Selection of Sites

The settings for this study included (a) homes wherein home schooling took place; (b) a church library, wherein some home schooling took place on a limited scale; (c) a department at a business, which served as the primary site of home schooling for one family; and (d) the different places where home schoolers gather for group events (see previous section Research Methods). According to LeCompte and Preissle (1993), "ethnographers must work in settings where behavior occurs naturally. They must go to their participants" (p. 95). The fact that the investigator conducted research on home schoolers in their own homes, at other places wherein home schooling took place, and at group events is evidence that this criteria was met in this research study.

Analysis of the Data

The data gathered in the qualitative portion of this study were analyzed using a tailored version of Wolcott's (1994) three-phase approach: description, analysis, and interpretation. Given the necessarily limited scope of this article, however, only the analysis and interpretation of data are presented and discussed here.

The Home Schooling Mother–Teacher

Analysis and Interpretation of the Interview Data

Analysis

As I studied, read, and reread the transcripts of these interviews, certain elements seemed to emerge again and again. Any subject or topic area that surfaced in more than one interview was considered an element, or finding, and is therefore presented as a microcategory. The larger categories—within which entire interviews clearly belonged and could be placed—are presented as macrocategories. The microcategories are detailed in the following section.

Microcategories. The 11 categories that emerged from the nine interviews conducted included (a) "Flexibility," (b) "Home Schooling as a Stress Reducer," (c) "Socialization," (d) "Children Actually Teach Themselves," (e) "Other Home Schoolers," (f) "The Public and/or Private Schools," (g) "Housework," (h) "Concerns Regarding Personal Shortcomings as a Teacher," (i) "Testing Home Schoolers," (j) "Attention Deficit Disorder," and (k) "Racial Tensions in the Public Schools." As was noted previously, each of these elements surfaced in at least two different interviews.

Macrocategories. When considering these interviews on a larger scale, clear similarities and some startling differences began to emerge and form two distinct categories of home schooling mothers, categories that I termed the *classic home schoolers* and the *pseudo home schoolers. Pseudo* was chosen as the appropriate term for the latter group because one of its definitions is "apparently similar" (Morris, 1985, p. 999). In that all of the participants interviewed were home schooling their children—at least in the technical sense—they are apparently similar. However, as the following discussion makes clear, several surprising and important differences existed between some of the participants interviewed.

Two of the interviews—the ones with "Cissy" (P7-Ped) and "Susie" (P8-Ped-Info4)—clearly had a different feel to them. Although both women were pleasant, neither one displayed the sometimes fervent, impassioned enthusiasm for home schooling evidenced by the other interviewees. Further meditation on these interviews—along with frequent review of the transcripts and field notes—revealed other ways in which Cissy's and Susie's interviews were similar to each other, but different from the other seven interviews. For example, when I interviewed all the other home schooling mothers, the children were eager to talk to me—showing me some of their projects, playing a musical instrument for me, voluntarily engaging me in conversation, and otherwise displaying

195

S. A. McDowell

an open and friendly attitude toward "the lady who came to talk about home schooling." I could not help but notice the different attitudes displayed by Cissy's and Susie's children. Cissy's home-schooled daughter had informed her mother that she "didn't want to talk to me," and, when I actually met the daughter during the course of the interview, she would not make eye contact with me or respond in any way to my smile and greeting. Similarly, Susie's children—whom I met briefly before they left for other activities—although mannerly, clearly did not want to talk to me. They barely smiled, and everything about their facial expressions and body language fairly screamed, "Get me out of here—I don't want to talk to her."

I found this particular aspect of the interviews to be extremely interesting. Despite the fact that I stressed to all the participants prior to the interviews that I would be interviewing home schooling mothers only and would not be interviewing the children, almost all the children of the other seven participants were eager to show or tell me something about their schooling. Whereas Cissy's and Susie's children were, in effect, pushing me away, the other interviewees' children were almost—sometimes literally—embracing me. I might have thought this difference in attitude to be a factor of the children's age, as both Cissy's and Susie's children were teenagers, were it not for the fact that three of the other home-schooled children were also in their teenage years.

It also came to light during analysis of these interviews that, out of all 11 categories discussed previously, Cissy and Susie made comments only about 4, those 4 including opinions about the public schools (Cissy), other home schoolers (Cissy), racial tensions in the public schools (Cissy), and housework (Susie). None of the other most frequently raised topics (e.g., flexibility, home schooling as a stress reducer, socialization issues, etc.) emerged from the interviews with Cissy and Susie.

Another obvious similarity between Cissy and Susie is the fact that they both have full-time jobs, despite their home schooling responsibilities. Although several of the other interviewees worked on a part-time basis, their responsibilities in no way interfered with their ability to be home with their children on a consistent basis. "Laura's" part-time business was operated from her home, and both "Evelyn's" and "Blanche's" part-time positions at the church library included time to work with their children. Even "Janice," who managed to run a highly successful business, informed me that not only is she able to price her products at any time of the day or night as is convenient for her, but she also takes her daughters with her on business trips. It could be argued that Cissy's daughter is also with her mother for a better portion of the day, but the extent of Cissy's actual involvement with her daughter during the work day is unclear.

The Home Schooling Mother–Teacher

Perhaps the most profound difference in these two sets of interviews has to do with the actual reason for home schooling. Whereas home schooling was a choice carefully considered and ultimately decided on by the other home schoolers, Cissy and Susie seemed to find themselves, or at least to feel themselves, forced into home schooling. Cissy obviously felt great frustration with her daughter's progress in public school and saw home schooling as an option that she was more or less forced into by her daughter's poor academic performance. Whereas other home schoolers also experienced frustration with the public schools, they seemed to feel irritated with the schools, not with their children. In brief, Cissy seemed to feel that having to home school was her daughter's fault—that her daughter's lack of achievement had forced her into an educational alternative that, as she informed me, she had heretofore clearly disdained. One of Cissy's comments—that if her daughter did not do her work and tried to "call her bluff" again (by not doing well in school), she would "pull her butt out of school so fast it would make her head spin!"—even makes it sound as if she used home schooling as a form of punishment. That Susie was also forced into home schooling as an educational option is obvious, as her son was expelled from public school, and private schools—as she informed me—were less than willing to accept him as a result.

Obviously, then, both Cissy and Susie were forced—in one way or another—into home schooling their children. It is also interesting to note that the adoption of home schooling as the educational alternative of choice did not result in any immediately perceivable lifestyle change for either. Both continued their full-time occupations, presumably making minor adjustments as necessary to accommodate their new responsibilities. Such a schooling arrangement is a far cry from that of the other interviewees, for whom home schooling is more or less a full-time job in and of itself.

Clearly, Cissy and Susie form a very different class of home schooling mothers, a class that some home schoolers would likely argue does not even involve real home schooling. As a result, Cissy and Susie fall into the pseudo home schoolers category, and all the rest of the home schoolers interviewed fall easily into the classic home schoolers category, based on the similarity of (a) the interaction with the participant and their family and (b) the content of discussion.

In sum, the components emerging from analysis of the interviews included two major elements—the microcategories and the macrocategories. As noted previously, the microcategories are flexibility, home schooling as a stress reducer, socialization, children actually teach themselves, other home schoolers, housework, public/private schools, personal shortcomings as a teacher, testing home schoolers, attention deficit disorder, and racial tensions in the public schools; macrocategories are classic home

197

S. A. McDowell

schoolers and pseudo home schoolers. How this analysis of the interview data may best be interpreted is addressed in the following section.

Interpretation

What is the perceived impact of home schooling on the family in general and the mother in particular, according to data gleaned from the interviews? From analysis of the interviews and their emergent categories, it is clear that those home schoolers who feel forced to home school their children (the pseudo home schoolers) are quite unlike the classic or mainstream home schoolers, and that this difference is reflected in both their children's demeanors and, possibly, in the quality of the relationship between parent and child. It is quite possible that an undercurrent of anger exists—in that the child somehow "forced" the parent to accept the additional responsibility of home schooling—and that this anger permeates the home schooling process and the parent–child relationship in a manner that is detrimental to both. Clearly, the manner in which the decision to home school is reached greatly influences the overall positive or negative "feel" of the home schooling process and, as a result, the perceived impact of home schooling on the mother–teacher and the family.

Most of the microcategories that emerged in analysis of the interview data deal directly with the perceived impact of home schooling on both the mother and the family. Insofar as the family is concerned—especially the children—the home schooling mother–teachers interviewed clearly believed that their children were positively impacted in terms of family flexibility; socialization; dealing with diagnosed attention deficit disorder; and the problems confronted in the public/private schools, including racial tensions.

In regard to the mother–teacher herself, although the elements of personal shortcomings as a teacher and housework were clearly concerns for many home schooling mothers, the other "jewels" (Janice—P1-Id) received from home schooling were obviously believed to outweigh these somewhat negative factors. These positive elements include, as previously set out, flexibility, children being able to teach themselves, and home schooling as a stress reducer.

In sum, then, the data gleaned from the interviews informed us that, despite any negatives discussed, many classic home schoolers find home schooling to be more of a stress-reducing, rather than a stress-inducing, educational alternative. The reasons for this include the flexibility ascribed by home schooling mothers to the adoption of home schooling, as well as the freedom from worry—worry about what might happen physically and/or emotionally to their children during the school day, worry about what cur-

198

The Home Schooling Mother–Teacher

riculum might be taught to their children, and so forth. Granted, concern about their children's learning continues unabated during home schooling, but at least the mothers know how and what their children are being taught. This combination of family flexibility and less worry concerning their children's welfare turns the process of home schooling—at least for many home schooling mother–teachers—into an actual stress-reducer.

Analysis and Interpretation of the Observational Data

Analysis

As noted, the six observations included attendance at and/or participation in (a) the home schooling curriculum fair in Knoxville, Tennessee; (b) a church service at the self-titled Church with the Home Schooling Heart; (c) a "Learning How to Learn" Seminar, Part I; (d) a second "Learning How to Learn" Seminar, Part II; (e) the 13th Annual MTHEA Conference; and (f) a home schooling skate party. During the observations, certain elements emerged consistently. These elements included noted characteristics of home schooling parents, as well as their home-schooled children.

At each observation, the home schooling parents were observed to be pleasant, relaxed, and friendly in their demeanor. These same characteristics were shared with their children, who were observed to behave in similar fashion in many differing situations (e.g., the curriculum fair, church services, the conference, skating party, etc.). In both the curriculum fair and the skating party observations, home schooling parents also proved themselves to be eager to help others.

Another characteristic of home schooling parents that emerged from many of the observations has to do with how very well-informed the vast majority of these people appear to be concerning home schooling regulations, legal issues, and research. Intelligent discussion of these issues and other pertinent matters could be overheard at the curriculum fair, the church service, and even the conference. The final characteristic that emerged is closely tied to this last one, as it has to do with the fact that home schoolers are not only very well-informed as a group, but they seem determined to remain well-informed. That this is true is evidenced by their willingness to attend the numerous informative seminars and workshops offered at the curriculum fair and the conference, as well as the seminars offered as part of a Wednesday night church service.

In sum, then, analysis of the observational data revealed that both home schooling parents and their children are consistently pleasant, relaxed, and friendly. Further analysis indicated that, as a group, home schoolers are

199

S. A. McDowell

eager to be helpful to others, very well-informed, and determined to remain well-informed.

Interpretation

According to information gleaned from analysis of the observational data, home schooling parents and their children are consistently pleasant, relaxed, and friendly. These data coincide precisely with the interpretation of interviews advanced previously—that is, that home schooling acts for many as a stress-reducing agent.

Analysis and Interpretation of the Document Data

Analysis

The documents used in this portion of the research included three newsletters from three home schooling organizations, a literature review of home schooling magazines, and a visit to 61 home schooling web sites on the Internet. The one quality common to all these differing documents was their clearly informative purpose. All of the newsletters, magazines, and Internet sites were, first and foremost, providers of information regarding all facets of home schooling.

Another emerging element—the element of home schooling promotion—was seen most obviously in the professionally produced and nationally distributed *Family Christian Academy Newsletter*, although many of the home schooling magazines could be termed, arguably, as promotional as well. The importance of encouragement of home schoolers as an element also surfaced most notably in the magazines and occasionally on the Internet web sites.

Document analysis revealed, then, that the informational aspect of the documents was a universal one, that the promotional aspect could be found in both newsletters and magazines, and that encouragement as an emerging element could be found in both magazines and Internet sites.

Interpretation

Despite the presence of articles dealing with stress and similar issues in many of the magazines analyzed in document analysis, it does not necessarily follow, according to the interview and observational data, that home

The Home Schooling Mother–Teacher

schooling mother–teachers experience any more stress than the average individual living in modern-day America. In fact, many of the home schooling mothers, by their own admission, experience much less stress as a result of home schooling than they did beforehand.

Summary

In essence, the interpretation of the analyzed data from the interviews, observations, and data analysis confirms—or at least, in the case of document analysis, does not disallow—the basic finding that for many home schooling mother–teachers, home schooling acts as a stress-reducing educational alternative. An in-depth examination and detailed discussion of all the findings gleaned from the qualitative data is presented in the following section.

Summary of Qualitative Findings

What is the perceived impact of home schooling on the family in general and the mother–teacher in particular? In the qualitative portion of this research study, research in the form of (a) nine interviews with home schooling mother–teachers who chose to home school for a variety of reasons, (b) observations of six different home schooling events, and (c) analysis of documents (including three newsletters from different home schooling organizations, home schooling magazines, and 61 different home schooling web sites on the Internet) provides a solid basis from which to draw appropriate conclusions.

Data drawn from these three areas of research should serve to either confirm or repudiate the central thesis emerging from the data. In the classic triangulation of results, analysis of the interview, observation, and document analysis data should reveal similar—or at least not contradictory—findings. At first glance, the findings from all the research areas in this study do not appear to converge particularly well. I would argue, however, that they do.

As was noted earlier, the results of both the interview analysis and the observation analysis reinforce the finding that—at least for classic home schoolers—home schooling can act as a stress-reducing agent. The only research area that would not seem to confirm this finding is the document analysis, which included analysis of several magazine articles that dealt with issues of stress in home schooling. As was noted in the literature review, however, the number of articles, letters to the editor, and so forth detailing the stresses of home schooling was much lower than of those

S. A. McDowell

proclaiming the joys and "pluses" of home schooling. Apparently, then, the presence of "stress" articles in home schooling magazines does not, in and of itself, bear witness to the fact that home schooling increases a mother–teacher's stress level. Such articles simply may seek to help the mother–teacher with the stresses she may encounter, although these stresses actually may be "less stressful" than those she encountered prior to adoption of home schooling.

In the final analysis, the data gleaned from analysis of the qualitative data provide the following response to the research question guiding this study (i.e., What is the perceived impact of home schooling on the family in general and the mother–teacher in particular?) and include the following elements:

1. Classic home schoolers (those who choose home schooling as their educational alternative and who do not work full-time outside the home) apparently experience home schooling differently and in a more positive manner than do pseudo home schoolers (those who feel "forced" into home schooling and who continue to work on a full-time basis outside the home).

2. Many classic home schoolers perceive home schooling to have a positive impact on their families, especially in terms of (a) family flexibility; (b) socialization; (c) dealing with diagnosed attention deficit disorder; and (d) the problems confronted in the public/private schools, including problematic racial tensions.

3. Many classic home schooling mother–teachers perceive home schooling to have a positive impact on their personal lives, in that the addition of home schooling apparently serves as a stress-reducing educational alternative. This positive aspect of home schooling obviously outweighs the negatives of housework problems and concerns about personal shortcomings as a teacher. Clearly, the element of control that home schooling introduces has much to do with the perceived lessening of stress levels.

Discussion

The quantitative methodology informed us, among other things, that the home schooling mother–teachers who participated in the survey judged the impact of home schooling on their families and themselves to be a positive one, while from the qualitative methodology emerges, among other things, a theory of home schooling as a stress-reducing educational alternative. If, indeed, home schooling can and does function as a stress-reducing endeavor for the mother–teacher, does this fact alone account for the overwhelmingly positive response from mother–teachers

The Home Schooling Mother–Teacher

concerning home schooling's impact found in the results of both quantitative and qualitative methodologies? Possibly, but not necessarily, and certainly not probably. One possible answer to this question can be found, I believe, in the highly empowering process of social integration.

Social integration involves and pertains to several aspects of an individual's life, the chief of which may be termed _social capital_. According to Coleman (1987), social capital is made up of "the norms, the social networks, and the relationships between adults and children that are of value for children's growing up" (p. 36). It is a regrettable fact that the norms and values of parents are not always afforded the attention they should or could be by public school professionals when policies are decided and implemented, as Crowson (1998) noted:

> Despite many observations of progress in school-community relations, there remain indications, however, of a deeply significant and yet inadequately addressed problem. In a nutshell, the central remaining test in a successfully adaptive professionalism (vis-à-vis parents and the community) lies within a single construct …: governance. (p. 57)

Crowson (1998) also discussed the lack of empowerment of parents by educational professionals, due, at least in part, to the fact that

> the need to preserve strong norms of professional discretion against privacy-minded parents and narrow-minded communities has been a theme of professionalism in education since the work of Waller (1932). Generations of school officials have been trained around the dangers of losing control to the politics of their communities. Even modern-day efforts to be much more inclusive (in recognition of the importance of parents for effective learning) have typically ended up as subtle sets of exclusions. (p. 63)

In undertaking home schooling, I believe that home schooling mother–teachers are simply taking themselves out of the sometimes tense, often antagonistic school–community equation. They are taking for themselves that which was not freely offered—that is, power, governance, and control as concerns important aspects of their children's education. In taking charge, however, mother–teachers not only assume control of their children's education, but they also assume a new level of control in their own lives, because home schooling affords them the opportunity to more fully integrate and implement into their lives their personal values, norms, and beliefs about their roles and the appropriate enactment of those roles. In sum, then, the element of social integration that home schooling can of-

203

S. A. McDowell

fer can be an extraordinarily empowering one to the mother–teacher. It is the "feminist" element presented and discussed at the beginning of this article. This element, in combination with the stress-reducing aspects of home schooling, helps to explain, if only in part, the surprisingly consistent and overwhelmingly positive response from mother–teachers in regard to home schooling and its impact.

Conclusions

What can be concluded from this research study? Bearing in mind that both the quantitative and qualitative portions of the project are extremely limited in their generalizability—in that the quantitative survey was a nonprobability one that used a convenience-type sampling and that qualitative research is almost inherently nongeneralizable—the following conclusions may be loosely and generally drawn:

1. Mother–teachers perceive home schooling to have a positive impact on both their families and themselves. Indeed, some mother–teachers seem to indicate that home schooling acts as a stress-reducing educational alternative. It also may be argued that the element of social integration that the home schooling process allows can be a highly empowering one to the mother–teacher.

2. Insofar as survey response is concerned, there is no statistically significant difference in mother–teacher response by (a) reason given for home schooling, (b) income level, (c) number of children home schooled, or (d) number of years spent home schooling.

3. The major stressors in the lives of home schooling mother–teachers involve housework and concerns about their children learning what they need to be learning.

4. Those home schooling mother–teachers who are "forced" or who "feel" forced into home schooling experience the process of home schooling in a more negative way than do those home schoolers who would be considered traditional (classic) home schoolers.

5. Generally speaking, home schooling mother–teachers were found to be (a) pleasant, relaxed, and friendly; (b) eager to be helpful; (c) very well-informed; and (d) determined to remain well-informed; home-schooled children also were found to be pleasant, relaxed, and friendly.

There is little doubt that home schooling is an important and rapidly growing educational movement. Some observers of the educational establishment even predict that the influence exerted by this movement will not only increase but also spread into areas other than education, as Belz (1997) noted:

204

The Home Schooling Mother–Teacher

What special interest group in American society right now may be most effective at lobbying the U.S. Congress? If you guessed that it's a band of educators, you'd be right. But if you picked the National Education Association—the very liberal union of public school teachers that is so active in public affairs—you might well be wrong these days. For according to Rep. William Goodling (R–PA), a 22-year veteran of Congress and chairman now of the influential Education and Labor Committee, the home schoolers of our country, and especially those associated with the Home School Legal Defense Association, have developed more expertise than any other group in getting the attention of our nation's lawmakers. …

I would suggest that Rep. Goodling's high praise of home schoolers for their ability to win points in Congress may represent no more than the tip of an iceberg—that it's only a precursor of other ways in which home schoolers may more and more shape society far out of proportion to their numbers and acceptability to the rest of society.

That will happen only partly because of the effectiveness of the educational methodology these people are committed to. It will happen even more because of the kind of people they tend to be, and the things they believe about matters other than education. (p. 5)

Given the rapidly expanding size of the home schooling movement and its concurrently increasing influence on a national level, research into the many aspects and facets of the home schooling movement is essential. It is to be hoped that this study, which probed the perceived impact of home schooling on the family in general and the mother–teacher in particular, may shed some light, albeit a faint one, on the increasingly important and increasingly vocal home schooling family.

References

Belz, J. (1997). Rebels of the best kind: As educational structures change, keep your eyes on the homeschoolers. *World, 12*(23), 5.

Coleman, J. S. (1987, August/September). Families and school. *Educational Researcher, 16*(6), 32–38.

Crowson, R. L. (1998). Community empowerment and the public schools: Can educational professionalism survive? *Peabody Journal of Education, 73*(1), 56–68.

Glaser, B. G., & Strauss, A. L. (1967). *The discovery of grounded theory: Strategies for qualitative research.* Chicago: Aldine.

Kutter, P. O. (1987). The home schooling movement in central Kentucky. *Home School Researcher, 3*(4).

LeCompte, M. D., & Preissle, J. (1993). *Ethnography and qualitative design in educational research* (2nd ed.). New York: Academic.

Lincoln, Y. S., & Guba, E. G. (1985). *Naturalistic inquiry.* Newbury Park, CA: Sage.

S. A. McDowell

Lines, P. M. (1991). Home instruction: The size and growth of the movement. In J. Van Galen & M. S. Pitman (Eds.), *Home schooling: Political, historical, and pedagogical perspectives* (pp. 9–41). Norwood, NJ: Ablex.

Mayberry, M., Knowles, J. G., Ray, B., & Marlow, S. (1995). *Home schooling. Parents as educators.* Thousand Oaks, CA: Corwin.

McDowell, S. A. (1998). *Home sweet school: The perceived impact of home schooling on the family in general and the mother–teacher in general.* Unpublished doctoral dissertation, Peabody College of Vanderbilt University, Nashville, TN.

Merriam, S. B. (1988). *Case study research in education: A qualitative approach.* San Francisco: Jossey-Bass.

Miles, M. B., & Huberman, A. M. (1994). *Qualitative data analysis* (2nd ed.). Thousand Oaks, CA: Sage.

Morris, W. (Ed.) (1985). *American heritage dictionary.* (2nd ed.). Boston: Houghton Mifflin.

Page, L. A. (1996). *Beliefs and practices of home schoolers about responsibility in a democracy.* Unpublished doctoral dissertation, Peabody College of Vanderbilt University, Nashville, TN.

Van Galen, J. A. (1986). *Schooling in private: A study of home education.* Unpublished doctoral dissertation, University of North Carolina at Chapel Hill.

Wolcott, H. F. (1994). *Transforming qualitative data: Description, analysis, and interpretation.* Thousand Oaks, CA: Sage.

Wordsmyth English dictionary [Online]. (1999). Retrieved June 1, 1999, from the World Wide Web: http://www.wordsmyth.net

Whither the Common Good? A Critique of Home Schooling

Chris Lubienski

This analysis shows home schooling to be part of a general trend of elevating private goods over public goods. The discourse around home schooling centers on issues of individual rights and private benefits, rather than the public good. Yet, the public has an interest in education because there are unavoidable aspects of education that make it a public good. However, home schooling denies this public interest. It undermines the common good in two ways. First, it withdraws not only children but also social capital from public schools, to the detriment of the students remaining behind. Second, as an exit strategy, home schooling undermines the ability of public education to improve and become more responsive as a democratic institution. Thus, home schooling is not only a reaction to, but also a cause of, declining public schools. Therefore, it diminishes the potential of public education to serve the common good in a vibrant democracy.

The discourse around home schooling often focuses on the rights of parents to educate at home, their responsibilities to their children, and the beneficial results. Those debating home schooling give much attention to the academic achievement of children educated at home and possible in-

CHRIS LUBIENSKI *is Assistant Professor in the Department of Curriculum and Instruction, College of Education, Iowa State University, Ames.*

Requests for reprints should be sent to Chris Lubienski, Department of Curriculum and Instruction, E155 Lagomarcino Hall, Iowa State University, Ames, IA 50011. E-mail: chris100@iastate.edu

C. Lubienski

fringements on the right to choose that form of education. Here, however, I focus not only on the rights of those choosing home schooling, but also on the aggregate social effects of those individual choices. To that end, I examine the nature of home schooling as a reaction to the state of public education and consider the community's responsibilities to the individual. Conversely, I suggest that the individual has responsibilities regarding the education of the community and the sustenance of the common good. The elevation of individual choice epitomized by home schooling may be more than simply the reaction to institutional decline; it may be part of the problem as well. This has considerable implications for democracy and the common good.

This analysis begins by reviewing the relation of home schooling to public education, showing that it is largely a reaction to the perceived decline in the state of public schools. However, education has public effects—good or bad. Therefore, I argue that, in addition to its private benefits, education is a public good, and thus the public has an interest in how it is provided. However, home schooling effectively negates that interest. It undermines the common good in two related ways. First, because home school families tend to be articulate, active, and interested in their children's education, students in public schools could benefit from educational experiences that include the participation of such influences. Consequently, these students are deprived of access to social capital when families make the rational decision to remove their children from a common educational experience to home school, to the detriment of the greater good.

Second, this pattern of private decisions undermining the public good also happens on an institutional level. In that respect, I use Hirschman's (1970) framework of exit and voice to consider different options available for improving education. I conclude that the recognition of the public-good aspects of education can strengthen democratic channels and their ability to improve responsiveness to public preferences. On the other hand, continued use of the exit option through home schooling undermines deliberative democracy as well as public education as an institution with the potential to serve the common good.

Home Schooling and Public Education

Parents express different reasons for home schooling. Van Galen (1991) characterized the movement in terms of faith-driven "ideologues" and libertarian or practice-oriented "pedagogues." Virtually all observers see the movement as predominantly consisting of the former. People engaged in home education are overwhelmingly White, more often than not evangeli-

208

A Critique of Home Schooling

cal or fundamentalist Protestant Christians, relatively wealthy, and well educated (Rudner, 1999). Home-schooled children usually enjoy the benefits of stable, two-parent families that can afford to survive on one income so that one parent—almost always the mother—can stay home (Ray, 1997b; Rudner, 1999).

Nevertheless, people from a variety of backgrounds home school, and the decision to do so represents a significant sacrifice on the part of the parents in terms of time, energy, and (in many cases) the opportunity for a second income. Indeed, under present circumstances, home schooling represents a rational individual choice for these individuals from among several options. However, the ability to make such as choice is dependent on having the means—the time and resources—to sacrifice. In fact, that sacrifice can be seen as an investment in one's child. Thus, whether arising from a religious or libertarian mandate or an assertion of a preferred pedagogy, we can safely surmise that, in practice, the willingness to make such a sacrifice or investment arises from the decision to focus one's attention on one's own child. This is part of a general trend with active and affluent parents to pursue the best possible advantages for their own children—even if it means hurting other children's chances (Kohn, 1998). Even self-described liberal, middle-class mothers who profess a loyalty to the idea of equality of educational opportunity are willing to negate such ideals in practice if, by doing so, they can increase educational advantages for their own children (Brantlinger, Majd-Jabbari, & Guskin, 1996).

Home schooling epitomizes this trend. In that respect, home schooling is largely a reaction against the typical democratic means of educating our young people: public schooling. Lines (1991), for example, suggested that home schooling is, among other things, "a flight from modern American schools" (p. 9). Thus, people in the home schooling movement react explicitly to the perceived state of public education by asserting individual rights to educate their own child. For instance, home schoolers often express concern about leaving their child in an unsafe neighborhood school, surrounded by nefarious influences (e.g., Klicka, 1995). This is evident in the Florida Department of Education's survey of home schooling families, which found that respondents' primary reason for home schooling was the parents' perceptions of the public school environment (Kantrowitz & Wingert, 1998; Lyman, 1998). Other advocates of home schooling point to the perceived mediocrity of academic achievement in public schools (Finn & Gau, 1998; Whitehead & Crow, 1993). Still others (a) argue that public schools do not teach values, or do not teach the values the critics prefer; or (b) are concerned not just with what the institution teaches but with the values of other students (e.g., Ballmann, 1995; Klicka, 1995). Farris (1997) summarized these reasons for exiting neighborhood schools: "Most home

209

C. Lubienski

schooling families have chosen this form of education because of the dangers of the public school—academic failure, moral decay, and physical safety" (p. 5; see also Holt, 1981).

Therefore, the home schooling movement can be seen largely as a mass exodus from public education. It is not the intent of this article to defend the state of public education. Instead, this analysis of home schooling focuses on the aggregate effects of individual choices on the ability of public schools to support the public good. However, it would be a mistake to assume that home schooling is simply the result of individual decisions to leave public schools when, in fact, well-organized groups promote that flight from public institutions. Groups like the Christian Coalition, Focus on the Family, the Home School Legal Defense Association, and the Rutherford Institute not only protect the rights of home schoolers, but also, along with the Bradley Foundation, advance an agenda under the banner of "parental rights" (Miner, 1996). For example, writing in his *Focus on the Family* newsletter, home and Christian schooling advocate James Dobson (1994) quotes Cal Thomas in reacting to one recent effort to reform public education this way:

> "How should parents respond to this latest government power grab? Just as they would if they knew their children's school was on fire—they should get them out, fast." ... The National Education Association, which supports every anti-family cause from homosexual activism to abortion and condom-mania, has finally achieved the prize it has pursued for decades: control of the nation's children. (p. 1)

Dobson's organization has a mailing list with upwards of 4 million families, and his radio show reaches about 5 million listeners. Similarly, Citizens for Excellence in Education (CEE) sponsors "Rescue 2010" for the 20 million Christian children in public schools. CEE—claiming 350,000 parents across the United States, in 1,680 chapters—argued that "CHRISTIANS MUST EXIT THE PUBLIC SCHOOLS" (B. Simonds, 1998; see also R. Simonds, 1999). Likewise, home schooling pioneer Reverend Ray Moore promotes "Exodus 2000," under the belief that *"ALL Christians should immediately remove their children from the government schools"* (Dominick, n.d.; see also Moore, 1997).[1]

Hence, if home schooling is largely a reaction to the state of public education, it also reflects rational, individual decisions within a constrained set of circumstances. But, in view of the influential groups promoting

---

[1]For the CEE proposal, see http://www.webcom.com/webcee/strategy.html; for Moore's campaign, see http://exodus2000.org/.

A Critique of Home Schooling

moral mandates for home schooling, it would be inaccurate to suggest that it is simply the product of independent, individual choices. Therefore, although the present analysis does not defend the state of public education, neither does it intend to criticize the individual decisions of home schoolers. Instead, I explore the systemic context of home schooling as organized exit from public schools, which, I argue, undermines public education's singular potential to serve as a democratic institution promoting the common good.

Education as a Public Good

Traditionally, education has served both private and public ends. For example, schooling aids the individual in employment potential and provides private businesses with trained employees. But schools also embody democratic ideals of equality and are used to promote civic values, as well as to sort people in the interest of "social efficiency" (Labaree, 1997b). As people increasingly configure publicly funded education to meet the needs of their own children, home schoolers proceed from the insight that the institution of public education cannot adequately serve their children in the ways they want them served.

Yet, although it provides private benefits to students, schooling is also a public good—something we increasingly forget. This is not a new insight. For years, people have associated the wide distribution of schooling with progress, an informed citizenry, assimilation into shared values, lower birthrates, lower crime rates, and so forth—as well as (for better or for worse) AIDS prevention, abstinence, inculcation of entrepreneurial values, teaching a shared language, providing hot meals, and other social services and agendas. In view of wider effects, economists refer to the "externalities" of mass education to explain the general societal benefits that accrue from the wide diffusion of education. In an age in which we like to think of relations in economic, transactional terms, these externalities can be understood as benefits enjoyed by parties outside the immediate customer–provider arrangement of the student and the school. In this sense, "society" is a "consumer" of education, enjoying the benefits of an educated populace.

Although such externalities could be enjoyed regardless of whether education was provided through public or private means, the public-good aspect of education is most obviously evident in the area of public schools. Public schools are configured to serve more than simply the individual private interests of their immediate users (students and their families). Thus, governance and funding are shared throughout the community—by users

211

C. Lubienski

and nonusers, future employers, parents, nonparents, future parents, and parents whose children are no longer in school.

However, the private aspects of education are ascendant, as people increasingly view schooling as a means to individual social and economic advancement (Labaree, 1997a, 1997b). As a private good, consumers can seek what is best for them regardless of the effects their choices have on others. In elevating individual choice and widening the scope of decisions we make as individual private decisions, we increasingly neglect community considerations of how our actions affect others and deny their rights to voice their concerns. In schooling, it is important to consider the extent to which charter school, choice, and home schooling activists have created an atmosphere—through a rhetoric of education as a private good—in which parents feel the unconstrained freedom or even moral mandate to choose privatized education for their children. Typically, such activists do not publicly discuss the wider social consequences of individual choices. Thus, we have a system in which parents make a decision without considering the common good.

Yet, if we neglect the public-good aspects of education in pursuing education for our own children, we will still have to deal with the unavoidable negative impact of public education as a diminished public good—more poorly educated students, less social cohesion and tolerance, and other consequences of poor education. Thus, as Labaree (in press) notes, we can exit the public schools, but we cannot escape the positive or negative realities of public education as a public good.

Education and the Public Interest

Yet, if education is a public good, then the public also has an interest in its provision. We all have a right, indeed a responsibility, to demand some say in how any child is educated. This is true not just in cases in which our tax dollars are supporting that education. In a society that claims to be democratic, there is an inherent social interest in some degree of common education for tolerance, understanding, and exposure to difference, as well as to moderate secessionist and radical tendencies.

There is a long-standing recognition of the importance of the public interest in education. Sir Humphrey Gilbert, the founder of England's first colony in North America, referred to Plato in arguing that "the educacion of children should not altogether be under the puissance of their fathers, but under the publique power and aucthority, becawse the publique have therein more Interests then their parentes" (as cited in Kaestle, 1973, p. 16). Indeed, the public concern not only with the wide diffusion but with the nature of education is also evident in the earlier colonial laws mandating schooling in the New England colonies. Leading up to the common school

A Critique of Home Schooling

reforms, this public interest was increasingly thought to be carried through public schools in the Republic, as Carter (1826/1969) argued: "Every private establishment ... detaches a portion of the community from the great mass, and weakens or destroys their interest in those means of education which are common to the whole people" (p. 24). Of course, the common school reformers institutionalized the public prerogatives in public education, largely by appealing to the need for sustaining the public good in a democracy, but also by appealing to the private interests of employers (when politically expedient). In doing so, they reinforced the legacy of competing public and private interests that has since driven public education. Various subsequent reforms and trends have tipped the scales toward the public or private good aspects of public schools, but both have survived to produce a creative tension in the purpose of schools.

Although the public interest in education underlies much of the way we think about schooling, it is often only an implicit consideration. On the other hand, recent reform efforts and movements such as home schooling explicitly focus on the private interest of students and their families. However, on reflection, the public interest is apparent to most people, including home schoolers. If parental control is good for one family because it removes them from the public-interest effects of other parents' choices, is it good for all? Subsequently, I argue that, on a practical level, it is not. However, on a more philosophical level, people agree that unregulated parental control is not an absolute right, because other people have to deal with the consequences of a parent's decisions. In one famous essay, Friedman (1955) reminded us that extremes allow us to test principles in their purest form. If we do that with home schooling, we could ask: Are most people—or even most home schoolers—prepared to forego public influence on the education of children if even one child is being instructed at home by Nazis, Shining Path guerrillas, advocates of race war, pedophiles, Satanists, or some other cultists? And what if the parents are just alcoholics, people caught in a cycle of poverty or a culture of dependency, or people in the chronic habit of making bad choices? We generally recognize a community sense of moral responsibility for the child, as well as the fact that we will have to deal with the fruits of that education when the child reaches adulthood in a democratic society. Home schoolers consistently argue against "state" or "government" involvement in their children's education. But, ideally, in a democracy the public is the state.

Perhaps two other examples from outside education help illustrate the public interest in a common good. Issues of public safety, justice, and punishment or correction of criminals are generally held to be a public good. There is an obvious public interest in how we pursue this good. If someone commits a publicly defined crime against another person, does the victim

213

C. Lubienski

personally get to decide on the punishment ? No. Because we recognize a general public interest in meting out justice—the public's safety has been injured. Other people also have a say in the type and severity of punishment because we believe that society in general should decide how to keep order, what is evil, what is forgivable, how to discipline, how to deter certain activities, what to forgive, and so forth. When people unilaterally "privatize" the administration of this public good, we call them "vigilantes."

Similarly, in health care, the "state" sometimes tries to assert a claim over medical decisions. For example, the state often attempts to intervene when sick children need medical attention. This conflicts with the beliefs of some people regarding medical practices. Yet, the public has an interest in preventing the spread of disease and in securing health care for minors unable to make their own decisions. For instance, people who are injured sometimes refuse blood transfusions due to religious beliefs. Generally, we recognize the right of an adult to make such a personal decision. However, when a child is injured and in need of a blood transfusion to survive, we see a gray area in which two sets of rights and responsibilities conflict—the right of the parents to raise a child in line with their personal beliefs and the public's responsibility to ensure that individuals do not die because of other people's choices. Likewise, some people claim that they have the individual right to choose when and how to end their lives. This is a hotly contested issue, and others seek to use the power of the state to prevent such decisions, seeing them as an affront to the public good. Often, the state asserts a right to make medical decisions in such cases. Does this conflict with the rights of some Christian Scientists or "right-to-die" advocates, for instance? Yes. Does it save some lives? Most likely. Do we, as a society, have an interest in violating people's rights to promote public health, individual life, and even public morality? Probably. However, unlike most medical practices, education policies can be influenced through voting. Some may call this "state intervention." Most people call it democracy.

But in education, home schooling, by its very nature, denies this public interest by acknowledging no mechanism, no legitimate public interest, in the education of "other people's children." This is ironic because education is arguably the institution most open to public input through traditions of local control, elections, millages, and school conferences. Furthermore, as a public good with the potential for vibrant democratic control, public schools are one of the last remaining means of resisting centrifugal social forces.

The Privatization of a Public Good

Thus, there is a chronic and often creative tension between private and public goals for education. Whereas the pursuit of education is often

A Critique of Home Schooling

driven by the desire for individual private benefits, those private interests are counterbalanced by the public interests, which can justify constraints on individual choices through the shaping of institutional options. Yet, home schooling denies the public's interest and responsibilities and privatizes the social aspect of education to the most atomistic level—as strictly a family concern. In focusing on individual rights to choose, home schooling demands all the advantages of education as a private good but nullifies the public good.

Hence, home schooling does not simply throw off balance the symbiosis between public and private interests in education. It throws it out. Perhaps that is why, despite the remarkable growth of home schooling and its forceful public advocacy by influential leaders, 57% of Americans still feel that home schooling is "a bad thing for the nation" (Rose, Gallup, & Elam, 1997, p. 50). By focusing only on the benefits for one's own children, home schooling represents a very radical form of privatization of a public good. Home schooling is both a more benign and more destructive form of privatization: benign because it does not put a claim on public resources (as do for-profit charter schools, for instance), and destructive in that it is a more fundamental form of privatization. It privatizes the means, control, and purpose of education and fragments the production of the common good not simply to the level of a locality or ethnic group, but to the atomized level of the nuclear family.

Obviously, some would see that as a good thing. One could argue that complete and radical privatization to its greatest degree—home schooling—is a better approximation of democracy because it removes statist bureaucracy and responds to citizens at the most local level. However, this ultra-individualistic conception is a very thin democracy indeed, inasmuch as it absolutely denies even the most minimal community interest in democratic schooling. Furthermore, advocates could contend that home schooling promotes the common good by cultivating future leaders for the benefit of all. This is a very elitist argument that identifies potential leaders on the basis of the fact that they happen to be one's own child, and it necessarily excludes others from that vision. Some, like Holt (1981), ask if it is so bad if the affluent remove their children from school, because, at least educators can attend to poor kids with "undivided attention" (p. 326). Of course, the common school reforms were largely a reaction to such a system, in which the children of the poor were often left to "public" and "charity" schools and others pursued private educational options according to their means. If such a situation were untenable then, we might want to consider how such a segregated system could be any more appropriate now.

Home schoolers could argue that (a) the strengths of their results contribute to the common good by providing a better-educated populace in

C. Lubienski

general, and (b) a wider acceptance of home schooling would increase overall academic achievement. Again, this argument turns its back on those left in the neighborhood schools. It assumes that the aggregate of individual choices automatically lead to the greatest good—that is, I can best help my neighbor by focusing on myself—an arguable proposition. Furthermore, it limits its definition of the purpose of schools to academic goals and denies the use of schools for other socially defined ends: assimilation, desegregation, cohesion, or whatever we collectively value.

Finally, home schoolers could argue that they are not undercutting the potential for the democratic production of the public good. They are only asking for classically liberal democratic rights to be free from interference, while not necessarily denying democratic responsibilities. For example, some critics of home schooling charge that, in focusing on their own, these parents are turning their backs on fellow citizens and denying the social contractual obligations of a republican conception of a democratic society. (After all, as Blakely & Snyder, 1997, perceptively asked in their analysis of gated communities, Can there be a social contract without social contact?) Yet, home schoolers argue that, by focusing on their own families, they are not turning their backs on the social contract (Ray, 1997b). Instead, they are reconstituting their rights at an individual and family level so that they may contribute to the community as autonomous individuals—as defined by those who founded the Republic (Lines, 1994; Williamson, 1989).

But this is a tenuous assertion, from both historical and libertarian perspectives. The antifederalist emphasis on civil liberties from government intervention, championed by home schooling, was not the only (much less dominant) view of the social contract at the beginning of the nation (Sandel, 1996). Classic debates over the social contract suggest that it was one of several competing understandings of the individual's role in society in the late 18th century. Leaders like Thomas Jefferson probably embraced a more republican–communitarian conception of social obligations—tied to the Scottish Enlightenment's focus on virtuous acts of benevolence toward others in the community—rather than the liberal Lockean conception of freedom from state interference (Matthews, 1984; Wills, 1978).

Second, it is debatable, even from a libertarian perspective (e.g., Holt, 1981), to claim that home schooling strengthens the common good by creating autonomous individuals. Home schooling defines liberty largely as freedom from other people's choices (in the form of the state) rather than freedom to make choices—an autonomy that is cultivated through critical thinking skills and independence from the coercion of others, including that of parents. Obviously, most people accept the notion that we do not hold children to be autonomous. However, they are also not their parents' property (Brighouse, 1997). To become truly autonomous individuals,

A Critique of Home Schooling

children's independence of views cannot be grounded in a unit as self-contained as the family but must be based in the larger community, which (for better or for worse) is more closely reflected in the classroom than the home (Durkheim, 1961).

The Price to Individuals of Maintaining Education as a Public Good

If, then, education is a public good, and the public has a consequent interest in the provision of that good, we might consider the distribution of costs for maintaining that public good. It is my contention that there are, indeed, real and opportunity costs associated with education as a public good. Although some of these are financial, the price of education as a public good also involves social costs. I outline these costs in this section, and I go on to argue that home schooling privatizes the personal benefits of education while asking others to disproportionately bear the social burdens of education as a public good. Thus, home schooling undermines the common good by distributing costs inequitably and, therefore (as I demonstrate later), it undermines the ability of society to pursue the common good through democratic channels.

In most conceptions of democracy, there are individual rights, accompanied by various civic responsibilities. That is, the idea of democracy becomes hollow and can collapse if individuals define democracy only in terms of their individual rights but neglect the public good—the prerequisite civil society of democratic discourse, community participation, voting, and other activities, that may have little individual payoff but can serve to strengthen the democratic polity.

Yet, increasingly, people are pursuing a consumer model of public life, withdrawing from areas that potentially represent social costs to them, while still pursuing public benefits—that is, we want to enjoy public goods but avoid private costs. This is the not in my backyard (NIMBY) ethic applied to democracy. We want better government but do not want to personally research the issues and take the time to vote. We want safe streets, but do not want to "get involved," serve on a jury, or pay taxes for public safety services, and we certainly do not want a prison in our neighborhood. We want a stable community but do not make the effort to talk with our neighbors.

As Olson (1965) and Hardin (1968) demonstrated, a resource or endeavor maintained as a common or collective good will deteriorate if based only on voluntary cooperation in a system of self-interest. If support is left up to individuals solely on a voluntary basis, although all can enjoy

217

C. Lubienski

the benefits, some will avoid paying their fair share. Therefore, we often decide to compel people who enjoy that good to share in the costs—opportunity or real costs. For the most part, the financial costs of public education are publicly distributed—that is, public authorities decide on the tax burdens for the support of mass education, and then, in the absence of voluntary support, compel payment through legal means. Similar systems are evident for other public goods such as roads, public and national security, and so forth.

However, in the case of education as a public good, there are other costs involved, and these are not distributed by a public authority so much as through private choices. Without requiring participation, social institutions such as public education require social and political capital to promote effectiveness and maintain consequent public support for their survival as public goods. These costs are less tangible than a tax bill but still very real. Such costs can include, for example, the time and effort spent advocating for one's child and hoping to make the school a better institution (to avoid the costs of an institution in a state of decline). There are opportunity costs involved with being around people of varied abilities, values, and backgrounds.

Peer Effects

These opportunity costs become apparent when we consider a child's classmates (and their families)—sometimes called "peer group effects." There is an established and rich research tradition, at least since the Coleman Report, that identifies the family background of an individual student and the family background of the other students in the school as the primary determinants of student achievement (Coleman et al., 1966; Epple & Romano, 1998; Jencks, 1972). Although these influences may be suggested by the students' economic indicators, they are closely associated with the cultural characteristics and values students bring to the classroom—punctuality, respect for authority, persistence, delayed gratification, and other such attributes that are (for better or worse) valued and rewarded by the education system. This research indicates more than a singular link between the individual's socioeconomic status (SES) characteristics and his or her own academic achievement. It demonstrates the importance of the SES characteristics of the classmates on a student's achievement as well, and, conversely, the effects of an individual's SES on his or her classmates—that is, the positive values, abilities, skills, and preferences brought to school by a student also determine the likelihood of other students' academic success. The peer group informs a student's edu-

A Critique of Home Schooling

cational and career aspirations and sets patterns well into adult life (e.g., Wells & Crain, 1994).

According to Putnam (1996), education level is a proxy for SES factors but also the best predictor of civic engagement. Furthermore, more highly educated people are more likely to contribute to the community because of their economic position, but more so because of the skills, abilities, and values they have received from home and school. Although there are many indicators that researchers use to discern the background SES characteristics—family income, books in home, parental education levels, computer use, and so forth—much of the research returns to the value of parental involvement in education (Coleman & Hoffer, 1987; Lareau, 1989). "Parental involvement" speaks to how parents value schooling, participate in their child's schooling, and impart or model those values to their children. In schools, high levels of parental involvement are associated with the all-important social capital in and around schools that, for many researchers, explains the superior academic achievement of students in private schools over public schools (Coleman & Hoffer, 1987; Steinberg, Brown, & Dornbusch, 1996). As Ray (1999) noted, "Home schooling, generally speaking, is, de facto, parent involvement" (p. 34).

Opportunity Costs

However, if parental involvement and certain associated values lead to better education for the individual and immediate peers, those families choosing to school at home have both a definite advantage and potential responsibility. Yet, home schooling emphasizes the former and neglects the latter (Franzosa, 1991; see, e.g., Holt, 1981; Williamson, 1989)—NIMBY democracy, in which the benefits are privatized and the costs are transferred to those remaining in the public sphere.

Certainly, those bringing more cultural capital to the school are asked to bear a greater portion of the opportunity costs, when they could use their skills to obtain more private benefits from education elsewhere. The opportunity costs of foregoing other educational options are real enough to the parents. There is a price to pay in potential gain in leaving a child in a neighborhood school when a selective school would better advance the child's potential. Yet, as those with the most advantageous SES characteristics to cultivate for personal use, they also have the most to share. And the loss of their advocacy, skills, values, and cultural capital represents real—not just opportunity—costs to those remaining in the neighborhood school.

Hence, whereas financial costs often are distributed through publicly constituted democratic authority, social and political costs often are paid

219

C. Lubienski

or avoided because of private decisions. When parents make a decision regarding their child's education, they are doing so largely to avoid costs (or to take advantage of opportunities). Thus, the logical choice to remove a child from one school and place him or her in another district, a magnet school, a private school, or some other option is a private prerogative that is exercised to avoid costs and maximize opportunities. Home schooling clearly illustrates this phenomenon.

Individual and Shared Costs, Voluntary Cooperation, and
Aggregate Consequences

The private decision to pursue a better educational experience for one's own child is a rational decision on an individual level in a system based on self-interest. However, the sum of these individual decisions, in the aggregate, can have negative consequences. Game theory offers insights into these dynamics and their consequences. The purpose of game theory is to provide models to predict human behavior in various circumstances, to discern likely outcomes. As with choosing an education for one's own child, we cannot assume simply that a choice is discrete and isolated, but instead that it is made (or not made) in response to what other "players" choose. Thus, for example, a parent probably would not decide to remove a child from a school if other people's choices had resulted in a school that exactly matched what that parent was looking for in terms of beliefs, parental participation, pedagogical preferences, and so on. So game theory analyzes rational, self-interested individual (and group) choices and patterns of choices in the context of what other people do or are expected to do.

One famous game, the Prisoners' Dilemma, can help us analyze the exercise of individual rights and responsibilities around a shared good such as public education—in this exercise, the "good" is to avoid prison time. It shows how outcomes are shaped not only by our actions but also by our actions in strategic interaction with the choices of others. In this game, two (or more) individuals are arrested and isolated in separate cells, unable to communicate. Assume that the prosecutor has enough physical evidence to put the prisoners away for only 1 year each. However, with testimony, a conviction for this crime carries up to 10 years in prison. Each prisoner has only two options: (a) admit guilt, and, in doing so, give evidence against the other; or (b) claim innocence. If a prisoner is willing to plead guilty and thereby testify against the other, the prosecutor will bargain: The prisoners will split the 10-year sentence if each pleads guilty; but, if one admits and the other denies, the one pleading guilty can go free, and the other will serve the full sentence. The prisoners know their options and the conse-

220

quences, but they cannot communicate. The possibilities are represented in Table 1.

Of course, in that scenario, the best overall outcome for the players (represented by the least amount of prison time) would be for each to serve only 1 year. However, to achieve this outcome, the prisoners must each, in isolation, forego the possibility of getting out of jail free, at the partner's great expense. Individually, the obvious strategy is to admit guilt, so that an individual serves no more than 5 years and possibly none at all. But, in the absence of cooperation, loyalty can carry a heavy cost. The players cannot communicate, but even if they could, there is an incentive to withdraw unilaterally from any agreement. Loyalty may lead to the greatest overall good, but only by assuring that each party shares part of the costs—if possible, some kind of binding contract between the players (e.g., Hardin, 1968; Olson, 1965). Played several times, strategies of betrayal and retaliation can serve an individual player. However, if the game is repeated indefinitely (which is more similar to social interaction), computer models show that voluntary cooperation emerges as the dominant strategy (Coulson, 1994).

What this exercise demonstrates in the context of education is that, when participating in a common good, individuals have a logical incentive to avoid costs, even at the expense of others. Even if voluntary cooperation is the best overall approach, there are individual incentives to pursue the best outcome for a given student, which can override the common good. In the current climate of treating education as a consumer good for its individual, private benefits, home schooling reflects this dynamic. Like the Prisoners' Dilemma, sharing the social costs of education—instruction in groups of varied abilities, values, and attributes (i.e., classrooms)—can lead to the general good of enhanced outcomes for the greater whole. Unlike the Prisoners' Dilemma, however, some people come to the decision with a greater share of potential benefits (in terms of SES) that can be realized both individually or collectively. Thus, they have an even greater incentive than is represented

Table 1
The Prisoners' Dilemma

	Options for Prisoner B	
	Admit	*Deny*
Options for Prisoner A		
Admit	–5, –5	0, –10
Deny	–10, –0	–1, –1

Note. Matrix represents outcomes for Prisoners A, B.

C. Lubienski

in the game to forego voluntary cooperation (or any social contract-type arrangement with others in the school), to more effectively pursue maximized opportunities—as any individual rational consumer should do. However, in doing so, the desirable attributes and skills exhibited by home schooling families are removed from the classroom where others may benefit, and, as with the Prisoners' Dilemma, the costs to those remaining in the shared arrangement are intensified in the form of declining social capital, diminished peer group effects, and so forth.

The Price of Exit for the Public Good

What, then, is the solution to this unwieldy entanglement of inequitably distributed private prerogatives and benefits and public costs? If we want to enjoy the public good aspects of education (and we all do) and not have to pay the high price for diminished or negative externalities of mass education, we need to guarantee a generally wide and adequate level of education across the population. The dilemma here is that the focus on private goods leads to more effective education for some, but it injures the opportunities for many others. Yet, because no one seems to be happy with the status quo, there are two obvious alternatives within the options outlined in this analysis: expand home schooling to more, if not all, people, or increase participation in the institution of public education to make it more effective.

More Participation in Home Schooling, or Public Schooling

Some home schooling advocates promote an even greater expansion of home schooling as an effective approach for education, to the point of questioning the legitimate need for public schools (e.g., Ray, 1997a). For example, Farris and Woodruff (1999) noted that, although home-schooled children tend to come from relatively affluent and well-educated families, even poorer and less-educated home schooling families appear to do quite well academically. Their success appears to contrast with the lower achievement of similarly situated students in the public schools. Indeed, Ray (1997a) suggested "the possibility that students 'left behind' in state schools might be better off if they were moved on to home or private education."

The anti-public school proposal is, in my view, inadequate, and such arguments miss a crucial point. There is an essential difference between home schooling parents engaging in home schooling and every family home schooling. Home school parents are self-selected, defined by the primary SES characteristic of interest and involvement in their child's educa-

222

tion. Although interest in education is unequally distributed across the public school population, virtually 100% of home schoolers, by definition, demonstrate an active interest in their child's education. So, when we look at high test scores for a home school student, we are seeing, among other things, the fruits of a highly motivated, active, and interested parent participating in the life of the child.

Thus, we need to be cautious in concluding on the basis of relatively high test scores for home school students that there is "something inherent to the modern practice of home education that could (or does) ameliorate the effect of background factors that are associated with lower academic achievement when students are placed in conventional public schools" (Ray, 1999, p. 36). The selection effects confound the treatment effects in a self-selected group necessarily defined by high parental involvement and desirable cultural capital.

Hence, home schooling cannot be expected to level inequities that arise from differences in home backgrounds, but instead is an indicator of those inequities. As the research on home backgrounds demonstrates, it would be sadly misguided to assume that all parents share those characteristics that account for academic success of home schoolers. "Treatments" external to the home (i.e., schools) have the potential to level the inequities arising from differentiated home backgrounds. Home schooling for all is unlikely to serve as a successful strategy, and it would appear that the continued growth of home schooling increasingly will erode the educational experiences for the vast majority of students. If applied on a broad scale, home schooling likely would exacerbate these inequities. Indeed, even if universal and academically beneficial, it likely would have detrimental effects on the vitality of democracy in pursuing the common good (as I argue in the conclusion).

Therefore, we need to refocus our attention on the institution of public education and its potential for serving the public good. To that end, Hirschman's organizational analysis is quite helpful. As a political economist, Hirschman is well positioned to offer useful insights into questions of public and private goods, individual and collective costs, and the confluence of such factors. Indeed, *Exit, Voice, and Loyalty: Responses to Decline in Firms, Organizations, and States* (Hirschman, 1970) is considered a classic in the field. In his analysis, when an institution such as public education fails to accommodate the views of those it is intended to serve, they have two options: exit or voice. Although both expressions of dissatisfaction have the potential to produce improvements in the organization, they are different in their essence. Hirschman saw voice as a political response—a willingness to remain in the organization and fight. Exit is associated with economic organizations. With exit, consumers have the power to force

223

C. Lubienski

changes on organizations by withdrawing their patronage and money—"voting with their feet" through flight. One response is messy, public, and confrontational. The other is clean and private, and it avoids nasty conflicts (Labaree, in press).

However, although these are the options that dissatisfied individuals have, organizations often are designed to be responsive to one or the other form of expression, which does not always match the individual's likely response. This is demonstrated in Table 2. In cases in which individual response matches institutional receptivity (Quadrants 1 and 4), there are effective patterns of responsiveness to expressed preferences. But in Hirschman's (1970) analysis, dysfunction can arise when dissatisfaction is likely to cause one response, but the organization is sensitive to the other (Quadrants 2 and 3). In those cases, responsiveness is ineffective, and the organization is likely to be inefficient. For example, a business enterprise is, by its nature, susceptible to exit, because losing customers to competitors hurts its relative market position, and its customers are most likely to respond with exit if they are not satisfied (Quadrant 1). However, in the event that a business has monopolistic control of a market, exit is less likely in view of lack of alternatives for consumers, and the business is not suited to respond effectively to voice. The result is an unresponsive and inefficient monopoly (Quadrant 2).

Table 2
Roles of Exit and Voice

	Decline Arouses Primarily	
	Exit	*Voice*
Organization is sensitive primarily to		
Exit	Competitive business enterprise	Organizations where dissent is allowed, but is "institutionalized"
	#1	#2
Voice	Public enterprise subject to competition from an alternative mode, lazy oligopolist, etc.	Democratically responsive organizations commanding considerable loyalty from members
	#3	#4

Note. From *Exit, Voice and Loyalty* by A. O. Hirschman. Copyright © 1970 by the President and Fellows of Harvard College. Reprinted by permission of Harvard University Press. See also Larabee (in press).

A Critique of Home Schooling

Similarly, public organizations in the political sphere usually are intended to be responsive to voice. Democratic deliberation and the organized expression of views are ideally the means for changing political institutions (Quadrant 4). However, when an organization is designed to be responsive to voice but arouses exit, it is in a state of dysfunction (Quadrant 3).

Of course, public education is in such a position. Under Hirschman's (1970) framework, public education usually is located in Quadrant 3, because it is designed to respond to political pressure, but often it incites dissatisfied users to leave for private options such as home schooling. In inducing that type of response, education is provided as a public good but treated as a private good by those exiting. And indeed, as with other private goods (toothpaste, restaurants, cars, etc.) that provoke a consumer-type response, individuals exit for private reasons and do not typically need to consider the effects of their choice on other consumers.

However, as a public good, schools are designed to be responsive to voice through school board elections and meetings, parent advocacy, and even bond issues, as these provide the opportunity for citizen preferences to be heard. Public schools generally are not designed to be directly responsive to exit, because—as a public good—they have a semimonopoly status and are not immediately penalized in financial terms for the loss of a student. Thus, pathology results. Indeed, as Hirschman (1970) noted, under present conditions of semimonopoly status for public schools and partial escape options for some parents (at least for those with means), schools often fail to respond to consumer exit. In fact, being primarily responsive to political pressure, schools may prefer or even encourage dissatisfied and vocal parents to home school to get rid of "difficult" individuals.

More Exit, or Voice

If we characterize public education in Hirschman's (1970) description of a lazy public monopoly, a few possibilities are evident. The status quo of public education is inherently unsatisfying for many, because it reflects an unwieldy combination of an economic paradigm (for users) and a public-democratic paradigm (for the institution). Thus, there are basically two alternatives. Reform means moving the institution of public education in the direction of a purer economic paradigm, or a purer political paradigm.

Obviously, many reformers currently propose the former. Proponents of charter schools, vouchers, and other forms of school choice advocate making education more of a private good to be pursued individually. Consequently, they advocate making schools more like businesses, in which

225

C. Lubienski

each school succeeds or fails based on attracting and retaining students. Although this is not the time for a comprehensive discussion of such reform proposals, it is interesting to note that under Hirschman's (1970) framework, these plans would remove education from the democratic or political paradigm of voice to the economic sphere responsive to exit. Indeed, Hirschman worried that Americans traditionally elevate the exit option as the preferred approach almost by default (see chap. 8). This clearly is reflected in the predominance of economic values in school choice proposals, as reformers seek to depoliticize education—making it more efficient and responsive to exit. Yet, although economists see politics as a messy, indirect, and inefficient form of expression compared with voting with one's feet, Hirschman facetiously noted,

> A person less well trained in economics might naively suggest that the direct way of expressing views is to express them! ... But what else is the political, and indeed the democratic, process than the digging, the use, and hopefully the slow improvement of these very channels? (p. 17)

Therefore, one significant consequence of moving toward exit is that it undermines the democratic potential of the institution to respond to citizens' voices—and not just the preferences of immediate users. This is important if we are to sustain public education as a public good for each member of society and not just for parents with children of school age at any given time. When people exercise their exit option for individual advancement, they undercut the ability of the institution to improve as a democratic institution. Atrophy sets in on the institutional ability to respond to democratic voice. And public education is denied its role as one of the last remaining means with at least the potential to sustain the public good directly.

Coercion, or Voluntary Cooperation

What, then, are the possibilities for enhancing the ability of public education to respond to voice? The most obvious and untenable position is coerced participation. By requiring parents to send their children to public schools and, even more so, by controlling the distribution of desirable SES characteristics so as to more equitably benefit all children (i.e., busing), we can coerce parental involvement from the most active parents because their children would be captured by public schools. This, however, is unconstitutional, politically indefensible, and generally distasteful to many (Trotter, 1998; Tyack, 1968).

A Critique of Home Schooling

The other possibility is the voluntary cooperation suggested by game theory. If people were voluntarily to forego capitalizing on private advantages arising from family characteristics and agree to enrich the peer effects of others, the greater good could be enhanced, and an institution with the potential for promoting the common good could be reinvigorated through the strengthening of the voice mechanism. Of course, this is the scenario we have now, and people are largely dissatisfied with the current situation. The growth of home schooling demonstrates that increasing numbers of families are exercising the exit option and refusing to participate voluntarily in the shared costs of public education.

However, this is also the approach with the greatest possibilities for fulfilling the potential of public education in pursuing the common good. Home schoolers have demonstrated amazing energy and advocacy skills in pursuing education for their own children. They display a remarkable array of publications, newsletters, alerts, political advocacy, and networking to support and sustain their efforts. If such activism and resources were brought to bear on a public institution such as public schools, the general public good would benefit. Of course, some would say their substantive participation is not welcomed by the public schools (Ray, 1999). That may be so. Hirschman's (1970) model suggests that, inasmuch as that is the case, part of the reason for that is the preference for flight over staying and demanding to be heard. Schools are one of the most accessible institutions in a democratic society, found in almost every neighborhood, open to public scrutiny of their performance and mistakes, and designed to respond to multiple forms of democratic expression (although that responsiveness may be decaying from disuse). Indeed, people probably can have a much greater influence and an impact more immediate to their lives by voting in a school board election than in voting in elections for national offices.

Implications

Home schooling is largely a reaction against the perceived state of public schooling. This analysis defends not the status quo of public education but its singular potential, which is largely denied by the essence of home schooling.

Of course, much of the discussion around home schooling centers around competing conceptions of democracy (Welner, 1999). What is interesting here is that, for many, home schooling represents a retreat into individualism after unsuccessful efforts to reform public education more to their liking (Franzosa, 1991; see, e.g., Holt, 1981). However, in embracing the exit strategy, home schoolers indicate a preference for an economic-style approach to public life—one in which education is treated as a

C. Lubienski

private good and in which conflicts over the nature of that good are likewise privatized away from open conflict. Ironically, the flight from the coercive nature of public authority can precipitate greater state coercion. In lieu of a viable social contract, patterns of betrayal and retaliation require that the state apparatus is called in to mediate and suppress conflict in an increasingly fragmented society (Margolis, 1998). Furthermore, the elevation of economic over democratic models undermines not just public institutions such as schools but also vibrant, public democracy itself.

Ideally, democracy is the implicit agreement to mediate disputes without violence (Wink, 1992). Implicitly, but more important, it is the agreement to disagree, if necessary, but to remain party to the process. Democracy assumes a social contract between citizens, not necessarily to agree with each other, but to agree to disagree without threatening the integrity of the polity. At the very least, democracy is the implicit agreement to talk, not to flee or literally fight with other members of the democratic body; to carry on informative and meaningful debate; to tolerate difference in views of other members of the body; to employ established and previously agreed-on due processes for mediating conflicts; and to respect the will of the majority and the rights of the minority. Thus, under this conception, democracy is a form of conflict management—not the conflict avoidance that is evident with privatized education experiences. Conflicts are necessary and encouraged as healthy expressions of diversity, but constrained within previously agreed-on parameters.

Hence, home schooling is a flight from the public production of values in a pluralist society. Because we cannot reach a consensus about moral issues (which are reflected in how we educate), people tend to retreat from the idea of public production of civic virtue (Sandel, 1996). The classically liberal, negatively defined rights of individuals to be free from external interference have come to mean that individuals define their own "good" in private processes like home schooling, divorced from politics. According to Sandel (1996), if the discussion of what constitutes a public good is transferred from the public sphere to the private sphere—from the public space of schools to private decisions in homes—we promote a hollow political culture bereft of substantive deliberation. But it is undesirable, if not impossible, to remove the political aspects of public education if it is to be a publicly produced good, as Cremin (1990) noted,

> Aristotle explicated the relationship in the classic discussion of education he included in the *Politics*. ... It is impossible to talk about education apart from some conception of the good life; people will inevitably differ in their conceptions of the good life, and hence they will inevitably dis-

A Critique of Home Schooling

agree on matters of education; therefore the discussion of education falls squarely within the domain of politics. (p. 85)

Home schooling is a relativistic retreat from the public discourse, which is bankrupted of its former role as the space where people had the right and civic responsibility to participate in the public–political production of conceptions of the "good life"—evident in the value of civic participation and virtue in early republicanism (Lasch, 1995; Sandel, 1996).

Thus, we might do well to consider more fully the wider consequences of multiple individual decisions in education based primarily on private interests. Indeed, in a research discourse primarily concerned with academic achievement and individual rights, there is relatively little recognition given to the idea of the common good. The common good becomes supplanted by the aggregate of our individual actions, which are directed only toward private, individual (or family) considerations. Therefore, it is difficult to demonstrate that such a system will enhance the common good when it is treated as nothing more than a hopefully positive byproduct of self-interested actions. Hence, we also might consider critically the roles of advocacy organizations in promoting these private decisions. In fact, the aggregate effects appear to supplant democratically constituted authority, not just with individual authority, but also with the might of private home schooling advocacy organizations based on membership rather than citizenship.

As an extreme form of privatizing the purpose of education, home schooling denies democratic accountability and disenfranchises the community from its legitimate interest in education. This denial of the public interest does not only affect the education of home schoolers, but it also erodes the ability of the community to express its interest in the education of those remaining in the public schools as well. Certainly, public schools fail often in many areas. But they fail publicly, as public institutions, and, in that, we at least have the potential to address the issue.

References

Ballmann, R. E. (1995). *The how and why of home schooling* (Rev. ed.). Wheaton, IL: Crossway.

Blakely, E. J., & Snyder, M. G. (1997). *Fortress America: Gated communities in the United States.* Washington, DC: Brookings Institution/Lincoln Institute of Land Policy.

Brantlinger, E., Majd-Jabbari, M., & Guskin, S. L. (1996). Self-interest and liberal educational discourse: How ideology works for middle-class mothers. *American Educational Research Journal, 33,* 571–597.

Brighouse, H. (1997). Two philosophical errors concerning school choice. *Oxford Review of Education, 23,* 503–510.

C. Lubienski

Carter, J. (1969). *Essays upon popular education, containing a particular examination of the schools of Massachusetts, and an outline of an institution of the instruction of teachers.* New York: Arno Press and the New York Times. (Original work published 1826)

Coleman, J. S., Campbell, E. Q., Hobson, C. J., McPartland, J., Mood, A. M., Weinfeld, F. D., & York, R. L. (1966). *Equality of educational opportunity.* Washington, DC: National Center for Educational Statistics.

Coleman, J. S., & Hoffer, T. (1987). *Public and private high schools: The impact of communities.* New York: Basic Books.

Coulson, A. J. (1994). Human life, human organization and education. *Education Policy Analysis Archives, 2*(9) [Online]. Retrieved November 14, 1997 from the World Wide Web: http://olam.ed.asu.edu/epaa/v1992n1999.html

Cremin, L. A. (1990). *Popular education and its discontents.* New York: Harper & Row.

Dobson, J. C. (1994, May). *Focus on the Family (Newsletter),* 1–7.

Dominick, M. (n.d.). Exodus 2000: The time has come for Christians to remove their children from public schools. *Cutting Edge Ministries Web Site* [Online]. Retrieved June 18, 1999 from the World Wide Web: http://cuttingedge.org/news/n1142.cfm

Durkheim, E. (1961). *Moral education: A study in the theory and application of the sociology of education* (E. K. Wilson & H. Schnurer, Trans.). New York: Free Press.

Epple, D., & Romano, R. E. (1998). Competition between private and public schools, vouchers, and peer-group effects. *American Economic Review, 88*(1), 33–62.

Farris, M. P. (1997). *The future of home schooling: A new direction for Christian home education.* Washington, DC: Regnery.

Farris, M. P., & Woodruff, S. A. (1999, April). *The future of home schooling.* Paper presented at the annual conference of the American Educational Research Association, Montreal, Canada.

Finn, C. E., & Gau, R. L. (1998). New ways of education. *The Public Interest, 130,* 79–92.

Franzosa, S. D. (1991). The best and wisest parent: A critique of John Holt's philosophy of education. In J. Van Galen & M. A. Pitman (Eds.), *Home schooling: Political, historical, and pedagogical perspectives* (pp. 121–135). Norwood, NJ: Ablex.

Friedman, M. (1955). The role of government in education. In R. A. Solo (Ed.), *Economics and the public interest* (pp. 127–134). New Brunswick, NJ: Rutgers University Press.

Hardin, G. (1968). The tragedy of the commons. *Science, 162,* 1243–1248.

Hirschman, A. O. (1970). *Exit, voice, and loyalty: Responses to decline in firms, organizations, and states.* Cambridge, MA: Harvard University Press.

Holt, J. C. (1981). *Teach your own: A hopeful path for education.* New York: Delacorte/Seymour Lawrence.

Jencks, C. (1972). *Inequality: A reassessment of the effect of family and schooling in America.* New York: Basic Books.

Kaestle, C. F. (1973). *The evolution of an urban school system: New York City 1750–1850.* Cambridge, MA: Harvard University Press.

Kantrowitz, B., & Wingert, P. (1998, October 5). Learning at home: Does it pass the test? *Newsweek,* 64–70.

Klicka, C. J. (1995). *The right choice: The incredible failure of public education and the rising hope of home schooling: An academic, historical, practical, and legal perspective* (Rev. ed.). Gresham, OR: Noble.

Kohn, A. (1998, April). Only for my kid: How privileged parents undermine school reform. *Phi Delta Kappan, 79,* 568–578.

Labaree, D. F. (1997a). *How to succeed in school without really learning: The credentials race in American education.* New Haven, CT: Yale University Press.

Labaree, D. F. (1997b). Public goods, private goods: The American struggle over educational goals. *American Educational Research Journal, 34*(1), 39–81.

230

A Critique of Home Schooling

Labaree, D. F. (in press). No exit: You can run but you can't hide from public education as a public good. In L. Cuban & D. Shipps (Eds.), *Reconstructing the common good in education: Coping with intractable American dilemmas.* Stanford, CA: Stanford University Press.

Lareau, A. (1989). *Home advantage: Social class and parental intervention in elementary education.* London: Falmer.

Lasch, C. (1995). *The revolt of the elites and the betrayal of democracy.* New York: Norton.

Lines, P. (1991). Home instruction: The size and growth of the movement. In J. Van Galen & M. A. Pitman (Eds.), *Home schooling: Political, historical, and pedagogical perspectives* (pp. 9–41). Norwood, NJ: Ablex.

Lines, P. M. (1994). Homeschooling: Private choices and public obligations. *Home School Researcher, 10*(3), 9–26.

Lyman, I. (1998, September 14). Not home alone. *National Review, 50*(17), 30–34.

Margolis, E. (1998, February). *The threat of educational reform: Schools, socialization, and the state.* Paper presented at the annual conference of the Sociology of Education Association, Monterey, CA.

Matthews, R. K. (1984). *The radical politics of Thomas Jefferson: A revisionist view.* Lawrence: University of Kansas Press.

Miner, B. (1996). Conservatives push the campaign for "parental rights." In R. Lowe, B. Miner, L. Miller, B. Peterson, & R. Tenorio (Eds.), *Selling out our schools: Vouchers, markets, and the future of public education* (pp. 68–69). Milwaukee, WI: Rethinking Schools.

Moore, E. R. (1997, May 26). Letter to C. Jarvis, Executive Vice President of Focus on the Family. *Exodus 2000 Project Web Site* [Online]. Retrieved June 25, 1999 from the World Wide Web: http://exodus2000.org/fotf.htm

Olson, M. (1965). *The logic of collective action: Public goods and the theory of groups.* Cambridge, MA: Harvard University Press.

Putnam, R. D. (1996, Winter). The strange disappearance of civic America. *The American Prospect, 7*(24), 34–49.

Ray, B. D. (1997a, June 23). The strengths of home schooling. *TheSite.com* [Online]. Retrieved January 8, 1999 from the World Wide Web: http://www.zdnet.com/zdtv/thesite/0697w1994/life/life1614_062397.html

Ray, B. D. (1997b). *Strengths of their own—Home schoolers across America: Academic achievement, family characteristics, and longitudinal traits.* Salem, OR: National Home Education Research Institute.

Ray, B. D. (1999, April). *Home schooling: The ameliorator of negative influences on learning?* Paper presented at the annual conference of the American Educational Research Association, Montreal, Canada.

Rose, L. C., Gallup, A. M., & Elam, S. M. (1997, September). The 29th annual Phi Delta Kappa/Gallup poll of the public's attitudes toward the public schools. *Phi Delta Kappan, 79,* 41–50.

Rudner, L. M. (1999). The scholastic achievement and demographic characteristics of home school students in 1998. *Education Policy Analysis Archives, 7*(8) [Online]. Retrieved April 24, 1999 from the World Wide Web: http://epaa.asu.edu/epaa/v7n8/

Sandel, M. J. (1996). *Democracy's discontent: America in search of a public policy.* Cambridge, MA: Harvard University Press.

Simonds, B. (1998). Letter to "Christian parents, grandparents, and all who follow Jesus." *Citizens for Excellence in Education/National Association of Christian Educators Web Site* [Online]. Retrieved March 6, 1999 from the World Wide Web: http://www.webcom.com/webcee/strategy.html

Simonds, R. (1999, May). *President's report.* Costa Mesa, CA: National Association of Christian Educators/Citizens for Excellence in Education.

Steinberg, L. D., Brown, B. B., & Dornbusch, S. M. (1996). *Beyond the classroom: Why school reform has failed and what parents need to do.* New York: Simon & Schuster.

231

C. Lubienski

Trotter, A. (1998, December 2). Teachers propose integrating schools by socioeconomic status. *Education Week, 18,* 5.

Tyack, D. B. (1968). The perils of pluralism: The background of the Pierce case. *American Historical Review, 74*(1), 74–98.

Van Galen, J. (1991). Ideologues and pedagogues: Parents who teach their children at home. In J. Van Galen & M. A. Pitman (Eds.), *Home schooling: Political, historical, and pedagogical perspectives* (pp. 63–76). Norwood, NJ: Ablex.

Wells, A. S., & Crain, R. L. (1994). Perpetuation theory and the long-term effects of school desegregation. *Review of Educational Research, 64,* 531–555.

Welner, K. M. (1999, April). *Homeschooling and democracy: Exploring the tension between the state and parents.* Paper presented at the annual conference of the American Educational Research Association, Montreal, Canada.

Whitehead, J. W., & Crow, A. I. (1993). *Home education: Rights and reasons.* Wheaton, IL: Crossway.

Williamson, K. B. (1989). *Home schooling: Answering questions.* Springfield, IL: Thomas.

Wills, G. (1978). *Inventing America: Jefferson's Declaration of Independence.* Garden City, NY: Doubleday.

Wink, W. (1992). *Engaging the powers.* Minneapolis, MN: Fortress.

PEABODY JOURNAL OF EDUCATION, 75(1&2), 233–255
Copyright © 2000, Lawrence Erlbaum Associates, Inc.

The Future of Home Schooling

Michael P. Farris and Scott A. Woodruff

Anyone who saw the cover picture of the cute little girl on the October 5, 1998 issue of *Newsweek* under the caption "Home Schooling, More Than a Million Kids and Growing: Can It Work for Your Family?" knows that home schooling exists. Whether people love it or fear it, they recognize that it is a well-established part of the American educational landscape—one that is growing rapidly. It is this rapid growth, perhaps more than any other single factor, that justifies an inquiry into the future of home schooling. What is inherent in the nature of home schooling that lends insight into its future? What data and studies are available from which trends can be discerned? What is distinctive about home schooling in the present that presages a distinctive future? This article touches on these issues and

MICHAEL P. FARRIS *is the Founder and President of the Home School Legal Defense Association, Purcellville, Virginia.*

SCOTT A. WOODRUFF *is an Attorney with the Home School Legal Defense Association, Purcellville, Virginia.*

Portions of this article are from *The Future of Home Schooling*, by M. Farris, 1997, Washington, DC: Regnery. Copyright 1997 by M. Farris. Reprinted with permission.

An earlier version of this article was presented at the 1999 Annual Meeting of the American Educational Research Association, Montreal, Canada.

Requests for reprints should be sent to Michael P. Farris, Home School Legal Defense Association, Box 3000, Purcellville, VA 20134. E-mail: sally@hslda.org

233

M. P. Farris and S. A. Woodruff

draws from a variety of resources without attempting an exhaustive review of the literature[1] pertaining to research on home schooling.

An Overview of the Current State of Home Schooling

Home Schoolers' Academic Achievements

Although the academic success of a form of education should not be judged by a few standouts, the home school movement has produced standouts, nonetheless. Thirteen-year-old home schooler Rebecca Sealfon was the 1997 champion of the National Spelling Bee sponsored by Scripps Howard. Thirteen-year-old John Kizer won second place in the National Geographic Society's 1998 National Geography Bee. Seventeen-year-old home schooler Timothy Stonehocker won first place in the Algebra II division of the Illinois State High School Math Contest in 1998. Home-schooled 7-year-old Faith Nejman-McNea won first place in her age group in a literary contest that attracted 38,000 contestants (Crump, 1998). Thirteen-year-old home schooler David Beihl won the 1999 National Geography Bee. But is this height without breadth?

On March 23, 1999, the *Education Policy Analysis Archives* published the results of the largest[2] study of home school students ever undertaken. Dr. Lawrence M. Rudner (1999) authored the report, titled *Scholastic Achievement and Demographic Characteristics of Home School Students in 1998*.[3]

In spring 1998, parents of 39,607 home school students who obtained testing services through Bob Jones University Press Testing and Evaluation Service were asked to allow the results of their children's tests to be made available for this study.[4] Of that number, parents representing 20,760[5] students agreed (without knowing the test results) and also re-

[1] For a review of earlier research on academic and demographic characteristics of home school students, see Ray (1999).

[2] The largest sample previously studied for academic performance and demographic traits was 5,402 home-schooled students. This study by Ray (1997) was based on data collected during the 1994–1995 and 1995–1996 academic years.

[3] Rudner's research and report were supported by a grant from the Home School Legal Defense Association, Purcellville, Virginia. The study was published in *Education Policy Analysis Archives* and is available online at http://epaa.asu.edu/epaa/v7n8.

[4] A number of home school parents have their children tested via standardized tests. For some parents, this is a tool for independently evaluating the academic progress of the student. For others, state law mandates it. Bob Jones University Press Testing and Evaluation Service is the largest single provider of testing services for home school families (see Rudner, 1999, p. 4).

[5] On page 4 of Rudner (1999), this figure is cited as 20,790, but this apparently is a typographical error (Rudner, personal communication, March 1999).

The Future of Home Schooling

turned usable demographic questionnaires. The Iowa Tests of Basic Skills were administered to children in kindergarten through eighth grade. The Tests of Achievement and Proficiency were administered to children in Grades 9 through 12. The answers to these questionnaires and the results of the achievement tests provided the data for Rudner's (1999) report.

Rudner's (1999) results demonstrate that home school families are a distinctive segment of the American population. They are distinguished not only by high academic achievement (suggesting that home-schooled standouts are not an aberration), but also by family characteristics.

Figures 1 through 6 show the exceptional academic performance of home-schooled children based on the tests administered. Six separate academic subtests were given, each with its own set of norms: composite with computation (this subtest is a blend of all other subtests, but independently normed; Lawrence M. Rudner, personal communication, March 1999), reading total, language, mathematics total with computation, social studies, and science. The median scores nationally and for home-schooled children are expressed as a percentile[6] and compared grade by grade. The 50th percentile is the national median of all students.

Rudner's (1999) report noted that home schoolers compare favorably with other forms of private education:

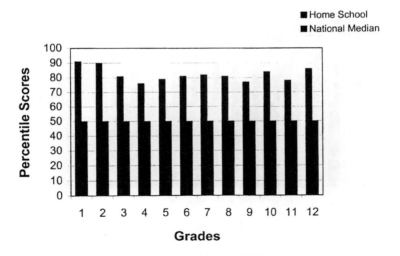

Figure 1. Composite subtest.

[6]The percentile recorded is the national percentile that corresponds to the median scaled score of a given subtest (Rudner, 1999, p. 14).

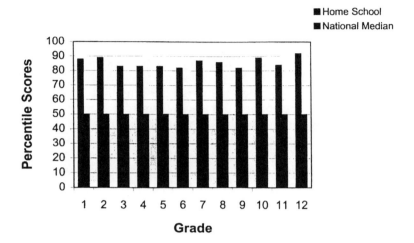

Figure 2. Reading subtest.

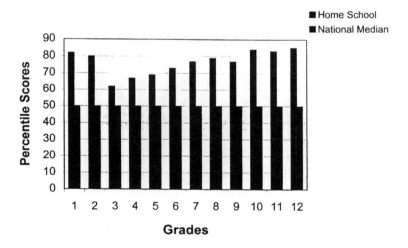

Figure 3. Language subtest.

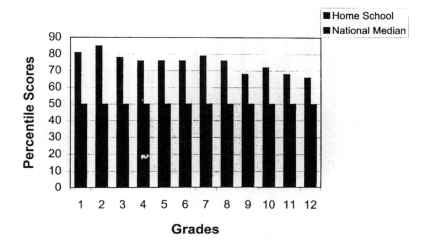

Figure 4. Math subtest.

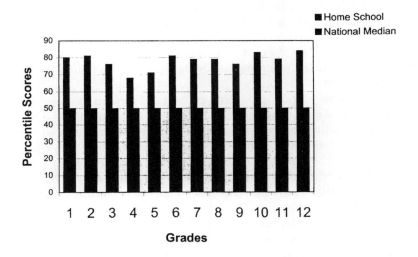

Figure 5. Social studies subtest.

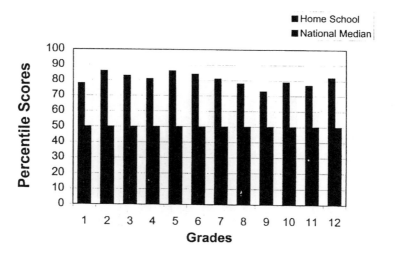

Figure 6. Science subtest.

At each grade level, the performance of home school students is above the performance levels of students enrolled in Catholic/private schools. ... a composite scale of 250, for example, is typical of a home school student in grade six, a Catholic/private school student in grade seven, and students nationwide in the later stages of grade eight. (p. 16)

Furthermore, the data show that "students who are home schooled for their entire academic life do better than students who have been home schooled for only a few years" (p. 18).

Although home schooling parents are better educated as a group than the general population (Rudner, 1999, p. 25), the children of home schooling parents with the least education still score well above national norms. Rudner stated, "At every grade level, the mean performance of home school students whose parents do not have a college degree is much higher than the mean performance of students in public schools" (p. 32).

Furthermore, although home schooling parents are wealthier than the general population (see Rudner, 1999, p. 25), scores for children of home schooling parents in the lowest specified income bracket (less than $35,000 per year) easily surpass national norms (p. 22). Home-schooled students whose parents were in this income bracket ranked, on average, at the 76th percentile (by deduction from data regarding Grades K through 10; Rudner, 1999, p. 22).

The academic advantages of home education are very substantial and are especially noteworthy for the children of the least wealthy and least educated, who do not typically surpass national achievement norms.

The Future of Home Schooling

Socialization

Question: "Don't you think home schooling might have a negative impact on the socialization process? I don't want my children growing up to be misfits."

"I wish I could home school my daughter. She has been teased so cruelly at school that she is now in professional counseling."

Most Americans harbor two antagonistic and irreconcilable drives within their psyche: the drive to conform and the drive to be different. Although we admire the standouts in our society—the heroes, the inventors, the artists, the literary geniuses, the ordinary citizen risen to prominence—we simultaneously feel a need to be like others, to conform, to be one of the crowd, and to go with the flow. Although we build monuments to George Washington and Martin Luther King, Jr., many Americans cherish the notion that they are the same as everyone else around them. Home schooling offers a unique contribution to this never-ending dialogue.

Home-schooled children spend much more time around their parents than do their public and private school counterparts. Most home school parents emphasize the teaching of values that have been honored by time and tradition. Because of this, most home-schooled children likely will enter adulthood with a set of personal values that closely conforms to that of their parents.

On the other hand, home-schooled students receive much individualized academic attention. The educational program is tailored to the needs and strengths of the individual child. The home-schooled child can pursue his or her own academic interests in a way not possible in a classroom setting. These factors are likely to result in adults who, in some ways, are truly distinctive and unique. Home-schooled students, therefore, will be both more conformed and less conformed than their classroom-educated counterparts. If the question of socialization is truly only a question of whether home-schooled students will be "different," the answer is both yes and no.

The first quotation with which this section was introduced reflects the angst of a conformity-minded parent who does not want her child growing up being an oddball or socially stigmatized or constantly feeling inferior because she is different. This question appeared in the syndicated popular advice column of James C. Dobson (1998), *Dr. Dobson Answers Your Questions*. For this parent, being like others is a virtue, and being different is a social hazard.

The second quotation at the introduction of this section is a close paraphrase of a statement made to Scott Woodruff by a participant in a truancy

239

M. P. Farris and S. A. Woodruff

proceeding against a Midwestern home school family. For that parent, socialization was a vice that was destroying the child, crippling her emotionally and devastating her to such an extent that professional therapy was necessary. The cruelty of what was occurring in the classroom and playground in the absence of effective adult supervision[7] probably will leave a permanent mark on that child's self-esteem. She will enter adulthood forever feeling different, unworthy, unpopular, and unacceptable. Ironically, she will enter adulthood feeling like the "misfit" that the first-quoted parent feared might be the result of home schooling.

The word *socialization* is derived from the Latin root *socius*, which means a companion, fellow, partner, associate, or ally (Whitney, 1914). The same root is found in our words *association* and *society*. At its fundamental level, therefore, socialization relates to the idea of how we learn to get along with others. There is nothing in the root of the word that implies a peer or an equal or someone of the identical age or status. Socialization, therefore, is only erroneously used to refer to the process of getting along with a peer group.

A study conducted in West Virginia in 1992 compared 30 home schooling families with 32 conventionally schooling families whose children were between the ages of 7 and 14. The author of the study, Lee Stough, concluded that home-schooled children "gained the necessary skills, knowledge and attitudes needed to function in society ... at a rate similar to that of conventionally schooled children" (Stough, as cited in Aiex, 1999). Stough continued,

> In so far as self-concept is a reflector of socialization, it would appear that few home schooled children are socially deprived, and that there may be sufficient evidence to indicate that some home schooled children have a higher self-concept than conventionally schooled children. (Stough, as cited in Aiex, 1999)

It is contrary to logic to assert that the social skills a child will need as an adult are best taught in a classroom, where the child is surrounded only by students of his or her own age, as Fedoryka (as cited in Clark, 1993) noted:

> I really didn't consider it proper for my child to spend a year of her life learning how to be an 11-year-old, then another year of her life learning how to be a 12-year-old, another year learning how to be a 13-year-old.

---

[7]According to Barbara A. Bliss (as cited in Aiex, 1999), "Protection during early, developmental years for purposes of nurturing and growth is evident in many areas: plant, animal, and aquatic. Why should it be considered wrong or bad in the most vital arena, human development?"

The Future of Home Schooling

... She has a mother at home. I'd rather she learn to be like her mother, and have plenty of time to do it. (p. 303)

If the goal of socialization is to produce adult social skills, it makes little sense to use classmates as teachers.

Doctoral candidate Larry Edward Shyers reported in 1992 the results of a study of self-concept among 140 children aged 8 and 9 years. Seventy home-schooled children and 70 traditionally schooled children were evaluated using the Piers–Harris Children's Self-Concept Scale, which measures self-esteem. Although his study[8] found no difference in self-esteem between the two groups,[9] the trained observers found that the home-schooled children had significantly fewer behavior problems than traditionally schooled children when playing with mixed groups of children. This supports the conclusion that children with greater parental contact have better-developed social skills, helping confirm the validity of the assumptions inherent in Fedoryka's intuitive statement.

Mike Mitchell, Dean of Enrollment at Oral Roberts University (ORU), surveyed 212 home-schooled students enrolled at ORU. He found that nearly 80% were in at least one club or organization, 88% were involved in at least one outreach ministry, and more than 90% played intramural sports (Klicka, 1998). Home-schooled graduates appear to be socially engaged at the college level, as well.

Children who have completed a program of home-based education and entered adulthood are sanguine concerning how home education taught them to relate to others. J. Gary Knowles of the University of Michigan studied 53 adults who had been educated at home. He came to the following conclusion:

I have found no evidence that these adults were even moderately disadvantaged. ... two-thirds of them were married, the norm for adults their age, and none were unemployed or on any form of welfare assistance. More than three-quarters felt that being taught at home had actually helped them to interact with people from different levels of society. (Knowles, as cited in Layman, 1998)

---

[8] As cited in Bunday (1995).

[9] An earlier similar study by John Wesley Taylor using the same test measured significantly higher self-esteem among the home-schooled group (The Moore Foundation, Box 1, Camas, WA 98607). A complete copy is available via University Microfilms International, 300 North Zeeb Road, Ann Arbor, MI 48106.

M. P. Farris and S. A. Woodruff

In the words of Dobson (1998), "To accuse home-schoolers of creating strange little people in solitary confinement is nonsense."

Those who raise the question of socialization may be concerned about home school families and children becoming isolated. This concern is unfounded. Home school families "rely heavily on support groups as a resource for planning field trips and maintaining personal contact with like-minded families" (Layman, 1998, p. 8). Smith and Sikkink (1999) of the sociology department of the University of North Carolina at Chapel Hill said,

> Of all types of non-public education, home schooling as a practice—by so closely uniting home, family, education, and (usually) religious faith—might seem the most privatized and isolated from the concerns of the public sphere. But in fact, most home schoolers are not at all isolated. Indeed, most are embedded in dense relational networks of home schooling families; participate in local, state, regional, and national home schooling organizations; and engage in a variety of community activities and programs that serve the education of their children. Home schooling families meet together at playgrounds; frequent local libraries, museums, and zoos; organize drama productions, science projects, and art workshops; enroll their kids in YMCA soccer and swimming classes; organize home school association picnics and cook outs; and much more. Home schooling families also frequent home education conferences and seminars; pay close attention to education-related legislative issues; share political information with each other; and educate themselves about relevant legal concerns. Far from being privatized and isolated, home schooling families are typically very well networked and quite civically active.

All objective evidence indicates that home-schooled children are well-adjusted members of society. To the extent that home-schooled children are different from others, it appears to be a socially positive difference.

Two Trends in Home Schooling

Classical Education

> Classical learning is ideally suited for the training of cultural leaders, and that is what we so desperately need (Wilson, 1994)

Home schoolers of the future should judge their success not by the degree to which they surpass the struggling government schools, but by how

The Future of Home Schooling

closely they come to obtaining for their children the full potential of home schooling itself.

The present academic success of home education may owe much to the wide variety of excellent curricula that are available.[10] Nonetheless, it may be that the fullest potential of home schooling as an academic endeavor will be achieved when the content and methods of classical education become firmly rooted in the home school movement.

Classical education has a content component and a process component. The content component consists of study of the great thinkers and writers of Western civilization. It involves bringing the great wealth of Western thought out of the vault into which it was put as expectations of student intellectual ability dropped simultaneously with the advance of compulsory education laws and the rapid growth of government schools in the late 19th and early 20th centuries. The books that added to the intellectual and cultural wealth of Western civilization, and thereby altered its course, are presented to the student for study. This includes the works of Homer, Sophocles, Plutarch, Virgil, Augustine, Aquinas, Chaucer, Machiavelli, Calvin, Shakespeare, Milton, Locke, Adam Smith, de Tocqueville, Tolstoy, and C. S. Lewis.

It is hoped that students familiar with these riches will draw on their lessons when, as adults, they make decisions for themselves, their families, their communities, their country, and their civilization. Their own wisdom will be augmented by the wisest of men our civilization has produced. This will allow them to identify and defeat old errors cropping up in new disguises.

With regard to the process component of classical education, studies generally are divided into two main components: the trivium (primary and secondary education) and the quadrivium (university training). The trivium is composed of three subparts: Grammar, Dialectic, and Rhetoric. The Grammar stage teaches basic facts and skills, the Dialectic stage steeps children in logic and helps to teach them the reasoning behind many of the facts they learned in the Grammar period, and the Rhetoric stage focuses on the children's ability to present their worldview in a pleasing and logical manner. In simple terms, Grammar teaches facts, Dialectic teaches reasoning, and Rhetoric teaches presentation.

After the basic skills of reading, writing, and math are begun, the child is ready at about age 9 to launch into the Grammar stage of the trivium. During the Grammar stage of life, "children possess a great natural ability to memorize large amounts of information even though they may not understand its significance," educator and author Fritz Hinrichs (1995) ob-

---

[10] According to Jane S. Preis (as cited in Aiex, 1999), "In 1987, in one home-schooling catalog alone more than 300 suppliers of home-schooling materials are listed."

243

served. He continued, "This is the time to fill them full of facts, such as the multiplication table, geography, dates, events, plant and animal classifications; anything that lends itself to easy repetition and assimilation by the mind." This is a great time to encourage children to memorize numerous and even lengthy passages from the Bible. In some rabbinical traditions, boys are expected to memorize the entire Pentateuch.

Both Hinrichs and classical education proponent Dorothy Sayers strongly encouraged the study of Latin or Greek during the Grammar period. Sayers (1947/1999) argued for Latin in the following terms:

I will say it once, quite firmly, that the best grounding for education is the Latin grammar. I say this, not because Latin is traditional and medieval, but simply because even a rudimentary knowledge of Latin cuts down the labor and pains of learning almost any other subject by at least 50 percent. It is the key to the vocabulary and structure of all the Teutonic languages, as well as to the technical vocabulary of all the sciences and to the literature of the entire Mediterranean civilization, together with all its historical documents. (as cited in Farris, 1997, p. 11)

Sayers also argued for the study of a modern foreign language during the Grammar stage.

Some may be concerned about the emphasis on memorizing a great many facts during the Grammar stage. But children need to memorize the basic facts of grammar, history, geography, art, addition, subtraction, multiplication, and division simply because they are necessary tools for further learning. Sayers (1947/1999) defended memorization during the Grammar period:

Anything and everything which can be usefully committed to memory should be memorized at this period, whether it is immediately intelligible or not. The modern tendency is to try and force rational explanations on a child's mind at too early an age. Intelligent questions, spontaneously asked, should, of course, receive an immediate and rational answer; but it is a great mistake to suppose that a child cannot readily enjoy and remember things that are beyond his power to analyze. (as cited in Farris, 1997, pp. 11–12)

Students are being encouraged to memorize and master this material, not as an end in itself but to lay a foundation for lifelong learning.

Around age 11, most children are ready to move on to the second stage of classical education—the Dialectic. The first stage focused on the child's observation and memory. In the second stage, the emphasis is on a child's ability to engage in discursive reason, as Hinrichs (1995) wrote:

The Future of Home Schooling

It is during this stage that the child no longer sees the facts that he learned as merely separate pieces of information but he starts to put them together into logical relations by asking questions. No longer can the American Revolution merely be a fact in history but it must be understood in the light of the rest of what the child has learned.

A formal course in logic is ideal at this stage of a child's education. It is a time to teach cause-and-effect, steps of reasoning, and how to make proper inferences.

The sentence most used by a teaching parent during the Dialectic period should be, "Why do you say that?" Children should be taught to present a logical and defensible explanation for every assertion they make. If a child writes an essay that proclaims, "America is the greatest nation on earth," he should be prepared to defend his or her conclusion. Current events are useful for starting discussion and debate.

The Rhetoric stage occurs at around 14 to 16 years of age. Hinrichs (1995) said, "The child moves from merely grasping the logical sequence of arguments to learning how to present them in a persuasive, aesthetically pleasing form." Sayers (1949/1999) also called this period the Poetic age, because during this period "the student develops the skill of organizing the information he has learned into a well-reasoned format that will be both pleasing and logical" (as cited in Farris, 1997, p. 14). In the Rhetoric stage, children should be asked two questions, "How can you say that more clearly?" and "How can you say that in a manner your audience will find more pleasing?"

Students who are inclined toward the sciences and mathematics should be encouraged to begin their specialization while still studying some literature and history. The reverse is true for those gifted in the humanities. Sayers (1947/1999) said, "The scope of Rhetoric depends also on whether the pupil is to be turned out into the world at the age of sixteen or whether he is to proceed to the university" (as cited in Farris, 1997, p. 15).

Although many home-schooled children aspire to careers in the "public square," not all of them will. Some will not want to become ministers, lawyers, statesmen, or journalists. Not everyone requires the same degree of polished rhetorical skills so essential in the public arena. But all adults need to be able to communicate ideas and information in a rational and pleasing manner. Such skills are useful in any job, in situations as diverse as talking to an appliance repairman or interacting with other members of a church board.

Classical education is not neutral. It takes definite philosophical sides. And all that is old is not necessarily good. A heavy dose in the literature and history of the Founding Fathers as well as the writings of great Americans in the intervening years must be included to make a truly ideal program for the modern American home schooler.

245

M. P. Farris and S. A. Woodruff

Even for parents who do not wish to pursue classical education in all its fullness, it offers insights that can be applied usefully to other types of programs. The content portion of classical education can be adapted by taking care to include study of a number of the great thinkers of Western civilization in the overall curriculum. The process component can be adapted by emphasizing acquisition of facts and knowledge in the early years, emphasizing reasoning, logic, and relationship in the middle years, and emphasizing communication and persuasiveness in the later years.

Although difficult to measure, it appears that the classical approach is gaining popularity among home schoolers. There are now around a dozen providers of organized classical education programs, scarcely any of which existed 10 years ago. In government schools, teaching methods and content are often driven by political pressure or the popularity of trendy but unproven theories in teachers' schools. Home schoolers are not subject to these pressures. The popularity of classical education will continue to grow commensurate with its ability to prove its merits to the home school community.

Technology's Helping Hand

The Internet is transforming how we think about commerce. It soon will transform how we think about education. America's twin passions for things excellent and things efficient seem to have merged in the Internet.

The Internet's first benefit to home schooling is near-instant access to information and knowledge. Scott Woodruff's family recently finished reading Louisa May Alcott's *Little Women*, in which one of the principal characters contracts scarlet fever. A 12-year-old member of the Woodruff family was given an assignment to research scarlet fever and give an after-dinner presentation the following night. By using the Internet, he was able to obtain the information he needed, with plenty of time left over for outlining his presentation. A few days later, the family observed an uncared-for dog in the neighborhood with large, bald patches in its coat. This same 12-year-old was assigned a research project on mange, and a day or two later, he gave an after-dinner presentation on his findings with the Internet supplying his information.

A word of caution is in order. Just as you would not ask your child to walk alone across one of our largest cities, it would be very unwise to ask your child to walk through the metropolis of the Internet without parental guidance and protection. The Internet has made the access to every-

The Future of Home Schooling

thing—including evil—much easier. It is hoped that future developments in programming and rating systems will allow parents a far greater degree of control over what appears on the family computer monitor when children are conducting research over the Internet.

The Internet's second benefit to home schooling is making classroom-style instruction available in the student's own home. Mike Farris teaches a constitutional law course over the Internet for home school students in high school. The students purchase textbooks as in a typical class. In addition to listening to recorded lectures, there are periodic live chat sessions between the teacher and all the students. There is also a bulletin board or forum where students can post questions or comments for response. Students send their tests via the Internet to the teacher, who grades them and sends the results back.

Fritz Hinrichs of Escondido Tutorial Services (www.gbt.org) offers a full classical curriculum using live Internet audio and video technology courses. Students from all parts of the country hear each other speak and discuss issues in a conference-call format. The students see the teacher's face and "raise their hands" by typing an exclamation point. Hinrichs recently taught class on location in Europe, showing his students photographs related to the topic taken with a digital camera. It is a paperless classroom, where writing assignments are handed in electronically, graded, and returned electronically. It is expected that more of this method of transmitting instruction will occur in the future.

The following advertisement appeared in *Home School Computing* magazine (now a section of *The Teaching Home* magazine). "Brighten Your Future ... Earn High School Credit with HOMER," the ad proclaimed. This computer-based course offering instruction in business education, English, mathematics, science, social studies, and vocational education is available through the North Dakota Department of Public Instruction—the same department that waged a bitter war on home schoolers throughout the 1980s, leading to criminal prosecution of several families. For this department to go from being one of the worst enemies of home education in the entire country to selling computer-based instruction to home schoolers throughout the nation is an absolutely amazing turnaround and convincing evidence of how Internet technology is changing home education (Farris, 1997).

Even for families not wishing to go "online," a computer and appropriate software can enhance significantly some aspects of home instruction. The quality of educational software spans a wide gamut from nearly useless to thoroughly challenging. Software companies know that putting the word *education* in front of a software product will get the attention of a certain segment of the public immediately. Use of the word *educational* has

247

M. P. Farris and S. A. Woodruff

been used both as a fig leaf[11] to cover up weak content and as a proud announcement of the introduction of genuinely worthwhile software. There are several published sources of help for parents looking for reasonably objective evaluations of educational programs, and we may expect that there will be more as time goes on.

An appropriate program can adeptly perform both routine drills and advanced instruction and give instant feedback. Part of the pleasure of home schooling is the opportunity for a rich and frequent interaction with one's children. High-tech educational programs will never replace this aspect of home schooling. However, they may allow parents to concentrate their time on the aspects of home schooling that are most beneficial and enjoyable.

An additional mode of high-tech learning is direct-broadcast satellite television. The advantage of this mode is the strong visual impact of watching and listening as a high-caliber instructor presents a lesson while the student watches from home. Its primary disadvantage is the absence of significant interaction between the student and other students and the instructor. In this respect, it offers little over the traditional classroom except additional choice of content. Nonetheless, this use of technology will continue to be available and grow as it is selectively used to enhance the home school program.

The availability of high-technology teaching aids makes home education a more attractive option for some. At the same time, the demand for such high-tech solutions will help spur the growth of educational technology. Technology and home education will help each other grow.

The Future of the Individual and Implications for Society

The modern phase of home education is now roughly 20 years old. It has grown during that time from fewer than 100,000 students to more than 1 million students (Ray, 1999). All, or nearly all, of the parents who are now educating their children at home were themselves educated in a traditional school. Within the next decade, we will observe the phenomenon of second-generation home schooling. How will this second generation of home schoolers affect the home education movement in America? Although no amount of speculation can substitute for empirical data, we can perhaps get an answer to the question by first asking how home schooling has affected these soon-to-be second generation home schoolers.

---

[11]"Home schoolers are looking for real educational tools, not vitamin-enriched games like Carmen San Diego which offer an educational value which is minimal at best" (S. Somerville, Esq., as cited in Farris, 1997, p. 74).

The Future of Home Schooling

In doing this analysis, it is important to remember that the object of both parenting and education is not simply to improve the condition of a child, but to produce in him a mature adult. Three aspects of life distinguish adulthood from childhood: marriage, career, and citizenship. We turn to an examination of these three to examine the likely future of home education.

Marriage

Home education gives the second generation a much higher likelihood of a happy and successful marriage than their traditionally schooled counterparts. Both the philosophy and the practice in which they have been immersed will logically tend to produce more committed and responsible marriage partners.

Fedoryka (as cited in Clark, 1993) noted, "The philosophy of self-realization, self-affirmation, self-fulfillment, and self-esteem is the dominant philosophy today, not only of our society and culture as a whole, but specifically of the schools" (p. 306). We should not expect a high proportion of children who grow up under teaching that places the gratification of self at the pinnacle of moral authority to be responsible and committed marriage partners. Furthermore, government schools are not permitted to teach the religious principles that marriage is ordained by God and that God hates divorce.

Most home school families, on the other hand, teach with reverence the sanctity of a lifelong union of one man and one woman and the virtue of preferring others before oneself (see, e.g., Rom. 12:10, King James Version). For faith-based home schoolers, especially, this concept is grounded in the strong Scriptural disapproval of divorce and strong approval of lifelong, faithful marriage (also see Matt. 19:9; Mark 10:9; Heb. 13:4).

Rudner (1999, pp. 6–7) reported that 97.2% of home school families are led by a man and woman who are married to each other, 25 percentile points higher than the national average. Divorce is not unknown in the home school community, but anecdotally it is comparatively rare. A recent workshop on the law related to divorce and home schooling attracted less than a dozen listeners, although the state conference on home schooling of which it was a part was attended by more than 5,000.

Rudner (1999, pp. 6–7) reported that home school families typically have more children than the national average. Nationwide, 78.8% of families have only one or two children. Among home school families, only 37.9% have so few. Nationwide, only 20.4% of families have three or more children. Among home school families, however, 62.1% have families of

249

M. P. Farris and S. A. Woodruff

this size. This may reflect an optimism and confidence that the marriage bond on which the family is based will endure.

This suggests that not only are home-schooled children being taught a philosophy that will tend toward producing more committed and responsible marriage partners, but a high proportion are witnessing this doctrine lived out in their own families. They are seeing their families, under the protection of the parental commitment to the marriage, procreate much more fruitfully than is typical nationwide. They are seeing the home filled with optimism and purpose. They are seeing the marriage covenant as the foundation for all home life and the home as the center of all educational life. The importance of the marital union is thus held high.

It is reasonable to expect that the next generation of home-schooled adults will respond to the principles they have been taught and the practices they have observed. We may justifiably anticipate stronger family units, a lower divorce rate, and a higher procreative rate among second-generation home schoolers.

Career

Home schooling's impact on the career potential of the next generation of home schoolers can best be gauged by their success in college. A survey of 1,657 home schooling families with 5,402 students found that 69% of the students went on to further formal education after high school graduation, essentially identical in proportion to the 71% of traditionally educated students who continue their schooling (Ray, 1997, p. 11). The 1998–1999 ACT average composite score for college-bound home-schooled students was 22.7 (see http://www.act.org/news/data/99/t9.html). For traditionally schooled students, it was only 21 (see http://www.act.org/news/data/99/t9.html). Because many colleges rely heavily on the ACT score, we can infer that home-schooled students have a stronger chance of getting into better colleges and receiving more scholarships. These educational opportunities will give home-schooled students an advantage when they start their careers. As of June 1998, the Home School Legal Defense Association counted 717 colleges that had accepted home schoolers.

Thomas M. Rajala, Director of Admissions at Boston University, sent the following letter to home school leaders in Massachusetts in 1991: "Boston University welcomes applications from home schooled students. We believe students educated at home possess the passion for knowledge, the independence, and the self-reliance that enable them to excel in our intellectually challenging programs of study" (as cited in Klicka, 1998, p. 3).

A 1995 study at Bob Jones University concluded that home-schooled college students perform "as well as, if not better than, their convention-

The Future of Home Schooling

ally educated counterparts" (as cited in Klicka, 1998, p. 5). A 1994 study at Oral Roberts University indicated that home schoolers had approximately the same scores on preadmission standardized tests as other students who were admitted at that institution. Home-schooled students, however, had a college grade point average (GPA) of 3.02, whereas the overall GPA was 2.76 (as cited in Klicka, 1998).

In 1997, Doctors Rhonda Galloway and Joe Sutton (1997) released the results of a 4-year study comparing how home-schooled college students achieve in five areas—academic, cognitive, spiritual, affective–social, and psychomotor—as compared with other students. The study tracked 180 students—60 graduates from home school programs, 60 from public schools, and 60 from Christian schools. In the area of academic achievement, home-schooled students ranked first in 10 out of 12 indicators.

Knowles (as cited in Layman, 1998) of the University of Michigan studied 53 adults who had been home schooled to gauge the impact of home education. He found that none of them was unemployed or on any form of welfare (p. 10).

We can reasonably conclude that the success of home schoolers in getting into and excelling in college will produce significant employment success. Business leaders do not have high expectations of the product of government schools. A *Fortune* magazine survey of CEOs in 1990 found that 76% believed public schools made American workers worse, not better. A survey of human resource officers that same year revealed that 64% did not believe public schools were producing competent workers (Practical Home Schooling Staff, 1994). Home schooling has prepared them well for success in college and in the workforce.

Citizenship

After every national election, the popular media decry the fact that only a small percentage of citizens who are qualified to vote actually exercise their right. Will second-generation home schoolers fall in with the large segment of our society that has withdrawn from even the most rudimentary expression of civic life, or will they chart their own course?

Once again, there are the standouts. A March 1999 survey conducted by the Home School Legal Defense Association revealed that 35 home schoolers held elected office at the state or national level at that time. But what level of civic involvement is typical for home school families?

In 1996, the National Center for Education Statistics of the U.S. Department of Education surveyed a nationally representative sample of 9,393 parents with school-age children (Smith & Sikkink, 1999). The survey

M. P. Farris and S. A. Woodruff

asked whether the parents (a) were members of a community organization; (b) participated in an ongoing community service activity; (c) went to the public library for books, tapes, lectures, or story hours, or to use library equipment; and (d) voted in a national or state election in the previous 5 years. The survey also asked parents if they had done any of the following during the last 12 months: wrote or telephoned an editor or public official; signed a petition; attended a public meeting; contributed money to a political candidate, party, or cause; worked for a political cause; or participated in a protest or boycott.

The results showed that in one category, attendance at public meetings, home schoolers and public schoolers ranked equally. In all other categories, home schoolers surpassed public schoolers (Smith & Sikkink, 1999; see also http://www.unc.edu/~cssmith/firstthings/index.htm for all the statistics discussed herein). This difference in level of civic involvement could not be accounted for by difference in education, income, age, race, family structure, region, or the number of hours per week that parents worked.

It is not surprising that home schoolers participate heavily in the political process. Home schoolers have had to fight and labor to establish the freedom to educate their children at home. They remember the criminal prosecution of home schoolers in the late 1970s. They remember the trips to various courts of appeal. They are constantly aware that there are groups in our society that would restrict or abolish this right. Every year legislation is introduced that would take away cherished educational liberties. The home schooler often has the perspective of a minority, of a reformer, of one who stands to lose the most precious things in his or her life at the stroke of a legislative pen.

Second- and third-generation home schoolers probably will participate in civil processes at a rate similar to their parents. Unlike their parents, however, they will have received the advantages inherent in a home-based program of education. How will these better-educated but equally active citizens affect America's political culture?

Our nation was birthed in direct response to a tyrannical monarchy. The American Revolution was inspired and led by well-educated men who could rightly understand the issues of the day and persuasively communicate them to their fellow countrymen. Because only persons who can think independently can envision an independent nation, the primary secular purpose of education in American society has always been to produce persons who can think independently and communicate persuasively.[12] This

---

[12]See, for example, Maine Revised Statutes Annotated 20–A §5001–A (7): "Compulsory education is essential to the preservation of the rights and liberties of the people and the continued prosperity of our society and our nation" (p. 534).

The Future of Home Schooling

is in contrast to the purpose of the highly centralized education common in totalitarian states, which is to create a compliant population that supports the government's agenda.

Because the character and continued existence of our republic hinge on the ability of our citizens to think independently of the government, it must be recognized that all genuine education is potentially subversive in that it may lead a person to disagree with his or her government. This subversive tendency is, paradoxically, the only safeguard of our liberty this side of the Divine. We cherish our right to disagree with our government. We need it.

It is, therefore, a potential or actual conflict of interest for the government to control education. The extent of the conflict increases in direct proportion to the degree of governmental, and especially federal, control. Precisely because it is not controlled by the government, home schooling is uniquely situated to foster the continuation of our rich and honorable tradition of civil opposition, preserving the things we value most in a free society and eliminating the things that threaten the foundation of liberty. Because the government does not control the views home-schooled students are taught, those students will be able to develop independent views of how society should be reformed.

The exceptional academic performance of home schoolers suggests that they will have the necessary mental faculties of reason, logic, and judgment to understand properly the contentious and weighty issues of the day. Those who pursue the classical education program may be especially well-equipped to present their cases to the public.

Home school graduates' domestic happiness will be a source of strength when advocating unpopular minority views. This home-educated citizen, well prepared for college and career, will rarely, if ever, see his or her independence dulled by reliance on government charity for a means of support.

Although their parents' civic activism may have been primarily oriented toward defending the right to educate one's children at home, we can reasonably expect that second- and third-generation home-schooled citizens will broaden the scope of the purposes for which they participate in the political process. They will articulate, espouse, popularize, and establish many successful reform movements of the future. They will make their mark on American political culture.

Conclusion

Americans love success. The current rapid growth of home schooling is partly attributable to the academic and college success home school gradu-

M. P. Farris and S. A. Woodruff

ates have enjoyed. As those graduates demonstrate success in their careers, their marriages, and their social and civic involvement, Americans will observe it, and the growth of home schooling will be enhanced.

As home school methods and materials mature, academic success will be further enhanced, which will lead to further growth. As home schoolers become a larger proportion of the population, their ability to protect their liberties will grow. The legal environment for home schoolers will improve, leading to more growth.

In short, as large as the home school movement is today, it is only a shadow of what it will be 20 years from now. Because the future of individual home schoolers is bright, the future of the movement is bright. This promises a brighter future for America.

References

Aiex, N. K. (1999). Home schooling and socialization of children. *ERIC Digest* [Online] (ERIC Document Reproduction Service No. ED 372460 94). Retrieved January 13, 1999 from the World Wide Web: http://www.ed.gov/databases/ERICDigests/ed372460.html or http://www.geocities.com/Athens/Forum/2780/aiex.html

Bunday, C. M. (1995). *What about socialization? It's a great reason to keep your child out of school!* [Online]. Retrieved March 28, 2000 from the World Wide Web: http://learninfreedom.org/socialization.html

Clark, M. K. (1993). *Catholic home schooling: A handbook for parents.* Rockford, IL: Tan.

Crump, S. (1998, August 12). Parma girl's win is one for the books. *Cleveland Plain Dealer*, p. 7B.

Dobson, J. (1998, August 27). Home-schooled kids are "social." *Observer.*

Farris, M. (1997). *The future of home schooling.* Washington, DC: Regnery.

Galloway, R. S., & Sutton, J. P. (1997, October). *College success of students from three high school settings: Christian school, home school, and public school.* Paper presented at the National Christian Home Educators Leadership Conference, Boston.

Hinrichs, F. (1995). *Why classical education?* [Online]. Retrieved March 28, 2000 from the World Wide Web: http://www.gbt.org/clasced.html

Klicka, C. J. (1998). *Special report: Home school students excel in college.* Purcellville, VA: National Center for Home Education.

Layman, I. (1998). Homeschooling: Back to the future. *Cato Policy Analysis, 294* [Online]. Retrieved March 28, 2000 from the World Wide Web: http://www.cato.org/pubs/pas/pa-294.html

Maine revised statutes annotated (Vol. 11). (1993). St. Paul, MN: West Publishing Co.

Practical Home Schooling Staff. (1994). Public education is doomed, Part II. *Home Life* [Online]. Retrieved March 28, 2000 from the World Wide Web: http://www.home-school.com/Articles /PubEdDoomedII.html

Ray, B. D. (1997). *Home education across the United States: Academic achievement, family characteristics, and longitudinal traits.* Salem, OR: National Home Education Research Institute.

Ray, B. D. (1999). *Home schooling on the threshold: A survey of research at the dawn of the new millennium.* Salem, OR: National Home Education Research Institute.

Rudner, L. M. (1999). *The scholastic achievement and demographic characteristics of home school students in 1998.* Purcellville, VA: Home School Legal Defense Association.

The Future of Home Schooling

Sayers, D. (1999, September/October). The lost tools of learning. *The Teaching Home,* 35–37. (Original work published 1947)

Smith, C., & Sikkink, D. (1999). Is private schooling privatizing? *First Things* [Online]. Retrieved March 28, 2000 from the World Wide Web: http://www.firstthings.com/ftissues/ft9904/smith.html

Stough, L. (1992). *Social and emotional status of home schooled children and conventionally schooled children in West Virginia.* Unpublished master's thesis, University of West Virginia. (ERIC Document Reproduction Service No. ED 353 079)

Wilson, D. (1994). Classical education. *Practical Home Schooling Magazine* [Online]. Retrieved March 28, 2000 from the World Wide Web: http://www.home-school.com/articles/ClassicalEducation.html

Whitney, W. D. (Ed.). (1914). *Century Dictionary.* New York: Century.

PEABODY JOURNAL OF EDUCATION, 75(1&2), 256–271
Copyright © 2000, Lawrence Erlbaum Associates, Inc.

The Cultural Politics of Home Schooling

Michael W. Apple

If one of the marks of the growing acceptance of ideological changes is their positive presentation in the popular media, then home schooling clearly has found a place in our consciousness. It has been discussed in the national press, on television and radio, and in widely circulated magazines. Its usual presentation is that of a savior, a truly compelling alternative to a public school system that is presented as a failure. Although the presentation of public schools as simply failures is deeply problematic,[1] it is the largely unqualified support of home schooling that concerns me here. I am considerably less sanguine.

MICHAEL W. APPLE *is the John Bascom Professor of Curriculum and Instruction and Educational Policy Studies, University of Wisconsin, Madison.*

Requests for reprints should be sent to Michael W. Apple, University of Wisconsin, Department of Curriculum and Instruction, 225 North Mills Street, Madison, WI 53706. E-mail: apple@education.wisc.edu

[1]It is important that we remember that public schools were and are a victory. They constituted a gain for the majority of people who were denied access to advancement and to valued cultural capital in a stratified society. This is not to claim that the public school did not and does not have differential effects. Indeed, I have devoted many books to uncovering the connections between formal education and the recreation of inequalities (see, e.g., Apple, 1990, 1995). Rather, it is to say that public schooling is a site of conflict, but one that also has been a site of major victories by popular groups. Indeed, conservatives would not be so angry at schools if public schools had not had a number of progressive tendencies cemented in them.

256

Cultural Politics

In a relatively short article, I cannot deal at length with all of the many issues that could be raised about the home schooling movement. I want to ask a number of critical questions about the dangers associated with it. Although it is quite probable that some specific children and families will gain from home schooling, my concerns are larger. They are connected to the more extensive restructuring of this society that I believe is quite dangerous and to the manner in which our very sense of public responsibility is withering in ways that will lead to even further social inequalities. To illuminate these dangers, I have to do a number of things: situate home schooling within the larger movement that provides much of its impetus; suggest its connections with other protectionist impulses; connect it to the history of and concerns about the growth of activist government; and, finally, point to how it actually may hurt many other students who are not home schooled.

At the very outset of this article, let me state as clearly as I can that any parents who care so much about the educational experiences of their children that they actively seek to be deeply involved are to be applauded, not chastised or simply dismissed. Let me also say that it is important not to stereotype individuals who reject public schooling as unthinking promoters of ideological forms that are so deeply threatening that they are—automatically—to be seen as beyond the pale of legitimate concerns. Indeed, as I demonstrated in *Cultural Politics and Education* (Apple, 1996), there are complicated reasons behind the growth of antischool sentiments. As I showed there, there are elements of "good" sense as well as bad "sense" in such beliefs. All too many school systems are overly bureaucratic, are apt not to listen carefully to parents' or community concerns, or act in overly defensive ways when questions are asked about what and whose knowledge is considered "official." In some ways, these kinds of criticisms are similar across the political spectrum, with both left and right often making similar claims about the politics of recognition (see Fraser, 1997). Indeed, these very kinds of criticisms have led many progressive and activist educators to build more community-based and responsive models of curriculum and teaching in public schools (Apple & Beane, 1995).

This said, however, it is still important to realize that although the intentions of critics such as home schoolers may be meritorious, the effects of their actions may be less so.

Although there are many home schoolers who have not made their decision based on religious convictions, a large proportion have. In this article, I focus largely on this group, in part because it constitutes some of the most committed parents and in part because ideologically it raises a number of important issues. Many home schoolers are guided by what they believe are biblical understandings of the family, gender relation-

257

M. W. Apple

ships, legitimate knowledge, the importance of "tradition," the role of government, and the economy. They constitute part of what I have called the "conservative restoration," in which a tense alliance has been built among various segments of "the public" in favor of particular policies in education and the larger social world. Let me place this in its larger context.

Education and the Conservative Restoration

Long-lasting educational transformations often come not from the work of educators and researchers, but from larger social movements that tend to push our major political, economic, and cultural institutions in specific directions. Thus, it would be impossible to understand fully educational reforms over the past decades without situating them within, say, the long struggles by multiple communities of Color and women for both cultural recognition and economic redistribution (see, e.g., Fraser, 1997). Even such taken-for-granted things as state textbook adoption policies—among the most powerful mechanisms in the processes of defining "official knowledge"—are the results of widespread populist and anti-Northern movements and especially the class and race struggles over culture and power that organized and reorganized the polity in the United States a century ago (Apple, 2000).

It should come as no surprise, then, that education is again witnessing the continued emergence and growing influence of powerful social movements. Some of these may lead to increased democratization and greater equality, whereas others are based on a fundamental shift in the very meanings of democracy and equality and are more than a little retrogressive socially and culturally. Unfortunately, it is the latter that have emerged as the most powerful.

The rightward turn has been the result of years of well-funded and creative ideological efforts by the right to form a broad-based coalition. This new alliance, what is technically called a *new hegemonic bloc*, has been so successful in part because it has been able to make major inroads in the battle over common sense—that is, it has stitched together different social tendencies and commitments creatively and has organized them under its own general leadership in issues dealing with welfare, culture, the economy, and—as many know from personal experience—education. Its aim in educational and social policy might best be described as "conservative modernization" (Dale, 1989). In the process, democracy has been reduced to consumption practices. Citizenship has been reduced to possessive individualism. And a politics based on resentment and a fear of the "Other" has been pressed forward.

Cultural Politics

There are a number of major elements within this new alliance (for more detailed discussion, see Apple, 1996). The first, *neoliberals,* represent dominant economic and political elites who are intent on "modernizing" the economy and the institutions connected to it. They are certain that markets and consumer choice will solve all of "our" social problems, because private is necessarily good and public is necessarily bad—hence, their strong support of vouchers and privatized choice plans. Although there is clear empirical evidence about the very real inequalities that are created by such educational policies (Lauder & Hughes, 1999; Whitty, Power, & Halpin, 1998), this group is usually in leadership of the alliance. If we think of this new bloc as an ideological umbrella, neoliberals are holding the umbrella's handle.

The second group, *neoconservatives,* are economic and cultural conservatives who want a return to "high standards," discipline, "real" knowledge, and what is in essence a form of Social Darwinist competition. They are fueled by a nostalgic and quite romanticized vision of the past. It is often based on a fundamental misrecognition of the fact that what they might call the classics and "real" knowledge gained that status as the result of intense past conflicts and often were themselves seen as equally dangerous culturally and just as morally destabilizing as any of the new elements of the curriculum and culture they now castigate (Levine, 1996).

The third element is made up of largely White working-class and middle-class groups who mistrust the state and are concerned with security, the family, gender and age relations within the home, sexuality, and traditional and fundamentalist religious values and knowledge. They form an increasingly active segment of *authoritarian populists* who are powerful in education and in other areas of politics and social and cultural policy. They provide much of the support from below for neoliberal and neoconservative positions, because they see themselves as disenfranchised by the "secular humanism" that supposedly now pervades public schooling. They are also often among those larger numbers of people whose very economic livelihoods are most at stake in the economic restructuring and capital flight that we are now experiencing.

Many home schoolers combine beliefs from all three of these tendencies; but it is the last one that seems to drive a large portion of the movement.

Satan's Threat

For many on the right, one of the key enemies is public education. Secular education is turning our children into "aliens" and, by teaching them to question our ideas, turning them against us. What are often accurate concerns about public schooling that I noted earlier—its overly bureaucratic

M. W. Apple

nature; its lack of curriculum coherence; its disconnection from the lives, hopes, and cultures of many of its communities; and more—are here often connected to more deep-seated and intimate worries. These worries echo Pagels's (1995) argument that Christianity historically has defined its most fearful satanic threats not from distant enemies but in relation to very intimate ones. "The most dangerous characteristic of the satanic enemy is that though he will look just like us, he will nevertheless have changed completely" (Pagels, as cited in Kintz, 1997, p. 73).

Some of the roots of this can be found much earlier in the call of conservative activist Beverly LaHaye for the founding of an organization to counter the rising tide of feminism. In support of Concerned Women of America, she spoke of her concern for family, nation, and religion:

> I sincerely believe that God is calling the Christian women of America to draw together in a spirit of unity and purpose to protect the rights of the family. I believe that it is time for us to set aside our doctrinal differences to work for a spiritually renewed America. Who but a woman is as deeply concerned about her children and her home? Who but a woman has the time, the intuition, and the drive to restore our nation? … They may call themselves feminists or humanists. The label makes little difference, because many of them are seeking the destruction of morality and human freedom. (as cited in Kintz, 1997, p. 80)

It is clear from this quotation what is seen as the satanic threat and what is at stake here. These fears about the nation, home, family, children's "innocence," religious values, and traditional views of gender relations are sutured together into a more general fear of the destruction of a moral compass and personal freedom. "Our" world is disintegrating around us. Its causes are not the economically destructive policies of the globalizing economy (Greider, 1997), not the decisions of an economic elite, and not the ways in which, say, our kind of economy turns all things—including cherished traditions (and even our children)[2]—into commodities for sale. Rather, the causes are transferred onto those institutions and people that are themselves being constantly buffeted by the same forces—public sector institutions, schooling, poor people of Color, other women who have struggled for centuries to build a society that is more responsive to the

---

[2]I am thinking here of Channel One, the for-profit commercial television show that is in an increasingly large percentage of our middle and secondary schools. In this "reform," students are sold as a captive audience to corporations intent on marketing their products to our children in schools (see Apple, 2000, and Molnar, 1996).

Cultural Politics

hopes and dreams of many people who have been denied participation in the public sphere, and so on.[3]

As I noted at the beginning of this article, however, it is important not to stereotype individuals involved in this movement. For example, a number of men and women who are activists in rightist movements believe that some elements of feminism did improve the conditions of women overall. By focusing on equal pay for equal work and opening up job opportunities that traditionally had been denied to women who had to work for pay, women activists had benefitted many people. However, for authoritarian populists, feminism and secular institutions in general still tend to break with God's law. They are much too individualistic, and they misinterpret the divine relationship between families and God. In so doing, many aspects of civil rights legislation, the public schools' curricula, and so many other parts of secular society are simply wrong. Thus, for example, if one views the Constitution literally as divinely inspired, then it is not public institutions but the traditional family—as God's chosen unit—that is the core social unit that must be protected by the Constitution (Kintz, 1997, p. 97). In a time of seeming cultural disintegration, when traditions are under threat and when the idealized family faces ever more externally produced dangers, protecting our families and our children are key elements in returning to God's grace.[4]

Even without these religious elements, a defensive posture is clear in much of the movement. In many ways, the movement toward home schooling mirrors the growth of privatized consciousness in other areas of society. It is an extension of the "suburbanization" of everyday life that is so evident all around us. In essence, it is the equivalent of gated communities and of the privatization of neighborhoods, recreation, parks, and so many other things. It provides a "security zone" both physically and ideologically. Kintz (1997) described it this way:

> As citizens worried about crime, taxes, poor municipal services, and poor schools abandon cities, the increasing popularity of gated communities, ... fortress communities, reflects people's desire to retreat. ... They want to spend more of their tax dollars on themselves instead of others. ... Further, they take comfort in the social homogeneity of such

---

[3]Of course, the very distinction between "public" and "private" spheres has strong connections to the history of patriarchal assumptions (see Fraser, 1989).

[4]This is a particular construction of the family. As Coontz (1992) showed in her history of the family in the United States, it has had a varied form, with the nuclear family that is so important to conservative formulations merely being one of many.

261

M. W. Apple

communities, knowing that their neighbors act and think much as they do. (p. 107)

This "cocooning" is not just about seeking an escape from the problems of the "city" (a metaphor for danger and heterogeneity). It is a rejection of the entire idea of the city. Cultural and intellectual diversity, complexity, ambiguity, uncertainty, and proximity to "the Other"—all these are to be shunned (Kintz, 1997, p. 107). In place of the city is the engineered pastoral, the neat and well-planned universe where things (and people) are in their "rightful place" and reality is safe and predictable.

Yet, in so many ways, such a movement mirrors something else. It is a microcosm of the increasing segmentation of America society in general. As we move to a society segregated by residence, race, economic opportunity, and income, "purity" is increasingly more apt to be found in the fact that upper classes send their children to elite private schools; where neighborliness is determined by property values; where evangelical Christians, ultraorthodox Jews, and others only interact with each other and their children are schooled in private religious schools or schooled at home (Kintz, 1997, p. 108). A world free of conflict, uncertainty, the voice and culture of the Other—in a word I used before, *cocooning*—is the ideal.

Thus, home schooling has many similarities with the Internet. It enables the creation of "virtual communities" that are perfect for those with specialized interests. It gives individuals a new ability to "personalize" information, to choose what they want to know or what they find personally interesting. However, as many commentators are beginning to recognize, unless we are extremely cautious, "customizing our lives" could radically undermine the strength of local communities, many of which are already woefully weak. As Shapiro (1999) put it,

> Shared experience is an indisputably essential ingredient [in the formation of local communities]; without it there can be no chance for mutual understanding, empathy and social cohesion. And this is precisely what personalization threatens to delete. A lack of common information would deprive individuals of a starting point for democratic dialogue. (p. 12)

Even with the evident shortcomings of many public schools, at the very least they provide "a kind of social glue, a common cultural reference point in our polyglot, increasingly multicultural society" (Shapiro, 1999, p. 12). Yet, whether called personalizing or cocooning, it is exactly this common reference point that is rejected by many within the home schooling movement's pursuit of "freedom" and "choice."

262

Cultural Politics

This particular construction of the meaning of freedom is of considerable moment, because there is a curious contradiction within such conservatism's obsession with freedom. In many ways this emphasis on freedom, paradoxically, is based on a fear of freedom (Kintz, 1997, p. 168). It is valued but also loathed as a site of danger, of "a world out of control." Many home schoolers reject public schooling out of concern for equal time for their beliefs. They want "equality." Yet it is a specific vision of equality, because coupled with their fear of things out of control is a powerful anxiety that the nation's usual understanding of equality will produce uniformity (Kintz, 1997, p. 186). But this feared uniformity is not seen as the same as the religious and cultural homogeneity sponsored by the conservative project. It is a very different type of uniformity—one in which the fear that "we are all the same" actually speaks to a loss of religious particularity. Thus, again there is another paradox at the heart of this movement: We want everyone to be like "us"—"This is a 'Christian nation'"; "Governments must bow before 'a higher authority'" (Smith, 1998); but we want the right to be different—a difference based on being God's elect group. Uniformity weakens our specialness. This tension between (a) knowing one is a member of God's elect people and thus, by definition, different; and (b) also being so certain that one is correct that the world needs to be changed to fit one's image, is one of the central paradox's behind authoritarian populist impulses. For some home schoolers, the paradox is solved by withdrawal of one's children from the public sphere to maintain their difference. For still others, this allows them to prepare themselves and their children with an armor of Christian beliefs that will enable them to go forth into the world later on to bring God's word to those who are not among the elect. Once again, let us declare our particularity, our difference, to better prepare ourselves to bring the unanointed world to our set of uniform beliefs.

Attacking the State

At the base of this fear both of the loss of specialness and of becoming uniform in the "wrong way" is a sense that the state is intervening in our daily lives in quite powerful ways, ways that are causing even more losses. It is not possible to understand the growth of home schooling unless we connect it to the history of the attack on the public sphere in general and on the government (the state) in particular. To better comprehend the antistatist impulses that lie behind a good deal of the home schooling movement, I need to place these impulses in a longer historical and social context. Some history and theory is necessary here.

One of the keys to this is the development of what Clarke and Newman (1997) have called the "managerial state." This was an active state that

M. W. Apple

combined bureaucratic administration and professionalism. The organization of the state centered around the application of specific rules of coordination. Routinization and predictability are among the hallmarks of such a state. This was to be coupled with a second desirable trait, that of social, political, and personal neutrality rather than nepotism and favoritism. This bureaucratic routinization and predictability would be balanced by an emphasis on professional discretion. Here, bureaucratically regulated professionals such as teachers and administrators still would have an element of irreducible autonomy based on their training and qualifications. Their skills and judgment were to be trusted, if they acted fairly and impartially. Yet fairness and impartiality were not enough; the professional also personalized the managerial state. Professionals such as teachers made the state "approachable" by not only signifying neutrality, but by acting in nonanonymous ways to foster the "public good" and to "help" individuals and families (Clarke & Newman, 1997, pp. 5–7).

Of course, such bureaucratic and professional norms were there not only to benefit "clients." They acted to protect the state by providing it with legitimacy. (The state is impartial, fair, and acts in the interests of everyone.) They also served to insulate professional judgments from critical scrutiny. (As holders of expert knowledge, we—teachers, social workers, state employees—are the ones who are to be trusted because we know best.)

Thus, from the end of World War II until approximately the mid-1970s, there was a "settlement," a compromise, in which an activist welfare state was seen as legitimate. It was sustained by a triple legitimacy. There was (largely) bipartisan support for the state to provide and manage a larger part of social life, a fact that often put it above a good deal of party politics. Bureaucratic administration promised to act impartially for the benefit of everyone. And professionals employed by the state, such as teachers and other educators, were there to apply expert knowledge to serve the public (Clarke & Newman, 1997, p. 8). This compromise was widely accepted and provided public schools and other public institutions with a strong measure of support because, by and large, the vast majority of people continued to believe that schools and other state agencies did in fact act professionally and impartially in the public good.

This compromise came under severe attack as the fiscal crisis deepened and as competition over scarce economic, political, and cultural resources grew more heated in the 1970s and beyond. The political forces of conservative movements used this crisis, often in quite cynical and manipulative—and well-funded—ways. The state was criticized for denying the opportunity for consumers to exercise choice. The welfare state was seen as gouging the citizen (as a taxpayer) to pay for public handouts for those who ignored personal responsibility for their actions. These "scroungers"

Cultural Politics

from the underclass were seen as sexually promiscuous, immoral, and lazy, as opposed to the "rest of us," who were hard-working, industrious, and moral. They supposedly are a drain on all of us economically, and state-sponsored support of them leads to the collapse of the family and traditional morality (Apple, 2000). These arguments may not have been totally accurate, but they were effective.

This suturing together of neoliberal and neoconservative attacks led to a particular set of critiques against the state. For many people, the state was no longer the legitimate and neutral upholder of the public good. Instead, the welfare state was an active agent of national decline, as well as an economic drain on the country's (and the family's) resources. In the words of Clarke and Newman (1997):

> Bureaucrats were identified as actively hostile to the public—hiding behind the impersonality of regulations and "red tape" to deny choice, building bureaucratic empires at the expense of providing service, and insulated from the "real world" pressures of competition by their monopolistic position. Professionals were arraigned as motivated by self-interest, exercising power over would-be costumers, denying choice through the dubious claim that "professionals know best." Worse still, ... liberalism ... was viewed as undermining personal responsibility and family authority and as prone to trendy excesses such as egalitarianism, anti-discrimination policies, moral relativism or child-centeredness. (p. 15)

These moral, political, and economic concerns were easily transferred to public schooling, because for many people the school was and is the public institution closest to them in their daily life. Hence, public schooling and the teaching and curricula found within it became central targets of attack. Curricula and teachers were not impartial, but elitist. School systems were imposing the Other's morality on "us." And "real Americans" who were patriotic, religious, and moral—as opposed to everyone else—were suffering and were the new oppressed (Delfattore, 1992). Although this position fits into a long history of the paranoid style of American cultural politics and was often based on quite inaccurate stereotypes, it does point to a profound sense of alienation that many people feel.

As I mentioned previously, there are elements of good sense in the critique of the state made by both right and left. The government has assumed all too often that the only true holders of expertise in education, social welfare, and so forth are those in positions of formal authority. This has led to a situation of overbureaucratization. It also has led to the state being "colonized" by a particular fraction of the new middle class that

265

M. W. Apple

seeks to ensure its own mobility and its own positions by employing the state for its own purposes. However, there is a world of difference between acknowledging that there are some historical tendencies within the state to become overly bureaucratic and to not listen carefully enough to the expressed needs of the people it is supposed to serve, and a blanket rejection of public control and public institutions such as schools. This not only has led to cocooning, but it also threatens the gains made by large groups of disadvantaged people for whom the possible destruction of public schooling is nothing short of a disaster. The final section of my analysis turns to a discussion of this last point.

Public and Private

We need to think relationally when we ask who will be the major beneficiaries of the attack on the state and the movement toward home schooling. What if gains that are made by one group of people come at the expense of other, even more culturally and economically oppressed groups? As we shall see, this is not an inconsequential worry in this instance.

A distinction that is helpful here is that between a politics of redistribution and a politics of recognition. In the first (redistribution), the concern is for socioeconomic injustice. Here, the political–economic system of a society creates conditions that lead to exploitation (having the fruits of your labor appropriated for the benefit of others), economic marginalization (having one's paid work confined to poorly paid and undesirable jobs or having no real access to the routes to serious and better-paying jobs), and/or deprivation (being constantly denied the material that would lead to an adequate standard of living). All these socioeconomic injustices lead to arguments about whether this is a just or fair society and whether identifiable groups of people actually have equality of resources (Fraser, 1997, p. 13).

The second dynamic (recognition) is often related to redistribution in the real world, but it has its own specific history and differential power relations as well. It is related to the politics of culture and symbols. In this case, injustice is rooted in a society's social patterns of representation and interpretation. Examples of this include cultural domination (being constantly subjected to patterns of interpretation or cultural representation that are alien to one's own or even hostile to it), nonrecognition (basically being rendered invisible in the dominant cultural forms in the society), and disrespect (having oneself routinely stereotyped or maligned in public representations in the media, schools, government policies, or in everyday conduct; Fraser, 1997, p. 14). These kinds of issues surrounding the politics of recognition are central to the identities and sense of injustice of many

Cultural Politics

home schoolers. Indeed, they provide the organizing framework for their critique of public schooling and their demand that they be allowed to teach their children outside such state control.

Although both forms of injustice are important, it is absolutely crucial that we recognize that an adequate response to one must not lead to the exacerbation of the other—that is, responding to the claims of injustice in recognition by one group (say, religious conservatives) must not make the conditions that lead to exploitation, economic marginalization, and deprivation more likely to occur for other groups. Unfortunately, this may be the case for some of the latent effects of home schooling.

Because of this, it is vitally important not to separate out the possible effects of home schooling from what we are beginning to know about the possible consequences of neoliberal policies in general in education. As Whitty et al. (1998) showed in their review of the international research on voucher and choice plans, one of the latent effects of such policies has been the reproduction of traditional hierarchies of class and race—that is, the programs clearly have differential benefits in which those who already possess economic and cultural capital reap significantly more benefits than those who do not. This is patterned in very much the same ways that the stratification of economic, political, and cultural power produces inequalities in nearly every socioeconomic sphere. One of the hidden consequences that is emerging from the expanding conservative critique of public institutions, including schools, is a growing antitax movement, in which those who have chosen to place their children in privatized, marketized, and home schools do not want to pay taxes to support the schooling of "the Other" (Apple, 1996).

The wider results of this are becoming clear—a declining tax base for schooling, social services, health care, housing, and anything "public" for those populations (usually in the most economically depressed urban and rural areas) who suffer the most from the economic dislocations and inequalities that so deeply characterize this nation. Thus, a politics of recognition—"I want to guarantee 'choice' for my children based on my identity and special needs"—has begun to have extremely negative effects on the politics of redistribution. It is absolutely crucial that we recognize this. If it is the case that the emergence of educational markets has consistently benefited the most advantaged parents and students and has consistently disadvantaged both economically poor parents and students and parents and students of Color (Lauder & Hughes, 1999; Whitty et al., 1998), then we need to examine critically the latent effects of the growth of home schooling in the same light. Will it be the case that social justice loses in this equation, just as it did and does in many of the other highly publicized programs of "choice"?

267

M. W. Apple

We now have emerging evidence to this effect, evidence that points to the fact that social justice often does lose with the expansion of home schooling in some states. A case in point is the way in which the ongoing debate over the use of public money for religious purposes in education is often subverted through manipulation of loopholes that are only available to particular groups. Religiously motivated home schoolers are currently engaged in exploiting public funding in ways that are not only hidden, but in ways that raise serious questions about the drain on economic resources during a time of severe budget crises in all too many school districts.

Let me say more about this, because it provides an important instance of my argument that gains in recognition for some groups (say, home schools) can have decidedly negative effects in other spheres, such as the politics of redistribution. In California, for example, charter schools have been used as a mechanism to gain public money for home schoolers. Charter school legislation in California has been employed in very "interesting" ways to accomplish this. In one recent study, for example, 50% of charter schools were serving home schoolers. "Independent study" charter schools (a creative pseudonym for computer-linked home schooling) have been used by both school districts and parents to gain money that otherwise might not have been available. Although this does demonstrate the ability of school districts to use charter school legislation strategically to get money that might have been lost when parents withdraw their children to home school them, it also signifies something else. In this and other cases, the money given to parents for enrolling in such independent study charter schools was used by the parents to purchase religious material produced and sold by Bob Jones University, one of the most conservative religious schools in the entire nation (Wells, 1999).

Thus, public money not legally available for overtly sectarian material is used to purchase religious curricula under the auspices of charter school legislation. Yet, unlike all curricula used in public schools that must be publicly accountable in terms of its content and costs, the material purchased for home schooling has no public accountability whatsoever. Although this does give greater choice to home schoolers and does enable them to act on a politics of recognition, it not only takes money away from other students who do not have the economic resources to afford computers in the home, but it also denies them a say in what the community's children will learn about themselves and their cultures, histories, values, and so on. Given the fact that a number of textbooks used in fundamentalist religious schools expressly state such things as Islam is a false religion and embody similar claims that many citizens would find deeply offensive,[5] it

[5]See Re'em (1998) for an interesting analysis of some of this content.

268

Cultural Politics

does raise serious questions about whether it is appropriate for public money to be used to teach such content without any public accountability.

Thus, two things are going on here. Money is being drained from already hard-pressed school districts to support home schooling. Just as important, curricular materials that support the identities of religiously motivated groups are being paid for by the public without any accountability, even though these materials may act in such a way as to deny the claims for recognition of one of the fastest growing religions in the nation, Islam. This raises more general and quite serious issues about how the claims for recognition by religious conservatives can be financially supported when they may at times actually support discriminatory teaching.

I do not wish to be totally negative here. After all, this is a complicated issue in which there may be justifiable worries among home schoolers that they are not being listened to in terms of their values and culture. But it must be openly discussed, not lost in the simple statement that we should support a politics of recognition of religiously motivated home schoolers because their culture seems to them to be not sufficiently recognized in public institutions. At the very least, the possible dangers to the public good need to be recognized.

Conclusion

I have used this article to raise a number of critical questions about the economic, social, and ideological tendencies that often stand behind significant parts of the home schooling movement. In the process, I have situated it within larger social movements that I and many others believe can have quite negative effects on our sense of community, on the health of the public sphere, and on our commitment to building a society that is less economically and racially stratified. I have suggested that issues need to be raised about the effects of its commitment to cocooning, its attack on the state, and its growing use of public funding with no public accountability. Yet, I also have argued that there are clear elements of good sense in its criticisms of the bureaucratic nature of all too many of our institutions, in its worries about the managerial state, and in its devotion to being active in the education of its children.

In my mind, the task is to disentangle the elements of good sense evident in these concerns from the selfish and antipublic agenda that has been pushing concerned parents and community members into the arms of the conservative restoration. The task of public schools is to listen much more carefully to the complaints of parents such as these and to rebuild our institutions in much more responsive ways. As I have argued in much greater

M. W. Apple

detail elsewhere, all too often, public schools push concerned parents who are not originally part of conservative cultural and political movements into the arms of such alliances by their (a) defensiveness, (b) lack of responsiveness, and (c) silencing of democratic discussion and criticism (Apple, 1996). Of course, sometimes these criticisms are unjustified or are politically motivated by undemocratic agendas (Apple, 1999). However, this must not serve as an excuse for a failure to open the doors of our schools to the intense public debate that makes public education a living and vital part of our democracy.

Luckily, we have models for doing exactly that, as the democratic schools movement demonstrates (Apple & Beane, 1995). There are models of curricula and teaching that are related to community sentiment, that are committed to social justice and fairness, and that are based in schools where both teachers and students want to be. If schools do not do this, there may be all too many parents who are pushed in the direction of antischool sentiment. This would be a tragedy both for the public school system and for our already withered sense of community that is increasingly under threat.

References

Apple, M. W. (1990). *Ideology and curriculum.* Boston: Routledge & Kegan Paul.

Apple, M. W. (1995). *Education and power* (2nd ed.). New York: Routledge.

Apple, M. W. (1996). *Cultural politics and education.* New York: Teachers College Press.

Apple, M. W. (1999). *Power, meaning, and identity.* New York: Peter Lang.

Apple, M. W. (2000). *Official knowledge* (2nd ed.). New York: Routledge.

Apple, M. W., & Beane, J. A. (Eds.). (1995). *Democratic schools.* Washington, DC: Association for Supervision and Curriculum Development.

Clarke, J., & Newman, J. (1997). *The managerial state.* Thousand Oaks, CA: Sage.

Coontz, S. (1992). *The way we never were: American families and the nostalgia trap.* New York: Basic Books.

Dale, R. (1989). The Thatcherite project in education. *Critical Social Policy, 9*(3), 4–19.

Delfattore, J. (1992). *What Johnny shouldn't read.* New Haven, CT: Yale University Press.

Fraser, N. (1989). *Unruly practices.* Minneapolis: University of Minnesota Press.

Fraser, N. (1997). *Justice interruptus.* New York: Routledge.

Greider, W. (1997). *One world, ready or not.* New York: Simon & Schuster.

Kintz, L. (1997). *Between Jesus and the market.* Durham, NC: Duke University Press.

Lauder, H., & Hughes, D. (1999). *Trading in futures: Why markets in education don't work.* Philadelphia: Open University Press.

Levine, L. (1996). *The opening of the American mind.* Boston: Beacon.

Molnar, A. (1996). *Giving kids the business.* Boulder, CO: Westview.

Pagels, E. (1995). *The origin of Satan.* New York: Random House.

Re'em, M. (1998). *Young minds in motion: Teaching and learning about difference in formal and non-formal settings.* Unpublished doctoral dissertation, University of Wisconsin, Madison.

Shapiro, A. (1999, June 21). The net that binds. *The Nation, 268,* 11–15.

Cultural Politics

Smith, C. (1998). *American evangelicalism*. Chicago: University of Chicago Press.
Wells, A. S. (1999). *Beyond the rhetoric of charter school reform*. Los Angeles: Graduate School of Education and Information Studies, University of California, Los Angeles.
Whitty, G., Power, S., & Halpin, D. (1998). *Devolution and choice in education*. Philadelphia: Open University Press.

Home Schooling for Individuals' Gain and Society's Common Good

Brian D. Ray

People have been competing to control the education of children since the first Homo sapiens was born. Regardless of genteel and resourceful language and rationales promoting consensus building and democratic decision making during the past century and currently, historians of institutional education have revealed that education is typically a realm of contention. Education in the United States is no exception; history supports this claim. In like manner, the discussions about parent-led, home- and family-based education—home schooling—are simply a continuation of the struggle over who will control what goes into the minds and affects the hearts of children—the future full-fledged citizens of any nation.

Whether more persons should choose to home school is, at first glance, an insignificant issue, because currently about 89% of all 52 million U.S. conventional school students in kindergarten through Grade 12 are in state-run institutions, with the other 11% in private schools (U.S. Department of Education, 1998); only another estimated 1.2 million to 1.7 million are home educated (Lines, 1998; Ray, 1999). The issue, however, goes to the core of the centuries-old debate over who should be in the primary position of influence in the educational lives of children and what effect the answer has on society.

BRIAN D. RAY *is Founder and President of the National Home Education Research Institute.*

Requests for reprints should be sent to Brian D. Ray, National Home Education Research Institute, Box 13939, Salem, OR 97309. E-mail: bray@nheri.org

Individuals' Gain and Society's Common Good

Both individual children and society are powerfully affected by today's educational arrangements for the younger generation. In essence, this article is about what is the best educational arrangement that should be promoted in America. An important starting place is to keep in mind that there is nothing that de facto supports the claim that a democratically mandated, tax-funded, and state-run institutional approach to controlling individual children's education is inherently the best approach to education in America. This is the nation made up of a liberty-loving people in a republic that is based on the fundamental premises, among others, that (a) all persons are created equal, (b) all persons are endowed by their Creator with certain unalienable rights (i.e., life, liberty, and the pursuit of happiness), (c) the government shall make law that neither establishes a religion nor prohibits the free exercise of religion, and (d) governments are to be limited in their powers (Declaration of Independence; U.S. Constitution, Article I and X).

I am aware that scholars who put their faith in certain theoretical frameworks used for analysis of statements like the preceding (and the ones later in this paragraph) might accuse me of insensitivity and various self-serving, -centric-, myopic-, and power-based interests and paradigms. I am also aware that discussions about education and its reform, both recently and during the 1800s, have been laced with references to the alleged wants and needs of all kinds of particular groups (i.e., arbitrarily and subjectively selected subcategories of the human species). This constant cacophony of discord essentially revolves around what one group wants (or is told by someone else it should have) that another group has. Germane to this article, it should be noted that the preponderance of this debate and jostling for power, position, and entitlement occurs within and around the state-run school system (i.e., financed by individual citizens' tax payments at the county, state, or federal level). Either much less of this kind of debate occurs within the private school community, scholars and the media simply do not report on it, or both. Almost none occurs within the home education community. Considering this background of discord, especially within the state-run school system, the realm of careful thought about education may be helped by putting less emphasis on stereotypical skin color-, ethnic-, class-, gender-, sexuality-, and greed-based language, arguments, and polemics about groups. Rather, individual children and parents might be better served by rationales based on the concepts of the inherent worth of every person's life, altruism motivated by a balance of merit and grace, personal responsibility to help those who are in dire need and have little ability to help themselves, and voluntary giving rather than the government compelling one person to aid another. With these things in mind, I proceed to consider the benefits of home schooling to both individuals and to society.

B. D. Ray

Contemporary home-based education is not a novel form of education; rather, it is centuries old and both predates and outdates institutional schooling as most American children experience it today (Gordon & Gordon, 1990; Ray, 1999; Shepherd, 1986). Although an age-old practice, home-based education waned to near-extinction by the late 1970s in the United States. Because the institutionalization of education has so completely prescribed and constrained the educational experience and thinking of five generations of Americans, including those scholars, educational practitioners, policymakers, and laypersons today writing about home schooling and reading this article, my task is to make a simple presentation that will stimulate my readers to consider seriously that the schooling and institutions we ourselves have experienced and promoted are likely not the best thing for either individuals or for the ordered society with the least possible intrusion from the state. I think that today, as the millennia change, claims such as "I went to institutional schools and I turned out okay, didn't I ...?," "Public schools are what made America great" (Mungeam, 1993; see also Glenn, 1988), "Private education creates more divisiveness," and "We all know that the public common school best serves the common good" are hollow incantations that do little good in addressing the historical and pressing needs of any individual child or nation or humans in general. It is time for education reform-saturated researchers, philosophers, sociologists, teachers, policymakers, and parents to reconsider "the way it is" and consider "the way it might be."

I submit to the reader that five general areas of evidence and reasoning support the claim that home schooling is a good, if not the best, form of education for individuals and for society's common good. These five areas are (a) learned children who become learned adults, (b) children who are psychologically and socially healthy who become adults who are psychologically and socially healthy, (c) hardy and hearty families, (d) liberty in a just society with a nondominant state, and (e) persons with reliable character and value systems.

Learned Children

Discussions about educational reform over the past 20 years frequently have included concepts such as equity, access, race, and gender and ignored or deemphasized academic learning, despite the fact that one of parents' and students' primary interests today—as it has been throughout history—is that children learn how to read, write, compute, and know and understand some basics in the areas of science, history, and geography. It is the ability to read, write, compute, and generally communicate that historically has been one of the primary keys in terms of enabling an individual, in most countries, to do

Individuals' Gain and Society's Common Good

what he or she desires to do and to lead others along a preferred path. In this regard, then, how do the home educated appear to be doing?

The balance of research to date suggests that home-based education has a positive effect on children's academic achievement as compared to the achievement of those in classroom-based institutional schools. A few researchers have found no significant differences between the achievement of the home educated and of those in state-run schools. Most scholars, however, have found the home educated to be outperforming the public schooled whether the study has been local, state-specific, nationwide in the United States (e.g., Ray, 1990, 1997; Rudner, 1999), or in other countries (Priesnitz & Priesnitz, 1990; Ray, 1994; Rothermel, 1999). Typically, the home educated score at the 65th to 80th percentile on standardized achievement tests. More complete reviews of research on academic achievement clearly support the conclusion that the home educated are doing remarkably well (e.g., Ray, 1999; see also Ray, 2000/this issue).

Although these studies have been largely descriptive in nature and not causal comparative, statistical analyses suggest that even when background demographic traits are controlled, students taught mainly by their parents do well (Ray, 1990, 1997; Rudner, 1999; Russell, 1994). Various studies provide evidence that factors such as parent education level, family income, gender of student, degree of regulation of home schooling by the state, and whether the parents ever have been certified teachers show weak relation to these children's achievement. An increase in studies that more carefully control background variables (as did, e.g., Coleman, Hoffer, & Kilgore, 1982) eventually will tell us more about the effect of home schooling on achievement (Cizek, 1993; Ray, 1988; Wright, 1988).

Considering the characteristics that intrinsically may be a part of home schooling (e.g., individualization of curriculum for each student, increased academic engaged time, high levels of social capital, as delineated in Ray, 2000/this issue), it is not surprising that the home schooled do well in terms of the three Rs, science, history, and geography. As Good and Brophy (1987) noted, private individualized tutoring—which, in many ways, is home-based education—"is the method of choice for most educational purposes, because both curriculum (what is taught) and instruction (how it is taught) can be individualized, and because the teacher can provide the student with sustained personalized attention" (p. 352).

Psychologically and Socially Healthy Persons

Americans, like those in other nations, value psychological and social health for their children in addition to good academic performance. Defi-

275

B. D. Ray

nitions of psychological and social health are likely to be very dependent on the theoretical orientation of the person doing the defining. Most adults, however, have a general idea of what it means to be healthy in these respects. A general and useful definition is that psychologically and socially healthy persons have (a) an efficient perception of reality, (b) an ability to exercise voluntary control over behavior, (c) positive self-esteem and acceptance by those around them, (d) an ability to form affectionate relationships, and (e) an ability to use their energy productively (Atkinson, Atkinson, Smith, Bem, & Nolen-Hoeksema, 1996, pp. 511–512; see also Meier, Minirth, & Wichern, 1982). Although less research has been performed in the domain of the psychological and social health of the home educated than in the realm of academic achievement, several of the preceding factors have been examined. Four areas of related research on the home educated suggest that they are doing as well or better than their conventionally schooled peers.

First, it should be emphasized that home schooling is actually home-*based* education. The parents are most often the primary decision makers about the daily activities, whether academic or social, of the children, and the majority of younger children's time is spent with their families. These children engage, however, in activities with a wide range of persons and groups and environments outside the confines of the home and family (Medlin, 2000/this issue; Ray, 1990, 1997; Wartes, 1987). In addition, as the children grow older, they spend an ever-increasing amount of time with persons and in places outside the home and family. The research base and my 15 years of close observation of the home schooling community indicate that the vast majority of home-educated children are nowhere near being socially isolated.

Second, research shows that home-educated children are healthy in terms of psychological and emotional health (Carlton, 1999; Medlin, 2000/this issue; Ray, 1999). They apparently have positive self-esteem and self-worth and live in psychologically sound families (Allie-Carson, 1990).

Third, one can infer from the research that those being home educated are doing well socially. Whether their well-being is related to interacting with others (Shyers, 1992), leadership potential (Montgomery, 1989), or being in families that are civically active (Smith & Sikkink, 1999; cf. Traviss, 1998), research indicates the home educated are doing as well or better than those in conventional schools (Medlin, 2000/this issue).

Finally, limited research to date suggests that the home educated are successful as young and older adults (Medlin, 2000/this issue). For example, home-educated girls are becoming young women who develop personal voice and " … the strengths and the resistance abilities that give them such an unusually strong sense of self" (Sheffer, 1995, p. 181). More generally, they are

Individuals' Gain and Society's Common Good

doing well in terms of academics just prior to and in college (ACT, 1997; Galloway & Sutton, 1995; Ray, 1997, 1999; Rudner, 1999), and many colleges are recruiting them actively (Ray, 1999). They are doing well in terms of critical thinking (Oliveira, Watson, & Sutton, 1994), leadership in college (Galloway & Sutton, 1995), and general life activities (Knowles & Muchmore, 1994).

In sum, studies indicate that home-schooled children and adults who were home educated are psychologically and socially healthy. As mentioned with regard to research on academic achievement, these studies have been mainly descriptive in nature and not causal comparative.

Hardy and Hearty Families

Humans throughout the centuries have recognized that families (i.e., a father, a mother, and children) are the core functional unit of society (Blankenhorn, 1995; Carlson, 1993; Popenoe, 1996; Wiggin, 1962). Healthy families make for healthy societies. Popenoe (1996) wrote that the empirical evidence "shows that by far the best environment for childrearing is in the home and under the care of the biological parents" (p. 214), and, generally speaking, the main generator of close, warm, and enduring relationships for individuals is marriage and the family. "Numerous studies show now ... [that] a strong family structure is anti-poverty insurance" (Olasky, 1996, pp. 192–193; see also, e.g., Tucker, Marx, & Long, 1998; White & Kaufman, 1997). Especially pertinent at this time in American history when almost 30% of all children are born out of wedlock, Blankenhorn (1995) emphasized the necessity of parents, fathers in particular, investing energy and resources in their children: "Paternal investment ... is an essential determinant of child and societal well-being" (p. 251). Furthermore, the research evidence has made clear that parent involvement in a child's life is crucial—perhaps the most significant factor—to a child doing well in the world of schooling and academics (Coleman, 1991; Coleman & Hoffer, 1987; Henderson & Berla, 1994; U.S. Department of Education, 1987, 1994). Of particular interest to those who emphasize the wants and needs of special groups, many researchers have pointed out the special importance of parent involvement in the lives of minority children. For example, Chavkin (1993) reported, "Unfortunately, the educational system has been less successful in educating this growing minority population than it has the majority population" (p. 1); parent involvement clearly improves student academic achievement, and minority students and children from low-income families have the most to gain from such involvement (p. 2).

Not only have members of the modern intellectual class (e.g., researchers) found that strong families are good for children and society, centuries

277

B. D. Ray

of core belief systems (i.e., religions) have told people that families are important to the well-being of humans. One should note that I am using in this article a functional definition of religion—that is, *religion* generally means a set of beliefs that deal with ultimate concerns. As Baer (1998) explained, "Secular descriptions of reality ... can function just like supernatural descriptions" (p. 107). With this in mind, one can say that religions have held for millennia that the family is an institution ordained by something or Someone greater than individual humans, and the family—both as an institution and particular groups of persons—is to be promoted and defended against degradation and loss of function.

For example, Christianity and Judaism, two religions significantly related to the history and traditions of the United States, both accord great importance to parents and the family. Meyer (1929/1983) wrote regarding education in ancient Israel:

All education is at first religious in the sense that religious motives and ideas predominate in the educational efforts of all primitive peoples. ... Here lies the explanation of the religious-educational character of Hebrew national life, and here, too, the secret of Israel's incomparable influence upon the religious and educational development of the world. The religion of Israel was a vital religion and it was a teaching religion. ... The home was the only school [including learning to read and write] and the parents the only teachers. (p. 901)

Modern traditional Jewish thinkers concur:

With respect to education, however, the traditional Jewish sources speak unequivocally, laying down a number of clear principles relevant to the current debate: (1) *Parents must have responsibility and control* ... (2) *Teachers and schools are agents of parents* ... control and responsibility remain with the parents. ... The "education establishment" always remains accountable to parents. (3) *Education should inculcate values as well as knowledge.* Because of this, the Jewish tradition does not see education as purely secular. (Pruzan, 1998, p. 2; see also Lapin, 1993, 1999)

Likewise, traditional Christians today (including both Catholics and evangelicals) concur that parents have the primary and final rights and duties regarding the education of their children (e.g., Adams, Stein, & Wheeler, 1989; Ball, 1994; Clark, 1988; DeJong, 1989; Hardon, 1998; Hocking, 1978; Klicka, 1993; Skillen, 1998).

Based on more limited knowledge, I also understand that traditional Muslims today agree that the primary authority and duty regarding the

Individuals' Gain and Society's Common Good

education of children lies with parents (see, e.g., http://www.ArabesQ.com). Finally, I think it is clear that the large majority of adults in the United States today, regardless of what faith they might espouse (i.e., be it more natural- or supernatural-based), philosophically agree that parents hold the primary right and duty regarding children's education and are, ultimately, the ones best equipped to make educational decisions (cf. Phi Delta Kappa International, 1998).

Research does not yet clearly show whether home schooling creates hardy and healthy families. There is evidence, however, that this may be the case (Allie-Carson, 1990; Carlson, 1993, 1995; Lines, 1994; Romm, 1993; Smith & Sikkink, 1999).

If parent involvement in the lives of children is so critical—based on both research on children's academic success and major religious worldviews—and home-based education is essentially the epitome of parent involvement, then the vast majority of educators, ministers of faith, and parents should be rushing to embrace its practice. During the past 2 decades, in fact, there has been a rush toward home schooling by a relatively significant percentage of parents, but hardly by a majority of educators and ministers of faith. I do not have space in this work to address ministers of faith, but I must take space for the question of why, perhaps, educators are not more ardently advancing the practice of parent-led and home-based education. One might make a good case that the primary reason is the control of a colossal amount of money from taxation (e.g., Brimelow & Spencer, 1993; Lieberman, 1997; Toch, 1991). However, I do not expand on this possibility in this article. Giving educators some benefit of the doubt, I think that at present the answer mainly has to do with their personal conceptions of what is the common good with respect to liberty in a just society with a nondominant state.

Liberty in a Just Society With a Nondominant State

With respect to social and political life, liberty means several things: A person shall not be encumbered with respect to what he believes; the government shall neither try to stop a person from believing something nor try to make a person believe anything (U.S. Constitution). Liberty means that every person is allowed to be as kind and generous as he or she wants to be to any other person or group. A person is not allowed to harm another in any way that clearly violates a clear and unambiguous standard.

Within a freedom-loving nation such as the United States, liberty also entails the idea that a person's rights of life, liberty, and the pursuit of happiness will be guarded in a way that is clear and unambiguous (e.g., all adult persons

279

B. D. Ray

may vote, any person may sit at the front of a room in a public-access building); it does not mean the government may coerce private persons to give money (e.g., via taxes), jobs, or privileges to other individuals or groups. Liberty means that the government shall not violate the private spaces and relationships of others (e.g., the home, the family, private business) unless there is clear and probable cause that something unlawful is taking place therein. Liberty does not mean, as some believe, license to do whatever one wants to do as long as it does not "clearly harm someone else."

It is clear that society ultimately must make choices of morality on many issues and correspondingly create and uphold law (Bauman, 1999). Each faith tradition, whether more anthropocentric or more theocentric, uses different approaches and standards regarding moral goodness. Judeo-Christian tradition would say that true liberty is attained in thought and action consistent with supernaturally revealed truth that should be the basis of a government's law and is therefore protected by the law. In a freedom-loving nation comprised of individuals with disparate worldviews (e.g., orthodox Jews, Marxists, neoliberals, and New Age adherents), passionate but respectful disagreement about the definition of liberty will continue for a long time. Perhaps more than liberty, justice has been the focus of American thinkers and policymakers during the past 2 decades.

As with the term *liberty*, justice's definition largely depends on one's worldview, one's functional religious presuppositions (see, e.g., Apple, 1993; Skillen, 1998; Welner, 1999). *Justice* has been defined in many ways:

According to the Romans, justice meant "giving to each its due." Plato and Aristotle conceived of justice as the proper ordering of society, resulting from the rule of reason over passion in public deliberation. The biblical tradition ties justice to righteous conduct—that which is consistent with God's commandments, a proper respect toward the Creator and His creatures. Many today stress the concept of justice as "fairness." (Skillen, 1998, p. 1)

Although I cannot solve the debate here, I suggest that a just society is one in which government officials treat all individuals impartially and in accordance with all law that is constitutional and moral (i.e., good); the government punishes anyone who harms another person (see, e.g., Olasky, 1996, Appendix B; Old Testament, Rom. 13:3–4, New American Standard). A just society is not one in which the government is authorized to force one person or group to give something (e.g., money, a job, more control over capital) to another person or group; that is to say, a just society does not mean one in which those in power—be they political representatives, think-tank sages, university professors, or union leaders—use the

Individuals' Gain and Society's Common Good

force of law and the state to try to create a society that has an absence of differences in things like amount of money earned, kinds of jobs held, or "one's relationship to the control and production of cultural and economic capital" (Apple, 1982, p. 505) when compared by persons' skin color, ethnic background, religion, gender, or sexual practices. For example, a just society is not one that assumes the state has an obligation to meet an indeterminate number of unspecified "needs of all children" (e.g., Clinton, 1996, pp. 128–145; Welner, 1999, p. 2). The nuanced difference between protecting a right and assuring that a person obtains a benefit may be vague, and I again recognize that there may be passionate but respectful disagreement in a constitutional republic about what is a just society.

Fervent wrangling over the definitions of liberty and justice in the context of this nation's and the world's common good will continue. There is often little one can do, in the end, to make another person accept one's own definitions. This is the "nice" thing—the convenient and relaxing thing—about America; everyone may have his or her own opinion. There are many individuals and groups who know, however, that there is a way to ensure that others will accept particular definitions of liberty and justice (or other concepts such as the common good, correct social theory, the best functional religion for a nation). They merely give the state power to create and enforce a system that retains the appearance of noncoercion but effectively guarantees the majority of the population will be under the control of the state and will come to espouse these particular worldviews and notions of liberty and justice. State-controlled schools may be the perfect system to meet these ends.

To the advantage of those who want to use state-run schools to meet their desired ends, I recognize (and I think others hold a similar view; see, e.g., Baer, 1998; Ball, 1994; Everhart, 1982) that the state-run school system has become essentially the "default setting"—the natural, normal, unchallenged choice, so to speak—for most Americans. The implicit assumptions are so pervasive in the thinking and writing of Americans, even among those who are advocates of parental rights, duty, and ultimate authority with respect to children's education, that they often talk about "withdrawing" or "taking children out of" the state school system (e.g., Welner, 1999, p. 2). These terms are even used to describe parents who never sent their children away from themselves and a home-based environment to be taught and directed by the strangers and experts at the state institutions. The practice of sending children to state schools and the language that accompanies it is entrenched in America. It is the "what is," not necessarily the "what ought." Although this language is now ingrained, it is notable that the majority of American parents would choose private or home schooling rather than state-run schools if they thought they genuinely had

281

B. D. Ray

the choice (Carper & Layman, 1997; Glenn, 1988, p. 284; Havermann, 1998; Phi Delta Kappa, 1998). Of special interest to those who focus on particular groups in the state-run system, Black adults appear to be more interested in authentic choice than do White adults (Glenn, 1988; McDowell, Sanchez, & Jones, 2000/this issue; Phi Delta Kappa, 1998).

Debate about the role of the state in education in America has been strong for well over a century (Arons, 1983; Ball, 1994; Everhart, 1982; Glenn, 1987, 1988; McCarthy, Oppewal, Peterson, & Spykman, 1981; McCarthy, Skillen, & Harper, 1982; Richman, 1994; Spring, 1990; Toch, 1991). I submit that those who promoted voluntary education under the authority of parents and First Amendment free associations and who opposed state-run schooling during the early history of the United States (e.g., the Voluntaryists; Glenn, 1988) were correct; the instruction, education, and indoctrination of children never should have been given over to the state and its agents. The practice of such has caused ceaseless strife among Americans, as Sowell (1993) explained, and it naturally causes the reduction of diverse and free thinking in the people of the United States (Ravitch, 1992). It appears that the desire of many proponents of state-run education over the past 200 years has been to control individuals and "the Other"—individuals or other groups of persons who think differently from oneself—to use the term in a way probably not intended by some (e.g., Apple, 1998).

Historical accounts provide insight regarding the motivations behind advocates of state-run education. For example, McCarthy et al. (1981) explained that Thomas Jefferson had tension in his thought

> between his theoretical commitment to individualism and his pragmatic bent toward collectivism. ... Jefferson did not take a direct route to the state [guaranteeing societal order]. He turned instead to the school as the primary institution to guarantee the order and freedom he desired in society. In Jefferson's thought the school gave up its autonomy to the state and became little more than a department of the state. And Jefferson saw nothing wrong with indoctrinating students into a philosophy of government as long as it corresponded to his understanding of orthodoxy.
>
> Benjamin Rush ... saw that Jefferson's program was but another form of sectarianism. ... [But] he followed the same route into pragmatic collectivism that Jefferson followed. (p. 85)

Rush unabashedly predicted that "our schools of learning, by producing one general and uniform system of educator, will render the mass of the people more homogeneous and thereby fit them more easily for uniform and peaceable government" (McCarthy et al., 1981, p. 86).

Individuals' Gain and Society's Common Good

Horace Mann was able to accomplish in the mid-1800s what Jefferson was not able to do in the late-1700s. As McCarthy et al. (1981) wrote, "Mann was successful in that he convinced enough people that a system of public schools which championed a supposedly nonsectarian religion was essential to the well-being of the social, economic, and political order of the state" (p. 86; see also McCarthy et al., 1982). Glenn (1988), likewise, historically and lucidly uncovered much of the thinking that has been behind the advocacy of state-run education in several nations; his findings also corroborate the kinds of thinking exhibited by Jefferson and Rush, as just noted.

It is crucial to recognize that many individuals holding notions that the state should be in control of future adult citizens are from this century, not only from past ones. For example, Wiggin (1962), of the University of Maryland, described herself as liberal in religion and in politics and firmly believes "that the proper place for a child or youth in a republican society is in a public elementary or secondary school" (p. viii) and that state-run schools are "a gigantic moral enterprise" (p. 36) in which society transmits to its citizens the correct answer to questions such as: "Who is an American? ... What should this American know and what should be his behavior? ... [and] How may he be a good American citizen?" (p. 36). A professor of education stated in 1981, "Public schools promote civic rather than individual pursuits" and "Each child belongs to the state" (as cited in Richman, 1994, p. 51). Winnie Mandela promised to South Africans in the early 1990s free and compulsory education and stated, "Parents not sending their children to school will be the first prisoners of the ANC [African National Congress] government" (Richman, 1994, p. 51). Apple (1993) explained the struggle that leads up to what becomes the "official knowledge" to be transmitted to future generations of students: "a *selective tradition* operates in which only specific groups' knowledge becomes official knowledge [of texts used in public schools]" (p. 65). A then-advocate of re-Christianizing state-run schools, Simonds (1993) promoted doing "indirect evangelism" in public schools by influencing the selection of curriculum materials that give a biblical view and omitting materials that promote nonbiblical views. He also stated that students "should be taught patriotism and the traditions of Western culture, as well as principles of self-government and democracy," and the "Judeo-Christian philosophy of life ... should be included in textbooks and the teaching process as a matter of history and the basis for our values, and ethical practices" (p. 109). More recently, an educator and official at the Oregon State Department of Education whose area of authority is home schooling told me that the state, not the parents, should have ultimate authority in making sure that a child receives an education according to the state's demands (D. Perkins, personal communication, May 17, 1999).

B. D. Ray

Not all persons' desires to use state-run schools for control and social change are as obvious as some of those in the preceding paragraph. For example, a thinker such as Apple (1993, 1996) provides elaborate analyses of the complex issues involved and power being exerted within the realm of America's state-run schools and claims commitment to an ethical and political principle that, among other things, dignifies human life, sees others not as objects to be manipulated, and considers all persons acting as *"co-responsible subjects* involved in the process of democratically deliberating over the ends and means of *all* of their institutions" (Apple, 1993, p. 3). Regarding such seemingly virtuous goals, two very important things must be considered. First, it is common knowledge that a relatively small percentage of citizens—especially parents with school-age children—have ever (especially during the past 50 years) democratically deliberated over the nature and power relationships of state-run schools in any local, meaningful, and effective way. They are not the ones—and never have been, at least in recent history—deciding the nature of state-run schools or the official knowledge being promulgated therein. Second, the same persons who say others should not be manipulated or coerced with power also advocate the state's continuation as the proprietor of indoctrination. As an example, we can read what Apple (1996) had to say about state-controlled schools:

> Many of us have quite ambivalent feelings about the place called school. All of us who care deeply about what is and is not taught, and about who is and is not empowered to deal with these issues, have a contradictory relationship to these institutions. We want to criticize them rigorously and yet in this very criticism lies a commitment, a hope, that they can be made more vital, more personally meaningful and socially critical. If ever there was a love/hate relationship, this is it. ... I certainly do not want to act as an apologist for poor practices [in schools]. Yet, during an era when—because of rightist attacks—we face the massive dismantling of the gains (limited as they are) that have been made in social welfare, in women's control of their bodies, in relations of race, gender, and sexuality, and in whose knowledge is taught in schools, it is equally important to make certain that these gains are defended. Thus, there is another clear tension in this volume. I want to both defend the idea of a *public* education, and a number of the gains that do exist, and at the same time to criticize many of its attributes. (pp. xv–xvi)

If by those like Apple "public" schools mean tax-funded and state-controlled schools, then there appears to be an inherent self-contradiction in their arguments in favor of peaceful democratic deliberation and against inequalities and dominating powers. On the one hand,

284

Individuals' Gain and Society's Common Good

they are disturbed that "the Others" (e.g., "rightists") have prevailed at times past in state-run schools and are now prevailing in too many ways (Apple, 1996, 1998, p. xvi), and they argue for nonmanipulative practices in society. On the other hand, they say they are glad they have made gains in certain areas (e.g., women's control over their bodies and whose knowledge is taught in schools) and want to hold on to those gains—gains that often have been attained via powerful political moves and the manipulation of others. My hypothesis (based on what I have read and experiences such as those I have had with educators at professional conferences like the annual meetings of the American Educational Research Association for more than a decade) is that these same persons who advocate state-run schools and the elimination of coercion and manipulation would like to teach children in state-run schools many specific attitudes and beliefs—that these people hold to be true—that are strongly objected to by "the Others" of different worldviews or religious persuasions. In other words, I infer that they are glad when they, or others who believe as they do, prevail in getting their way in the polity, curriculum, and official knowledge of the state-run schools.

Although it is difficult and risky to ascertain the motives of contemporaries, history provides both perspective and motivation to do so. I suggest that many of today's proponents of state-run education are no different from their colleagues of the past. Thankfully, scholars have pointed out that some of the most appalling regimes in memorable history were enamored with using state-run schools to control the thought of children and thus, eventually, the nation (Ravitch, 1992; Richman, 1994). By compelling children to be schooled and then only funding schools that are controlled by the state, a government is inherently acting inequitably toward one group of persons—those who do not want or choose not to put their children under the indoctrinating authority of the government. This coercive use of different scales for different persons is to be detested, and it violates the universally accepted golden rule (Prov. 16:11, 20:23; Matt. 7:12, New American Standard). In addition to other arguments about why state-controlled schools should exist and why children should attend them, some have argued that this is a way to protect children from their parents (e.g., their ineptitude, abuse, narrow-mindedness, crude influence). In response to this line of thought and to the others, it is important to remember certain things, as Skillen (1998) made plain:

> While it is true that public law should not misidentify the family as a totalitarian enclave in which parents may do anything and everything whatever to their children, it is also true that every public-legal attempt to "liberate" minor children from parents makes the minors subject to

B. D. Ray

whatever legal, medical or other authority is then authorized to direct or influence their actions. Thus, not only are the children not liberated from all external authorities, but one of the most important non-governmental institutions of society is thereby weakened by the overwhelming power of the state. The family as an institution suffers injustice, as does the child who was created first for family life and, via the family, for eventual adult maturity and personal independence.

In sum ... I would argue that the failure to identify human beings correctly as persons-in-community and the family as the foremost community for children, when combined with the failure to discriminate properly in law between adults and minor children, leads to the publicly unjust treatment of families and children. (pp. 3, 5)

Today's advocates of state-run education view the schools as a way to enact their vision of the good life, the good society, the common good. These schools are a way to keep millions of children (i.e., future adult citizens) under the tutelage of those who can teach them to think and act as they allegedly should.

However, in a nation that claims to be liberty-loving and an advocate of citizens' free thinking, there can be no room for an arrangement in which the state puts its citizens under its own particularistic and value-laden teaching. The functions of instruction, education, and indoctrination should be left in the hands of the private, personal, particular, and peculiar worlds of parents and their families and their volitionally funded and privately managed free associations. Any wrong behaviors that might proceed from teachings of these parents and their free associations would be tempered by clear and consistent law and related punishment for the violation thereof.

But, in the end, perhaps the discussion about who should have the main control over children's instruction and education does not revolve around one's conception of liberty in a just society with a nondominant state and to what extent and how one group should control another. Perhaps the conflict most essentially revolves around which values and beliefs (i.e., faith or religion; McCarthy et al., 1981, p. 111) should prevail in our society.

Persons With Reliable Character and Value Systems

There was a time when I thought—and most people still do think—that all Americans agree on the goodness of some basic traits such as honesty, faithfulness, dependability, kindness, and helpfulness. At this point in American history, and that of Western culture in general, however, it is dif-

286

Individuals' Gain and Society's Common Good

ficult to say that we can even agree about the absolute goodness of these traits. Intellectual faith systems such as metaphysical naturalism (Johnson, 1995), post-modernism, and sociobiology seem to call into doubt anything of durability and stability in the realm of human ethics and morality. I hope to see an increasing percentage of our society possessing beliefs and expressing behaviors that are good. Among other things, these beliefs include treating all human beings as created equal: "They need no title or qualification beyond their simple humanity in order to command respect for their intrinsic human dignity, their 'unalienable rights'" (Keyes, 1999). But it is now clear that Americans are having great difficulty agreeing on even the character traits that so many once thought were fundamental. Intimately related to this goal, the quintessential issue regarding any child's education actually may be what value system or worldview should be taught to him or her, not what is the socially accepted definition of justice or whether honesty is always the best policy.

Proponents of compulsory schooling law and state-controlled schools, whether "leftists" or "rightists," are working, perhaps unwittingly, to make sure that something called the "common curriculum"—the one approved by those in positions of power—is taught to all (or most) children. Advocates of these government institutions hope they will long be the ones in positions of power. Conversely, most proponents of home schooling and parental choice and authority only want to make sure that their personally chosen curriculum is taught to their children. These folks are not asking the state or anyone else for money or power to teach their curriculum to anyone else. They are asking the state and their neighbors to assume that they, the parents, have the best interests of their children and society's common good in mind. In fact, these parents are only asking the state, and their neighbors and thinkers who empower and influence the agents of the state, to let them go about their lives peaceably and quietly in the privacy of their homes and communities with their children. Advocates of home-based education are familiar with the golden rule and the big issues of liberty and justice for all in society. These parents want the state to allow individual citizens to choose freely when and how they will help other parents.

In Closing

Home schooling allows parents, in a context of nurture and high social capital, to choose freely a unique and effective education for their children. Each year a child grows older gives the parents and the child more opportunity to forge stronger bonds and a richer, relationally developed curricu-

B. D. Ray

lum. Parents and children in such an arrangement, under no compulsion or coercion from the state, are allowed to escape the hidden curriculum of others and of the state, choose texts for learning, and work together in their communities as they "see work–family–religion–recreation–school as an organically related system of human relationships" (Tyack, 1974, p. 15).

The battles over power and domination that riddle state-run schools cannot sap home schooling parents and their children of their strength, consume their energy, and destroy their zest for learning. Zeal for social justice, liberty, the common good, and being right with one's Creator can be approached from an environment of security, strength, and stability while the ever-maturing child year after year steps out into larger and more expansive spheres of challenge, democratic deliberation, and creative service to others.

The voices of those who are anti-home schooling, anti-parents' rights, and antichoice and of those who assert that home schooling causes "balkanization," "divisiveness," "social anarchy," "narrow-mindedness," "fundamentalism," "segregationism," and "possessive individualism" are increasingly hollow and impotent. Evidence supporting their claims is (and always has been) scarce to nonexistent (e.g., Caldwell, 1999; L. Berg, organizational specialist, National Education Association, personal communication, July 28, 1999). Furthermore—and tragically for this nation's children and to the chagrin of the proponents of state-run schools—the power struggles, illegal drug deals, racism (Greene & Mellow, 1998), violence, philosophical contention, religious censorship, lack of parent involvement, low academic achievement, high dropout rates, premarital sexual activities, teachers' and bureaucratic antiparental power (Baker & Soden, 1998), and greed-based high-stakes labor disputes that are associated with the halls and culture of public schools and so powerfully overshadow the significant incidents of success and joy therein make the common criticisms of parent-led home schooling look very wan and insignificant.

I have explained that the research evidence on home-educated children's learning, psychological and social health, and success in adulthood supports the inference that home schooling has very positive effects. Research and theory also suggest that home schooling is associated with, if not causes, strong and healthy families. I have argued that persons who desire liberty in a just society will embrace and advocate home-based education as the educational option of preference. Also, although several ideas I present and promote in this article may be outside the majority view of contemporary educators, thinkers, and those who publish in the field of education, I have documented that these ideas are certainly neither neoteric nor outside the realm of reasonable and bona fide discourse. Finally, I have posited that although debates over the meanings of and how to advance liberty and justice may continue forever, the issue of how we should make education available to children and youth is essentially a matter of which value system or worldview should be taught to them and who will control the decision; it should be their parents, not the state.

Home schooling is done out of intense care and concern for today's children. Research is clear that home schooling is chosen to (a) assure that children are academically successful, (b) individualize teaching and learning for each child, (c) enhance family relationships, (d) provide children guided and reasoned social interactions with youthful peers and adults, (e) keep children safe in many respects, and (f) transmit particular values and worldviews to the children (Ray, 1999). Parents do not engage in home education, by and large, to aid some group (be it a majority, minority, disadvantaged, or advantaged one). It is done for today's children, knowing that if they benefit, then society as a whole ultimately will benefit and thus the common good will be served.

Home schooling is a potent way of education and a rich social experience that had all but vanished by 1980 from the consciousness of the American people. Family-based and parent-led education is now back in strength and dynamism. Hundreds of thousands of people in America (and other countries) are enthusiastically developing the thesis that it liberates children and families. Home schooling gives parents and children an opportunity to escape the multiple dominating powers and special interest groups who constantly vie for control within the dominion of state-controlled schooling.

Although I have attempted in this article to put relatively little emphasis on subcategories of humans, it is critical to note in this age of such emphasis that both leftists and rightists, light-skinned and dark-skinned, poor and wealthy, those with special needs and those with talented and gifted children, and theists and humanists are joining the ranks of home schooling. Research and anecdotes indicate that involvement of a diversity is presently accelerating. Home schooling is very open to the public. It frees children and families from the coerced consensus-building processes of the state-run schools. It gives individuals and groups the freedom to help others in direct, personal, immediate, and effective ways. Based on research and philosophical reasoning, I believe that in the long run home-based education academically and psychologically benefits children, emancipates persons to choose their social and political lives freely, and advances the common good of any nation.

References

ACT [formerly American College Testing]. (1997). *ACT high school profile; Home schooled composite report; HS graduating class 1997.* Iowa City, IA: Author.

B. D. Ray

Adams, B., Stein, J., & Wheeler, H. (1989). *Who owns the children? Compulsory education and the dilemma of ultimate authority.* Austin, TX: Truth Forum.

Allie-Carson, J. (1990). Structure and interaction patterns of home school families. *Home School Researcher, 6*(3), 11–18.

Apple, M. W. (1982). Education and cultural reproduction: A critical reassessment of programs for choice. In R. B. Everhart (Ed.), *The public school monopoly: A critical analysis of education and the state in American society* (chap. 14, pp. 503–541). Cambridge, MA: Ballinger.

Apple, M. W. (1993). *Official knowledge: Democratic education in a conservative age.* New York: Routledge.

Apple, M. W. (1996). *Cultural politics and education.* New York: Teachers College Press.

Apple, M. W. (1998). Are markets and standards democratic? *Educational Researcher, 27*(6), 24–28.

Arons, S. (1983). *Compelling belief: The culture of American schooling.* New York: McGraw-Hill.

Atkinson, R. L., Atkinson, R. C., Smith, E. E., Bem, D. J., & Nolen-Hoeksema, S. (1996). *Hilgard's introduction to psychology* (12th ed.). New York: Harcourt Brace.

Baer, R. A. (1998). Why a functional definition of religion is necessary if justice is to be achieved in public education. In J. T. Sears & J. C. Carper (Eds.), *Curriculum, religion, and public education: Conversations for an enlarging public square* (pp. 105–115). New York: Teachers College Press.

Baker, A. J. L., & Soden, L. M. (1998). The challenges of parent involvement research. *ERIC/CUE Digest, 134.* (ERIC Document Reproduction Service No. 419 030 98)

Ball, W. B. (1994). *Mere creatures of the state?: Education, religion, and the courts, a view from the courtroom.* Notre Dame, IN: Crisis.

Bauman, M. (1999). The falsity, futility, and folly of separating morality from law. *Christian Research Journal, 21*(3), 20–23, 36–41.

Blankenhorn, D. (1995). *Fatherless America: Confronting our most urgent social problem.* New York: Basic Books.

Brimelow, P., & Spencer, L. (1993, June 7). The National Extortion Association? *Forbes.*

Caldwell, D. K. (1999, January 30). Death to the schools: Leaders of religious right calling for a Christian exodus out of public education. *Dallas Morning News*, 1G.

Carlson, A. C. (1993). *From cottage to work station: The family's search for social harmony in the industrial age.* San Francisco: Ignatius.

Carlson, A. C. (1995). Preserving the family for the new millennium: A policy agenda. *The Family in America, 9*(3), 1–8.

Carlton, B. (1999). A systemic view of the socialization of home schoolers. *Private School Monitor, 20*(3), 7–9.

Carper, J. C., & Layman, J. (1997, Winter). Black-flight academies: The new Christian day schools. *Educational Forum, 61*, 114–121.

Chavkin, N. F. (Ed.). (1993). *Families and schools in a pluralistic society.* Albany: State University of New York Press.

Cizek, G. J. (1993). The mismeasure of home schooling effectiveness: A commentary. *Home School Researcher, 9*(3), 1–4.

Clark, G. H. (1988). *A Christian philosophy of education* (2nd rev. ed.). Jefferson, MD: Trinity Foundation.

Clinton, H. R. (1996). *It takes a village: And other lessons children teach us.* New York: Simon & Schuster.

Coleman, J. S. (1991). *Policy perspectives: Parental involvement in education.* Washington, DC: U.S. Department of Education, Office of Educational Research and Improvement.

Coleman, J. S., & Hoffer, T. (1987). *Public and private high schools: The impact of communities.* New York: Basic Books.

Individuals' Gain and Society's Common Good

Coleman, J. S., Hoffer, T., & Kilgore, S. (1982). *High school achievement: Public, Catholic, and private schools compared.* New York: Basic Books.

DeJong, N. (1989). *Education in the truth.* Lansing, IL: Redeemer.

Everhart, R. B. (Ed.). (1982). *The public school monopoly: A critical analysis of education and the state in American society.* Cambridge, MA: Ballinger.

Galloway, R. A., & Sutton, J. P. (1995). Home schooled and conventionally schooled high school graduates: A comparison of aptitude for and achievement in college English. *Home School Researcher, 11*(1), 1–9.

Glenn, C. L. (1987). "Molding" citizens. In R. J. Neuhaus (Ed.), *Democracy and the renewal of public education* (pp. 25–56). Grand Rapids, MI: Eerdmans.

Glenn, C. L. (1988). *The myth of the common school.* Amherst: University of Massachusetts Press.

Good, T. L., & Brophy, J. E. (1987). *Looking in classrooms* (4th ed.). New York: Harper & Row.

Gordon, E. E., & Gordon, E. H. (1990). *Centuries of tutoring: A history of alternative education in America and Western Europe.* Lanham, MD: University Press of America.

Greene, J. P., & Mellow, N. (1998, September). *Integration where it counts: A study of racial integration in public and private school lunchrooms.* Paper presented at the meeting of the American Political Science Association, Boston. (Available at www.schoolchoices.org/roo/jay1.htm)

Hardon, J. (1998). Father Hardon on home schooling. *Seton Home Study School, 15*(11), 4–5.

Havermann, J. (1998, May). A private rescue mission. *Citizen, 12*(5), 16–17.

Henderson, A. T., & Berla, N. (Eds.). (1994). *A new generation of evidence: The family is critical to student achievement.* Washington, DC: National Committee for Citizens in Education.

Hocking, D. L. (1978). The theological basis for the philosophy of Christian school education. In P. A. Kienel (Ed.), *The philosophy of Christian school education* (Rev. ed., pp. 7–28). Whittier, CA: Association of Christian Schools International.

Johnson, P. E. (1995). *Reason in the balance: The case against naturalism in science, law, and education.* Downers Grove, IL: InterVarsity.

Keyes, A. (1999, July 30). The armed defense of liberty. *WorldNetDaily.com* [Online]. Retrieved July 30, 1999 from the World Wide Web: www.worldnetdaily.com/bluesky_keyes/19990730_xcake_the_armed_.shtml

Klicka, C. J. (1993). *The right choice.* Gresham, OR: Noble.

Knowles, J. G., & Muchmore, J. A. (1994, April). *"Yep? We're grown-up home schooled kids—and we're doing just fine, thank you very much."* Paper presented at the annual meeting of the American Educational Research Association, New Orleans, LA.

Lapin, D. (1993, November). Parents versus the state. *Crisis.*

Lapin, D. (1999). *America's real war.* Sisters, OR: Multnomah.

Lieberman, M. (1997). *The teacher unions.* New York: Free Press.

Lines, P. M. (1994). Homeschooling: Private choices and public obligations. *Home School Researcher, 10*(3), 9–26.

Lines, P. M. (1998). *Homeschoolers: Estimating numbers and growth.* Washington, DC: U.S. Department of Education, Office of Educational Research and Improvement, National Institute on Student Achievement, Curriculum, and Assessment.

McCarthy, R., Oppewal, D., Peterson, W., & Spykman, G. (1981). *Society, state, and schools: A case for structural and confessional pluralism.* Grand Rapids, MI: Eerdmans.

McCarthy, R. M., Skillen, J. W., & Harper, W. A. (1982). *Disestablishment a second time: Genuine pluralism for American schools.* Grand Rapids, MI: Eerdmans.

McDowell, S. A., Sanchez, A. S., & Jones, S. S. (2000/this issue). Participation and perception: Looking at home schooling through a multicultural lens. *Peabody Journal of Education, 75*(1&2), 124–146.

Medlin, R. G. (2000/this issue). Home schooling and the question of socialization. *Peabody Journal of Education, 75*(1&2), 107–123.

B. D. Ray

Meier, P. D., Minirth, F. B., & Wichern, F. (1982). *Introduction to psychology and counseling.* Grand Rapids, MI: Baker Book House.

Meyer, H. H. (1983). Education. In J. Orr (Ed.), *International standard Bible encyclopedia* (Vol. 2, pp. 900–905). Grand Rapids, MI: Eerdmans. (Original work published 1929)

Montgomery, L. R. (1989). The effect of home schooling on the leadership skills of home schooled students. *Home School Researcher, 5*(1), 1–10.

Mungeam, F. (Executive Producer). (1993, December 5). *Town hall show.* Portland, OR: KATU Television.

Olasky, M. (1996). *Renewing American compassion: How compassion for the needy can turn ordinary citizens into heroes.* New York: Free Press.

de Oliveira, P. C. M., Watson, T. G., & Sutton, J. P. (1994). Differences in critical thinking skills among students educated in public schools, Christian schools, and home schools. *Home School Researcher, 10*(4), 1–8.

Phi Delta Kappa International. (1998). *The 30th annual Phi Delta Kappa/Gallup poll of the public's attitudes toward the public schools* [Online]. Retrieved April 13, 2000 from the World Wide Web: http://www.pdkintl.org/kappan/kp9809-1a.htm

Popenoe, D. (1996). *Life without father: Compelling new evidence that fatherhood and marriage are indispensable for the good of children and society.* New York: Free Press.

Priesnitz, W., & Priesnitz, H. (1990, March). *Home-based education in Canada: An investigation.* Unionville, Ontario: The Alternative Press. (Available from The Alternative Press, 195 Markville Road, Unionville, Ontario L3R 4V8, Canada)

Pruzan, A. (1998). *Toward tradition on educational vouchers/school choice.* Mercer Island, WA: Toward Tradition.

Ravitch, D. (1992). The role of private schools in American education. In P. R. Kane (Ed.), *Independent schools, independent thinkers* (pp. 20–26). San Francisco: Jossey-Bass.

Ray, B. D. (1988). Home schools: A synthesis of research on characteristics and learner outcomes. *Education and Urban Society, 21*(1), 16–31.

Ray, B. D. (1990). *A nationwide study of home education: Family characteristics, legal matters, and student achievement.* Salem, OR: National Home Education Research Institute.

Ray, B. D. (1994). *A nationwide study of home education in Canada: Family characteristics, student achievement, and other topics.* Salem, OR: National Home Education Research Institute.

Ray, B. D. (1997). *Strengths of their own—Home schoolers across America: Academic achievement, family characteristics, and longitudinal traits.* Salem, OR: National Home Education Research Institute.

Ray, B. D. (1999). *Home schooling on the threshold: A survey of research at the dawn of the new millennium.* Salem, OR: National Home Education Research Institute.

Ray, B. D. (2000/this issue). Home schooling: The ameliorator of negative influences on learning? *Peabody Journal of Education, 75*(1&2), 71–106.

Richman, S. (1994). *Separating school and state: How to liberate America's families.* Fairfax, VA: Future of Freedom Foundation.

Romm, T. (1993). *Home schooling and the transmission of civic culture.* Unpublished doctoral dissertation, Clark Atlanta University, Atlanta, GA.

Rothermel, P. (1999, Summer). A nationwide study of home education: Early indications and wider implications. *Education Now,* (24), 9.

Rudner, L. M. (1999). The scholastic achievement and demographic characteristics of home school students in 1998. *Education Policy Analysis Archives, 7*(8) [Online]. Retrieved April 13, 2000 from the World Wide Web: http://epaa.asu.edu/epaa/v7n8/

Russell, T. (1994). Cross-validation of a multivariate path analysis of predictors of home school student academic achievement. *Home School Researcher, 10*(1), 1–13.

292

Individuals' Gain and Society's Common Good

Sheffer, S. (1995). *A sense of self: Listening to homeschooled adolescent girls*. Portsmouth, NH: Boynton/Cook.

Shepherd, M. S. (1986, September). The home schooling movement: An emerging conflict in American education [Abstract]. *Home School Researcher, 2*(3), 1.

Shyers, L. E. (1992). A comparison of social adjustment between home and traditionally schooled students. *Home School Researcher, 8*(3), 1–8.

Skillen, J. W. (1998). Justice and civil society. *The Civil Society Project, 98*(2), 1–6. (Available from The Civil Society Project, 3544 N. Progress Ave., Suite 101, Harrisburg, PA 17110)

Simonds, R. L. (1993). *A guide to the public schools: For Christian parents and teachers, and especially for pastors*. Costa Mesa, CA: Citizens for Excellence in Education.

Smith, C., & Sikkink, D. (1999, April). Is private schooling privatizing? *First Things, 92*, 16–20.

Sowell, T. (1993). *Inside American education: The decline, the deception, the dogmas*. New York: Free Press.

Spring, J. (1990). *The American school: 1642–1990* (2nd ed.). White Plains, NY: Longman.

Toch, T. (1991). *In the name of excellence: The struggle to reform the nation's schools, why it's failing, and what should be done*. New York: Oxford University Press.

Traviss, M. P. (1998, Fall). Racial integration and private schools: A summary of two of Dr. Jay Greene's articles. *Private School Monitor, 20*(1), 9–10.

Tucker, C. J., Marx, J., & Long, L. (1998, April). "Moving on": Residential mobility and children's school lives. *Sociology of Education, 71*, 111–129.

Tyack, D. B. (1974). *The one best system: A history of American urban education*. Cambridge, MA: Harvard University Press.

U.S. Department of Education. (1987). *What works: Research about teaching and learning* (2nd ed.). Washington, DC: U.S. Government Printing Office.

U.S. Department of Education. (1994). *Strong families, strong schools: Building community partnerships for learning*. Washington, DC: Author.

U.S. Department of Education, National Center for Education Statistics. (1998, February). *Mini-digest of education statistics, 1997*. Washington, DC: Author.

Wartes, J. (1987, March). Report from the 1986 home school testing and other descriptive information about Washington's home schoolers: A summary. *Home School Researcher, 3*(1), 1–4.

Welner, K. M. (1999, April). *Homeschooling and democracy: Exploring the tension between the state and parents*. Paper presented at the annual meeting of the American Educational Research Association, Montreal, Quebec, Canada.

White, M. J., & Kaufman, G. (1997). Language usage, social capital, and school completion among immigrants and native-born ethnic groups. *Social Science Quarterly, 78*, 385–398.

Wiggin, G. A. (1962). *Education and nationalism: An historical interpretation of American education*. New York: McGraw-Hill.

Wright, C. (1988, November). Home school research: Critique and suggestions for the future. *Education and Urban Society, 21*(1), 96–113.

The Home Schooling Movement: A Few Concluding Observations

Robert L. Crowson

In 1932, Willard Waller (*The Sociology of Teaching*) warned of the importance of distinguishing clearly between school and not-school. Otherwise, the special concerns of parents (vis-à-vis their own children), alongside community power inequities, would intrude heavily on the abilities of educators to be fully professional, to avoid favoritism and particularism, and to be effectively neutral.

Waller likely would be much surprised today to learn that a successful buffering of school from not-school is now given some credit (e.g., by Apple, 2000/this issue) for fueling the home schooling movement (see also Sarason, 1995). A rather unresponsive and notoriously bureaucratized profession apparently has not yet learned how to be adequately user-friendly.

Waller might be even more surprised to learn that the not-school, in very rapidly growing numbers (as noted by Ray, 2000a/this issue), is currently assuming the role of the school. What is the deep significance here? For parents to serve their children as pedagogues is not at all new, historically (see Carper, 2000/this issue); but the social and institutional implica-

ROBERT L. CROWSON *is Professor in the Department of Leadership and Organizations, Peabody College of Vanderbilt University, Nashville, Tennessee.*

Requests for reprints should be sent to Robert L. Crowson, Department of Leadership and Organizations, Box 514, Peabody College of Vanderbilt University, Nashville, TN 37203. E-mail: robert.l.crowson@vanderbilt.edu

Concluding Observations

tions of the home schooling movement (at this time of much turbulence in education's policy environment) should be examined closely.

This issue of the *Peabody Journal of Education* has done an excellent job of beginning to do just that. Historically informative tensions between religious beliefs, family preferences, and the development of the common schools are cleanly and succinctly sketched by James Carper (2000/this issue). Tyler and Carper (2000/this issue) combine in a highly instructive (and thoroughly readable) story of Zan Peters Tyler's personal political odyssey in South Carolina. The South Carolina case demonstrates that historically significant tensions persist—in a clear recognition by individuals, lawmakers, and educators that deep political "stakes" can be involved in home schooling legislation; that parental "clout" is already very much a force to be reckoned with in this state policy arena; and that the continuing "hold" of a home schooling minority on applicable state regulatory structures can be a key to successful policy implementation.

It is interesting to note that home schooling is by no means limited to the American context. There are also deep roots, with considerable success, in western European nations that are traditionally much less given to local control than is the United States. An informative summary by Taylor and Petrie (2000/this issue) notes the accommodate-the-home but protect-the-child flavor of enabling legislation in much of Europe—while observing the hard line against nonschool schooling taken in Germany. It would be well to learn much more about the politics and rationale of Germany's oppositional position.

As would be expected in a volume addressing such a value-laden issue, there are a number of articles that respond to the popular criticisms of home schooling (with "hard" data and with solid points of argument). Brian Ray (2000b/this issue) examines the key does-it-work question with valuable evidence that indeed it does, often for the same reasons that have been identified as keys to school improvement (e.g., high expectations, individualized curricula, direct instruction). Richard Medlin (2000/this issue) is effective in assembling research that counters the complaint that home schooling limits the social development and social adjustments of children; and Jacque Ensign (2000/this issue) offers evidence that home schooling also can work very effectively for children with special needs (from learning disabilities to giftedness).

There is just a bit of the let's-make-believers of the readership to some of the it-works articles. Such a tendency in this issue is nicely leavened, however, by pieces by McDowell, Sanchez, and Jones (2000/this issue) and by McDowell (2000/this issue) alone, which observe that the ethnic breakdown among home schoolers is, perhaps problematically, highly disproportionate to the larger society and that home schooling is not quite the

295

R. L. Crowson

"pleasant" experience for every mother–teacher that a rather romanticized literature implies. Also, to the great credit of the editorship of this issue, some intellectually powerful and insightful critiques of home schooling are offered by Chris Lubienski (2000/this issue) and by Michael Apple (2000/this issue). I refer in more depth to their work in the next few pages.

Finally, two of the most intriguing and informative pieces in this issue are the articles by Patricia Lines (2000/this issue) and Paul Hill (2000/this issue). Lines provides a review and some specific examples of trends in the development of "partnerships" between public schools and home schoolers. Her piece is evidence that the movement has decidedly come of age if, indeed, public officials are now making adaptive responses to parental school-them-at-home initiatives. It is also a possible hint, as Lines suggests, of a paradigm to come in the provision of much greater, parent-friendly programmatic flexibility in public education. When a movement begins to influence significantly the "mainstream," it is truly something worth a focusing of our attention.

Paul Hill (2000/this issue), on the other hand, claims that home schooling is not at all likely to "meld back" into mainstream public education. Home schoolers dread much of the accompanying paraphernalia of public schooling (e.g., bureaucratization, unionized teachers, lax discipline). This is not to suggest though, continues Hill, that "something like schools" will fail to develop. As home schoolers continue to rely more and more on one another, new less conventional but decidedly school-like institutions will evolve (out of what is increasingly a privatization thrust in America). Thus, Hill too sees home schooling as a window into a "broad movement," with ramifications far beyond the actual (although not insignificant) numbers of adherents and participants.

Some Additional Thoughts

Both Lubienski (2000/this issue) and Apple (2000/this issue) recognize fully that home schooling is a development of significance. Both, however, have deep concerns. Chris Lubienski wraps a strong piece of criticism around the tension between private benefits and public goals. When families deeply imbued with high-achievement attributes and expectations opt out, pulling their children away from the communal arena, they are removing themselves from a societal burden that we all share—to contribute to the larger "public good." Peer effects in classrooms are lost to the children of less well-prepared families, a privatization of economic interests displaces collective benefits, and "flight" is used to express dissatisfaction when the democratic use of "voice" might have led to societally beneficial change (in the organization and delivery of schooling).

Concluding Observations

Sharing much the same set of concerns, Michael Apple (2000/this issue) finds home schooling to be just one small element in a larger, very powerful social movement. There is good sense to be found in a legitimate concern for children and in a reaction to the bureaucratization of public education. However, disturbingly, this movement also reflects a pulling away from social equality and community toward stratification and "cocooning." There is a retreat from democratic discussion and criticism into strategies, says Apple, of "possessive individualism."

There may be less that is new to today's privatization of interests or to today's cocooning than Lubienski (2000/this issue) and Apple (2000/this issue) would imply. We learned long ago from C. M. Tiebout (1956) that Americans are adept at "voting with their feet" for educational services that match their individual preferences—usually in just-like-us communities of folks with similar tastes, similar incomes, and similar prejudices. To be cocooned, whether by choice or through lack of choice, is already a long and well-established tradition.

Nevertheless, there is, again, a sense (shared by Elshtain, 1995; Hawley, 1995; Murphy, 2000; and others) that a significant social movement is indeed in process—of which home schooling is just one part. Joseph Murphy noted a national mood of public cynicism about and an alienation from government-initiated activity, including a "widespread perception that the state is overinvolved in the life of the citizenry." Indeed, Brian Ray's (2000b/this issue) discussion of liberty and justice in a "non-dominant state," in this issue, provides a well-articulated sense of the essential, underlying mood.

Thus, the trend in America is away from "the state" as a means to achieve one's personal goals (e.g., access, equality, or communality)—and toward the individual and family unit as instruments of their own opportunities (Murphy, in press). Indeed (so goes the argument), it may be the state's job, if doing much of anything, to stand aside, to remove marketplace impediments from the self-seeking and self-fulfilling journeys of individuals. "Choice"—not just whether to home school but whether to charter school, attend a magnet, receive a voucher, return from busing to "the neighborhood," go to a workplace school, or join a for-profit school—seems decidedly to be the operant ideology in today's increasingly differentiated array of options for education.

In an atmosphere—indeed, an ideology (Crowson, 1999)—of individualism and choice, it is hard to fault an option for families that (as the editors' introduction notes) "is thriving; its ranks are swelling, and its children—according to the most current research—are flourishing." Farris and Woodruff (2000/this issue) are quite correct in concluding that home schooling is now "a well-established part of the American educational landscape." Evidence

297

R. L. Crowson

is surfacing of exceptional academic performance, of enhanced family to-getherness, of no loss in "social skills," of a valuable growth in "network-ing" among home schooling families, of a boom in available home-study materials and resources, and perhaps even a "carryover" (claim Farris & Woodruff) into more successful marriages and careers.

Among those who study the politics of social movements, an observa-tion can be offered that home schooling seems to be rapidly becoming "in-stitutionalized" in American society (see Crowson, Boyd, & Mawhinney, 1996). Differences between the states in the laws regulating home school-ing are starting to wash out; federal rules governing eligibility for student financial aid are being eased for home schoolers; home schoolers increas-ingly are willing to compare themselves against "mainstream" measures of accomplishment (e.g., standardized test scores); some accommodations are surfacing between public school administrators and home schoolers; and indeed (as Lines, 2000/this issue, notes), the jargon of public school re-form is now beginning to include home schooling or "independent study" as an acceptable option among reform alternatives.

In fact, insufficiently addressed in this issue are some concerns and pos-sible issues of significance that should receive added attention as home schooling does reach an "institutionalized" status. Just a few hints of po-tential strains to come are mentioned by the authors. Carper's (2000/this issue) article asks how a growing diversity (particularly in religious be-liefs) may influence the movement and "its relation to the state." Farris and Woodruff (2000/this issue) point out that home school families have tended to be "a distinctive segment of the American population" (i.e., somewhat wealthier and better educated), with a fairly common sense of curriculum (i.e., what's most worth learning). As the movement broadens and deepens, however, it may experience centrifugal forces that push away from its current distinctiveness.

In addition, Lines's (2000/this issue) interesting compilation of adaptive "partnerships" between home schooling families and the public schools forecasts a potential future wherein home schooling could become "co-opted" back into public-sector programming. In short, to be "accepted" and "legitimized" as an educational movement pulls home schooling into an entirely new realm of relationships and problems. Even if, as Hill (2000/this issue) suggests, the institutionalization that occurs takes a privat-ized direction all of its own, the very fact of institutionalization is itself of significance. Success as a movement carries its own deep threats to those forces that created and sustained the movement in the first place.

On the other hand, if Lines (2000/this issue) is quite correct that the adapting and co-opting that is beginning to occur "could become the model for tomorrow's education," then the significance of home schooling

Concluding Observations

is no longer to be found in its distinctiveness. The movement instead might receive central credit as a deviant "tail" that ends up wagging key pieces of "the dog" of public education. Indeed, Hill (2000/this issue) also recognizes that home schooling is less a threat to public education than a now-significant "force that will change it." For a social movement initiated by families (indeed, by just a small "niche" of dissenting families) to begin to shake successfully the larger institution of public education—that is a potential "story" of educational reform well worth much attention and deep analysis.

Indeed, it is apparent in reading this important set of articles for the *Peabody Journal of Education* that, again, home schooling has decidedly "come of age" as a vital topic of policy analysis and academic research. No longer to be ignored or to be regulated to an out-of-the-loop set of topics for scholarly inquiry, home schooling is now a movement of significance and power. We need to give it much more attention and seek a much deeper level of balanced, objective understanding than has been the case to date.

References

Apple, M. W. (2000/this issue). The cultural politics of home schooling. *Peabody Journal of Education, 75*(1&2), 276–271.

Carper, J. C. (2000/this issue). Pluralism to establishment to dissent: The religious and educational context of home schooling. *Peabody Journal of Education, 75*(1&2), 8–19.

Crowson, R. L. (1999, April). *The turbulent policy environment in education.* Paper presented at the annual meeting of the American Education Research Association, Montreal, Canada.

Crowson, R. L., Boyd, W. L., & Mawhinney, E. (Eds.). (1996). *The politics of education and the new institutionalism.* New York: Falmer.

Elshtain, J. B. (1995). *Democracy on trial.* New York: Basic Books.

Ensign, J. (2000/this issue). Defying the stereotypes of special education: Home school students. *Peabody Journal of Education, 75*(1&2), 147–158.

Farris, M. P., & Woodruff, S. A. (2000/this issue). The future of home schooling. *Peabody Journal of Education, 75*(1&2), 233–255.

Hawley, W. D. (1995, Summer). The false premises and false promises of the movement to privatize public education. *Teachers College Record, 96,* 735–742.

Hill, P. T. (2000/this issue). Home schooling and the future of public education. *Peabody Journal of Education, 75*(1&2), 20–31.

Lines, P. M. (2000/this issue). When home schoolers go to school: A partnership between families and schools. *Peabody Journal of Education, 75*(1&2), 159–186.

Lubiensky, C. (2000/this issue). Whither the common good? A critique of home schooling. *Peabody Journal of Education, 75*(1&2), 207–232.

McDowell, S. A. (2000/this issue). The home schooling mother–teacher: Toward a theory of social integration. *Peabody Journal of Education, 75*(1&2), 187–206.

McDowell, S. A., Sanchez, A. R., & Jones, S. S. (2000/this issue). Participation and perception: Looking at home schooling through a multicultural lens. *Peabody Journal of Education, 75*(1&2), 124–146.

R. L. Crowson

Medlin, R. G. (2000/this issue). Home schooling and the question of socialization. *Peabody Journal of Education, 75*(1&2), 107–123.

Murphy, J. (2000, February). Governing America's schools: The shifting playing field. *Teachers College Record, 102*(1), 57–84.

Ray, B. D. (2000a/this issue). Home schooling for individuals' gain and society's common good. *Peabody Journal of Education, 75*(1&2), 272–293.

Ray, B. D. (2000b/this issue). Home schooling: The ameliorator of negative influences on learning? *Peabody Journal of Education, 75*(1&2), 71–106.

Sarason, S. B. (1995). *Parental involvement and the political principle: Why the existing governance structure of schools should be abolished.* San Francisco: Jossey-Bass.

Taylor, L. A., & Petrie, A. J. (2000/this issue). Home education regulations in Europe and recent U.K. research. *Peabody Journal of Education, 75*(1&2), 49–70.

Tiebout, C. M. (1956, October). A pure theory of local expenditures. *Journal of Political Economy, 64*, 416–424.

Tyler, Z. P., & Carper, J. C. (2000/this issue). From confrontation to accommodation: Home schooling in South Carolina. *Peabody Journal of Education, 75*(1&2), 32–48.

Waller, W. (1932). *The sociology of teaching.* New York: Wiley.